MARYLAND A to Z

MARYLAND A to Z

A TOPOGRAPHICAL DICTIONARY

BY

MARION J. KAMINKOW

MAGNA CARTA BOOK COMPANY
5502 MAGNOLIA AVENUE
BALTIMORE, MARYLAND 21215
U.S.A.
1985

I S B N: 0-910946-26-4

Library of Congress Cataloging in Publication Data

Kaminkow, Marion J.
   Maryland A to Z.

   Bibliography: **p**.
   Includes index.
   1. Names, Geographical—Maryland—Dictionaries.
2. Maryland—History, Local—Miscellanea. I. Title.
F179.K36 1985   917.52'003'21   85-3042
ISBN 0-910946-26-4

INTRODUCTION

Much has been written on American local history, and it seems as though the time has come to pause and look at what has already been published, and to summarize it all, as far as possible, in a single work.

To this end, starting with Maryland, the compiler scanned books on local history, pamphlets, tourist folders, newspapers, magazines etc. in all libraries of the state which have local history collections, copied information from historical markers, and questioned oldest inhabitants. A large proportion of the places have been visited in person to check for accuracy; but the project has taken several years, and as every compiler knows, facts go out of date overnight, so the task is never done.

The idea was inspired by *The King's England,* by Arthur Mee, a set of 41 volumes covering the counties of England, which was published in the 1930's and 40's. But whereas *The King's England* listed only towns and villages, *Maryland A to Z* lists also localities, counties, collective areas, ghost towns, lakes, rivers, mountains, hills, railroads, parks, dams, airports, institutions, and anything else that has a name.

A very few brief explanations are necessary:

Location. Each place is pinpointed by the distance from its county seat or nearest metropolis, and the distances are strictly as the crow flies from county courthouse or city hall; they will be longer by road.

Population. This is taken from the 1980 census and is given for all incorporated towns, regardless of size, but only for unincorporated towns if their population is over 1,000.

Name. The origin cannot always be found. Sometimes it can be guessed at, for we find that the majority of place names which can be traced fall into categories, some of which are: Indian words; the name of the first post-master, the first settler, an early large landholder or an early railroad depot manager; the previous home town of the first post master, the first settler, or an early large landholder or an early railroad depot manager; an industry; caprice.

Boundaries. These are given as they stand today. It is common knowledge that many of them, especially those of counties, are quite different now from when they were formed.

Other compilers, intimately familiar with another state, may wish to take up the task. A suggested title for the whole series is *THE PEOPLES' U.S.A.*

Maryland A to Z has something of interest to everybody, whether they are travelling or staying at home, and we dedicate it to Maryland's people, particularly the researchers who have gone before and discovered most of the information which is summarized here.

CONTENTS

Map of Maryland Counties   viii

The State of Maryland   xi

Maryland A to Z   1

Addenda   368

Selected Bibliography   373

Index   380

Supplementary Index   402

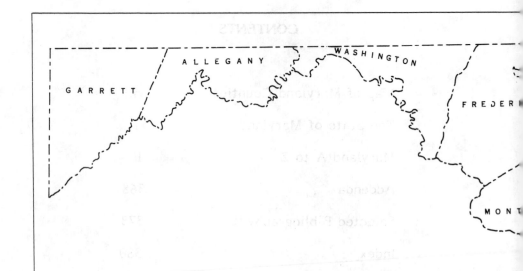

COUNTIES OF MARYLAND

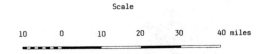

Scale

10   0   10   20   30   40 miles

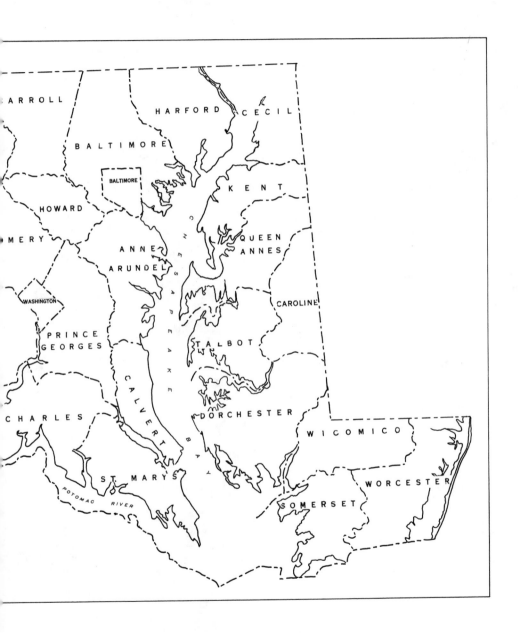

THE STATE OF MARYLAND

One of the thirteen original colonies.
Named for Queen Henrietta Maria, wife of Charles I of
    England.
Nicknames: The Free State. The Old Line State.
State Capital: Annapolis.
Area: 12,303 square miles, of which 9,874 are land. 42d in
    size.
Population: 4,216, 975 19th in size.
Counties: 23 plus Baltimore City.

Location

Maryland is one of the Middle Atlantic States, lying between parallels 37° 53' and 39° 43', deeply indented by the
Chesapeake Bay.   It is bounded on the north by the
Mason-Dixon Line, which separates it from Pennsylvania; on
the east by Delaware and the Atlantic Ocean; on the south
by Virginia and West Virginia; on the west by Virginia. Its
extreme east-west dimension is 240 miles and its extreme
north-south dimension is 125 miles, narrowing to under 2
miles near Hancock.

Maryland extends across three main geographical
provinces.   The western counties lie in the Appalachian
Province, a region of mountains and valleys;   the central
portion lies in the Piedmont Province, a region of rolling
hills;   the southern and eastern portions lie on the Coastal
Plain, a level area much dissected by rivers and estuaries.

Climate

The climate is generally temperate.   Winter temperatures average from 25°-45° and summer temperatures average from 65°-85° except in the mountains where the range is
somewhat more extreme.   The normal average precipitation
is 41.31 inches.

History

Maryland was granted to George Calvert, First Lord Baltimore, a Catholic, in 1632 by King Charles I, but neither he nor his son Cecilius, or Cecil, the Second Lord Baltimore, ever set foot on the territory. Colonists, under the leadership of Leonard Calvert, brother of the Second Lord Baltimore, set out from England in the Ark and the Dove and arrived in the Potomac River on March 27th, 1634, and established a settlement which they named St. Mary's.

Charles, the Third Lord Baltimore, spent much time in the colony, becoming involved in boundary disputes with Pennsylvania and losing the colony to the Crown in 1692; it was returned to his grandson, the Fifth Lord Baltimore, a Protestant, in 1715. The Sixth and last Lord Baltimore died in 1771 and the colony descended to Henry Harford, his illegitimate son, for a few years.

No major battles took place in Maryland during the Revolutionary War but the state saw much action during the War of 1812, when the British landed at several points on her territory. They were repulsed at the Battle of North Point, and the National Anthem was created during the attack on Fort McHenry.

During the Civil War, Maryland was allied with the North but there was much sympathy with the South in the southern areas of the state. Many conflicts took place on Maryland soil, the most important being the Battle of Sharpsburg, or Antietam, on Sept. 16-17, 1862, when the Confederates were forced to retreat across the Potomac.

Minerals

In earlier times iron ore, chrome and copper were mined in Maryland and several ornamental building stones were quarried. Quarrying today is in sand, gravel and clay on the coastal plain, crushed marble and limestone for road building and cement in the middle part of the state. The western counties still yield coal, mostly by strip mining, although deep mining was important in earlier times.

Agriculture

Agriculture is approximately 60% livestock raising and 40% crops, mainly corn and soybeans, with some tobacco, wheat, fruits and vegetables. Livestock raising is mainly broiler chicken production, in which the state ranks 6th in the country, and dairy farming.   Seafood production consists of fish, crabs, oysters and clams.

Industry

Industry is centered mainly around Baltimore, whose port ranks 4th in the nation, dominated by steel production, manufacture of metal products and food processing.   Near Washington, D.C. the occupations are mainly concerned with government departments, which have decentralized into Maryland, and research and development agencies.

Transportation

U.S. rail passenger transportation started in Maryland. The B.& O. Railroad was chartered at Baltimore in 1827 and before long there was a rail network serving almost every town and village in the state.   Passenger rail transport today consists of the Amtrak eastern corridor service, a daily train from Washington to the west and a few commuter trains to Washington from Baltimore and Brunswick.   The roads of Maryland are consistently good, all paved, and by-passing most towns and villages.

ABERDEEN   (Harford) Pop. 11,533 Incorp. 1892
10 miles SW of Belair, sprawling on both sides of U.S.40. It was originally composed of three small villages: Halls Cross Roads, Aberdeen and Mechanicsville.   The first house was built by Mr. Winston of Aberdeen, Scotland, in 1835.

Aberdeen Proving Ground, a Federal installation, opened in 1917, occupies 75,000 acres on a neck of land fronting on the Chesapeake Bay.   5,722 people live on the Proving Ground, and a mult-million dollar Nuclear Pulse Reactor is located here.

The U.S.Army Ordnance Museum is maintained on the Proving Ground, consisting of the most complete and comprehensive collection of arms and military vehicles in existence today, from the Revolutionary War to the Vietnam War. It is open to the public Tuesday thru Friday, 12-5 and Sat. and Sun 12-5.   Get map and pass at the Military Police gate. (See also **OLD BALTIMORE)**

ABINGDON   (Harford)
6½ miles SE of Bel Air on route 7, the old road to Phila-delphia.   The town was laid out by the Paca family in 1779, and William Paca the "Signer" was born at Chilberry Hall, south of here in 1740.   Small stones mark the four corners of the estate and a plaque marks the former entrance.   The first silk hat factory in America stood at the corner of Paca and Washington Streets.

Cokesbury College, named for Bishops Asbury and Coke, and the first Methodist College in America had a short-lived existence here.   The cornerstone was laid in 1785 and an impressive three-story building erected, only to be burned to the ground in 1795.   The bricks were carted away for other Methodist structures and the bell is in Goucher Hall, Baltimore.   The site, on an eminence east of the town, is marked, and there is a model of the building under the trees.

ACCIDENT (Garrett) Pop. 237. Incorp. 1916

16 miles N of Oakland. Named from a tract surveyed and claimed by two separate individuals. A log house built here by the Drane family still stands and is the oldest dwelling in the county. A more recent construction is the compressor of the Texas Eastern gas storage facility which encompasses 34,000 leased acres with natural gas storage capacity of 63.5 billion cubic feet.

Two miles northeast of the town is the Bear Creek Fish Rearing Station, where trout are raised for stocking the local streams. The station is open to visitors, who may view the pools on different levels, fed by natural springs and crowded with fish.

ACCOKEEK (Prince George's) Pop. 3,894

18 miles southwest of Upper Marlboro. The village itself is lost amid new developments. Excavations here show that the area was inhabited by Indians and Paleo-Indians. The excavations are not open to the public, but artifacts are on view at the local library. Four miles west of here is the National Colonial Farm. (See **BRYAN POINT**)

ADAMSTOWN (Frederick)

8 miles southwest of Frederick. It was called Davis' Warehouse until 1840, when the name was changed; Adam was the first name of the B. & O. Railway agent, and the town was centered around the station. The area is slated for urban development.

2 miles northeast of here is St. Joseph's Church, which marks the center of what was once the vast estate of Charles Carroll of Carrollton, one of the Maryland "signers", who owned most of the valley south of Frederick. (See also **DOUBS**)

ADELINA (Calvert)

5 miles southwest of Prince Frederick. South of here, on route 508 is the Taney Place, where Roger Brooke Taney (1777-1864), whose name is associated with the Dred Scott decision, was born. (See **FREDERICK**) The house, which was built in 1750, is private and not open to the public.

ADELPHI (Prince George's) Pop. 12,530

An old grist mill on the bank of the Northwest Branch

of the Anacostia River has given its name to a northeastern Washington D.C. suburb. The mill, built in 1796, is now used as a community activities building in North West Branch Park. It is located off New Riggs Rd. (MD 212) north of University Boulevard East (MD 193)

AGNER (Caroline)

9 miles southeast of Denton. It was once called Chestnut Woods, and later, Chestnut Grove, a name still borne by the church. John Agner once kept a store and post office here, and the town took his name.

AIKEN (Cecil)

14 miles southwest of Elkton. It was originally a station on the B. & O. Railroad called Frenchtown, but the railroad later renamed it for the oldest resident.

AIREY (Dorchester)

Village and railroad station 6 miles southeast of Cambridge formerly called Aireys. It was originally located half a mile below its present location, but moved in order to be on the railroad. Here, in 1781, the first Methodist sermon was preached in Dorchester County at the home of Henry Airey, by Freeborn Garrettson (1752-1827) an itinerant Methodist preacher. He was arrested and confined in Cambridge jail for preaching the doctrine of John Wesley, who was considered to be a Tory.

ALLEGANY COUNTY. County seat: Cumberland. Pop. 80548 Area: 440 square miles.

The county was formed in 1789 and the name was taken from an Indian word said to mean "beautiful stream." Its boundaries are: north, the Mason-Dixon Line; south, the Potomac River; east Sideling Hill Creek; west, a straight line from the summit of Big Backbone Mountain to the middle of the mouth of the Savage River.

The western fifth lies on the Appalachian Plateau, and the eastern four fifths in the Ridge and Valley Province (q.v.) The county was opened up by the railroads and the C.& O. Canal, both of which served the coal industry. Most of the deep coal mines of the county are exhausted, but strip mining is still practised. Corn, grains and hay are raised for local consumption and there is some tree-fruit growing and dairying. (Map on next page)

ALLEGANY GROVE (Allegany)

5 miles west of Cumberland. This area of development was originally a camp meeting ground, used for religious and entertainment purposes. The Tabernacle was in the center and summer cottages and tents were laid off in streets, while two railroad stations were erected to bring in visitors. Only a stone marker with the date 1890 near the corner of Simpson Ave. and Hemline Ave. marks the spot now.

ALLEGHENY PLATEAU

The broad table land of the Appalachian Mountains whose eastern margin in Maryland is Dans Mountain. The plateau extends far beyond the western boundary of Maryland. (See **DANS MTN., BACKBONE MTN.**)

ALLEN (Wicomico)

8 miles southwest of Salisbury. It was named in 1884 after a local family, but previously it was named Upper Trappe, and in the 1790's it was known as Brereton.

ALLVIEW ESTATES (Howard) Pop. 2,314

6 miles southwest of Ellicott City. A new housing development on route 29.

ALTAMONT (Garrett)

9 miles east of Oakland. Named for its high location on

Backbone Mountain and well known in railroad circles, since it is the summit of the famous seventeen mile grade, which carries the Baltimore and Ohio Railroad over the Appalachians. A marker beside the tracks tells that the summit is 2,628 ft. above sea level. When the new station was built at Oakland, the old one was hauled here, but has long since gone, and only a cottage or two remains in the vicinity. Some Civil War activity took place nearby and some of the railway property was damaged by the Confederates.

AMCELLE (Allegany)
6 miles southwest of Cumberland, and the base of the Celanese Fiber Co. from which the name is derived. The factory was opened in 1924 and employed nearly 10,000 workers in its heyday. Today it is almost defunct.

AMOS MILL (Harford)
15 miles northwest of Bel Air, near Norrisville. An 18th century grist mill on Island Branch. Operations ceased only at the death of John Amos in 1973, although the mill wheel looks as though it has been rusty and still for decades.

ANACOSTIA RIVER
A tributary of the Potomac, which enters it two miles south of the U.S. Capitol. Its two branches, Northeast and Northwest, join just north of Bladensburg, which was once a busy port before the river became silted up around 1800. Anacostia River Park embraces both branches and part of the main river in the stream valley. Kenilworth Aquatic Gardens form part of the east bank within the D.C.boundary.

ANDREWS AIR FORCE BASE (Prince George's) Pop. 10,064.
10 miles south of the U.S. Capitol. The base was completed in 1943 and used as a pilot training center during World War II, at which time it was called Camp Springs Air Force Base, after a nearby village. It was enlarged in 1962, when it took in the Anacostia Naval Air Station, and now covers 4,420 acres and employs over 10,000 military personnel. It is the principal arrival and departure point for foreign dignitaries and Air Force I is based here. The name comes from Lieutenant General Frank M. Andrews, commander of European Operations for all Army Air Forces.

ANNAPOLIS   Maryland State Capital and seat of Anne Arundel County. Pop. 31,740

Approximately mid-way between the Pennsylvania and Virginia borders, Annapolis is situated on an inlet of the Chesapeake Bay. It is Maryland's most fascinating town and attracts historians, artists, photographers, boating enthusiasts and sightseers; it has inspired numbers of photographic histories, and the name is known throughout the country on account of the Naval Academy, which is situated adjacent to the town.

Thanks to a number of preservation enthusiasts, an organization called Historic Annapolis Inc. has been formed, which stands guard over the town and wages unending war with despoilers. Largely due to its efforts, changes have been halted and the town retains its atmosphere, although frequently clogged with cars.

Narrow streets lead from State Circle to City Dock, a large open space along the water front where promenades and seats allow visitors to view the activities of the work boats and pleasure craft, and the comings and goings of the Harbor Queen, a sightseeing boat which leaves every few hours in the summer for a trip down the Severn River and out into the Chesapeake Bay.

Facing the water and lining the narrow streets are various restaurants and shops, and at one end of the square is the Market House, recently restored and doing business in fruit, vegetables, seafood and snacks. Busses connect the town with Eastport, Baltimore and Washington.

Annapolis was founded about 1650 on the site of the present Maryland Yacht Club and became the state capitol in 1694, when it was called Anne Arundel Town, after the wife of Cecilius Calvert, second Lord Baltimore. The name was changed soon afterwards to honor Queen Anne. Annapolis grew and thrived and became one of the most active centers of governmental and social activity in the colonies. Fine town houses were built and also a center of Education, King William's School (now St. John's College) At various times the town was dubbed "The Paris of America," and "The Athens of America."

On Oct. 19, 1774, Annapolis staged its own tea tax protest when the owner of *The Peggy Stewart* was forced to burn his vessel at dockside; but it played a far more dignified role in the struggle for independence when the State House served as the Capitol of the U.S. from Nov.26,1783 to Aug.13,1784.

The economy of the town is based largely upon state and county government, tourism, pleasure boating and boat building, repairing and equipment.

SIGHTS TO SEE

THE NAVAL ACADEMY (Pop. 5,367)
The academy was established here as the Naval School, on the grounds of old Fort Severn, in 1845. It covers several hundred acres adjoining the town and is a community within a community. Between 800 and a thousand midshipment are graduated each year during the first week in June, known as June week, when the navy dominates the town. The grounds and parts of the Academy are open to visitors; a visitors' center supplies a tour leaflet, and there is also a gift shop.

Main points of interest are Bancroft Hall, the Chapel and the Museum. Bancroft Hall, the dormitory building boasts that it contains the largest dining hall in the world, where the entire student body can be served at a sitting. Each noon, (12.10 on Sats. and 12.30 on Suns.) the brigade forms in front of the hall. The Chapel contains many memorials and in the crypt are housed the remains of John Paul Jones, father of the American Navy. The Museum contains artifacts of naval history and marine paintings.

Other points of interest are the statue named Tecumseh and the foremast of the battleship Maine.

THE STATE HOUSE
The present building dates from 1772-9 and is the oldest state house in the country in continuous legislatve use. It served as the Capitol of the U. S. from Nov. 26, 1783 to Aug. 13, 1784; here George Washington resigned his commission on Dec. 23, 1783 and here the Treaty of Paris was ratified on Jan. 14, 1784. At the State House also was held, in 1786, the meeting of delegates from the colonies to consider the possibilities of a closer union, an event which gave rise to the Constitutional Convention.

The State House is open daily (except Christmas Day) 9-5 and there are free guided tours. A ceremony commemorating Ratification Day takes place each Jan. 14th.

THE OLD TREASURY BUILDING
On the State House grounds, this little edifice, built 1735-7, is the oldest public building still standing in Maryland.

ST. ANNE'S EPISCOPAL CHURCH

Standing in the center of Church Circle, the present building was erected in 1859 on the site of two earlier churches.   In the churchyard is buried Governor Eden, the last of Maryland's colonial governors.

a. Anne Arundel County Courthouse. b. Maryland State House. c. State Office Building.

GOVERNMENT HOUSE

The home of Maryland's governor stands in a circle of its own between State Circle and Church Circle. Originally a Victorian brick mansion, built in 1869, the wings were added in 1935 to give it a 17th century look. The governor holds open house on New Year's Day.

MARYLAND INN

Near the State House, the old inn, part of which dates from the 1770's, has hosted many visiting dignitaries; many of the state's legislators still lodge here during sessions. It was restored in the 1950's and still serves as an inn and restaurant.

ST. JOHN'S COLLEGE

This was founded in 1696 as King William's School, and chartered under its present name in 1784. It is a four year liberal arts college with an unusual curriculum based on the famous selection of Great Books. One of its notable students was Francis Scott Key. On the grounds stands the Liberty Tree, a large tulip poplar, known to be more than 400 years old.

THE CHASE-LLOYD HOUSE 22 Maryland Ave.
The house was begun in 1769 by Samuel Chase, one of Maryland's four "signers" and completed by Edward Lloyd, governor of Maryland and large landowner in 1809. Open daily 2-4 except Wed., Sun. and holidays.

THE HAMMOND-HARWOOD HOUSE 19 Maryland Ave.
Completed in 1774, the house is considered to be an outstandingly fine example of Georgian domestic architecture. Open Tues. thru Sat. 10-5, Sun. 2-5 (closes at 4 in winter)

THE PACA HOUSE 192 Prince George St.
Built in 1763-5, this house was the home of William Paca, one of Maryland's four "signers," who was three times governor of Maryland. It was rented out after his death and became a hotel; a large addition was added in 1907. In 1965 the house was rescued from demolition by Historic Annapolis, Inc. who have since performed miracles of restoration upon the house and spacious garden. The garden is open Mon.-Sat. 10-4 and Sun. 1-4 and the house is open for tours at certain times.

There is much more of the old and picturesque in Annapolis and visitors wishing to learn more can take a conducted walking tour starting daily from the Hilton Inn at 9.30 a.m. or the Wax Museum at 2 p.m.
Several festivals take place in Annapolis each year, beginning with the first week in June, which is the Naval Academy graduation celebratioin. The third week in June brings the Fine Arts Festival and the first week in August is the Maryland Clam Festival at City Dock. Heritage weekend, with tours of historic buildings and homes is the last weekend in September and the boat show comes in mid-October. Frostbite sailboat races, sponsored by the Annapolis Yacht Club take place every Sunday afternoon, Nov. to March. Walking tours, hunt breakfasts, craft demonstrations and other activities are arranged from time to time by Historic Annapolis, Inc.

ANNAPOLIS JUNCTION (Anne Arundel)

$3\frac{1}{2}$ miles northeast of Laurel.   In former times a line branched off the B. & O. Railroad here to Annapolis, and there was a busy station.   The branch line now goes only to Fort George Meade, and although the post office is still named Annapolis Junction, the vicinity served by a single morning and evening commuter train between Washington and Baltimore, is called Fort George Meade Junction.   The place was once called Centralia, since it is about midway between Baltimore, Annapolis and Washington.

ANNAPOLIS ROCK (Howard)

A locality in what is now part of Patuxent State Park. It was said, before the days of smog, that one could see the State House in Annapolis from the slight eminence.

ANNAPOLIS ROCK (Washington)

An overlook, elevation 1762 ft. on the crest of South Mountain, north of route 70, approachable by the Appalachian Trail.

ANNE ARUNDEL COUNTY.   County Seat: Annapolis, the State Capital.   Pop. 370,775   Area: 430 square miles.

Anne Arundel County was formed in 1650 and named after the wife of Cecil Calvert, Second Lord Baltimore.

It is bounded on the east by the Chesapeake Bay;   on the north by the Patapsco River and Baltimore City;   on the west by Deep Creek, a tributary of the Patapsco, the B.& O. Railroad line to Laurel, and the Patuxent River as far as Lyons Creek;   on the south by an irregular line from Lyons Creek to the vicinity of North Beach Park.

The county lies mostly on the coastal plain.   Its low shoreline is much dissected by rivers and their tributaries, around which are clusters of developments, many of which started life as summer colonies and public beaches but have now evolved into sprawling year-round communities and private beaches.

Population is dense in the northern part adjacent to Baltimore City and growing steadily in the areas around Annapolis.   The strip away from the shoreline remains relatively rural;   corn, grains, soybeans, tobacco and hay are raised.   (Map on next page)

ANNESLIE (Baltimore County)

6 miles due north of downtown Baltimore, just over the city line. It is named for a house built in 1840 by a certain Frederick Harrison, a civil engineer for the B.& O. and Northern Central Railroads, who named it after his wife, Anne. Residential development started here in 1922 and now completely surrounds the house, which still stands on its small re-maining acreage on a street east of York Rd.

ANTIETAM (Washington)

The village is about 3 miles south of Sharpsburg at the point where Antietam Creek enters the Potomac. It was originally built around a large iron works, for there were ore deposits nearby. The furnace was started in 1765 by J. Chapline, the founder of Sharpsburg; it closed finally in

1880 and very little remains of the complex except for a kiln, dated 1845, on the south side of Harper's Ferry Rd. In its heyday nine water wheels operated the machinery; there was a forge with a twenty-one ton hammer, a rolling mill, and and important nail factory. A large number of cannon used in the Revolutionary War was cast here, and most of the machinery for Rumsey's steamboat, first tested across the Potomac River at Shepherdstown, W.Virginia, was made here. The C.& O. Canal crosses the Antietam by a beautiful three-arched acqueduct at this point.

ANTIETAM CREEK (Washington)

Rises in Pennsylvania and meanders down the Great Valley, through Hagerstown, and enters the Potomac at the village of Antietam. It is notable for its picturesque bridges, fourteen of which were built before 1863. The Civil War Battle of Antietam was named for the stream, which flows past Sharpsburg (q.v.) where the battle took place.

APPALACHIAN MOUNTAINS

The mountainous area which lies west of the Piedmont Province and runs in a northeasterly - southwesterly direction from Maine to Georgia under many different local names. The portion of the area which is in Maryland consists of the Allegheny Plateau, the Ridge and Valley Province, the Great Valley and the Blue Ridge.

APPALACHIAN TRAIL

A foot trail along the crest of the easternmost range of the Appalachians, running from Maine to Georgia. In Maryland the trail enters the state at Penmar and follows the crest of South Mountain until it reaches the Potomac River at Weverton. After descending the abrupt slope, the hiker must follow the river westward along the C. & O. Canal towpath until he is able to cross the Potomac by the route 340 road bridge, and climb the steep face of Loudon Heights in Virginia.

APPEAL (Calvert)

14 miles southeast of Prince Frederick. $1\frac{1}{2}$ miles northwest of here on Milldridge Rd. is Hellen Creek Hemlock Preserve, owned by the Nature Conservancy and considered to be a prime natural area, the southernmost stand of hemlock.

ARBUTUS (Baltimore County) Pop. 20,163

5 miles southwest of Baltimore. This is an older suburb of individual houses, rowhouses and apartments, but there is much recent development also. A number of small factories are in the area.

ARCADIA (Baltimore County)

25 miles northwest of Baltimore. It was originally called Burke's Station, but re-named in 1879, although the post office continues to be called Upperco (q.v.) Sportsman's Hall, a skating rink here, is named after the original land grant.

ARNOLD (Anne Arundel) Pop. 12,285

4 miles northeast of Annapolis. The Anne Arundel County Community College is located here, which has helped to promote much surrounding development.

ASHLAND (Baltimore County)

14 miles north of Baltimore, formerly served by the Northern Central Railroad. It was a company town, belonging to the Ashland Iron Co. which started in 1837 and was the largest iron company in Maryland. The iron works ceased in 1880 after a fire, and the machinery was sent to Sparrow's Point steel plant. Around 1924 the whole village was purchased by Mano Swartz, a Baltimore furrier, who has since allowed needy families to live in the run-down houses. The church was founded in 1874 on the site of an attack by John Brown's raiders.

ASHTON (Montgomery) Pop. with Sandy Spring 2,659

9 miles northeast of Rockville. The village was originally settled by Quaker families and named in 1890. The name is a combination of two farms: Ashland and Clifton. Some development is taking place nearby.

ASPEN HILL (Montgomery) Pop. 47,455

A new development 4 miles east of Rockville.

ASPEN RUN (Carrroll)

5 miles northeast of Westminster. A developing community around a lake, and named for a stream. There will be a bandstand and club house on the shore.

ASSATEAGUE ISLAND (Worcester)

Stretches from the Ocean City Inlet to about fourteen miles below the Maryland-Virginia boundary, and is part of the Barrier Reef extending along the Atlantic coast. The island is about thirty two miles long and the width varies from one mile to one third of a mile. It is separated from the mainland by Sinepuxent Bay in the north and Chincoteague Bay in the south. Assateague's only connection with the mainland in Maryland is a bridge from Lower Sinepuxent Neck, ten miles south of Ocean City. Another bridge at the southern end of the island connects with the Virginia mainland.

The northern tip of the island is a wildlife management area, below which a state park extends for six miles. The state park portion of the island has two miles of ocean front and 311 camp sites open all year, much in demand in summer. South of the state park the island becomes a National Sea Shore for the rest of its length. The beach is one of the finest on the east coast and a prime angling spot. Visitors are urged to stay off the dunes, which provide protection from erosion.

ATKISSON RESERVOIR (Harford)

4 miles south of Bel Air. A small reservoir behind a dam on Winter's Run and forming the water supply for Edgewood Arsenal. It is surrounded by a primitive area.

AVALON (Baltimore County)

A location on the Patapsco River which now gives its name to an area of the Patapsco State Park. The area was once rich in iron ore and an important forge was built here by the enormously wealthy Dorsey family, who also built Belmont, described under **ELKRIDGE.**

AVALON (Talbot)

Village on Tilghman Island (q.v.) The land at this point was built up from oyster shells, which the packing companies dumped off the docks over the years. The Tilghman Seafood Packing Co., active here for 75 years, closed in 1975.

AVENEL-HILLANDALE (Montgomery & Prince George's)

Adjacent developments 8-10 miles north of the U.S. Capitol. Combined population is 19,686. (See **HILLANDALE**)

BACHMANS MILLS (Carroll)

6½ miles northeast of Westminster, at the head of Big Pipe Creek. The village was founded about 1780 and called Bowers Mills until purchased by Wm. & A. C. Bachman. An old railroad called the Bachman Valley line, used mainly for hauling iron ore, used to connect with the Western Maryland Railroad just north of the Pennsylvania border at Black Rock.

BACKBONE HILL (Somerset)

6 miles northeast of Princess Anne, on the lowest part of the Eastern Shore. A number of streams rise in this vicinity, which rises to the dizzying height of 40 ft.

BACKBONE MOUNTAIN (Garrett)

Backbone Mountain and its northern continuation, Meadow Mountain, form the divide of the Appalachian Range in Maryland. Rivers flowing eastward from here find their way into the Potomac and the Chesapeake Bay; rivers flowing westward make towards the Ohio.

The highest spot in Maryland, Hoyes Crest (q.v.) is on Backbone Mountain in the extreme southwest corner of the state. Table Rock (elev. 3,095 ft.) once a favorite picnic spot, is where route 50 crosses Backbone Mountain and is the highest spot on any Maryland Road (according to a road marker.) Allegany Heights, due south of Oakland, is where McCullough's path crossed it (q.v.) At Altamont (q.v.) the B.& O. Railroad reaches the top of its 17 mile climb.

Other summits are: Roth Rock, Conneway Hill, Kelso Gap and Eagle Rock, 3160 ft. about midway between Oakland and Kitzmiller (no view now as the top has been quarried off.)

BACK RIVER (Baltimore County)

An estuary emptying into the Chesapeake Bay north of

the Patapsco; its name is oddly compatible with the sewage disposal plant on its shores.

Back River Neck is the peninsular between Back River and Middle River. On the Neck are the following open spaces: Rocky Point (at the tip), Cox's Point, Turkey Point, Sue Creek, Breezy Point.

BACON HILL (Cecil)

3 miles west of Elkton. Captain John Smith called it Peregrine's Mount, but a large colonial landowner of the area, George Talbot, renamed it Beacon Hill, of which Bacon Hill is a corruption. There were frequent boundary disagreements in this part of Maryland in former times, and Talbot would use the beacon on the hill to summon his tenants to the fray.

BADEN (Prince George's)

11 miles south of Upper Marlboro. Bishop Claggett, first Episcopal Bishop ordained in America, was rector of St. Paul's Church here, 1780-86, and a memorial window honors him. St. Paul's was built in 1733 to replace the church at Mt. Calvert.

St. Paul's Church, Baden

BAINBRIDGE NAVAL CENTER (Cecil)

14 miles west of Elkton on a bluff above the Susquehanna River near Port Deposit. The center opened in 1942 on the grounds of the Tome School, a private school for boys, and covers 1,132 acres. Among other things, it was

the only WAVE recruit training command in the U.S.   A housing project was erected in 1954 with 720 houses for naval personnel and the population was given as 5,257 in 1970.   The center is now used by the Job Corps for teaching trades to about 1400 boys and girls.

The Tome School was started by Jacob Tome, a poor boy who arrived in Port Deposit on a raft, and made good.   He started a free school in the town, and after his death in 1898, money from his estate was used to found the far larger institute on the hill.   A brick and stone stairway leads up the face of the cliff from the town.   (See **PORT DEPOSIT**)

BALD FRIAR (Harford and Cecil)

The name of Bald Friar is on the map both east and west of the Conowingo Reservoir, a few miles below the Pennsylvania border.   It is said to be a corruption of the name of a one-time ferry owner called Fry.   Although both localities are over a mile from the water and contain nothing but a few residences, they are reminders of the important crossing of the Susquehanna River which existed before Conowingo Dam was built.   Both ford and ferry existed here in early times, and it was the lowest point of the river where heavy equipment could be taken across.

The most notable crossing of the river which took place here was that of Lafayette's and Rochambeau's troops on their way to Yorktown in 1781.   Some waded across, others took scows.   Lafayette's scow is said to have run aground and a soldier named Aquila Dean carried him across on his back.

BALTIMORE Pop. 786,775.   Incorp. 1797

Baltimore, the nation's tenth largest city and fourth largest port, was first laid out as a town in 1729, near the inlet called Northwest Branch of the Patapsco River on the west side of Jones Falls.   It was named for Lord Baltimore, the proprietor of Maryland, who in turn took his title from his estate in Ireland.   In 1745 it absorbed an older settlement called Oldtown, or Jonestown, on the east bank of Jones Falls and in 1768 it became the seat of Baltimore County, which covered a far larger area then than now.

The town by the water grew steadily, centered around seaborne trade and ship building.   It spread up and down the water front and eventually inland into the hills, which first became   farms,   then   resorts,   then   summer   homes   and

eventually suburbs.   By 1851 it was large enough to become
an independent city and the county seat was moved to
Towson.   A disastrous fire destroyed most of the downtown
area in 1904, but growth and annexations continued until the
present boundaries were reached in 1914.

Baltimore appears to greatest advantage when approached by water. A sight-seeing boat entering the five mile wide
estuary of the Patapsco River travels for ten miles between
the wharves and shipping, cranes, factories and warehouses
which make up the Port, dominated by the Sparrows Point
steel mills.   At length, as it rounds a bend, Fort McHenry
comes into view, on a point between the two branches of the
Inner Harbor.   Another bend, and the tall buildings of the
downtown area are revealed, dominated by the pink granite
U. S. F. & G. Building, with its well-proportioned horizontals,
and the smaller octagonal World Trade Center at the water's
edge, also with horizontal window lines.   In the background
the low hills of the Piedmont can be seen.   The last bend
and the panoramas are replaced by the serenity of the Inner
Harbor with its marinas for pleasure boats, walks, shops and
restaurants and the chequered hull of the Constellation.

Baltimore lies somewhat more to the west than the
other Atlantic ports, which gives it some trading advantage.
It was for this reason that the nation's first railroad, the
Baltimore and Ohio, started from Baltimore and turned its
sights westward.

The street numbering system of the city begins at
Charles and Baltimore Streets.

Government is by mayor and 16 city councillors.

The city supports a baseball team (The Orioles,) an ice-
hockey team (The Skipjacks) and a soccer team (The Blast.)

Baltimore panorama.

BALTIMORE - TOURS

Boats from Constellation Dock make hourly tours to Fell's Point and Fort McHenry in summer. Larger boats run a schedule of voyages out into the Chesapeake Bay, to Annapolis and to St. Michael's.

Alexander Tours have a $7.50 bus tour Monday, Wednesday and Friday at 10, 1 and 3; and a $15.00 tour on the other four days at 10. Call 664-5577 for reservations.

BALTIMORE - PARKS AND CEMETERIES

Carroll Park. Southwest Baltimore. Former home of Charles Carroll the Lawyer, acquired in 1890. Contains Mount Clare Mansion.

Clifton Park. East Baltimore. Formerly the summer estate of Johns Hopkins.

Cylburn Park. 4915 Greenspring Ave. 180 acres in northwest Baltimore purchased in 1942. Protected as a wild flower preserve. Contains mansion house and museum used for art and nature classes.

Druid Hill Park. 674 acre landscaped park acquired in 1860. It contains lakes (some now dried up), drives, walks, picnic pavilions and there are open areas for baseball and tennis. It also contains the 150 acre Baltimore Zoo, a natural history museum and conservatories with floral displays in season.

Gwynns Falls Park. An under-used, wooded park stretching for six miles along the stream valley. Together with Leakin Park it contains over 1,000 acres.

Herring Run Park. An open stream valley park, with playing fields, winding six miles through the city. With Armistead Gardens it covers 800 acres.

Leakin Park. Former estate of the Winans family who built the first Russian railroad from Moscow to St. Petersburg. It contains the mansion, called Crimea, open area for kite-flying, etc., wooded hillsides with trails, massive trees, and a stream valley. It is named for J.W.Leakin who provided the money for its purchase.

BALTIMORE – PARKS AND CEMETERIES continued

Loudon Park Cemetery.   Opened in 1853, it contains graves of Union and Confederate soldiers and the graves of Mary Pickersgill and some of the Bonaparte family.   It is believed to be the only cemetery which had trolley cars for transporting visitors 1905 - 1931.

Patterson Park.   Inner city park much used for soccer games. Consisting of 150 acres, it was Baltimore's first park.   It contains a pagoda.

Greenmount Cemetery.   Greenmount and North Aves.   Many local notables and historical figures are buried here, including the Booth family, with John Wilkes in an unmarked grave.

St. Paul's Cemetery.   Fremont Ave. and W.Lombard St. Walled and padlocked, it is the resting place of several notables including Tench Tilghman and Samuel Chase.

Westminster Churchyard.   Fayette and Green Sts.   Among other notable graves is that of Edgar Allen Poe.

Westminster Churchyard.   Poe's grave.

WYMAN PARK.   Once an estate belonging to a grandson of Charles Carroll.   Purchased by Johns Hopkins University in 1902.

BALTIMORE - HISTORIC HOUSES

Babe Ruth Birthplace. 216 Emory St. Contains exhibits and displays. Open 10-6 Thur. thru Tues. in summer;   10-4 Fri. thru Mon. in winter.

Carroll Mansion. 800 E. Lombard St. The town house of Charles Carroll of Carrollton, erected ca. 1815. Open Wed. thru Fri. 10.30 - 4.30. Sats. and Suns. 1-5.

Evergreen House. 4545 N.Charles St. Originally the home and estate of John Garrett of the B. & O. Railroad, it now belongs to Johns Hopkins University. Open weekday afternoons with more extensive opening the second Tues. of each month, 10-4.30.

Homewood. N.Charles St. near 34th St. on the campus of Johns Hopkins University. Erected in 1802 it belonged to the son of Charles Carroll of Carrollton.

Mother Seton House. 600 N.Paca St. Built in 1807 and occupied by Mother Seton 1808-9. (See **EMMITSBURG**) Open Sat. and Sun. 1-4.

Mount Clare Mansion. In Carroll Park. The oldest house and the only pre-revolutionary mansion standing in Baltimore. Its construction was begun in 1754 and it belonged to Charles Carroll the Barrister. Open Tues thru Sat. 11-4, Suns. 1-4.

H.L.Mencken House. 1524 Hollins St. The notable man of letters lived here most of his life. The house now belongs to the University of Maryland, but is open occasionally. Mencken's books and papers are in the Enoch Pratt Library.

Poe House. 203 Amity St. A small row house where Edgar Allen Poe lived and wrote during the years 1832-5. Open Sat. 1-4.

BALTIMORE - HISTORIC PLACES OF WORSHIP

Basilica of the Assumption. Cathedral and Mulberry Sts. The oldest Catholic Cathedral in the U.S. built in 1806. Tours are held on the second and fourth Sundays of each

BALTIMORE - HISTORIC PLACES OF WORSHIP continued

month after the 12.30 Mass.   The Basilica, which was formerly called the Cathedral, yielded its title when the new
huge Cathedral of Mary our Queen was built near the city
line at 5200 North Charles St.   This cathedral has tours on
Sundays at 1.30.

Lloyd St. Synagogue. Lloyd and Baltimore Sts. Built in 1845
it is the oldest synagogue in Maryland. It is open the first
and third Sunday of each month 1.30 -5.

Lovely Lane Methodist Church. St. Paul and 22d Sts. Built
in 1882-7 to replace the older church, it is considered to be
the Mother Church of American Methodism. It contains a
small museum.

Old Otterbein U.M.Church. Conway St. near Sharp St. Built
in 1785-6 it is the oldest church in Baltimore in continuous
use.

St. Paul's P.E.Church. Charles St. at Saratoga. The present
red brick church was built on the site of a small brick
church erected in 1729, the first place of worship in Baltimore, and the Mother Church of Baltimore Episcopalians.

BALTIMORE - IMPORTANT MONUMENTS

Battle Monument.   Calvert and Fayette Sts.   Erected
1815-25 on the site of the earlier court house. It was the
first monument in the U.S. dedicated to the slain in the War
of 1812, and since 1827 has been the symbol of the city.

War Memorial. At the opposite end of the plaza facing City
Hall. Dedicated in 1925, it is in the form of an auditorium,
which can be used for meetings. Around the walls are
inscribed the names of the dead.

Washington Monument. Mount Vernon Place and Monument
St. Erected 1815-1829, it was the first major monument to
George Washington, whose statue surmounts the column. Its
total height is 178 ft. There are some exhibits at the base,
and the column can be ascended by 228 stairs. Open Fri. to
Tues. 10-4.

Baltimore. Washington Monument.

BALTIMORE - BUILDINGS

Baltimore Arts Tower. 312-18 W.Lombard St. Originally the Bromo-Seltzer Tower built by the Emerson Drug Co. in 1911. It was then the tallest building in Baltimore, designed in imitation of the Palazzo Vecchio campanile in Florence and crowned with a blue alka-seltzer bottle. It now belongs to the city and has been converted to offices for cultural organizations.

Civic Center. Baltimore and Howard Sts. This municipally owned building with the pleated roof was opened in Oct. 1962. It has 160,000 sq. ft. of exhibit space and 44 meeting rooms. There are 10,000 permanent seats for spectators of the hockey and basketball games, circuses and concerts.

City Hall. Holiday St. at Fayette St. Built in 1867-75 in the French Revival style with a cast iron dome, it has recently been restored.

Convention Center. South Charles and Pratt Sts. A building of concrete, steel and glass, opened in Aug. 1979. It has

BALTIMORE - BUILDINGS continued

115,000 sq. ft. of unobstructed exhibit space, which can be divided into four separate halls, and 26 meeting rooms.

Custom House. Lombard and Gay Sts. Contains a striking mural on the first floor depicting the history of sailing vessels.

Enoch Pratt Free Library. Cathedral St. between Mulberry and Franklin Sts. The library was founded in 1886, although the present building dates from 1933 and contains nearly a million volumes. Its 12 street-level display windows are an unusual feature.

Fort McHenry. This National Monument and historic shrine, which is administered by the National Park Service, stands on the point formed by the two branches of the Baltimore Harbor. The Fort was named for James McHenry of Baltimore who served as Washington's first Secretary of War. He is buried in Old Westminster Cemetery in Baltimore. The bombardment of Fort McHenry, Sept. 12-14, 1814, climaxed the British attack on Baltimore and inspired the writing of the words of *The Star Spangled Banner*. A visitors' center is open seven days a week with film and explanation.

Harbor Place. Pratt and Light Sts. Developed by the Rouse Co., these two pavilions of glass and green metal were opened in July 1980. They house 120 outlets, on two floors, of specialty stores and restaurants, many with harbor views.

Johns Hopkins Hospital. 601 N. Broadway. World-famous institution founded by the Baltimore merchant and benefactor. The original building is flanked by huge additions.

Johns Hopkins University. N. Charles and 34th Sts. This privately-endowed, world-famous institute was founded in 1876 and is dedicated to research. Brochures for a walking tour are available at the information desk.

Lexington Market. Eutaw and Lexington Sts. Founded in 1782, this is thought to be the oldest continuously operating

BALTIMORE - BUILDINGS continued

market in the U.S. The first building was erected in 1803. Extensive renovations were made in 1952 and the new additions was opened in 1982. The market is open for shopping and eating Mon.-Sat. 8.30 to 6.

Loyola University. Charles St. at Coldspring Lane. Old established Catholic university.

McCormick Spice Co. 414 Light St. facing the harbor. It has a tea room and museum for visitors and sends a spicy aroma wafting over the city.

Maryland Institute. Mt. Royal Ave. at Lanvale St. Art school. Built 1905 of marble in the Roman Revival style.

Maryland National Bank Building. E.Baltimore and Light Sts. Built in the 1930's and the tallest building in Baltimore until 1974. The art deco features and mosaics on the first floor are worth examining.

Memorial Stadium. 33rd St. Completed Oct. 1954. Can seat 56,000.

Morgan State University. Hillen Rd. and Coldspring Lane. Founded 1867 as a Biblical Institute for blacks.

Peabody Institute. Mount Vernon Place. Founded in 1857 by George Peabody, a Baltimore philanthropist who also gave foundations in Boston and England, it is renowned for its Conservatory of Music and its unique scholars' library whose open balconies of stacks are a striking feature. Since 1983 the library has been administered by the Johns Hopkins University.

Shot Tower. The brick tower was built in 1829 for the production of shot by dropping molten metal from a height into water. The ground floor is open and houses some exhibits.

U. S. Fidelity & Guaranty Trust Co. Building. 100 Light St. This 35 story building, sheathed in pink granite is Baltimore's tallest building and was opened in mid-1974.

BALTIMORE - BUILDINGS continued

University of Baltimore.   Founded in 1924 it expanded in 1968 when it acquired and re-modelled a former car sales-room built in 1906.   It became a state institution in 1975 and is still expanding.   Student body is about 5,000.

University of Maryland Hospital.   Large modern complex with Davidge Hall as its nucleus.   Built in 1812, this hall is the oldest building in the country in continuous use as a medical center.

World Trade Center.   A five-sided building at the water's edge on Pratt St. opened in 1977.   The Maryland Port Authority occupies 4 of the thirty stories;   the rest is rented to Port related activities.   The "Top of the World" observation deck on the 27th floor is open seven days a week.

BALTIMORE - HOTELS AND RAILROAD STATIONS

Camden Station.   Was the largest railroad station in the world when the B.& O. opened it in 1851.   It has witnessed the departure of some historic trains, but is now used by only a few rickety commuters to Washington.

Pennsylvania Station.   Recently cleaned and renovated it is still a busy station used by all of Amtrak's east coast trains.

Mount Royal Station.   Connected with the Camden Station area by a tunnel under Howard St., this was a grand B.& O. station when it opened in 1896.   It closed to passengers in 1961 but has since been remodelled as part of the Maryland Institute, and its clock tower is still a landmark.

Lord Baltimore Hotel.   Built in 1928 it is now undergoing extensive restoration.   The ballroom and meeting rooms are decorated with murals depicting the history of Baltimore.

Belvedere Hotel.   Charles and Chase Sts.   A noble building, erected in 1903 and named after the Baltimore estate of John Eager Howard.   It no longer functions as a hotel but the restaurants have been re-modelled and re-opened.

BALTIMORE - MUSEUMS AND THEATERS

Aquarium. See **National Aquarium in Baltimore.**

Baltimore Maritime Museum. 1617 Thames St. Among the floating exhibits are a lightship and W W II submarine.

Baltimore Museum of Art. N. Charles St. at 31st St. Contains several notable collections including the Cone Collection of 19th Century French Art and a Maryland Wing. Open Tues.-Fri. 10-4 and Sat & Sun. 11-6.

Baltimore Museum of Industry. 1415 Key Highway. Has artifacts and demonstrations of Baltimore's industrial past in the fields of canning, garment manufacture, printing, shipbuilding, steel manufacture and others. Open Sat. 10-5 and Sun. 12-5.

Baltimore Public Works Museum. 701 Eastern Ave. Demonstrates the history of Baltimore's water supply and waste water treatment. Open Fri. 11-4. Sat. 12-4. Sun. 11-5.

Baltimore Fire Museum. Gay and Ensor Streets. Displays old fire-fighting equipment, helmets and other paraphernalia. Open Fri. and Sat. 7-9 and Sun. 1-5.

Baltimore Street Car Museum. 1901 Falls Rd. Contains a collection of street cars from 1880-1963 and a mile of track where some cars are operational. Open Suns. 1-5.

Baltimore & Ohio Railroad Transportation Museum. Pratt and Poppleton Streets. A unique museum housed in a huge roundhouse and adjoining buildings. There is a collection of locomotives dating from the earliest days of American railroading and other memorabilia. Here also is the nation's first railroad depot built in the early 1830's for the B.& O.'s pioneer passenger line to Ellicott City. Open Wed.-Sun. 10-4.

Center Stage. 700 N.Calvert St. The theater opened at this location in 1976 in the old Loyola High School, which had stood vacant since 1941. The building was remodelled with the help of grants from the city and state and several foundations.

BALTIMORE - MUSEUMS AND THEATERS continued

Flag House and Museum. 844 E.Pratt St. Once the home of Mary Pickersgill, who made the flag which flew over Fort McHenry in 1814 and inspired the writing of the National Anthem. Open Mon.-Sat. 10-4 and Sun. 1-4.

Lyric Opera House, formerly the Lyric Theater. Mount Royal Ave. and Cathedral St. Although elderly and plain it has recently received a sparkling new lobby and the accoustics are still excellent.

Maryland Historical Society. 201 W.Monument St. Contains a fine library of Marylandania, paintings, costumes and furniture. Its most striking exhibit is the original manuscript of the words of the Natiional Anthem.

Maryland Science Center. 601 Light St. This red brick, castle-like building at the south corner of the Inner Harbor was completed in 1976. It houses 106,000 square ft. of scientific exhibits and the Davis Planetarium. Open Mon.-Thurs. 10-5, Fri. and Sat. 10-10, Sun. 12-6.

Meyerhoff (Joseph) Symphony Hall. This elegant building is all curves; there are no flat walls or 90° angles. Opened in Sept. 1982, it is the home of the 96 member Baltimore Symphony Orchestra and has seating for 2,367 concert-goers.

Morris Mechanic Theater. Baltimore St. Opened in 1967 for the presentation of Broadway shows, it is an octagonal structure of ungarnished cement.

National Aquarium in Baltimore. Pier 3, E.Pratt St. This seven-level glass building topped by a glass pyramid was opened Aug. 1981. It houses over 5,000 sea creatures, while the pyramid contains a rain forest with tropical creatures. Ramps go below the tanks to view the sharks, while the seals can be viewed from the outside. Normally closes at 6 but is open to 10 Wed.-Sun. in summer.

Peale Museum. 225 Holliday St. Built 1813 as a museum by Rembrandt Peale, it served for a time as Baltimore City Hall. The first practical use of gas lighting was demonstrated here in 1816. It contains material relating to the

BALTIMORE - MUSEUMS AND THEATERS continued

history of Baltimore and paintings by the Peales, a noted family of American artists. Open Tues.-Sun. 10-4.

Pier 6 Concert Pavilion. A semi-openair theater with 2,000 seats under canvas where summer concert-goers can listen to symphony, pop, jazz or musical comedy.

U.S.F.Constellation. Constellation Dock, Pratt St. Built in Baltimore, the ship was launched in 1797, was the first ship of the U.S.Navy and saw action in the War of 1812. Open every day, 10-8 in summer, 10-4 in winter.

Walters Art Gallery. N.Charles St. near the Washington Monument. A collection of pictures and objects begun by William T.Walters and bequeathed to the city by his son in 1931. A modern addition has recently been added to exhbit more of the world-renowned collection. Open Tues.-Sun. 11-5. Free admission on Wed.

BALTIMORE - NEIGHBORHOODS

Ashburton. A northwestern suburb of beautiful single family homes inhabited mainly by black, upper middle class families. It takes its name from a city reservoir and filtratioin plant here.

The Block. The 400 block of E. Baltimore St. A strip of nightclubs, peep shows, adult book shops, etc. It enjoyed a greater reputation in the days of Burlesque.

Bolton Hill. A prestigious preservation district in the northern mid-town area consisting of several blocks of three-story spacious row houses.

Brooklyn. Pop.13,893. On the southwest bank of the Patapsco, it was evidently named because it was across the river from the city, as Brooklyn is to New York. It was laid out in lots by the Patapsco Co, in 1853 and annexed by Baltimore City in 1918; until then the Patapsco had been the Baltimore boundary.

BALTIMORE – NEIGHBORHOODS continued

Canton.   3 miles southeast of downtown Baltimore on the east bank of the harbor.   It was named by John O'Donnell who arrived with the first cargo of goods imported from China in 1785 and later planted a large peach orchard here for the making of peach brandy.   In 1828 the Canton Co. purchased the property and built wharfs, industries and its own railroad.   Today it is integrated into the Baltimore Port complex.

Charles Center.   A renewed area in downtown Baltimore consisting of One and Two Charles Center, which are tall buildings of offices and apartments, Charles Center South, Hopkins Plaza, with its square fountain, and Center Plaza, with its striking bronze sculpture "Energy" by Francesco Somaini, all connected by pedestrian walks and overpasses. The first building, One Charles Center, was opened in 1962.

Charles Village.   Several blocks on either side of N.Charles St. from 23d to 33d Sts. containing the Johns Hopkins University, the Baltimore Museum of Art, apartment houses and row houses.   Residents are a mixture of elderly and young professionals.

Cross Keys.   5100 Falls Road in northwest Baltimore. Named for a village and inn that once stood here, the Village of Cross Keys is an enclosed development built by the Rouse Co. who also built Columbia (q.v.) The village consists of an elegant shopping plaza, apartments, a high rise condominium, town houses and a hotel.

Dickeyville.   5 miles northwest of downtown Baltimore. It is hard to believe that this unique neighborhood of stone and white clapboard houses is within the city boundaries. The village was originally built around a mill operated by water power from the Gwynns Falls and owned by the Tschudy family.   Purchased by John Wethered in 1850, the village became Wetheredsville;   Wm. J. Dickey acquired it first by rent and then by purchase in 1872 and it became Dickeyville, although for a period in 1911 the name was changed to Hillsdale. During the Civil War the mill was confiscated as it was making cloth for Confederate uniforms;   the last

BALTIMORE - NEIGHBORHOODS continued

stone mill, which manufactured woollen and cotton cloth, still stands and is now a craft center. The stone houses are from the Wethered period, while the frame houses are from the Dickey period.

Eutaw Place.   Baltimore's finest street of town houses, constructed for the wealthy in the early 1900's. After World War II blight set in and some mansions were razed, but efforts are being made to save the rest.

Federal Hill.   The hill itself is a grassy elevation on the south side of the inner harbor, equipped with benches, paved walks and monuments. Between 1795 and 1895 a tower stood here from which ships were observed entering the mouth of the Patapsco, 15 miles away, and signals were sent to their owners by the raising of flags. Federal troops occupied it during the Civil War.   The surrounding area of brick row houses has received some attention recently and has been designated a preservation area.   There is a nice view of the city from the hill.

Fells Point.   The area surrounds the square where Broadway

Fells Point. Thames St.

BALTIMORE NEIGHBORHOODS continued

meets the harbor.   It was laid out as a separate town by
William Fell in 1763 and became part of Baltimore in 1773.
From 1750 to the 1830's it was a shipbuilding center;
Baltimore clipper ships, first built here in 1832, became
world renowned. Fells Point still has two marine piers.

Owing to the threat of demolition by an expressway, the
area acquired some publicity and is now a Preservation
District.   Among the old buildings, some of which antedate
1830, there are two small live theaters, numerous bars and
small restaurants, art gallery, market building, and the city's
Recreation Pier where activities are held, and which has a
fine view of the harbor from the roof.   The population is
equally   diverse ranging through seamen, artists, home-
steaders who are remodelling the old homes, down and outers
and well-heeled visitors.

Govans.   A northern middle class suburb of cottages and row
houses.   Originally it was a village on York Road called
Govanstown, from the local landowner, William Govans, who
received his tract in 1775.   It became part of Baltimore in
1918.

Guilford.   An affluent suburb east of Charles St. and south
of Coldspring Lane, which was developed just before World
War I.   The quiet, tree-shaded streets are bordered with
palatial residences of varied architecture.   Sherwood Gardens, the grounds of the John W.Sherwood House, which provide a nice display of azaleas and tulips in season, are now
maintained by the city.

Hamilton.   A suburb of cottages and duplexes in the northeast part of the city. It became part of Baltimore in 1918.

Hampden.   The area surrounding W.36th St. which is its main
shopping   area   and   still   retains   a   neighborhood   flavor.
Hampden originated as a mill town, a suburb of Woodberry,
in the Jones Falls valley.   Some of the stone mills still remain and the original mill-owner's home is on the hill above
the valley, now the S.P.C.A. headquarters.   The small houses
are of many styles and the population is mainly white, native, blue collar.

BALTIMORE - NEIGHBORHOODS continued

Highlandtown. Centering on Eastern Ave. east of Patterson Park, this is a neighborhood that was once typical of Baltimore, with its streets of neat brick or formstone-fronted houses, white marble front steps and painted window screens. Originally settled by Greeks, Poles, Italians and Germans, it still has a mainly white, working population.

Homeland. East of Charles St. on the northern fringe of the city this is one of Baltimore's wealthiest suburbs, with spacious homes on tree-shaded streets.

Inner Harbor. Literally the stretch of water lapping up to Pratt St. and Light St. Today the term applies to the whole re-developed district surrounding it. Once an area of wharves and shipping activities, it is now given over to promenades and elegant new buildings which attract throngs of people.

Little Italy. A small area south of Pratt St. and west of Eden St. A close-knit, family-oriented community of neat picturesque streets; outsiders are attracted by the numerous well-known Italian restaurants.

Locust Point. Originally this name applied to the whole peninsular between the Northwest and Middle Branches of the Patapsco River, previously known as Whetstone Point. Today it applies mainly to the area around Fort Avenue near Fort McHenry and the yards and piers of two of Baltimore's Marine Terminals. The north terminal was originally begun by the B.& O. Railroad in 1849 and was a port of entry for immigrants until World War I; the rail yards cover many acres. A community of row houses backs up the terminal.

Mount Vernon. The area surrounding the Washington Monument, which stands on a slight elevation on North Charles St. Four small parks containing fountains and statuary radiate from the monument; they are surrounded by elegant stone mansions, a stately Methodist Church, the Walters Art Gallery and the Peabody Institute.

Mount Washington. A suburb on Baltimore's northwestern slopes formed by the Jones Falls Valley. Originally a rural

BALTIMORE - NEIGHBORHOODS continued

development for wealthy citizens, the area is still heavily wooded with varied architecture on large lots. There is a small collection of boutique and specialty shops in the valley where the railroad station once stood.

Northwood. A large northern suburb of row houses built in the 1950's. One of Baltimore's first suburban shopping centers was built here.

Oldtown. Centering on North Gay St. this was originally a separate town, divided from Baltimore by Jones Falls. Belair Market, now covered, began in 1813 as an open air farmers' market. The area deteriorated badly but recently the 400 and 500 blocks of N.Gay St. have been closed to traffic and renovated as the picturesque Old Town Mall.

Pimlico. A northwestern suburb of mainly row houses with some groups of cottages, which has seen several population changes. The name is known nation-wide as the home of the race course, which attracts thousands of fans from March until May. The season culminates in the Preakness, one of the world's most prestigious horse races.

Port Covington. Fronting on the Middle Branch of the Patapsco River, this was one of the marine terminals of the Baltimore Harbor, dealing mainly in bulk shipments of coal and operated by the Western Maryland Railroad. There are seven piers and room for 3,000 railroad cars in the yards. Since the absorption of the W.M.R. by CSX, the whole complex has fallen into obsolescence.

Roland Park. A quiet affluent northwest suburb west of Charles St. on both sides of Coldspring Lane. It is an older community, planned by the Olmsteads, who designed Central Park; its own fake-Tudor shopping center on Roland Ave. is said to be the earliest suburban shopping center in the country. The slopes leading down to Jones Falls valley conceal winding, leafy streets.

Seton Hill. A small preservatiion area of quiet, narrow streets of row houses near the downtown area. It is named

BALTIMORE - NEIGHBORHOODS continued

for Mother Seton (See **EMMITSBURG.**) The area where the recently demolished St. Mary's Seminary stood has been converted into a small park.

Union Square.   A small square west of the downtown area, bounded by streets of tall row houses and designatedd a preservation district. The Mencken House, where H.L.Mencken, the writer, spent most of his life, is here. The fountain, which formerly stood in the center of the square has recently been replaced by a replica.

Waverly.   Centered on Greenmount Ave., which becomes York Rd. a few blocks to the north, Waverly was originally a village on the York Road. The Memorial Stadium is in the area; the surroundings, consisting of row houses and elderly frame cottages, are thoroughly integrated.

Windsor Hills.   A suburb originally developed among the hills and trees northwest of the city. Winding streets and spacious older homes side by side with newer houses and apartments provide homes in this integrated community for many of the workers at the Social Security Administration in Woodlawn.

Woodberry.   A community based on the mills which once lined the Jones Falls. The first silk mill in the U.S. was located here but there were also many woollen and cotton mills, which in later years specialized in cotton duck and sailcloth. Some of the great stone buildings remain, now rented out to various companies, and the mill workers' houses, built of the same sombre stone, form the nucleus of the village.

BALTIMORE COUNTY.   County Seat: Towson.   Pop. 655,615.   Area: 646 sq. miles.

Baltimore County was first formed in 1659 but has undergone several divisions since.   It was named for George Calvert's barony in Ireland from which he took his own title of Lord Baltimore.   It is bounded on the north by the Pennsylvania border;   on the east by the Little Gunpowder River and a line northwards from its source;   on the southeast by the Chesapeake Bay;   on the southwest by the Patapsco River and on the west by a straight artificial boundary.   All of the county lies on the Piedmont Plateau except for a small area in the southeast, which lies on the Coastal Plain, and where most of the industry is situated. Baltimore City is an independent division and is described separately.

In Baltimore City and County lives nearly half of Maryland's population. Many of the large residential developments and unincorporated towns adjoin the city, and much of the heavy industry and water-related activity lies in and just beyond the city.

North of Baltimore, between corridors of development, lie the Greenspring and Worthington Valleys where a number of farms and estates still survive and still foster the earlier traditions of fox-hunting and horse breeding and racing. Still further north the developments give way to rolling farmland, dissected by stream valleys. Two large reservoirs, Loch Raven and Prettyboy, on the Gunpowder River, form the area's water supply, while a third, Liberty, on the Patapsco River lies half within the county.

BALTIMORE HIGHLANDS (Baltimore County)

4 miles south of downtown Baltimore. It was a stop on the Baltimore and Annapolis Railroad and developed around the station, but it is now considered part of Lansdowne.

BALTIMORE PIKE

This early road was completed in 1822 from Cumberland to Baltimore and the name is still given to the present route 40 west where it passes through Baltimore's western suburbs. Old route 40 over South Mountain still follows the course of the old road, but elsewhere the roadbed has been re-located several times, the olders sections being designated route 144, route 99, Frederick Road or Old Frederick Road. Other parts have lost their identity beneath Interstate 70.

BALTIMORE-WASHINGTON INT'L AIRPORT (B. W. I.)

Before it received its present name, B. W. I. was known as Friendship Airport, the reason being that it was centered on a small community called Friendship. Many houses and road segments were obliterated before the airport was opened in 1950. It has twice undergone renovations and is capable of handling the largest jets.

A number of industries ring the airport, including the Aerospace Division and Systems Development Division of Westinghouse, which together employ 6,500 people.

BARCLAY (Queen Anne's) Pop. 187. Incorp. 1931.

13 miles northeast of Centreville.

BAR NECK (Talbot)

16 miles southwest of Easton at the lower end of Tilghman Island. A wild bird refuge is maintained here by the Tilghman Packing Co.

BARNESVILLE (Montgomery) Pop. 162. Incorp. 1888

15 miles northwest of Rockville. It was named in 1811 for a local landowner named Wm. Barnes who later moved to Ohio and founded another Barnesville in Belmont County.

Near Barnesville is the Al Marah horse farm, said to be the largest privately-owned Arabian horse farm in the world. It is open daily 9-4 for drives and walks. Nearby on Peachtree Rd. is the only Arabian horse museum in the U.S. It is open Tues. thru Fri. 9-5 and Sat. and Sun. 1-5 free.

In the churchyard of St. Mary's Church is a mass grave of workers who died of cholera while building the C. & O. Canal.

BARTON (Allegany) Pop. 723. Incorp. 1900.

16 miles southwest of Cumberland. This coal town in the George's Creek Valley was named for Barton-on-Humber, England, birthplace of the founder, Maj. Andrew Bruce Shaw. In 1810, after a heavy rainstorm, the populace was astonished to see "A mountain of coal" exposed in the area now known as Potomac Hollow, but the first mine was not opened until 1854.

BASKET SWITCH (Worcester)

8 miles northeast of Snow Hill. They say there was once a basket factory here and also a switch on the railroad, perhaps to serve the factory. The small village now has neither.

BATTLE CREEK CYPRESS SWAMP (Calvert)

6 miles southwest of Prince Frederick. The area is adjacent to Battle Creek, a river which was named by Robert Brooke, the first commander of Calvert County, after his wife's home at Battle in England. About a hundred acres of the swamp was acquired by the Nature Conservancy in 1955 and it is a registered National Landmark and a wild life sanctuary; the trees are believed to be the most northerly stand of bald cypresses in the country.

A raised boardwalk has been constructed through the

swamp from which the bulbous trunks and feathery leaves of the huge trees can be viewed without damage to the environment.   A small nature center is open Tues. to Sat. 10-4.30 and Sun. 1-4.30.   Closed Mon.

Bald cypresses at Battle Creek Cypress Swamp.

BAYNESVILLE (Baltimore County)
8 miles northeast of downtown Baltimore.   An old settlement which has been swallowed up in the developments adjoining Loch Raven Boulevard near the Beltway.

BAY RIDGE (Anne Arundel) Pop. 1,989.
4 miles southeast of Annapolis.   It is hard to believe that this Bayside community was advertised in the 1880's as an incomparable resort, with a beach stretching 4,000 ft., row boats for hire, picnic groves, pony rides, baseball ground, hotel, opera house, dancing pavilion, observatory, zoo, museum, restaurant (the largest in the country!) where the marine band played to diners, etc., etc.   Visitors were brought here by steamer to the covered pier, or by train.

Nothing of all this remains.   Until a few years ago, there was a beach and pool open to the public for a small fee.   This has now become a private club owned by the Bay Ridge Inn, which is open all year for private banquets, etc. The few streets of homes facing the water collectively own the remainder of the shore.

BAY VIEW (Cecil)

8 miles northwest of Elkton. From here one is supposed to be able to see the Chesapeake Bay (perhaps from the church tower.) Half a mile from the village is Gilpin's covered bridge over Northeast Creek, built around 1860 and restored 1959. The road has been re-aligned and no longer passes over the bridge. Just below it is Gilpin's Rocks, or Falls, named after Samuel Gilpin who settled the area in 1733 and built a mill here two years later. Numerous mills have stood at this spot over the years, and a dam here was once used to supply electricity to nearby towns.

BEALLSVILLE (Montgomery)

16 miles northwest of Rockville. It was previously called Beall's Crossroads. Near the village is the Monocacy cemetery which was chartered in 1872 on the site of Old St. Peter's Church, originally built in 1737. The church was re-built later, only to be badly damaged in the Civil War.

BEANTOWN (Charles)

8 miles northeast of La Plata. East of here, in the angle between routes 232 and 382 lived Dr. Samuel Mudd. This gentleman set the broken leg of John Wilkes Booth after his flight from Washington and as a result was accused of conspiracy and sentenced to life imprisonment; he was freed in 1869 on account of his heroism during the yellow fever epidemic. He is buried in St. Mary's Catholic cemetery, one mile south of Bryantown on route 232. Recent efforts have resulted in the clearing of his name.

BEAR CREEK (Baltimore County)

A creek which enters Baltimore Harbor and almost bisects Patapsco Neck. Sparrows Point Country Club fronts onto its east bank and several smaller public parks are on its banks and inlets, including: Bear Creek, Battle Grove, Inverness, Lynch Cove, Chesterwood, Merritt Point, Orchard and Fleming Parks, and Watersedge Beach.

BEAR ISLAND (Montgomery)

8 miles southwest of Rockville in the middle of the Potomac at Great Falls. It is a well-known study area for the local crystaline rocks.

BEAVER CREEK (Washington)

6 miles southeast of Hagerstown. The village school here is preserved as a small museum demonstrating the old type of rural school; it also includes a farm tool collection and millinery store, open Sun. afternoons June to Oct. 1. Just north of route I 70 is the Beaver Creek Fish Hatchery, belonging to the State Dept. of Game and Inland Fish. Opened in 1916 and re-built in 1948, it supplies rainbow trout to the area streams and fingerlings to other hatcheries. It is fed by a copious fresh water spring which maintains an even temperature year round.

BEAVER DAM (Baltimore County)

13 miles north of downtown Baltimore near Cockeysville. It exists today only in the name of a road and a swimming club whose pool fills the old Beaver Dam quarries. The marble quarries here were opened in the early 19th century and provided marble for the Washington Monument in Baltimore and part of the Washington Monument in Washington, D.C. as well as for many buildings in Baltimore, Towson, Philadelphia, Detroit and New York, to say nothing of the white marble steps so typical of the older sections of Baltimore City. One of the old quarry buildings still stands near the pool.

BECKLEYSVILLE (Baltimore County)

25 miles northwest of downtown Baltimore. A crossroads village named for George Beckley who built a paper mill here about 1800. Beckleysville Rd. used to cross George's Run, but part of it now lies under Prettyboy Reservoir.

BEL AIR (Allegany)

A housing development area between Cumberland and Westernport.

BEL AIR County Seat of Harford County. Pop. 7,814. With N. & S. Belair included: 13,504. Incorp. 1874.

Land was purchased for a courthouse here in 1782, in Scott's Old Field. Scott's house, demolished in 1930, was at the north end of town behind the present oil storage plant near the railroad tracks. The courthouse burned down and the present one was erected in 1858-9 and enlarged in 1904.

The Harford County Historical Society owns an

interesting house at 312 Kenmore Ave. Known as the Hay's House, it was probably built before 1711, saved from destruction in the 1960's, moved to this site and restored. Lafayette is said to have spent the night in it in 1784. The house is open to the public on the first Sun. of each month, 1-5 p.m.

The neighborhood of Bel Air has a theatrical history, since Edwin Booth was born not far from town (see **FOUNTAIN GREEN;**) the Harford Community College carries on the theatrical tradition with its drama group.

Several large housing developments have sprung up around the town, predominantly to the south, many of whose inhabitants commute to Edgewood Arsenal for their employment. There are some smallish industries around town including the manufacture of raincoats, jackets and ornamental railings.

BELAIR (Prince George's)

Belair started life as a suburb of Bowie, but now far exceeds that town in size and population, although it is still technically part of Bowie. It takes its name from an important colonial house, which was built in 1743 for Samuel Ogle, three times governor of Maryland; the next governor, Benjamin Tasker, also lived there for a time. The house, which is considered to be one of the best examples of Georgian architecture in Maryland, still stands proudly amid the interloping houses on Tulip Grove Drive, off the 2800 block Belair Drive; it is now the headquarters of the city, and can be visited during office hours, Mon. thru Fri. 8.30 - 5.00. The great avenue of tulip poplars which lined its driveway has also been spared, although it is difficult to walk down it without trespassing on some back yards.

The original estate was 3,600 acres and is considered to be the birthplace of horse-racing in America; during its long history of horse-breeding it produced several triple crown winners. Horse-breeding came to an end in 1955; in that year the owner, William Woodward, Jr. was accidently shot by his wife, who mistook him for a prowler at their home in Oyster Bay, N.Y. Three years later the estate was purchased by Levitt & Sons and the new Levitt Town of Belair was born.

One of the stables has been preserved and houses a museum of horse-racing memorabilia. It is located on Belair

Drive opposite the intersectioin of Tulip Grove Drive, and is open Suns. 2-4 during May, June, Sept. Oct. and at other times by appointment by calling 262-0695.

BEL ALTON (Charles)

4½ miles south of La Plata. It was founded in the 18th Century and is today a somewhat scattered place, although the surrounding countryside has changed little from the time when John Wilkes Booth, the assassin, hid out on the farm of Samuel Cox, about two miles from here. The Charles County Fair Grounds are a mile to the north.

BELCAMP (Harford)

8 miles southeast of Belair on route 40 at the head of the Bush River. The Bata Shoe Company's factory here, the largest industrial plant in Harford County, was started by Czech refugees just before World War II and employs 2500-3000 people. Bata has 97 plants in 91 countries, and this is their headquarters. It occupies less than 100 acres of the 1500 acres owned by the company, and plans are now under way to start building a new town for 10,000 people and an industrial park. The factory maintains a retail shoe outlet.

BELINDA SPRINGS (Washington)

14 miles south of Hagerstown. In the early 1800's this was a resort, owned by Jacob Gardenhour, who named it after his wife; the amenities included cottages, bath-houses, ten pin alleys, billiards and more. No trace remains of it on the map, and very little at the site.

BELTSVILLE (Prince George's) Pop. 12,760.

12 miles northeast of the U.S.Capitol. it was named by the B. & O. Railroad in 1839 for a local landowner, Truman Belt, and not, as could be supposed, because it is close to the Washington Beltway.

There are a number of small industries located here, but the name is chiefly associated with the Agricultural Research Center of the U. S. Dept. of Agriculture. The center consists of 10,000 acres, with over 600 buildings and countless plants and animals. Crops are studied both here and throughout the country; plant-breeding experiments carried out at Beltsville have revolutionized food production and given us the term "green revolution." The Beltsville turkey, a small bird for small families, is another of their products. A visitors' center is open daily 9-4 and free tours are available.

Nearby, on route 1, is the National Agricultural Library, an impressive building which is a prominent landmark for miles.

BENEDICT (Charles)

16 miles east of La Plata at the west end of the Patuxent River Bridge. The town was founded in 1683 and originally named Benedict Leonard Town, after the fourth Lord Baltimore. It is the only town on the Patuxent River in Charles County; it has a boat building industry for small craft and a small seafood industry. It is also a favorite hunting and fishing center, where boats can be rented.

Benedict water front.

Benedict was originally a far more important port; it had a customs house and was a prominent shipping point for tobacco until the early 1800's. In 1814 it achieved prominence when the British landed 5,000 troops there for the march on Washington. Lest any should doubt this fact, a British cannon ball was found embedded in an old house recently and other artifacts were unearthed during some renovations.

BENTLEY'S SPRINGS (Baltimore County)

26 miles north of downtown Baltimore. The name is derived from Charles W. Bentley, who owned a small summer

resort here, which attracted people from Baltimore to take the medicinal waters. A hotel and cottages were burnt down in 1868, and a rooming house, which replaced the hotel, was demolished in the 1950's. Trains which brought people from Baltimore along the Northern Central line have not passed through for many years, but the station sign still survives over the door of the general store.

BERKLEY (Harford)

12 miles northeast of Bel Air. After crossing the Susquehanna River at Bald Friar in 1781, Lafayette stayed with his troops at the estate of Col. James Rigbie near here. It is said that a mutiny was quelled before the southward march was resumed.

BERLIN (Worcester) Pop. 2,162. Incorp. 1868.

17 miles northeast of Snow Hill. Some think the name is a contraction of Burleigh Inn since the land around here was patented under the name of Burleigh.

Near here was born Stephen Decatur, naval hero of the War of 1812, who died in a duel (See **BLADENSBURG.**) There is a memorial to him on route 113 near the Stephen Decatur Memorial Park, just south of town and there are Decatur memorabilia in the museum at Snow Hill.

There is a large poultry processing plant here and several smaller businesses.

BERWYN HEIGHTS (Prince George's) Pop. 3,135. Incorp. 1896.

9 miles northeast of the U.S.Capitol. A Washington suburb which was originally laid out east of the B. & O. Railroad tracks in the 1880's under the name of Charlton Heights, after the first name of one of the developers. The town of Berwyn was later laid out in the 1890's on the west side of the tracks, where a village had previously been established. Charlton Heights changed its name to match the other development in 1896.

BETHESDA (Montgomery) Pop. 62,736.

8 miles northwest of the U. S. Capitol. The community was named in 1820 when the settlers built the Presbyterian Church, which was burnt in 1846 and rebuilt in 1850. The name refers to the healing pool mentioned in the Gospel of

St. John, and is an appropriate name for the suburb, since Bethesda today is the home of two great medical institutions, which are situated on either side of route 240: The Naval Hospital, and the National Institute of Health, which combines seven separate facilities, including the National Library of Medicine. Otherwise, Bethesda is basically residential, although a large firm produces tissue culture materials. North Bethesda has a population of 22,671.

BETHLEHEM (Caroline)
11 miles southwest of Denton. The tiny postoffice here only comes alive in December, when thousands of pieces of mail are received in order that they may be postmarked with a special stamp. The practise was started in 1938 by a teenager who advertised in a stamp collectors' magazine.

BETTERTON (Kent) Pop. 327. Incorp. 1906.
11 miles north of Chestertown, facing the Chesapeake Bay at the mouth of the Sassafras River. Old timers well remember when this was one of the finest beaches in Maryland and steamers used to bring holiday-makers across the Bay from Baltimore. The beach is still free to the public, but the parking is scarce, the beach is littered and what remains of the facilities is squalid and decaying. The county purchased the property in 1979 and improvements are planned.

BEVERLY BEACH (Anne Arundel)
7 miles south of Annapolis. This was once a family resort on the Chesapeake Bay, but the park is closed and the buildings rotting. The beach that remains is privately owned by the community.

BIG POOL (Washington)
16 miles southwest of Hagerstown. The Big Pool is a narrow lake, nearly two miles long and very deep in places, which parallels the Potomac River and is part of the C.& O. Canal. The canal engineers decided to make use of a natural ridge to create a lake by erecting a dike for the towpath and flooding the area between the ridge and the dike. At the northwestern end of the pool is a village of the same name. At the southeastern end is Fort Frederick State Park and small boats for hire.

BIG RUN STATE PARK (Garrett)
17 miles northeast of Oakland in the Savage River State

Forest on the northern tip of the Savage River Reservoir. The park covers 300 acres and primitive camping is permitted.

BIG SPRING (Washington)
12 miles west of Hagerstown. The spring still exists on private land in the village and so does the tiny railroad station. Commercial water bottling is done at Green Spring (q.v.)

Big Spring station on the old Western Maryland Railroad.

BILLMEYER WILD LIFE MANAGEMENT AREA (Allegany)
708 acres of forest land on Town Hill Mountain, managed for hunting.

BIRCHWOOD (Anne Arundel) Pop. 9,558
7 miles northwest of Annapolis. A conglomeration of summer settlements and new developments.

BIRDSVILLE (Anne Arundel)
8 miles southwest of Annapolis. A scattered community founded by an early settler named Bird. At All Hallows Church near here, the rector from 1784 to 1792 was Mason Locke Weems (1759-1825) a versatile character involved in literature and publishing as well as preaching. It was in his

biography of George Washington that the anecdote of the cherry tree first appeared, assuring immortality for a humble parson in an obscure parish. The church was built in 1727 on an earlier site. Some revolutionary soldiers are buried in the churchyard.

BIRDTOWN (Somerset)

19 miles southwest of Princess Anne, this tiny village was named for the Bird family. It is Maryland's southern-most community and is in danger of being washed away by the erosion of the shore in this flat part of the state - perhaps it has been by now.

BISHOPVILLE (Worcester)

22 miles northeast of Snow Hill. It is named for the Bishop family who settled here in the 1660's, but it was once called Milltown, as there was a mill on a tributary of St.Martin's River.   One of its citizens was Dr. George Bunting (1870-1959) the developer of *Noxema*.

BITTINGER (Garrett)

17 miles northeast of Oakland. Near this tiny place on route 495 is a maple sugar camp and a magnificent stand of giant maple trees.   Visitors are allowed to look into the sugar-making sheds where modern equipment is used.

BIVALVE (Wicomico)

16 miles southwest of Salisbury on the Nanticoke River. Its earlier name was Waltersville, but when the post office opened in 1887, the name was changed in honor of the oyster on which the town depended.   There is a tiny harbor on the Nanticoke River.

BLACK HILL (Cecil)

10 miles southwest of Elkton and 2 miles northeast of the village of Elk Neck. It is a small hill in the southern section of Elk Neck State Forest, which only appears high in relation to its flat surroundings.

BLACK HORSE (Harford)

12 miles northwest of Bel Air. A small village, which once boasted a tavern called the Black Horse, where George Washington stayed in 1773.   Recently an old inn sign of a

black horse was found, repaired and hung outside the house which stands on the site of the old tavern. The present house was built in 1849 by the tavern owner.

BLACK ROCK (Washington)

On the crest of South Mountain, north of route I 70, approachable by the Appalachian Trail. There was once a hotel here, now merely ruins, and the spot was popular for Fourth of July gatherings, picnics and orations.

BLACKROCK MILL (Montgomery)

12 miles west of Rockville on Seneca Creek, off route 28, a water-powered grist mill owned by the State. Restoration is planned.

BLACK WALNUT POINT (Talbot)

17 miles southwest of Easton at the lower end of Tilghman Island. Radar was tested here in its early days. The point is still government property and is inaccessible.

BLACKWATER WILD LIFE REFUGE (Dorchester)

12 miles south of Cambridge. The Department of the Interior maintains 11,216 acres here as a refuge for migratory wild fowl. The refuge was established in 1932 and is one of the chief wintering places for Canada geese using the Atlantic flyway, attracted by the tidal marshes, fresh water ponds, woods and some cropland. The bald eagle and the Delmarva fox squirrel are also found here.

An information center, open 9 - 4.30 displays photographs and exhibits of flora and fauna. Woodland walks, open drives and an observation tower are open to the public from dawn until dusk.

BLADENSBURG (Prince George's) Pop. 7,691. Incorp. 1854.

6 miles northeast of the U.S. Capitol. It was chartered in 1742 as Garrison's Landing on the Anacostia River, but was later named for Thomas Bladen, Maryland governor 1742-47. It was a busy port, shipping flour and tobacco until 1800, when the river began to silt up; but the town remained in business since it was situated on the main north-south highway (route 1.)

The Indian Queen was the principal inn; built in 1760, it operated until 1962, and after changing hands several times, was acquired by a conservation group who have restored and preserved it.   Another famous inn was the Palo Alto, which was known for cock-fighting.   Some say the term cocktail originated there.

In 1814 Bladensburg was the site of a battle in which the Americans were routed by the British, who marched on from here to begin their attack on Washington.   Fort Lincoln Cemetery has several interesting associations.   Under a large oak there is a spring house where Lincoln is said to have taken a drink.   A nearby marker designates the duelling ground where numerous duels were fought before duelling was outlawed;   Stephen Decatur was mortally wounded by James Barron in a duel here.   There is also a floral clock.

The huge concrete cross at the junction of routes 1 and 450 is a World War I memorial.

BLOCKHOUSE POINT (Montgomery)
9 miles west of Rockville, where a cliff meets the Potomac and the C. & O. Canal and towpath bend around the point.   It is believed that there was a frontier stronghold here once.

BLOODSWORTH ISLAND (Dorchester)
25 miles south of Cambridge in the Chesapeake Bay. This low swampy island, named for the Bloodsworth family, is now deserted and belongs to the Federal Government.

BLOOMING ROSE (Garrett)
A rural area in northwest Garrett County often mentioned by Meshack Browning.   Only a small church now bears the name.

BLOOMINGTON (Garrett)
19 miles northeast of Oakland on the west bank of the Savage River at its junction with the Potomac.   The town was laid out in 1849 and called Llangollen, after the town in Wales.   Some think the present name was chosen on account of the abundance of wild flowers on the hillsides which tower above the river.

The B.& O. Railroad crosses the Potomac at this point by an original stone and concrete arched bridge, built in 1851 and widened in the 1900's.   The Confederate Army prepared to blow up this bridge in 1864, and it is said that the holes drilled for blasting are still visible. The recently completed Bloomington Dam is upriver near Kitzmiller.

BLOSSOM POINT (Charles)

10 miles southwest of La Plata on a neck of land between Nanjemoy Creek and Port Tobacco River. The U.S. Government maintains a tracking station here and also its Diamond Ordnance Fuze Laboratories.

BLUE BALL (Cecil)

8 miles northwest of Elkton. This formerly important crossroads was named after the Blue Ball Tavern, which was established here about 1710 by Andrew Job. An historical marker tells us that Job's son married an indentured servant named Elizabeth Maxwell, who was a niece of Daniel Defoe. When Elizabeth's mother died in England, Defoe sent over the furniture. The long white building was a later tavern, now a private house.

BLUE MOUNT (Baltimore County)

22 miles north of downtown Baltimore. There is nothing much here except the Blue Mount Quarries, now water-filled. They were started around 1900 and the dark-colored serpentine was used extensively for road making.

BLUE RIDGE

The Blue Ridge in Maryland consists of South and Catoctin Mountains (q.v.) and the intervening Middletown Valley (q.v.) which form a ridge 1500 - 2000 ft. high running in a northeasterly, southwesterly direction and separated from the rest of the Appalachians by the Great Valley. The Blue Ridge of Virginia is not a direct continuation, but is offset slightly to the west. The northerly continuation of the Virginia Blue Ridge in Maryland is called Elk Ridge (q.v.)

BLYTHEDALE (Cecil)

13 miles west of Elkridge. It was called Whitaker's Mill in 1855 and later it became Independence, before the present name was adopted.

BODKIN POINT (Anne Arundel)

11 miles south of Annapolis. The point was well known to early mariners, as it marks the mouth of the Patapsco

River and the entrance to Baltimore Harbor. The point is on private land, backed by a large wooded area and fronted by a good beach, which has recently caught the attention of some developers.

BOHEMIA MILLS (Cecil)

Bohemia Mills is a small village 10 miles southeast of Elkton, while Bohemia River is a tributary of the Elk River. The name comes from Bohemia Manor, which was a grant of 4,000 acres given in 1662 to Augustine Herman (a native of Bohemia in Europe) for making a map of the Chesapeake Bay area. The land grant was increased to 6,000 acres in 1663 and the estate eventually grew to 200,000 acres. The map was a great success and copies of it were used into the nineteenth century.

Herman ran his estate on manorial lines from a manor house near St. Augustine (q.v.) A new house has been built on the site and his gravestone has been restored, although the actual site of the grave is unknown.

BOLIVAR (Frederick)

10 miles northwest of Frederick on old route 40. Above the village, Reno Monument Road passes through Fox Gap in South Mountain, and at this point stands a monument to General Reno who was killed during the Battle of South Mountain in 1862. Much carnage took place around here during the battle.

BOOKERS WHARF (Queen Anne's)

6 miles north of Centreville on the Chester River. The Peninsula Methodist Conference has about 200 acres here for a summer camp.

BOONESBORO (Washington) Pop. 1,908. Incorp. 1831.

10 miles southeast of Hagerstown on old, or alternate, route 40, which reached here in 1810, after crossing South Mountain. The town was laid out in 1788 by George and William Boone, said to be related to the famous Daniel, whose family may have emigrated to Kentucky from this part of Maryland. It was named Margarettsville after George Boone's wife. William Boone and his wife, together with other Boones, are buried in the Trinity Reform graveyard; Trinity Church was founded in 1750, before the town itself.

For its size the town has a good park and a nice little museum, collected and maintained by a single individual, but open to the public on Sunday 1-5, or by appointment. Washington Monument (q.v.) on top of South Mountain was built by the men of Boonesboro in 1827 and was the first public monument to George Washington (the Baltimore monument was not completed until 1829.) Several skirmishes took place here during the Civil War and the wounded were cared for in the churches of the town.

BORDEN SHAFT (Allegany)

2 miles south of Frostburg in the George's Creek Valley. This small mining town was named for the Borden family of New York, who formed a mining company here and opened a shaft, the first one in the area, in 1854. When the shaft became flooded, a tunnel was dug to Clarysville, where the water drained into Braddock's Run and polluted it.

BORING (Baltimore County)

21 miles from downtown Baltimore. The village was originally called Fairview, on a bend in the old Hanover Pike, which has since been re-aligned. Since there are six other Fairviews in Maryland, to say nothing of Point, Mountain, Summit, etc., the name was changed to that of the first postmaster. The post office had opened in 1880, but the change was not made until 1905 and one end of the village is still marked Fairview on the map.

BOWIE (Prince George's) Pop. 33,695 Incorp. 1874

16 miles northeast of the U.S.Capitol. It was founded in 1870 under the name of Huntington City, but was re-named in 1874 for Oden Bowie, governor of Maryland, who helped the Pennsylvania Railroad get its line into Maryland (See **POPE'S CREEK**) Bowie claims to be the second largest incorporated town in Maryland, with its overgrown suburb of **BELAIR**(q.v.)

The old town still exists along the railroad tracks and a number of buildings near the station have been converted into antique shops. This part of town has been designated the Huntington section and is due for rehabilitation.

Bowie is the home of the Maryland State Teachers' College, which was established in Baltimore in 1867 as the Baltimore Normal School, and moved here in 1908, when the state purchased it.   Originally it was a private college for training black teachers, but it is now an accredited state institution.

The town is fortunate in its recent acquisition of White Marsh Park.   Close to route 3, the park has an art center and indoor and outdoor sports of all kinds.

BOWLEY'S QUARTERS (Baltimore County)

An indeterminate location on a neck of land between Middle River and Seneca Creek, 13 miles east of Baltimore. It was named for Captain Daniel Bowley, who was born in Gloucestershire, England, in 1715.   It is said that he was en route for Jamaica when his ship collided with another vessel, bound for America; he was flung from his ship onto the deck of the other vessel and landed in America, where he remained!

BOYDS (Montgomery)

11 miles northwest of Rockville.   It was named for the founder, Capt. James A Boyd, a progressive farmer and railroad contractor who worked for the B. & O. Railroad.   Boyd spent much money hoping to create a flourishing town around what was then called Boyd's Station, and early writers extolled the beauty of the location, as it is on a slight elevation.   The town never amounted to very much however.

BOZMAN (Talbot)

11 miles west of Easton.   A tiny waterfront community thought to have been named for the Bozman family.   One of the family's members, John Leeds Bozman, published one of the first histories of Maryland.

BRADDOCK (Frederick)

4 miles west of Frederick on old route 40 where it begins to climb Catoctin Mountain.   The village is named for General Braddock, who marched this way in 1755 en route to Fort Cumberland;   a monument beside the road a little higher up the mountain marks this event.

BRADDOCK HEIGHTS (Frederick)

5 miles west of Frederick on the summit of Catoctin Mountain.   This community started as a summer resort built in 1896 by the company that operated the trolley lines over

the mountain between Frederick and Hagerstown. Some of the original cottages that formed part of the resort are still inhabited.

In addition to the cottages there used to be the Hotel Braddock, an auditorium for 1200 persons, a 40 ft. high observatory, dancing pavilion, cafe and amusements such as golf and tennis, all spread over 70 acres, with tables and paths illuminated at night by hundreds of electric lights. The park closed down in 1962 or 3; the trolley lines had already been removed, although the trolley station remains and is today a store and postoffice. A few derelict buildings also remain amid the ghostly overgrown walks.

BRADDOCK'S ROAD

In 1755 General Braddock built a road from Cumberland to Great Meadows, near Uniontown, Pennsylvania; it went over Haystack Mountain, closely following Nemacolin's Path, an old trail which in turn followed a wild life trace. The National Pike, now route 40, follows the general course of Braddock's Road, although it chose a different route out of Cumberland, following Wills Creek through the Narrows instead of over Haystack Mountain.

Part of Braddock's Road can be followed by taking Washington St. out of Cumberland. An old stone, supposed to have been erected by Braddock's troops in 1755, and later rescued from a stonemason who had intended to use it for steps, now stands on the grounds of Frostburg State College. It reads: *11 mi. to Fort Cumberland, 29 mi. to Capt. Smith's Crossings.* On the back of the stone is: *We will defend.*

BRANDYWINE (Prince George's) Pop. 1,319

10 miles southwest of Upper Marlboro. This insignificant village has given its name to a group of people, estimated to be about 5000 in number, scattered through Southern Maryland. Called the Brandywine People, they are neither white nor black, and in spite of several studies by anthropologists, their origin seems to be something of a mystery.

BREATHEDSVILLE (Washington)

7 miles west of Hagerstown. North of this small village is the Maryland Institute for Men and east of it is the

Devil's Backbone County Park, at the confluence of Antietam Creek and its tributary, Beaver Creek. Owing to their meanders, the streams appear to be flowing in opposite directions.

BREEZY POINT (Baltimore County)
12 miles east of Baltimore on Back River Neck. A small beach here is open to the public in season.

BREEZY POINT (Calvert)
7 miles northeast of Prince Frederick. This private beach is open on a fee basis, one of the few left around the Chesapeake BaY. There are camp sites, swimming, picnicking and boats for rent.

There is yet a third Breezy Point in Anne Arundel County on the Magothy River, 7 miles northwest of Annapolis.

BRENTWOOD (Prince George's) Pop. 2,988. Incorp. 1912.
5 miles northeast of the U.S.Capitol. It was originally called Highlands, but changed its name after the Civil War. North Brentwood, which adjoins it, is a separate town with a population of 758, incorporated in 1924.

BRETON BAY (St. Mary's)
An estuary which runs from Leonardtown to the Potomac River.

BRIDGEPORT (Carroll)
15 miles northwest of Westminster, where route 97 crosses the Monocacy River. A roadside marker tells that a corps of the U.S.Army camped around here in June, 1863.

BRIDGETOWN (Caroline)
11 miles northwest of Denton. It was once called Nine Bridges. Before the Civil War a large landowner and noted slave dealer named Marcy Fountain is thought to have had dealings here with the notorious Patty Cannon (See **RELIANCE**) He died in 1864 and is buried in the churchyard.

BRIGHTON DAM (Montgomery)
10 miles northeast of Rockville and a mile east of the village of Brighton, this dam on the Patuxent River forms the Tridelphia Reservoir (q.v.)

BRISTOL (Anne Arundel)

16 miles southwest of Annapolis. In the cemetery of St. James Church, a square brick building, is one of the oldest tombstones in Maryland, dated 1665.

BROAD CREEK (Queen Anne's)

An inlet on Kent Island half a mile south of the Bay Bridge. From the later half of the 17th century a ferry from Annapolis docked here, and there was a town of Broad Creek where the town of Stevensville now stands.

BROAD FORD DAM (Garrett)

This new dam on Broad Ford Run, northeast of Oakland, provides a lake and recreatioin area.

BROADFORDING (Washington)

5 miles northwest of Hagerstown. It was named for a crossing of Conococheague Creek, which is spanned by a five-arched bridge. That this insignificant village was once an important crossing is indicated by the fact that narrow Broadfording Road extends for many miles.

BROAD NECK PENINSULAR (Anne Arundel)

The area between the Severn and Magothy Rivers, once called Persimmon Point. Cape St. Claire, a new development, is the largest community on the peninsula.

BROOKEVILLE (Montgomery) Pop. 136. Incorp. 1890.

8 miles northeast of Rockville. Named for the Brooke family, who were early residents here, it is merely a few streets of stone houses. But its location of Georgia Ave. (route 97) leading straight out of Washington,D.C. put it in the path of President Madison, when he prudently left the capital during its brief occupation by the British on Aug.24 - 25, 1814. He and Richard Rush, his Attorney General, sheltered in the home of Caleb Bentley, which took the name of "Capital for a Day."

The Brookeville Academy opened here in 1815, added a top story in 1848 and moved to a larger structure one mile north in 1869. The original building now belongs to the American Legion. It is said that a law prohibiting the sale of intoxicants in the vicinity of the academy was the first of its kind in Maryland, perhaps to encourage visitors to partake of the area's chalybete springs.

BROOKLANDVILLE (Baltimore County)
9 miles northwest of downtown Baltimore on Falls Road. Nearby is the estate of Brooklandwood, which was originally one of several estates owned by Charles Carroll of Carrollton. Later, the estate was purchased by Isaac Emerson, the inventor of Bromo Seltzer, and now houses St. Paul's School, a preparatory school associated with Old St. Paul's Episcopalian Church in Baltimore. A little further north on Falls Road is Sater's Church, the oldest Baptist Church in Maryland, founded in 1742 and re-organized in 1865, after near extinction.

BROOKVIEW (Dorchester) Pop. 95. Incorp. 1953.
15 miles east of Cambridge. A ferry was established here over Marshyhope Creek (then called the Northwest Fork of the Nanticoke) in 1671 and for a while the town was called Crochet's Ferry. It was named Brookview about 1900 and a bridge was built over the creek in 1903. For some reason the town is said to have had a notorious reputation for drunkennes..

BROOMES ISLAND (Calvert)
8 miles southwest of Prince Frederick. It was named for the Broome (or Brome) family. It is a popular boating center, and there are camp sites, boat rental and a restaurant. Denton's oyster packing plant can be toured each Tuesday in season (which is usually Oct. - March) but the plant should be contacted in advance by calling 301-586-0300.

BROWNINGSVILLE (Montgomery)
16 miles northwest of Rockville. It was once a busy village with several businesses and mills along Bennett's Creek but there is little here today.

BRUCEVILLE (Carroll)
14 miles northwest of Westminster on Big Pipe Creek. The land was once owned by John Ross Key but he exchanged the property with Norman Bruce. Bruce's property then became Bruceville, and Key's property became Keysville. Bruceville is nearly deserted since the road was re-routed and only a few old stone houses, which were the homes of the workers in a nearby grist mill, remain. There is another Bruceville in Talbot County, 8 miles southeast of Easton.

BRUFF'S ISLAND (Talbot)

9 miles northwest of Easton. It is a point of land at the mouth of the Wye East River, no longer an island since the channel filled up. An old town called Doncaster, or Wye Town, was established near here, but only a few foundations remain.

BRUNSWICK (Frederick) Pop. 4,572. Incorp. 1890.

14 miles southwest of Frederick. The town was laid out in 1780 by Leonard Smith and originally called Barry Postoffice and later, Berlin; the railroad changed the name to Brunswick in 1890, as there was another Berlin in Maryland.

The town lies along the banks of the Potomac River between Catoctin and South Mountains and has long been a crossing point, first by ferry, then by a wooden toll bridge (erected 1859 and burnt by the Confederate cavalry two years later) and today by a high modern bridge.

The B.& O. Railroad and the C.& O. Canal reached Brunswick at about the same time, but it was the railroad freight yards that turned Brunswick into a boom town when they were first constructed in 1890. When the yards at the west end of town were constructed in 1906-7, in the days when the B. & O. was an individual rail company, the combined yards were said to be the largest freight yards belonging to a single company.

Brunswick was chosen as the site for freight yards as it is fairly level and is also east of all the big junctions disgorging freight on to the system. Although passenger traffic is limited to two Amtrak trains and a few commuter trains each day, and although most of the railroad repair work is now done elsewhere, the town still depends partly upon railroading, and operations at the round house are still worth watching. Freight trains also change crews here. There is not much other industry in town apart from a factory making mens' coats.

Crowds are drawn to Brunswick each August by the Potomac River Festival which celebrates both railroad and canal. Maryland's oldest and largest Veterans' Day Parade is also held here.

BRYAN POINT (Prince George's)

19 miles southwest of Upper Marlboro, fronting on the

Potomac River opposite Mount Vernon in Virginia. Nearby is the National Colonial Farm, a co-operative project of the Accokeek Foundation and the National Park Service. It is run as a typical 18th century farm, growing the early varieties of corn and other crops of the period and cultivated by hand with old-time implements. It is open June 1st to Labor Day, 10-5.

BRYANTOWN (Charles)

8 miles northeast of La Plata. Although its origin dates back to the early 18th century, its period of greatest prosperity was from 1820 to the 1880's, during which time it was a stage coach center, almost as important as La Plata. The railroad put a stop to all that when it by-passed the town in 1872.

BUCKEYSTOWN (Frederick)

6 miles south of Frederick. It was named for George and Michael Buckey who established a tannery here in 1775. Formerly it was served by a branch of the B. & O. Railroad, but the branch has long been derelict. Eastalco has a large aluminum plant nearby and on its grounds is Carrollton Manor House, not open to the public. The Buckingham School for needy boys was here from 1898 to 1944; six years after it closed, the Episcopal Church acquired the building and farm, and it is now the Claggett Diocesan Center.

BUCKTOWN (Dorchester)

8 miles southeast of Cambridge. Harriet Tubman was born of slave parents on a farm near here about 1820. She found freedom in flight to the north, aided by a Wilmington Quaker named Thomas Garrett, but returned to the Eastern Shore nineteen times and successfully led away about 300 slaves at the risk of her own life. During the Civil War she served as cook, nurse, scout and spy.

Greenbriar Swamp near here is thirty square miles of dense marsh grass and water, and is the scene of many legends and ghost stories.

BULL MOUNTAIN (Cecil)

11 miles southwest of Elkton near the mouth of the Northeast River. It was named for Thomas Bull who owned land near here in the 1600's. The forested hill is only 306 ft. high but appears like a mountain in relation to the flat surroundings.

BURKITTSVILLE (Frederick) Pop. 221. Incorp. 1894

12 miles west of Frederick at the foot of South Mountain. It was once called Harley's Postoffice but later named after Henry Burkitt who owned the surrounding land. In former times there was a tannery and a Seminary for Young Ladies here. An historical marker at the cross roads tells of the part played by the town in the Battle of South Mountain.

The small town is pretty and unspoilt by development; it is designated an Historical District.

BURNT MILLS (Montgomery)

8 miles southeast of Rockville on the North Branch of the Anacostia River. A rapid sand water filtration plant is located here, serving the Montgomery County water supply.

BURRSVILLE (Caroline)

5 miles east of Denton, almost on the Delaware border. Two earlier settlements were on this site, named Union Corner and Punch Hall.

BURTONSVILLE (Montgomery)

12 miles northeast of Rockville. It was named for Isaac Burton, the first postmaster, about 1850 and the original village stood where the shopping center now stands on route 29. Some developments have been built here and more are planned.

BUSH (Harford)

6 miles southeast of Bel Air on the Old Philadelphia Road. It was once a place of some importance called Harford Town and was the seat of Harford County 1773 - 1782 before the courthouse was moved to Bel Air. One house from this era remains, the Coach House Inn, now a private residence.

The town has another claim to fame in the "Bush Declaration" proclaimed in March 1775. This was the first Declaration of Independence ever adopted by an organized elected body in the country. It is inscribed on a plaque for the passing visitor to read.

BUTLER (Baltimore County)

18 miles northwest of downtown Baltimore. Only a few

houses remain here; but from the Butler flagstone quarries came buildings all over the state, to say nothing of walls, walkways and patios. Not much stone is now taken from the quarries but the Weaver Stone Co. buys stone from other locations and has a fine display of decorative stone work near their office.

Near Butler the Grand National Point to Point Horse Race is held each year on the third Saturday in April.

BUTTONWOOD BEACH (Cecil)
13 miles southwest of Elkton on the Elk River. A large trailer park is located here.

BUZZARD FLATS (Frederick)
A series of flat tops between Catoctin and South Mountains 12 miles northwest of Frederick. The vegetation here is unusual for the area.

BUZZARD ISLAND (Calvert)
A small island in the Patuxent River 5 miles southwest of Prince Frederick and 2 miles below the old Patuxent River Bridge. During the Civil War some families are said to have buried treasure here, but so far it has not come to light.

CABIN JOHN (Montgomery) Pop. with Brookmont 5,135

10 miles northwest of the U.S.Capitol. Some think the place was named after a hermit who lived nearby in a cabin, but the name of the stream here appears on older maps as Captain John's Branch.

Cabin John Bridge was built 1857-63 to carry the water conduit from Great Falls to Washington D.C. over Cabin John Creek. The conduit acts as an arch to support the bridge; it is 100 ft. high and has a span of 220 ft. and at the time of building it was the longest single span in the world. It still carries 20% of the D.C. water supply while vehicular traffic passes across the single lane of the bridge. There is a parking lot and a small enclave where visitors can view the span from above; it is difficult to view from below, for an expressway now passes under it. A plaque marks the bridge as being not only an historical landmark but an historic water landmark also.

Bobinger's Hotel was a popular restaurant at Cabin John for Washingtonians until it burnt down in the 1930's. Some say that Maryland fried chicken originated here, not in the manner of frying, but in the manner of Rosa Bobinger's arrangement of the chicken on the platter, with a curl of bacon on top.

Cabin John Regional Park has a mile-long miniature train, mini-farm and other amusements.

CALVERT (Cecil)

10 miles northwest of Elkton. The town was originally known as Brick Meeting House, or East Nottingham, and is situated on land that was a source of territory disputes between the proprietories of Maryland and Pennsylvania. The name Calvert is the family name of the Lords Baltimore and was adopted by the post office in 1880. It is said that the postmaster's wife picked the name, but it is believed that

the name was in use since the days of the boundary dispute, in order to lay greater claim to the territory.

An historic Friends' Meeting House has stood here since 1709 and been in continuous use ever since. William Penn selected the site himself, believing that it lay within his own boundaries. The brick part of the building now standing was erected in 1729, and the stone part in 1751. A marker relates how the building was used as a hospital for soldiers in 1778; those who died were buried in the nearby cemetery.

Lafayette's army encamped here en route from Elkton to the Susquehanna River crossing at Bald Friar.

In 1714 Benjamin Chandler settled in the village and established a business making clocks, compasses and other scientific instruments, which was carried on by his heirs until 1816.

CALVERT BEACH (Calvert)

A private beach 8 miles SW of Prince Frederick. (See **LONG BEACH**)

CALVERT CLIFFS (Calvert)

The Calvert Cliffs extend along the west shore of the Chesapeake Bay from near the Calvert County boundary in the north to Drum Point in the south, a distance of about 15 miles. They are fairly low, ranging from 40 ft. to 100 ft. in height, but conspicuous from the water, owing to the level nature of the surrounding terrain. They are notable for the large quantities of miocene fossils which are packed into the layers of clay, a phenomenon which has made them world renowned and a mecca for paleontologists.

Unfortunately there is little chance for the amateur collector to reach the cliffs from the landward side. Most of the beaches are privately owned, including the prime collecting areas belonging to the Chesapeake Ranch Club. A beach at Governor's Run is now private and fossil collecting is not allowed; it is not allowed either at the Calvert Cliffs State Park (open sunrise to sunset March 1 to Oct. 31) south of Lusby, even after the long walk from the car to the cliffs. The gas and electric plant near Lusby allowed parties of visitors and collectors while it was being erected, and maintains a small museum. Fossil specimens can also be seen in museums at Governor's Run and Solomons.

CALVERT COUNTY - County Seat: Prince Frederick. Pop. 34,638. Area: 216 square miles.

Calvert County was formed in 1650 and named for the family name of Lord Baltimore. It is Maryland's smallest county, with an area of 216 square miles on a peninsula 35 miles long whose average width is nine miles. It is bounded on the north by Anne Arundel County, on the east by the Chesapeake Bay and on the west by the Patuxent River which parallels the Bay. The terrain is flat and sandy.

The county's most notable feature is the Bay shoreline, where the Calvert Cliffs extend from above Chesapeake Beach to Drum Point. Collectors have been attracted to the area since 1824, although it was well known for 100 years previously.

The county remains rural and there is little industry apart from a few small boat building and oyster packing enterprises. Tobacco is still the chief cash crop; some corn, soy beans and grains are also raised.

CALVERTON (Montgomery and Prince George's) Pop. 7,649

A child-oriented suburb of Washington begun in 1961. Its 1,500 homes were all constucted by one developer.

CAMBRIDGE   Seat of Dorchester County.   Incorporated 1793. Pop. 11,703.

Cambridge is situated on the south shore of the Choptank River, 15 miles from its mouth and 33 miles from the eastern end of the Bay Bridge, but longer by road, owing to the indented coastline. Over 40% of Dorchester County's population lives here, and the town has always supported a large black community. It is the Eastern Shore's only deep water port; it has a 25 ft. channel and a 500 ft. pier to receive cargoes which consist largely of frozen fish for the processing plants.

Cambridge was founded in 1684 and laid out in 1687 when the county court was transferred there. It became a center for military operations of the lower Eastern Shore during the Revolution, and a number of revolutionary soldiers and statesmen are buried in the cemetery of Christ Episcopal Church. Five former Maryland governors sleep in the same churchyard.

The present courthouse was erected in 1854 and additions made in 1913. There are a number of old houses in the town, one of the most prominent being the Meredith House on Maryland Ave., which was built in 1760 and is now owned by the Dorchester County Historical Society, which maintains it as a museum, open Sundays 1-5.

Cambridge is a center for pleasure boating as well as for commercial shipping, and the Cambridge Yacht Club is famous for its sailing contests. Cambridge Creek, formerly called Hughes Creek, an inlet of the Choptank, is crowded with small boats, while boating regattas are common on the Choptank.   At the end of Water St. is a marina and a waterfront park where there is an interesting relic - a smoke stack from President Roosvelt's yacht "Potomac" which was used to house an elevator.

Factories produce wire cloth, electronic components, corrugated containers, and shirts.   There is a branch of Western Publishers, and several large canneries and seafood packers. The Eastern Shore State Hospital for the mentally ill is on a 390 acre farm nearby.

CAMP AIRY (Frederick)
15 miles north of Frederick on Catoctin Mountain.   A boys' camp with accomodation for 360 boys, which was started in 1924 and supported by a foundation.

CAMP DAVID (Frederick)
17 miles north of Frederick in Catoctin National Park. This facility is maintained by the U.S.Government for the use of presidents. Formerly called Shangri La by President Roosvelt, it was re-named Camp David by President Eisenhower in 1953, after his young grandson.

CAMP LOUISE (Washington)

13 miles northeast of Hagerstown on South Mountain. It was established in 1922 for Jewish girls.

CAMP SPRINGS (Prince George's) Pop. 16,118

8 miles southeast of the U.S. Capitol. The World Weather Center is located here, on the western edge of Andrews Airforce Base.

CAPITAL HEIGHTS (Prince George's) Pop.3,271. Incorp.1910.

5 miles east of the U.S. Capitol. One of Washington's older residential suburbs.

CAPITOL VIEW (Montgomery)

10 miles northwest of the U.S. Capitol. A residential suburb, which was originally centered around the B. & O. Railroad station. When it was developed in the 1880's a five-acre artificial lake was constructed and stocked with trout to attract wealthy Washingtonians.

CARDEROCK (Montgomery)

12 miles northwest of the U.S. Capitol. Here, at the Navy Ship Research and Development Center there is a mile-long covered building which houses a Model Basin, built in 1937. The Navy Aerodynamics Lab was opened here in 1944, and the Applied Math Lab in 1952.

CARDIFF (Harford)

12 miles north of Bel Air. It was formerly called South Delta, Delta being an adjoining town to the north across the Pennsylvania border. It was renamed for Cardiff in Wales by Welsh quarrymen who settled here to work the slate quarries for which the vicinity is noted. There is little demand for slate today, so the quarries are abandoned, and neighboring municipalities are eyeing them for use as refuse dumps.

In the middle of the town a road leads to a quarry in the local serpentine rock, formerly called the Green Marble Quarry. The pit opening here is impressive. Ornamental trim for numerous well-known building, including the Empire State Building, came out of it. But this quarry is also closed down; most serpentine is now obtained from Vermont.

CARLOS (Allegany)

A small mining town one mile west of George's Creek. Carlos Junction, also called National, is a mining town in George's Creek Valley, 4 miles south of Frostburg.

CARMICHAEL (Queen Anne's)

8 miles southwest of Centreville.   3 miles southeast of here is **WYE PLANTATION** (q.v.)

CAROLINE COUNTY. County Seat: Denton.   Pop.23,143. Area: 317 square miles.

The county was formed in 1773 and named for Lady Caroline Calvert, sister of the last Lord Baltimore.

It is bounded on the east by the Delaware boundary; on the west by the Choptank River and its tributary, Tuckahoe Creek; and on the south by various state roads. It is the only county on the Eastern Shore with no shoreline.

The county is basically agricultural and nearly all its small industries are related to agriculture in some form.

CARROLL COUNTY.   County Seat: Westminster.   Pop. 96,356. Area: 445 square miles.

Carroll County was formed in 1836. It was named after Charles Carroll of Carrollton, the longest surviving signer of the Declaration of Independence. It is bounded on the north by the Pennsylvania boundary; on the west by the Monocacy

River, Little Pipe Creek, Sam's Creek and the South Branch of the Patapsco River; on the east by the North Branch of the Patapsco to Glen Falls and then a line north, 17° east to the Pennsylvania line. It lies entirely within the Piedmont Province.

Many of the early settlers were German, followed by English, Irish and Scots. The county has at least two claims to fame: one is the birthplace of Francis Scott Key, author of the words of the Star Spangled Banner, and the other is an important shrine of Methodism, near Sam's Creek.

The county is predominantly rural, although there is some urban sprawl in the southern part. With Frederick County it leads the state in dairying and the growing of corn, wheat, barley and hay. A former occupation was the raising of vermifuge, which was distilled into wormseed oil at several distilleries in the county. The oil was used for curing hookworm in man and animals, and its cultivation was similar to that of tobacco; but its cultivation seems to have died out.

There are a number of diverse light industries around the towns, the most important being the Black and Decker plant at Hampstead and the Congoleum plant near Cedar-hurst. Several small factories put together garments cut out elsewhere.

The county was the scene of many troop movements in 1863, which inspired a book with the title: *Just south of Gettysburg.*

CARROLL ISLAND (Baltimore County)

15 miles east of downtown Baltimore. It is a neck projecting into the Gunpowder River. Baltimore society people founded a hunting club here in 1851 but the area today is part of the U.S.Military Reservation which encompasses Aberdeen Proving Ground and Edgewood Arsenal.

CARROLLTON (Frederick)

Carrollton was the 17,000 acre estate of Charles Carroll of Carrollton, the longest surviving signer of the Declaration of Independence, and Maryland's largest landowner at the time. He took the name of Carrollton to distinguish himself from others of the same name, but he did not live on the es-tate.

Carrollton covered most of the valley between the Monocacy River and Catoctin Mountain south of Frederick, and included some of Maryland's choicest farm land. Charles Carroll is portrayed in the B.& O. Railroad Museum in Baltimore, turning the first spadeful of earth to launch the nation's first railroad, which would later cross his estate from Frederick to Point of Rocks.

The estate has been broken up long since, but the older settlements are still along the railroad line. They are: Adamstown, Buckeystown, Doubs, Licksville, Limekiln, Point of Rocks and Tuscarora.

CARROLLTON (Carroll)

$4\frac{1}{2}$ miles southeast of Westminster. It was a pretty village in a deep gorge formed by the West Branch of the Patapsco River. Some of the houses and the tracks of the Western Maryland Railroad, which followed the stream, were several times ripped apart by flooding and little remains of the village today.

CASSELMAN BRIDGE (Garrett)

One half mile east of Grantsville, where route 40

crosses the Casselman River, and formerly a place of some importance known as Little Crossings. The Tomlinson family, who were large landowners in the area, had their residence nearby and there was also a distillery. The bridge was built in 1811 and for many years its 50 ft. stone arch was the longest single span bridge in the country. It carried the heavy traffic of the National Road until the 1930's when route 40 was completed. The bridge is now preserved by the state, surrounded by a mini-park and entered on the Register of Historic Places.

The Casselman River is of some interest to westward-bound travellers as it is the first river of any size to be found flowing westward instead of towards the Atlantic.

CASSELMAN HOTEL (Garrett)

One half mile west of Grantsville, it is one of the oldest hotels on the National Road in Maryland. Built in 1842 and originally known as Sterner's Tavern, it is an imposing brick structure. The coming of the railroads put most hotels on the road out of business, but this one remains today as a restaurant.

CATOCTIN FURNACE (Frederick)

12 miles north of Frederick at the foot of Catoctin Mountain. The complex contains a great mortarless stone wall, a huge stone furnace dating from the 18th century, some tiny log and stone dwellings, and the ruins of the manager's house, all owned by the State of Maryland and preserved as an Historical District.

Thomas Johnson founded the furnace about 1774 before he became the first elected governor of Maryland, and it later passed into the hands of his brothers. Several furnaces were in continuous operation until about 1905 and were the most important industry of the area for most of that time. The site was connected to Thurmont and Frederick by railroads, which transported hundreds of tons of pig-iron and household items such as pots, stoves and firebacks. The company also produced cannonballs in the Revolutionary War and the shafts for James Rumsey's steamboat, tested across the Potomac near Shepherdstown, W. Va. and also some iron plates for the Monitor at the time of the Civil War.

The materials to feed the voracious furnaces were close at hand. Hundreds labored to dig the iron ore in the vicinity; hundreds more denuded Catoctin Mountain of its forest trees, which were made into charcoal. The mountain slopes of Catoctin National Park are being allowed to regenerate themselves.

CATOCTIN MOUNTAIN (Frederick)

Catoctin is the mountain to which Whittier refers in the line: "Green-walled by the hills of Maryland." in his poem *Barbara Fritchie*. Together with South Mountain it forms the Blue Ridge in Maryland, which is slightly offset from the Blue Ridge of Virginia. Catoctin merges with South Mountain in the north and extends to the Potomac River at Point of Rocks in the south, where a rocky outcrop reveals the layers of greenstone of which it is partly composed.

On the heights above Thurmont part of the mountain is occupied by Catoctin National Park, which contains a number of marked trails to overlooks, a forbidden area containing Camp David, and a Demonstration Area where in the summer months there are displays of craft operations, such as quilting, broom-making and maple syrup refining. There is also a visitors' center on route 77, a self-guided nature trail, and a still, operating from a stream in the woods. Chimney Rock, Wolf Rock, Thurmont Vista and Hog Rock are all summits within the park.

Separated from the National Park by route 77 is Cunningham Falls State Park. The falls of Big Hunting Creek cascade down Catoctin Mountain to be captured further downstream in a man-made lake where swimming, fishing and boating are permitted and a fee is charged.

Six miles northwest of Frederick, the summit of Catoctin is occupied by yet another park - Gambrill State Park, where again there are hiking trails and views. Braddock Heights (q.v.) occupies the summit where old route 40 cross Catoctin; at Point of Rocks there is scarcely enough room between mountain and river for railroad and canal to squeeze by.

The lower slopes of the mountain are famous for their fruit, particularly apples and peaches. Six major streams flow down towards the Monocacy River from Catoctins slopes. In October, several towns at the foot of the mountain organize together for the Catoctin Colorfest weekend, and in February they hold the Winter Festival weekend.

CATONSVILLE (Baltimore County) Pop. 33,208

7 miles due west of downtown Baltimore. Named after Richard Caton, who married the eldest daughter of Charles Carroll of Carrollton, last survivor of the "Signers." Carroll gave the couple a house here named Castle Thunder, now, unfortunately demolished; it was situated on Frederick Road where the Public Library now stands and a picture of the house hangs in the library.

Catonsville was once served by its own branch railroad which terminated on Frederick Road opposite the White Coffee Pot Junior, but the track is now abandoned and partly overgrown.

The Townsend House at 1824 Frederick Road belongs to the Catonsville Historical Society and houses a small museum. It is open Wednesdays 11-3 and the first Sunday afternoon of each month.

The University of Maryland has an important branch in Catonsville and the Baltimore County Community College occupies an estate formerly called Hilton, which once belonged to the Glens of Glen Burnie. Catonsville is also the home of Spring Grove State Hospital.

CAVETOWN (Washington) Pop. 1,533

7 miles east of Hagerstown at the foot of South Mountain. There was indeed a cave here in bygone days, known variously as Bishop's Cave and Bushey's Cavern. It was located near route 66, north of the town near the large limestone quarry; but quarrying operations removed much of it in the 1920's and the rest collapsed. Only a small portion remains and it is too dangerous to enter.

This cave was the first to be discovered in Maryland and is mentioned as far back as 1748. For several years around 1823 it was illuminated and open to the public as a kind of beer garden at July 4th celebrations. According to reports, it was 500 ft. long and beautifully decorated with stalactites and massive columns, with a large lake at the end. A second smaller cave was discovered at the quarry in 1881.

CAYOTS (Cecil)

10 miles southeast of Elkton. Near here was the Labadie Tract, once the home of a small, much studied Dutch religious group known as the Labadists. The group settled here as a farming commune, with strict discipline but

poor organization, in 1683. After many scandals the group split up in 1727.

CEARFOSS (Washington)

Small village 4 miles northwest of Hagerstown, named after Daniel Cearfoss who, in 1877, was storekeeper and postmaster as well as farmer and drover. Previously the settlement was known as Stearn's Tavern and then Cunningham's Cross Roads.

CECIL COUNTY County Seat: Elkton. Pop. 60,430. Area: 374 square miles.

Cecil County was formed in 1674 and named for Cecil Calvert, Second Lord Baltimore. It is bounded on the north by the Pennsylvania state line, on the east by the Delaware state line, on the west by the Susquehanna River and the head of the Chesapeake Bay, and on the south by the Sassafras River. The northern part lies on the Piedmont and the southern part lies on the Coastal Plain, deeply dissected by Bay tributaries.

Cecil is usually considered to be one of the Eastern Shore counties and it is primarily agricultural, being engaged in dairying and the raising of corn, grains and soy beans.

CECILTON (Cecil) Pop. 581. Incorp. 1816

15 miles south of Elkton.   It was named for Cecil
Calvert, second Lord Baltimore, and previously called Cecil
Cross Roads.   Although   small,   Cecilton   is   the   most
successful attempt to found a town of this name; three pre-
vious sites had been selected at points along the Bohemia
River, but all had been failures.

Cecilton. Town offices and library.

CEDAR GROVE (Washington)

9 miles southwest of Hagerstown. At this small place
beside the Potomac River there is an old mill on Downey
Branch, which has been known by many different names. It
no longer works, but the owners permit camping, fishing and
picnicing for a small fee.

CEDAR HEIGHTS (Prince George's)

5 miles northeast of the U.S. Capitol. This was for many
years a neglected community, but until recently it boasted a
circular brick house.

CEDARDHURST (Carroll)

7 miles southeast of Westminster. At this village on the
North Branch of the Patapsco River, just above the far end
of Liberty Reservoir a large factory known as the Congoleum
Plant produces dry felt, which is sent to other plants as a
base for congoleum. The plant, which covers 155 acres and
employs about 300 people was started in 1913; at that time
the   station   on   the   railroad   which   serves   it   was   called
Asbestos.

CEDAR POINT (St. Mary's)

There are 19 Cedar Points in Maryland, plus one Cedar Point Neck, and 52 other places on the map containing the word Cedar. Cedar Point in St. Mary's County is now part of the Patuxent Naval Air Test Center. Cedar Point lighthouse, erected by the Coastguard in 1894, marked the mouth of the Patuxent River 15 miles east of Leonardtown. At that time the point was connected to the mainland by a narrow strip of land, but later the lighthouse became an island. It was abandoned in 1928, but as recently as 1981 the cupola was rescued and placed in the museum of the Naval Air Test Center.

CEDARVILLE STATE FOREST (Charles)

12 miles northeast of La Plata. Its 3510 acres are partly in Charles and partly in Prince George's Counties. The Piscataway Indians made this area their home in former times, and there is said to be an Indian burial gound in the forest. Within its boundaries is a state park with camping, fishing, hiking, hunting and picnicking facilities; the state uses this forest for demonstrations; charcoal kilns provide charcoal for other state forests and parks.

CENTREVILLE. Seat of Queen Anne's County. Pop. 2,018. Incorp. 1794.

Centreville. Queen Anne's County courthouse.

The name, of course, means Middletown, perhaps because the town was mid-way between Chestertown and Easton, which were both county seats before Centreville. Previously it had been called Chester Mill.

Centreville became the county seat in 1782 when the court was moved from Queenstown. The courthouse was completed in 1794 and the same building is in use today, being the oldest courthouse in continuous use in Maryland. Remodelling and repairing have left it looking unchanged. The statue of Queen Anne in front of the courthouse was unveiled in 1977.

Two houses in the town are owned by the County Historical Society: the Tucker House is a restored 18th Century home and Wright's Chance, on Commerce St. was originally built on a farm outside town and moved here in 1964. The latter is representative of Eastern Shore plantation homes. Both houses are open to the public on Fridays, 11-4, in summer.

CERESVILLE (Frederick)

4 miles northeast of Frederick. It was named after the Ceresville Estate and Mills on Israel Creek, a small tributary of the Monocacy. The name is appropriate for a village that has always been dominated by a flour mill.

CHALK POINT (Charles)

Chalk Point Generating Station, 6 mls. east of Hughesville is one of Potomac Edison's facilities. Three of its units burn coal, but in 1982 an oil-burning unit was added, the last major oil-fuelled generating unit to be built in the U.S.

CHANCELLOR POINT (St. Mary's)

A point projecting into the St. Mary's River two miles southwest of St. Mary's City and 14 miles southeast of Leonardtown. It was named for the 17th century owner, Philip Calvert, brother of the second Lord Baltimore, who was chancellor of the province at the time; for many years it was thought to have been the original landing place of the Ark and the Dove. There is a small public beach and a fine view of the river and the reconstructed state house at St. Mary's; also a nature center and trails.

CHAPEL POINT (Charles)

A point jutting out into the Port Tobacco River 5 miles southwest of La Plata. One half mile from the water, on a little hill, stands St. Ignatius Catholic Church and cemetery. Both the point and the church have direct associations with Father White, the Jesuit priest who arrived with the Maryland colonists on the Ark and the Dove in 1633, for it was he who named the point, after he converted a local Indian queen during a visit to Port Tobacco in 1639. The church was founded in 1641 but the present building, whose corner stone was laid by Bishop John Carroll, dates from 1798.

St. Thomas Manor was erected earlier than the present church, in 1741, as a Jesuit residence and is connected to the church by a brick passage, which is even earlier. The church is considered to be the oldest continuously active parish in the U.S.

CHAPTICO (St. Mary's)

10 miles northwest of Leonardtown. A cross-roads village named for the Chaptico, or Choptico Indians who formerly inhabited the area.

Chaptico. Christ Church.

Chaptico was designated a river port in 1683 at the head of a creek on the east side of the Wicomico River, and shipping continued until the early 20th century; but the creek is now silted up and most of the population scattered. From here, in 1689, John Goode organized a rebellion against Lord Baltimore.

Chaptico again saw action in 1814 when the British damaged the town. Christ Church, built in 1736 on a site dating from 1642, suffered much interior damage when their soldiers used it as a stable. It has undergone extensive repairs and the tower was added in 1913.

CHARLES COUNTY. County Seat: La Plata. Pop. 72,751. Area: 462 square miles.

Charles County was formed in 1658 and named for Charles Calvert, Lord Baltimore. It is bounded on the south and west by the Potomac River; on the north by a line drawn irregularly from a point on the Potomac opposite Mount Vernon to a point on the Patuxent River; on the southeast from a point on the Patuxent River to the Wicomico River estuary. It has 150 miles of shoreline on four rivers.

The county is mostly level plain and is still basically rural, although the opening of the Potomac River bridge in 1940 and the improvement of route 301 opened it up considerably. Tobacco is still the chief cash crop, although some grains, soy beans and sweet potatoes are also grown, with a certain amount of beef cattle raising, dairying and oystering.

Four tobacco auction warehouses are situated in the county, two in Hughesville, one in Waldorf and one in La Plata. They open the third week in April for 14 weeks, 5 days a week, from 9.30 until sold out. All leading cigarette manufacturers are represented at the sales, since the particular type of tobacco raised in the locality is incorporated into all tobacco mixtures.

CHARLESTOWN (Cecil) Pop. 721. Incorp. 1786

9 miles southwest of Elkton on the west bank of the Northeast River. It was named for Charles Calvert, Lord Baltimore.

The original town was laid out in 1742 when there were as yet no towns at the head of the Chesapeake Bay. Being accessible both by water and the Old Post Road, it became a thriving port, rivalling Baltimore, with two fairs a year attracting visitors from near and far. By the time of the Revolutionary War, however, Baltimore had overtaken the town in importance.

In the 1780's there was a small shipbuilding industry at Seneca Point, a mile from the town, and from 1781 to 1786 Charlestown became the seat of Cecil County, although no public buildings were erected, except a jail. When the county seat was removed to Elkton in 1786, some of the inhabitants dismantled their houses and shipped the materials to be re-erected in Baltimore. George Washington recorded several visits to the town and is known to have lodged there twice in 1795.

A Natioinal Historic District preserves fourteen

18th century homes, and each May a colonial fair is held patterned on that of 1774.

CHARLES TOWN (Prince George's)

Although not marked on any modern map, this was the first seat of Prince George's County, from 1696 to 1721. It was situated where Charles Branch and Western Branch meet just before joining the Patuxent, 3 miles southeast of Upper Marlboro. The name Mount Calvert was also applied to the town, Charles Calvert being the name of Lord Baltimore. Nothing remains of Charles Town now except an old house on private land named Mount Calvert.

CHARLOTTE HALL (St. Mary's) Pop. 1,901

15 miles northwest of Leonardtown. It is named for a school which stood here, and which in turn was named for Queen Charlotte of England. The locality was known from earliest times for its health-giving springs "The Coole Springs of St. Marie's" and the drinking of these waters appeared to cure an epidemic which swept the area in 1691. A few years later the colonial government built a small hospital here, which claimed to be the first publicly supported sanitarium in America.

Charlotte Hall. One of the several springs.

The springs are still there, in a little park opposite the main entrance to the school. Modern tests show that the water has no actual medicinal value, although it may have been purer than some of the local drinking water. Alas, it is no longer pure, and the springs are disfigured with notices warning against drinking from them.

Charlotte Hall Military Academy was established in 1774, although it did not actually open its doors until 1797, and the military program was introduced in 1850. In 1983 most of the buildings were demolished and the Charlotte Hall Veterans' Home was erected on the site.

There is not much to the village, but the few houses retain some charm.

CHARTWELL-ON-SEVERN (Anne Arundel)

10 miles northwest of Annapolis. A residential development built around the Chartwell golf and country club.

CHASE (Baltimore County)

14 miles northeast of downtown Baltimore near where the Pennsylvania Railroad crosses the mouth of the Gunpowder River. It was named for Charles Chase of New England, who came to Baltimore to collect a debt and received a tract of land in payment.

Chase once had a railroad station where parties alighted to hunt and fish around the Gunpowder estuary. That region is now the Hammerman Area of the Gunpowder State Park.

CHATOLANEE (Baltimore County)

11 miles northwest of downtown Baltimore in the Greenspring Valley. Here was once a hotel and summer colony which attracted well-heeled visitors from Baltimore. There was also a water-bottling operation from the springs forming the headwaters of the Jones Falls, which were believed to have restorative properties. Nothing remains now except five large frame houses approached by a private drive.

CHELTENHAM (Prince George's)

7 miles southwest of Upper Marlboro. Near here, on a 560 acre site, is the Naval Communications Station of the U.S.Government, which was started in 1938. It maintains around-the-clock communications with the Navy Department, ships at sea, and naval shore stations. Also near here is Boys' Village on a 1200 acre site. Started privately in 1872 as a refuge for young teen-aged boys, it was taken over by the state in 1937.

CHESAPEAKE AND DELAWARE CANAL (Cecil)

The canal connects Elk River, a tributary at the head of the Chesapeake Bay, to Delaware Bay, a distance of 14.7 miles, and shortens the distance between Baltimore and Philadelphia by almost 300 miles. The canal is used by about 40% of all arrivals and departures from Baltimore.

The C.& D. Canal was completed in 1829, although work had begun on it many years before, and it has been deepened and widened since. The government purchased the canal in 1919 and it is administered by the U.S. Army Corps of Engineers who also own 2,400 acres along the banks, part of which is used as a park and part as a wildlife management area. A new deepening plan is under study, but being delayed owing to environmental impact studies. (See **CHESAPEAKE CITY**)

C.& D. Canal bridge at Chesapeake City.

CHESAPEAKE AND OHIO CANAL

The C.& O. Canal was thought to be the answer to inland transportation when President Adams turned the first shovelful of earth at Georgetown, near Washington, D. C. in 1828. When the canal reached Cumberland in 1850, after crossing several mountain ranges and performing feats of engineering unsurpassed in its day, it was already outdated by the railroad. The canal follows the course of the Potomac River, negotiating a 605 ft. rise through 74 locks, many of which remain, plus 11 acqueducts across tributary streams and a 3,000 ft. long tunnel. Cargoes were mainly coal, in boats averaging 4 miles per hour, pulled by mules using ropes 224 ft. long.

Factors which put the canal out of business were railroad competition, depletion of Western Maryland coal and repeated floods, climaxing in the flood of 1924, which ended canal operations for good, while the railroads continued to flourish.

C.& O. Canal acqueduct across the Monocacy River.

The Federal Government acquired the canal in 1938 and it became an Historical Monument in 1961. Its entire length from Georgetown to Cumberland is a National Park; hikers and bikers instead of plodding mules are to be seen along the towpath, and there are facilities for camping at intervals.

CHESAPEAKE BAY
The Chesapeake Bay is in reality the drowned estuary of the Susquehanna River and is extemely important to the economy of Maryland. Its length is 185 miles (118 of them in Maryland) and its width varies from 3 to 22 miles; its greatest depth is 174 ft. near the southern tip of Kent Island. 46 principal rivers flow into it and 17 of Maryland's 23 counties, plus Baltimore City, border on it or its tidal estuaries

10,000 ocean-going ships navigate its waters each year,

many of them proceeding to the head of the Bay and navi-
gating the Chesapeake and Delware Canal which connects
the Bay to the Delaware Bay.   305,000 acres of tidal
marshes help produce food for acquatic life, which in turn
nourish the crabbing and oystering industries.

Another of the Bay's important functions is recreation,
which embraces fishing, boating, duck-hunting, crabbing, etc.
although beaches for swimming and relaxing are becoming
increasingly rare.   Nearly 114,000 boats are registered in
Maryland, almost 102,000 of them for pleasure.   The best
place to view the Bay from land is Sandy Point State Park.

Chesapeak Bay inlet, seen from Kent Island.

CHESAPEAKE BAY BRIDGE

Properly called the William Preston Lane, Jr. Memorial
Bridge, it crosses the Bay at a narrow point where Kent
Island projects from the Eastern Shore.   The two east-bound
lanes were opened in 1952, as one lane in each direction.
These soon proved inadequate and the three west-bound lanes
were added in 1973.

The bridge is 7.1 miles long, of which 4.3 are over
water. The highest part is 200 ft. above the water and there
are two spans for the two shipping channels of the Bay.
U.S. Highways 50 and 301 are routed over the bridge and the
toll booths are at the west end, the toll being $1.25 for a
private car.

CHESAPEAKE BEACH (Calvert) Pop. 1,408. Incorp. 1885

10 miles northeast of Prince Frederick. For many years this was a popular Bayside recreation spot, with hotel accomodation and many attractions. In 1900 a mile-long boardwalk was built and a railroad started bringing visitors from Seat Pleasant, near Washington; a harbor was dredged at the mouth of Fishing Creek in 1913. The Belvedere Hotel burnt down in 1923 and the railroad was closed in 1935, but the town survived for some time with rides, picnicking, fishing, boating and a swimming pool.

When the new lanes were added to the Bay Bridge, visitors were lured more and more to the Atlantic beaches. The attractions were swept away and the site became the Rod and Reel Club and Marina, catering to the boating and fishing crowd rather than to family outings. The old railroad station miraculously survives, high and dry on the parking lot, and has been made into a small musuem, open June to Oct. on Sats. and Suns. 1-4.

South of the town is the U. S. Naval Research Laboratory, conspicuous by its radio towers.

CHESAPEAKE CITY (Cecil) Pop. 1,031. Incorp. 1849.

6 miles southeast of Elkton, it lies on both sides of the Chesapeake and Delaware Canal, which is spanned by a lofty highway bridge here, high enough to allow shipping to pass beneath it. Most of the town lies on the south side of the canal and is little changed since the mid-19th century, when it sprang up around the canal operations. In those days machinery was needed to raise water for the nearby lock, but in 1927 the canal was lowered to sea-level, eliminating the several feet of difference in elevation between the two ends. The old Lock Pump House, which was erected in 1851 has been preserved and houses two original steam engines and a large scoop wheel which used to raise water to refill the lock. These engines were in use 1837 to 1927. The Pump House is open weekdays 8-4 and Suns. Easter to Thanksgiving, 10-5.30.

Chesapeake City no longer caters to the needs of commercial shipping but serves the pleasure craft which often pass through the canal. (See **CHESAPEAKE AND DELAWARE CANAL**)

CHESAPEAKE RANCH CLUB (Calvert)

19 miles southeast of Prince Frederick.   This large

estate consists of 4,500 acres, divided up into individual home sites, where many people have already built their homes. Privileges include access to private Bayside beaches, fishing and hunting.

CHESTER (Queen Anne's)

13 miles southwest of Centreville. A small scattered community on Kent Island. It has some small seafood packing houses.

CHESTERFIELD (Anne Arundel)

7 miles west of Annapolis. A place almost too insignficant to mention except that it was once a more important community named for an absentee landlord - Lord Chesterfield.

CHESTERTOWN. Seat of Kent County. Pop. 3,300. Incorp. 1806.

The town was once called New Town but the present name seems to have been associated with the locality from the earliest days. The first courthouse was built here in 1697, the town was laid out in 1706 and the name permanently adopted in 1780.

Owing to its situation on the wide Chester River, it became one of Maryland's leading ports before the Revolution. Foreign trade developed a wealthy society, and merchants constructed substantial homes beside the river along what was then called Front St. but is now Water St. It was also the political, trading, and shipbuilding center of the Upper Eastern Shore, for in addition to being a port, it was close to the north-south route which crossed the Chesapeake Bay at Rock Hall.

Several historical events took place in Chestertown. The brig *Geddes*, named after its owner, was the scene of a local "tea party" in 1774. The name *Episcopal* for the Church of England in America was adopted here, at the instigation of William Smith, rector of Emmanuel Church. The church, built in 1772, still stands.

William Smith was also the moving spirit in pursuading a number of financiers to donate an endowment for the founding of a college here, and George Washington, one of the donors, agreed to lend his name to the college, the only college so honored. Washington College was therefore erected in 1783-88; it was destroyed by fire in 1827 but re-built in 1845. The student body numbers about 800.

Chestertown. The Chester River Bridge.

Other points of interest are the Customs House and the Geddes-Piper House. The Customs House at 103 High St. dates from 1746 and is a building which was once attached to the Customs House proper (now demolished) and stands near the site where the "tea party " took place. The Geddes-Piper House at 101 Church Alley belonged to the owner of the brig Geddes, and is now the headquarters of the Kent County Historical Society, open on Sundays 2-4 during May to Oct. Water St. is still lined with venerable water-side homes.

A notable figure who was born in Chestertown is Charles Wilson Peale, Maryland artist and founder of a family of artists, whose work can be seen in the Peale Museum in Baltimore and other places.

In spite of its small size, there is some industry in the town, including Campbell's Soup, a company making valves and a seafood packer. Although the town has a prosperous appearance, there are a few streets of run-down houses at the edge of town.

A useful brochure of a walking tour of Chestertown is available from the Chamber of Commerce on Cross St. In May is held the Chestertown Tea Party Festival and a re-enactment of the incident described above. In October there is a candlelight walking tour of the town and some of its homes.

CHEVERLY (Prince George's) Pop. 5,751. Incorp. 1931.
6 miles northeast of the U.S.Capitol. This is one of Washington's older residential suburbs.

CHEVY CHASE (Montgomery) Pop. 25,421.
7 miles northwest of the U.S.Capitol. The suburb began as Chevy Chase Village, incorporated in 1910, which still remains an entity, with a population of 2,118. The name comes from an old English ballad and is taken from the French Chevauchée, meaning a border raid. The Village is bounded by Wisconsin Ave., Western Ave., and Bradley Lane; half the area consists of the country club, for formal landscaping was part of the original plan; it is said to be one of the first planned communities in the U.S.
At 8940 Jones Mill Rd. is the home of the Audubon Naturalists Society, a mansion with 40 acres of garden and wildlife sanctuary, open free to the public all year on weekdays.
Surrounding the Village is the modern suburb of Chevy Chase stretching as far as Kensington, where it is known as North Chevy Chase.

CHEWSVILLE (Washington)
5 miles east of Hagerstown. It is said that Col. Fitzhugh, who owned a nail factory here, named the town after a friend named Chew.

CHILDS (Cecil)
3 miles northwest of Elkton. It was called Spring Hill until 1886, when George W.Childs purchased a mill here and the B.& O. Railroad opened a station nearby.

CHILLUM (Prince George's) Pop. 32,775.
5 miles north of the U.S.Capitol. It takes its name from a former estate named Chillum Castle Manor, probably named after Chilham Castle in England. Pierre Charles L'Enfant, designer of Washington, D.C., died here and was buried in the grounds, but later re-interred at Arlington in 1911. The house is now a Catholic Theological Seminary named Resurrection Scholasticate.

CHIMNEY ROCK (Frederick)
An overlook on Catoctin Mountain in Catoctin National

Park, overlooking Thurmont at about 1500 ft. and approachable only by a foot trail. The inhabitants of Catoctin Furnace used to say that smoke occasionally appeared to rise from it, which meant that the mountain was protesting against those who stole its mineral treasures.

CHLORA POINT (Talbot)

10 miles southwest of Easton. It is thought to have been named for a local female landowner named Chlora. A ferry once ran from here to Castle Haven on the other side of the Choptank River.

CHOPTANK (Caroline)

15 miles southwest of Denton. A village on the river of the same name at the confluence of Big Hunting Creek. It was previously called Medford's Wharf and two or three steamers left here daily for Baltimore.

CHOPTANK RIVER

The Choptank rises in a large number of small springs on either side of the Delaware border in the vicinity of Marydel. It runs south for about 40 miles and, like many other Eastern Shore rivers, makes a sudden swing to the north before entering the Chesapeake Bay. The Choptank is spanned near Cambridge by the Governor Emerson C. Harrington Bridge, which was opened in 1935; Franklin D. Roosevelt's yacht, *Sequoia,* with the president on board, was the first ship to sail through the opening. The bridge is a renowned fishing spot and is usually lined with fishermen.

CHURCH CREEK (Dorchester) Pop. 130. Incorp. 1867.

6 miles southwest of Cambridge on a tributary of the Little Choptank River. The village was first named Dorchester Town, and later White Haven, but derived its present name from the early Protestant Church which was built here before 1680. The church was restored to its original appearance in 1850, when it received its present name of Old Trinity; it is the oldest Episcopal Church still standing in Maryland. In the burial ground are the graves of early settlers and revolutionary soldiers; also Anna Ella Carroll and Thomas King Carroll, her father. (See **KINGSTON**, Somerset County.)

Ship building was carried on in the area until the white

oak trees were exhausted, around 1875. One large tree, the Treaty Oak, said to be the tree under which a conference took place with the Indians in 1650, is preserved on the outskirts of the town.

CHURCH HILL (Queen Anne's) Pop. 247. Incorp. 1817.

8 miles northeast of Centreville. It is thought to be the oldest town in the county; the hill which gives it its name rises to the dizzying height of 80 ft. above sea level. St. Luke's Episcopal Church was completed in 1732, was gutted and used as a barracks and stables by Federal troops in the Civil War, but was renovated in 1881. The walls are original. Like many other colonial churches, it received gifts from Queen Anne of England, which it still possesses. In the churchyard is an old school, known as The Academy, dating from 1817.

CHURCHVILLE (Harford)

6 miles east of Belair. It was once called Lower Cross Roads, and was considered for the seat of Harford County.

About two miles northwest of town, the first graduate in medicine in the U.S. was born in 1741; he was first because his name was Archer and appeared first on the roll of graduates of Philadelphia School of Medicine in 1768. In about 1800 he built a house on the site of that in which he was born and named it "Medical Hall." It still stands on Medical Hall Road.

CLAGGETTSVILLE (Montgomery)

17 miles north of Rockville. Members of the Claggett family were here as early as 1665 and became prominent in the Revolutionary War, politics and banking. There is little here but the name.

CLAIBORNE (Talbot)

12 miles northwest of Easton. The village was established in 1886 by the Baltimore and Eastern Railroad when they built a line here to connect with a ferry from the western shore; the ferry terminal was later moved to Love Point in Queen Anne's County. The name is probably for William Claiborne, an early settler of the Eastern Shore (See Kent Island)

The strip of land to the north of here is called **RICH**

NECK and was once the plantation of Matthew Tilghman (1718-1790) who was called "The Patriarch of Maryland." He headed the Maryland delegation to Congress until 1776 and was president of the Maryland Convention which drew up the state's first constitution. The house still stands and the Patriarch is buried on the grounds.

CLARKSBURG (Montgomery)

13 miles northwest of Rockville. It was named for John Clark, a merchant, who erected the first house in 1780. According to Scharf, the Catawba grape was first cultivated here, introduced by a Mr. Jacob Scholl.

A stone by the roadside at the east end of the village marks the site of Dowden's Ordinary, where General Braddock stayed, April 15-17, 1755. The Communications Satellite Corporation is located here and much development is taking place.

CLARKSVILLE (Howard)

9 miles southwest of Ellicott City. Named for James Clark who started a hotel and store here in 1830. A company doing research in organic and inorganic chemicals employs up to 500 people nearby.

CLARYSVILLE (Allegany)

Clarysville Inn.

8 miles west of Cumberland. At this small town on the National Pike a group of buildings, erected in 1807, served as a Union hospital during the Civil War. The buildings surrounded the Clarysville Inn, once called the Eight Mile House, but are now demolished, although the inn remains, and is a restaurant. The lion's head fountain, mentioned by Scharf, was east of town on route 40 by an old ruined bar. No trace of it remains.

CLEAR SPRING (Washington) Pop. 499. Incorp. 1840.

12 miles west of Hagerstown on route 40 at the foot of Fairview Mountain. Once the dominant town of the area, it catered to wagon traffic preparing to negotiate the mountain ranges, or recovering after the descent. It is now by-passed by Interstate 70 and somewhat dormant. A sign on the main road indicates the spring for which it is named, behind some buildings, in a pathetic cement box. There is said to be a house whose front steps are made from several left-over Mason-Dixon markers. The first postoffice was established here in 1823.

Three miles to the northwest, Hanging Rock, a poor remant of its former self, stands beside the road. Hearthstone Mountain, further up the mountainside, has a fine view if you have the courage to drive up, ignoring the forbidding signs and the mysterious installations on top.

CLINTON (Prince George's) Pop. 16,438

9 miles southwest of Upper Marlboro at what was formerly an important crossroads. Previously it was known as Surrattsville, a name which is retained by the local schools and a nearby road. Mrs. Mary Surratt kept a tavern and postoffice here, which, in 1865 was rented out to John M. Lloyd and known as Lloyd's Tavern, while Mrs. Surratt went to live in Washington where she kept a boarding house.

That Lincoln's assassin, John Wilkes Booth, knew Mrs. Surratt is certain, for he stayed at her Washington boarding house sometimes. It is certain also that he and David Herold stopped briefly at Lloyd's Tavern after their flight from Washington in April, 1865. It is not certain that Mrs. Surratt was a knowing accomplice. Nevertheless she was tried, found guilty and hanged. The postoffice changed the name of the town to Clinton.

The Surratt Tavern still stands, a red building on Brandy-wine Road, south of route 223. It belongs to the National Capital Parks and Planning Commissioin and is open for tours Thurs. and Fri. at 11 and 3. Sat. and Sun. 12 and 4.

In Christ Episcopal Church in Clinton, the Greater Washington glass show is held each April. Not far from Clinton is Cosca Regional Park where there is fishing and boating on a spread of 500 acres.

CLOPPER (Montgomery)
7 miles northwest of Rockville. Near the village was Clopper's Mill, built in 1833 by Francis Clopper and burnt down in 1947.

COASTAL PLAIN
The Atlantic Coastal Plain stretches from Cape Cod to Florida. In Maryland it forms the counties of the Eastern Shore and the southern part of the state, lapping up against the hills of the Piedmont. The junction of the Coastal Plain and the Piedmont is most noticeable in the stream valleys, where the streams are narrow and swift across the hard rocks of the Piedmont, but become broad and placid across the soft sands and clays of the Coastal Plain.

COBB ISLAND (Charles)
20 miles southeast of La Plata at the tip of Cobb Neck to which it is connected by a road bridge. Cobb Neck is a peninsula between the Wicomico and Potomac Rivers. Small craft are manufactured here and there is a commerical marina.

COCKEYSVILLE (Baltimore County) Pop. 17,013
14 miles north of downtown Baltimore. It is named for John Cockey, a Baltimorean, who purchased lands here and along the Patapsco River in 1728 The white marble which was quarried in the vicinity for many years is known as Cockeysville Marble. (See **BEAVER DAM**) The Greater Baltimore Industrial Park has urbanized the area.

COLESVILLE (Montgomery) Pop.14,359
8 miles east of Rockville. Named for the Cole family, who were early settlers it was originally centered on what is now route 29. The ever-widening Washington suburbs are causing much development here.

COLLEGE PARK (Prince George's)   Pop. 23,614.   Incorp. 1945.

8 miles northeast of the U.S.Capitol.   As its name implies, College Park is the location of the University of Maryland, but the town does have some identity of its own, since there are a number of small industries, and some larger ones producing electronic equipment and tubing; but the campus on both sides of route 1 is the most prominent feature.

The university was founded as the Maryland Agricultural College in 1856 by Charles B. Calvert, a descendant of Lord Baltimore, who lived in the vicinity at Riverdale, and donated part of his estate for the purpose. The Rossborough Inn, built by the Ross family in 1798, still remains on the property, fronting on route 1.

The university still places emphasis on farming, in addition to its many other courses, and maintains an Agricultural Co-operative Extension Service for farmers state wide.   It also maintains six professional schools in Baltimore, several branches in the state and more than 200 educational centers in 22 countries for American military personnel in co-operation with the Department of Defense.

The College Park Airport, east of route 1 and the railroad tracks, was the first airport to be built in the U.S. and the first military training field in the world. The Wright brothers brought their laboratory here to improve their vehicle after its flight at Kittyhawk, and many flight experiments have been made here over the years. The airport can be viewed Fri. and Sat. 12-4.

COLMAR MANOR (Prince George's) Pop. 1,286. Incorp. 1924.

5 miles northeast of the U. S. Capitol.   One of Washington's older residential suburbs.

COLORA (Cecil)

15 miles northwest of Elkton.   A large number of Federal troops camped in the vicinity during the Civil War.

COLTON (St. Mary's)

8 miles southwest of Leonardtown at a point projecting into the Potomac River, which is four miles wide here. The Potomac River Museum is appropriately located here, since Saint Clement Island is within view. (q.v.)   The museum

illustrates the early history of Maryland life and is open daily 9-4 and weekends 12.40-4.30.

On can hire a boat and be taken out to St. Clement Island. The charge is about $2.00 per person but the boatman is unwilling to make the trip for less than four persons.

The blessing of the oyster fleet is held here each September, with entertainment and food.

COLUMBIA (Howard) Pop. 52,518

Columbia lies on both sides of route 29, 12 miles from Baltimore and about 26 miles from Washington, D.C. It is named after one of the small villages which it absorbed, which in turn was named for being on the Columbia Pike, the old road from Baltimore to Washington.

Columbia is a new town, a planned community consisting of nine villages around a main downtown and with a total land area slightly larger than Manhattan Island. The project was started by the Rouse Company in 1966, the first residents moved in during 1967 and the town is now considered to be complete. A tour from the visitors' center shows sightseers the layout: the Post Pavilion, where concerts are held, the Garland Dinner Theater, the boating lake, the shopping mall. Promotion material draws attention to the parks and fountains, woodland paths and village greens, culture, crowds, seclusion . . .

The industrial parks which support the population are separated from the residential areas and over 80 firms have located here, the largest being General Electric, manufacturing major appliances. Some of the other firms manufacture venetian blinds and drapery hardware, ski equipment and sportswear and there are research laboratories.

COLUMBIA BEACH (Anne Arundel)

11 miles south of Annapolis. A compact Bay-side community of single homes, inhabited by blacks and marked very private.

CONOCOCHEAGUE CREEK (Washington)

Conococheague Creek rises in Pennsylvania, follows a meandering course down the Great Valley and enters the Potomac at Williamsport. Some of its beautiful meanders are so pronounced that the stream flows almost due north at one point. It is spanned by several 18th century stone bridges, one of which, no longer used for traffic, can be seen from the route 40 bridge. (See **WILSON BRIDGE**)

CONOWINGO DAM

The dam spans the Susquehanna River ten miles from its mouth and provides electricity which flows to the Pennsylvania Power Company's bulk power sub-station near Philadelphia. It also acts as a bridge over the river for Route 1. An earlier Conowingo Bridge, a covered wooden structure about 3 miles to the north, was inundated in 1928 when the reservoir was filled.

The name comes from the Indian word meaning "At the rapids." The rapids extended downstream to the mouth of Deer Creek, and barred the progress of Captain John Smith, who travelled up the Susquehanna during his explorations. There is a locality named Conowingo on either side of the bridge, but the original village of Conowingo was inundated.

Construction of the dam started in 1926 and finished in 1928, at which time it was the largest power development ever built in one step. In 1962 four new generators were added, raising the capacity to 512,000 milowatts, nearly doubling its previous capacity.

A fishing platform extends the entire length of the downstream side of the powerhouse, for shad still come here in great numbers. The river bed is excavated for several hundred feet below the powerhouse to provide an adequate channel for the discharge of unneeded water when some of the 53 spillway gates are opened. If turbulence is expected from operations at the powerhouse, red lights flash and sirens sound below the dam to warn fishermen and boaters.

The powerhouse is open to visitors and there is a parking lot a short walk from the entrance on the west bank. (See also **SUSQUEHANNA RIVER**)

COOK POINT (Dorchester)

12 miles northwest of Cambridge, projecting into the mouth of the Choptank River. It was named for Ebenezer C.Cook, who inherited his estate here in 1711. Cook was a Maryland poet who enjoyed the title of America's only Poet Laureate, and whose best-known poem, published in 1708, was *The Sotweed Factor, or a Voyage to Maryland*. Sotweed was the name for tobacco.

COOKSVILLE (Howard)

13 miles west of Ellicott City on route 144, the old Baltimore Pike. There is an old inn with high chimneys just west of route 97, which has been restored as a dwelling and in which General Lafayette is said to have breakfasted during his return visit to America in 1825; it is also said that the chair in which he sat is still preserved by a Cook descendant. In 1836 there was a cavalry skirmish here.

CORAL HILLS (Prince George's)   Pop. 11,602.

5 miles southeast of the U.S. Capitol. One of the many residential suburbs that ring Washington, D.C.

CORBETT (Baltimore County)

18 miles north of downtown Baltimore. A minute village which only exists because the railroad company bought land from Isaac Corbett here.

CORDOVA (Talbot)

8 miles northeast of Easton. A jousting tournament has been held at St. Joseph's Church off Route 309 every August since 1868. Less romantically the area has a poultry processing plant.

CORNERSVILLE (Dorchester)

8 miles west of Cambridge and named after the Corner family of original settlers. There were once shipyards here on an inlet of the Choptank River.

CORRIGANVILLE (Allegany)   Pop. 1,020.

4 miles northwest of Cumberland at the junction of routes 35 and 36. It was named after its postmaster, Matthew Carrigan, and the name has since been modified.

Near here, when blasting for the Western Maryland Railroad was taking place in 1912, the famous Cumberland Bone Cave was discovered, containing fossil bones spanning a period of 50,000 years. There was a further important find in 1950.

COTTAGE CITY (Prince George's)   Pop. 1122. Incorp. 1924.

5 miles northeast of the U.S. Capitol. There was once a grist mill here, which figured in the Battle of Bladensburg. Development began around 1920 when a builder began constructing one-storied cottages.

COURTHOUSE POINT (Cecil)

A point jutting out from the east bank of the Elk River 7 miles southwest of Elkton. It is so called because the Cecil County courthouse was located here in 1719 after being removed from Jamestown on the Sassafrass River. The court met here until 1781, and an important ferry was operated across the Elk River. The point is now privately owned and cannot be visited.

THE COVE (Garrett)

A valley nestled atop the Appalachian Plateau, now occupied by contour farming. It can be viewed from route 219 between Keyser's Ridge and Accident, where there is a parking area and picnic tables.

COVE POINT (Calvert)

15 miles southeast of Prince Frederick, it is a point of land protruding into the Chesapeake Bay. At the tip stands a much-photographed lighthouse, which was built in 1828 and is the oldest light in Maryland and one of the few remaining tower lighthouses; its light flashes every ten seconds. Visitors are allowed to view the lighthouse from 9 to 6 each day in summer and 10 to 4 in winter but are not permitted to climb the tower.

A Liquified Natural Gas terminal constructed near here is now in mothballs although its bulk can be seen rising from the water. A nearer view is impossible as all the beaches in the area are private.

Cove Point Lighthouse.

COX'S POINT PARK (Baltimore County)

8 miles east of downtown Baltimore. A small waterfront park on the Back River in Essex. A regatta is held here in early August, competing for the Governor's Cup.

CRAMPTON GAP

18 miles southeast of Hagerstown where Gapland Road crosses South Mountain between Gapland and Burkittsville. It was named for Thomas Crampton, who settled in Pleasant Valley on the west side of the mountain and who was born at sea in 1735. Crampton Gap was one of the sites of the Battle of South Mountain during the Civil War, and is now occupied by Gathland State Park (q.v.) and the Townsend Memorial Arch.

CRANBERRY (Carroll)

2 miles northeast of Westminster. The Western Maryland Railroad named it when it put a depot here, on account of the large number of cranberries in the area. None are apparent today. Cranberry once boasted a grist mill and a whiskey distillery. It is due to get a shopping mall.

CRANESVILLE PINE SWAMP (Garrett)

9-10 miles northwest of Oakland in the extreme west of the state and mostly in West Virginia, at the headwaters of Muddy Creek. Botanists say that this noted botanical site has remnants of plants from a sub-arctic era. The Nature Conservancy owns a large part of it; there is an entrance a short way down the dirt road from Lake Ford, but the unusual vegetation can be viewed from the road. Eight acres of the area has been named a Natural History Landmark by the Department of the Interior.

CRAPO (Dorchester)

18 miles south of Cambridge. The town was originally called Woodlandtown and the origin of the present name is disputable. Some think it was named after a settler and others think that it was from the French *crapeau,* meaning amphibian, due to the number of croaking frogs in the surrounding marshes. The remains of a windmill were here until recently.

CREAGERSTOWN (Frederick)

11 miles northeast of Frederick. A formerly important cross roads town where the road running down the Monocacy Valley crossed the road from Baltimore to Pittsburg. It once had four taverns, a tannery and a brewery, although none is apparent today. Creagerstown is believed to have supplanted a village called Monocacy about a mile away.

CRELLIN (Garrett)

3½ miles southwest of Oakland in the valley of the Youghiogheny. It acquired its present name in 1896, having previously been called Sunshine and then Luransville. The first known settler is said to have been a certain John Smith.

The town was founded upon the lumber industry, which boomed in the late 1900's and denuded the surrounding hills. The Preston Lumber Co. opened a branch railroad from here to Hutton, which operated until 1960. By the 1920's the sawmills had been replaced by coal mining operations which lasted until the early 1960's. The individual homes are well preserved and do not give the appearance of an ex-coal town.

CRESAPTOWN (Allegany) Pop. 4,645

6 miles southwest of Cumberland. Named for Joseph Cresap, son of Daniel, a pioneer whose name is intimately associated with the area, and who is commemorated by a monument in Riverside Park in Cumberland. Joseph's house, extensively remodelled, still stands at 198 Oakwood Ave.

There is some residential and industrial development. Bel Air is a residential community one mile southwest of the town and there is a small firm producing precast concrete products.

CRESWELL (Harford)

5 miles southeast of Bel Air. On Creswell Rd. is the Bonita Farm, one of many horse breeding and training farms in Harford County. Visitors may watch horses being exercised on the track on Tues. and Thurs. mornings, 10-11.

CRISFIELD (Somerset) Pop. 2,924. Incorp. 1872

13 miles southwest of Princess Anne. The town was surveyed in 1663 and first called Somers Cove, later changed to honor John W. Crisfield (1808-97) whose greatest achievement

was the financing of the Eastern Shore Railroad in Maryland. This line formerly ended at Delmar on the Delaware border, and he succeeeded in bringing it down to Crisfield, although getting it to the water's edge was a difficult and costly task owing to the marshy nature of the ground. The problem was eventually solved by laying it on a bed of oyster shells. The Crisfield line is now derelict.

The arrival of the railroad led to a seafood boom in the 1860's and the growth of Crisfield into "The Seafood Capital of the U.S." as it still likes to call itself, although to the irreverent it is simply "Crabtown." Most activities are still related to the seafood industry, for the indented coastline is particularly favorable to oysters and crabs. In the early 1900's there were over 150 seafood processing plants here and it was a busy port of call for steamboats from Baltimore and other places.   Today the number of seafood packers numbers about 18, although there are some related industries such as the manufacture of boxes, barrels, crab pots, etc. and the raising of diamond backed terrapin. Other industries are a company which produces paint brushes and the Carvel Hall cutlery, which has a popular factory outlet shop.

Since the blue crab is so vital to the area, the University of Maryland's Natural Resources Institute oper-ates the Crisfield Seafood Laboratory.   The Crisfield Historical Museum on Main St. contains some material of in-terest. Somer's Cove Marina, opened in 1962 and belonging to the Maryland Port Authority, provides berths for about 144 boats.   Ferries depart from here to Smith Island (q.v.) and Tangier Island in Virginia.

People are attracted to Crisfield each Labor Day weekend by a festival known as the Hard Crab Derby. Started in a small way in 1948 it has become increasingly elaborate.   On the whole however, Crisfield is a shabby place. It suffered from the Hurricane of 1972 and many of the neighboring sandy beaches were destroyed or reduced in size.   The land is also sinking slowly and the marshes are encroaching upon the shore.

CROCHERON (Dorchester)
23 miles south of Cambridge, a marshy, desolate spot named for Nathan Crocheron, who settled here in the mid-19th century. Many of the residents are descended from

the inhabitants of Holland and Bloodsworth Islands, who settled here when their islands were evacuated owing to subsidence.   Some of their houses were moved here also.

CROFTON (Anne Arundel) Pop. 12,009
11 miles west of Annapolis. A residential development on route 3, which started in 1964 as a community of professional and managerial income groups, where membership of the social club was a condition of purchase.   Three years later the remainder of the tract was sold to Levitt and the condition was dropped.

CROOM (Prince George's)
$4\frac{1}{2}$ miles due south of Upper Marlboro. The village is in the heart of an agricultural area which was chosen for their estates by many prominent families of earlier times. At the Episcopal Church of St. Thomas, members of the Calvert family, relatives and descendants of the Lords Baltimore, are said to be buried under the chancel. In the churchyard are tombs bearing many other well-known Maryland names.

The church was served for a time by Rev. Thomas Claggett, who became the first bishop of the Protestant Episcopal Church to be consecrated in the U.S. He was buried here, but later was removed to the National Cathedral in Washington, D.C. There is a memorial to him in the churchyard, embellished with a new bronze bust.

Croom. Bust of Archbishop Claggett

CROPLEY (Montgomery)

13 miles northwest of the U.S.Capitol near the Potomac River. This insignificant spot could be called the center of Maryland's gold mining industry. In 1864, a member of a regiment which was encamped on a plateau behind the Old Anglers' Club, noticed flakes of gold dust in a stream where he was washing his skillet. Three years later he returned as a civilian and organized the Maryland Mining Co. Several gold mines were operated intermittently in the area until 1951 but the deposits were scanty. Some of the openings are still visible and there is said to be a small museum on Falls Rd. in the home of a former mine manager.

CROWNSVILLE (Anne Arundel)

7 miles northwest of Annapolis. Crownsville State Hospital is situated on 1,217 acres of land here. Originally a mental hospital for blacks, the obsolete buildings were plagued by escapes, riots and overcrowding before new buildings were dedicated in 1954 and 1960. It became integrated in 1962.

CRUMPTON (Queen Anne's)

16 miles northeast of Centreville. In earlier times this was the point on the Chester River where steamboats used to turn around. A rope ferry crossed the river in the 1750's and 60's and the place was called Callister's Ferry. The first bridge across the Chester River was erected at this point in 1865.

Two promoters from New Jersey tried to build a large town here, but without success. Later, in the 1870's, a fruit grower boasted that he had the largest peach farm in the world here, with 1,000 acres under trees.

Every Wednesday there is a large auction near Crumpton, starting about noon. The movie *Showboat* was filmed near Crumpton.

CRYSTAL BEACH (Cecil)

15 miles southwest of Elkton at the mouth of the Elk River. There are picnic grounds, cottages and a bath house. Crystal Beach Manor House stands on a hill and has been converted into a restaurant.

CRYSTAL GROTTOES (Washington)

10 miles southeast of Hagerstown on route 34. The caverns were discovered in 1920 as a result of quarrying operations for road material and were spared because of their beauty. Two years later they were lighted and opened to the public; the stone entrance house was built in 1942. The caves are a series of passages lined with beautiful formations and are the only caverns in Maryland open for visitors.

CUMBERLAND. Seat of Allegany County. Pop. 25,933. Incorp. 1815.

Cumberland lies at the eastern foot of the Appalachian Plateau in a bowl in the mountains. Its altitude is only 641 ft. above sea level, but it is surrounded by mountains up to 2,300 ft. in height.

Cumberland was founded by Thomas Beall (b.1734) near the point where Wills Creek cuts a pathway through the mountains and enters the Potomac. At this strategic location a frontier fort had been established in 1750, an outpost which served as a rendezvous and landmark for western expeditions and which became the base of operations against the French on the Ohio. A larger fort, Fort Pleasant, was built in 1754. When General Braddock arrived from England in 1755 to pursue the war against the French, he changed the name to Fort Cumberland, after his commander-in-chief, the Duke of Cumberland. It occupied the

Cumberland. Emmanuel Episcopal Church with First Presbyterian
Church in background.

small hill at the intersection of Baltimore St. and Washington St. where Emmanuel Episcopal Church, completed in 1851, now stands; the remains of its old tunnels are under the church and can be seen by permission.

The parade ground was on the opposite side of Washington St. where the Allegany County Library now stands, a building which once housed the Allegany County Academy. The Fort Cumberland Trail, starting at Greene and Washington Sts. encircles the fort boundary with a series of historical plaques.

Cumberland City Hall.

In the angle between Wills Creek and the Potomac River is Riverside Park; re-erected here is a small log house, known to have been used by Washington as his headquarters during the French and Indian War; a tape recording tells its story. Nearby is a monument to Col. Thomas Cresap, "pathfinder, pioneer and patriot," who is mentioned more fully in connection with **OLDTOWN.**

The old National Road to the west started in Cumberland, and the C.& O. Canal ended here. The B.& O. Railroad also ended here from 1842 to 1849 until a route was found to cross the Appalachian Plateau.

For many years traffic to and from the west flowed through Cumberland, either over Haystack Mountain

(Braddock's Road, q.v.) or through the celebrated Narrows (q.v.) but the new National Freeway (route 48) now soars over the town, leaping the railroad tracks which once caused endless traffic snarls. Will Rogers once described the town as a city built between two railroad tracks. It still is, but the Western Maryland Railroad at the west end of town no longer carries traffic, while the B. & O. at the other end of town, although busy with freights, carries only one Amtrak train each way per day.

Cumberland has always been a railroad town. The B. & O. still maintains shops here; its two main lines from the west still meet here, and train crews are still changed here. The railroad originally dubbed Cumberland The Queen City, and in 1872 built the large and elaborate Queen City Station and Hotel, popular with both railway passengers and revellers. In spite of all efforts to save it, the station fell to the wreckers in 1971; a postoffice and small station now occupy the site. Some of the relics went to collectors, some to the Greenbriar Hotel in West Virginia, while the panelling now adorns the dining room of the Algonquin Hotel in Cumberland.

The mainstays of Cumberland's economy are the Kelly-Springfield Tire Co., one of the earliest pioneers of the rubber industry, and the Pittsburg Plate Glass factory across the river. The Celanese plant, which was once so flourishing is now almost defunct.

Cumberland is still making decisions as to what to tear down and what to save in its downtown development. Some improvements have been made and some mistakes have occurred. Much of its history can be studied at History House, 218 Washington St., where the Allegany Historical Society maintains a small museum. The house is open May-Oct. on Sundays 1.30 - 4.30 and also by request.

CUNNINGHAM FALLS STATE PARK (Frederick)

The park occupies the summit of Catoctin Mountain south of route 77 about 12 miles northwest of Frederick. It was created in 1954 when the Federal Government deeded to Maryland 4,446 acres of its Catoctin Recreational Demonstration Area. The falls of Hunting Creek, which cascade down the mountainside are the main feature of the park and are named for an early owner of the land.

Below the falls, Hunting Creek has been dammed to

form a lake, where boating, swimming and fishing are allowed.   There are trails through the forest from the falls to the
lake.

Cunningham Falls

DAMASCUS (Montgomery) Pop. 4,129

15 miles north of Rockville. It is said to have once re-
joiced in the name of Black Ankle.   The present name is
taken from the original land grant and the town was founded
by Edward Hughes in 1816.   The Energy Research and Development Agency is located here on route 270 and much
building has taken place in the last 15 years, with individual
homes on half acre lots. County planners foresee an increase
in population here up to 25,000 people.

DANIELS (Howard and Baltimore)

4 miles north of Ellicott City.   Since nothing much remains of this town in the Patapsco Valley it seems odd to
devote space to it, but many people remember when it was a
thriving factory town.

There was an important textile mill here as far back as
1829, when it was run by Thomas Ely. James S. Gary took it
over in 1853 and renamed it the Albert Co. after his son,
and the village became Alberton.   The factory remained in
the family until 1940 when the whole town was bought by
the Daniels Company who changed the name of the town to
Daniels.   The factory turned out cotton duck cloth, laundry
hampers, conveyor belts and tarpaulins. In 1968, rather than
modernize the homes to conform to state regulations, the
Daniels Co. demolished all of them except the postoffice.

When hurricane Agnes arrived in 1972, the river took a
short cut across a bend and demolished the factory, paying
no heed to the fact that one of the town's many churches
was incorporated into it and that the whole complex was on
the National Register of Historic Places.

The railroad bridge has long since been repaired from
flood damage, but the demolished road bridge has never been
replaced and probably never will be since there are no longer
any residences in town.   The factory operations were moved

elsewhere and in 1977 a fire swept through what remained of the buildings.

DANS MOUNTAIN (Allegany)

This name is given to the southernmost section of the high ridge immediately west of Cumberland, the edge of the Appalachian Plateau.   It was named for Daniel Cresap, one of the sons of Thomas, of Oldtown, whose memorial is in Riverside Park in Cumberland.   Daniel Cresap met his death on the mountainside during an Indian conflict.

8,239 acres of the mountain comprises the Dans Mountain Wildlife Management Area and Refuge under the jurisdiction of the state.   A further 500 acres is devoted to Dans Mountain State Park, nine miles south of Frostburg. Both areas are approached from the George's Creek Valley.

Dans Rock Summit is an overlook which was once a popular place for outings.   One can drive up to the top from Midland, but owing to the re-alignment of route 36, the beginning of the road is somewhat obscured.   The appearance of the summit is marred by a burnt house, a fire tower and a government installation, but the view remains unchanged.

DANVILLE (Allegany)

Even although this place lies at the foot of Dans Mountain on route 220, it is not named for the mountain but for Brother Dan McNally, a minister, who died in a plane accident.

DARGAN (Washington)

18 miles due south of Hagerstown.   Nearby on Harper's Ferry Road is the farm where John Brown and his raiders gathered on the night before the raid at Harper's Ferry in 1859.   In those days it was called the Kennedy Farm, but it is marked on the map today as John Brown's Farm.   A marker indicates the spot but the farm is private.

DARLINGTON (Harford)

11 miles northeast of Bel Air, probably named for the town in England.   In the main street is Deer Creek Friends' Meeting House, which was founded in 1737, rebuilt in 1784 and restored in 1888.   Lafayette's army camped in Darlington on April 13th, 1781.   An important early industry of the town was the Susquehanna Power and Paper Co.

Nearby, on route 1, is the privately owned Octagon House, built by William Hensel, a ship's carpenter, in the early 18th Century. It has a "widow's walk," some false windows, a pie-shaped bathroom, and is believed to have been made from the wood of an old ship, brought from Baltimore by ox-cart.

DARES BEACH (Calvert)

4 miles northeast of Prince Frederick. A beach resort for local residents at an indentation in the Calvert Cliffs. It was an early center of Quakerism.

DARNESTOWN (Montgomery)

8 miles west of Rockville. It was named for William Darne. In 1869 the Andrew Small Male and Female Academy was established here from funds bequeathed to the Presbyterian Church by Andrew Small. The brick building stood on the site now occupied by the elementary school and was the largest school building in the county. Small is buried in the graveyard behind the church.

Like many other Montgomery County communities, Darnestown may expect to be swamped by new developments.

Darnestown. Grave of Andrew Small.

DAWSON (Allegany)

16 miles southwest of Cumberland. The sawtooth rocks at the end of Fort Hill Mountain, north of the village, are a point of interest.

DAWSONVILLE (Montgomery)

11 miles west of Rockville. It was named for the Dawson family, one of the largest landowners in the vicinity.

DEALE (Anne Arundel) Pop. 3,008

14 miles south of Annapolis on Rockhold or Rock Hole Creek, a Chesapeake Bay inlet. There are docking facilities for pleasure boating and fishing and there is a boat building company. Land amenities are few. Deale Beach is two miles to the east and faces the Bay but the beach is private.

DEAL ISLAND (Somerset)

18 miles west of Princess Anne, this low, marshy island is connected to the mainland by a bridge. The original name was Devil's Island, pronounced Deil's as in Scotland; and the town of Dames Quarter was at that time Damned Quarter. A dignitary of the Methodist Church insisted upon the new spelling in the 1830's.

Deale Island. The harbor at Wenona.

Deal Island was the scene of Methodist camp meetings for many years. A vigorous Methodist minister named Joshua Thomas (1776-1853) who had his headquarters here, is buried in St. John's graveyard beside the memorial chapel. His field of operations was the islands of the Chesapeake Bay, which he visited in his large log canoe named The Methodist and he was better known by his nickname -- The Parson of the Islands.

North America's only fleet of working sailboats is based here at the towns of Wenona, Chance and other localities. Every Labor Day races are held for the skipjacks and other workboats in Tangier Sound and many spectators are present. Two small seafood packing houses, fishing, crabbing and oystering provide employment for the majority of the inhabitants.

Little Deal Island to the south, now marshy and uninhabited once had twenty acres of arable land and was the home of Joshua Thomas. The Deal Island Wildlife Management Area is a large acreage of marshland on the nearby mainland, owned by the Maryland Department of Natural Resources.

DEEP CREEK LAKE (Garrett)

An artificial lake formed by a dam across Deep Creek, about 1.5 miles above its junction with the Youghiogheny and 7 miles north of Oakland. The dam was completed by the Pennsylvania Electric Co. in 1925, forming the lake, which covers six square miles, with 62 miles of shoreline, 95% of which is held by individuals and 5% by the state. A "Green Belt" ordinance prevents building close to the shore in order to preserve the lake's beauty, but there are numerous resort cottages in the area and ample opportunity for boating water skiing and other types of recreation.

10 miles north of Oakland and a mile north of Thayerville, off route 219, is the entrance to the 1800 acre State Park. Here the visitor can swim, picnic, boat, fish or hike. There is also a public fishing area near Deep Creek Lake Bridge. (See **McHENRY**)

DEER CREEK (Harford)

Deer Creek flows through a picturesque gorge at Rocks State Park (q.v.) and enters the Susquehanna about 4 miles below Conowingo Dam. It gives its name to a small hamlet 8 miles northeast of Bel Air.

DEER PARK (Garrett)

4 miles northeast of Oakland. The locality today is but a shadow of its former self, for Deer Park was a pleasure complex created in 1873 by John W.Garrett, president of the B. & O. Railroad. There was a commodious hotel on a slope above the railroad tracks with meadows sloping down to the station; gardens laid off in walks and drives and studded with pagodas, pavilions and rustic benches, all brilliantly lighted at night; a cleared summit above the hotel with an observatory, and a number of large summer cottages.

John W.Garrett died at his cottage; Grover Cleveland, the 22d president, came here for his honeymoon and the cottage which he occupied still stands and is inhabited. Graham Bell experimented with telephone communications between the Deer Park Hotel and a large hotel in Oakland.

A voluminous spring supplied the complex, and the water from the spring was used in the B.& O. dining cars for many years. It is invisible today, being roofed over by a commercial bottler who sold the bottled water until 1975.

DEFENSE HEIGHTS (Prince George's) Pop. 6,775

A suburb 7 miles northeast of the U.S.Capitol.

DELMAR (Wicomico) Pop. 1,232. Incorp. 1888

6 miles north of Salisbury, at the Maryland-Delaware line. The name, of course, is a combination of the two states, since part of the town and a further 943 inhabitants are on the Delaware side. The main street is the dividing line, and while the bank is in Maryland, most of the shops are in Delaware. This situation caused endless problems and rivalry in former times, but the town has matured and reached a working compromise over its public services.

Railroading has always played an important part in the town's history, for the tracks ended here until 1884, when they were brought down to Crisfield and then to Cape Charles. A reminder of railroading days is an old railroad signal in the shape of a ball, which was raised high to denote that the line was clear and so gave rise to the term "high balling." Near the ball is a small museum housed in a caboose, open Sat. and Sun. 2-4.

DENTON County Seat of Caroline County. Pop. 1,927. Incorp. 1802

Denton was named as the county seat in 1773, at which

time it was known as Pig Town. Understandably a change of name was required, and the name Edentown was proposed, after Lady Caroline Eden, the colonial governor's sister. However, the Revolution ·intervened and when the matter was finally settled in 1790 some compromise was made and the name became Edenton and finally, Denton. A courthouse was not started until 1793 owing to delaying tactics by the town of Greensboro (then called Choptank Bridge) which wanted to be county seat.

Denton has long been a crossing point of the Choptank River. The first bridge was built in 1811, replaced by an iron bridge in 1875, and by the present structure in 1913. Denton was also a port of call for ships, and the first steam ship from Baltimore called here in 1850. The Choptank is still navigable for small craft to this point, and the county maintains a launching ramp at Ganey's Wharf southwest of the town.

There are few older buildings remaining, but the town nevertheless retains its quiet rural atmosphere. Neck Meeting House, built in 1802 and used as a barracks by Union Troops during the Civil War, is open by request. Some small factories make metal signs and electric heating elements.

DETOUR (Carroll)
15 miles west of Westminster close to the point where Big Pipe Creek and Little Pipe Creek join to become Double Pipe Creek. The village was originally based upon a water mill and was called Double Pipe Creek Village, but in 1905 the Western Maryland Railroad decided that the name was too long and a vote was taken for a new name. What exactly is detoured could not be established.

DICKERSON (Montgomery)
17 miles northwest of Rockville. In the vicinity is a large Potomac Edison power plant, burning pulverized coal, whose tall chimeys are a landmark for miles. A small factory nearby produces cobalt 60.

DISTRICT HEIGHTS (Prince George's) Pop. 6,799. Incorp. 1936.
7 miles southeast of the U. S. Capitol. Land was purchased here in 1925 to begin the building of this older residential suburb.

DIVIDING CREEK

There are three Dividing Creeks in Maryland, two of them insignificant, but the thrid is a tributary of the Pocomoke River and divides Somerset from Worcester County.

An early Somerset County courthouse was situated west of the point where Dividing Creek joins the Pocomoke River, but when Worcester County was formed, the Somerset County courthouse moved to Princess Anne.

DONCASTER (Charles)

The village is 13 miles west of La Plata, but the name is mainly associated with Doncaster State Forest, which lies to the east of the village and covers 1,464 acres on both sides of route 6. The land was purchased by the state after a fire destroyed most of the original trees.

DORCHESTER COUNTY. County Seat: Cambridge. Pop. 30,623. Area: 573 sq. miles.

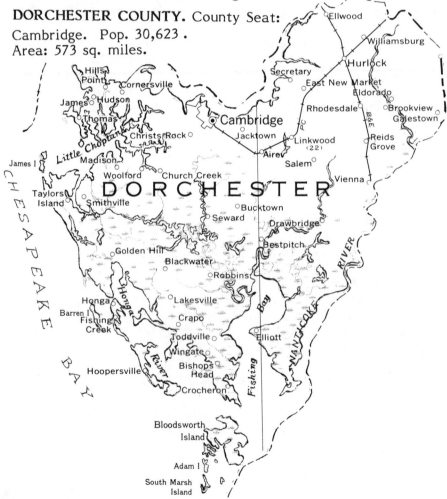

Dorchester County was formed in 1668 and named after the Earl of Dorset, a family friend of the Lords Baltimore. It is bounded on the north by the Choptank River and an irregular line to the Delaware border; on the east by a portion of the Delaware border; on the southeast by the Nanticoke River and on the west by the Chesapeake Bay.

One fifth of the county's area is water, but the land portion still makes it the largest of the Eastern Shore's counties. The land is level and large areas are swampy, while the remainder is agricultural, producing mainly barley, soybeans, chickens and most of Maryland's tomato crop. Over 40% of the population lives in Cambridge where there is some manufacturing, although there are also some farm-related industries in Hurlock and Vienna. Muskrat trapping is a sideline of the marshland areas.

DORSEY (Howard) Pop. 1,186

7 miles southeast of Ellicott City. It is named after the Dorsey family who played a prominent part in Maryland history and owned land and iron furnaces nearby. Several industrial parks have sprung up in the vicinity.

DOUBS (Frederick)

9 miles southwest of Frederick, in the Frederick Valley. It was named for Mr. Doub who operated a mill here; the mill originally belonged, like everything else in the valley, to Charles Carroll of Carrollton. Between here and Adamstown a branch of the B. & O. Railroad, now obliterated, ran southward to connect with the main line near Point of Rocks. This old line once served quarries producing the ornamental stone called calico marble, or Potomac marble, which decorates the interiors of many public buildings in Washington.

DOUGHOREGAN MANOR (Howard)

An estate 5 miles west of Ellicott City. The name, taken from the gaelic, means King's Gift, and the estate belonged to Charles Carroll of Carrollton, who preferred it to all his other estates, and spent most of his later years there. He is buried in the Catholic chapel which forms one end of the mansion. The estate, originally 10,000 acres, was granted to Carroll's grandfather by Lord Baltimore in 1707 and has been continuously in the possession of Carrolls to the present day. The acreage has diminished to about 2,400 and a development by the name of King's Gift is arising on part of the former estate.

DRUM POINT (Calvert)
18 miles southeast of Prince Frederick at the southern-most tip of Calvert County. There is a lighthouse at Drum Point, a hexagonal wooden structure on iron pilings, with an automatic light. A little way inland is Drum Point Pond, said to be notable for the diversity of its wildlife.

DUBLIN (Harford)
9 miles northeast of Bel Air and named after Dublin in Ireland. It was the central settlement of a large area inhab-ited by Scotch-Irish in the 18th century.

DUCKETT, T. HOWARD, DAM
The dam is about a mile upstream from Laurel on the Patuxent River and forms Rocky Gorge Reservoir, which stretches for about ten miles up the steep, narrow valley. The dam is named for the main founder of the Washington Suburban Sanitary Commission, and the reservoir provides a water supply for suburban Washington and the Maryland sub-urbs.

The dam can be seen from Interstate 95, but the reser-voir is out of sight; for a good view of the water, get off the Interstate at Brooklyn Bridge Rd., enter the gate, which is open 8-4 and ascend the observation platform near the parking lot. The reservoir holds over six billion gallons and the water is pumped two miles uphill to a filtration plant at Sandy Spring Rd. After filtering it is stored in circular tanks.

DUG HILL RIDGE (Carroll)
This is the name for the northeast trending ridge which runs between Westminster and Lineboro on the Pennsylvania border, and which forms part of the Piedmont watershed. Its southwesterly continuation is Parr's Ridge (q.v.)

DUNDALK (Baltimore County) Pop. 85,377
6 miles southeast of downtown Baltimore. It is named after Dundalk, Ireland, the birthplace of the father of William McShane, an industrialist who established a bell foundry here in 1895, although the Pennsylvania Steel Co.

had been established in the area since 1886. The streets of
Dundalk are named afer the streets of Dundalk in Ireland.

In 1916 the Bethlehem Steel Co. purchased 1,000 acres
to build houses for the workers of their Sparrows Point plant,
planning to erect an English-style community around a village green, but the plan was altered to accomodate the large
influx of steel workers in World War I.

There are numerous industries in Dundalk, including
Eastern Stainless Steel but it is best known for the Dundalk
Marine Terminal, part of the Port of Baltimore. The
Terminal occupies 435 acres and can berth twelve vessels at
one time; it handles three quarters of the Port's container-
ized cargo.

DUNKIRK (Calvert)

13 miles northwest of Prince Frederick. Green sand and
diatomite are extracted from a nearby quarry. On Ferry
Landing Rd. is the oldest Methodist Church in the county.

EAGLE HARBOR (Prince George's) Pop. 200. Incorp. 1929.

17 miles southeast of Upper Marlboro. A black peoples' summer resort on the Patuxent River.

EARLVILLE (Cecil)

15 miles southwest of Elkton. A little to the southeast of here on Grove Neck Rd. is Mount Harmon, a 386 acre 18th century plantation, now a wildlife center. It is open to individuals and groups 10-3 Tues. and Thurs. and Suns. 1-4 after May 15. A fee is charged.

EASTERN NECK (Kent)

Eastern Neck is a peninsula enclosed by a U-turn of the Chester River near its mouth. At the town of New Yarmouth there was a courthouse by 1674.

2,285 acre Eastern Neck Island is at the south end of the Neck and is connected to it by a bridge. Since 1926 the island has belonged to the U. S. Dept. of the Interior, who control a major refuge for migratory wild fowl -- 227 species have been recorded. Also on the island is the birthplace of Lambert Wickes, Revolutionary naval captain. A rather sorry wooden statue of Wickes stands in Rock Hall on route 20 at Main.

Statue of Lambert Wickes at Rock Hall.

EASTERN SHORE

This is the name given to the Maryland counties between the Atlantic Ocean and the Chesapeake Bay. A portion of the peninsula forms the State of Delaware and the southern tip is part of Virginia; the whole stretch of land is often called the Delmarva Peninsula.

The whole of the Eastern Shore lies within the coastal plain province and is flat and sandy. It was formerly a prime truck farming area; but corn, soy beans and chicken raising have largely replaced the fruits and vegetables for which it was once famous. In addition it was an area of large estates and "gracious living," but a new generation of sportsmen and corporations has taken over many of the old estates and mansions. They have discovered the recreational possibilities of the greatly indented coastline and its rivers, with many havens for pleasure craft, fishing, and duck and deer hunting although much commercial crabbing and oystering is still practised.

Methodism has a strong foothold on the Eastern Shore, but the former somewhat narrow and conservative outlook of "The Shore" is slowly giving way before the invasion of outsiders who now pour over the Chesapeake Bay Bridge to the Atlantic coastal resorts, or hurry north and south down the route which connects the population centers of the east coast to the Newport-News area of Virginia by means of the Bridge-Tunnel.

EAST NEWMARKET (Dorchester) Pop. 251. Incorp. 1832

9 miles northeast of Cambridge. This crossroads village was originally called plain Newmarket, but East was added in 1827 to avoid confusion with Newmarket in Frederick County.

There are several 18th century houses remaining in the town, one of the best examples being Friendship House or Hall, built around 1790. The New Market Academy was founded here in 1829, a direct forerunner of East New Market High School. There is a small cannery which operates in season.

EASTON. County Seat of Talbot County. Pop. 7,536. Incorp. 1790.

Easton was once known as Talbot Courthouse, later as Talbot Town, and it once served as the center of government for the entire Eastern Shore of Maryland, which probably gave it its present name. The first courthouse was built here in 1712, but the present structure dates from 1794, although the wings were added in 1957; it is one of only two Maryland courthouses dating from the 18th century, the other being at Centreville.

On the courthouse grounds stands a statue commemorating Confederate soldiers from Talbot County. Earlier the "Talbot Resolves" had been adopted on the same spot, a document whose sentiments were later incorporated into the Declaration of Independence.

The Brick Hotel, a leading hotel when it was built in 1812, stands at the intersection of Washington and Federal Streets. The Third Haven Meeting House stands in a peaceful grove reached by a narrow drive from South Washington St. Known to have been attended by William Penn, George Fox and Lord Baltimore, it was built in 1682 and is believed to be the oldest frame religious Meeting House in the United States.

Easton has an air of prosperity and caters largely to estate owners who do not depend upon farming for a living. The Academy of Arts exhibits works by local artists each April, and a waterfowl festival is held each November. The Historical Society and Museum at 25 S.Washington St. has a bookstore which is open Tues.-Sat. 10-4 and Sun. 1-4.

The large and attractive Tidewater Inn is a popular restaurant and hotel, more modern than it looks, for it was constructed in 1949 and enlarged in 1953.

EASTON POINT (Talbot)

A mile west of Easton on the north fork of the Tred Avon River. There is a marina here, and on the opposite shore are said to be the remains of a fort built to protect Easton in the War of 1812.

EAST PINES (Prince George's) Pop. with Riverdale Hts. 8,941

8 miles northeast of the U. S. Capitol. A Washington suburb near Riverdale that started in 1942 with ten homes. Two more sections were opened in 1943 and 1946.

EASTPORT (Anne Arundel)

A suburb of Annapolis one mile to the south of Horn

Point (q.v.) and connected to Annapolis by a bridge across Spa Creek. The first house was built here in 1857 by Henry Medford, but it received its name in 1888 from a developer whose native city was Eastport, Maine. Its main business is yachting.

EBBVALE (Carroll)

8 miles northeast of Westminster, and named for a village in Wales. Iron mines were once opened here, and provided freight for the Bachman Valley Railroad, which passed through the village.

ECKHART (Allegany)   Pop. 1,333

A scattered village on both sides of route 40, one mile east of Frostburg. Once known as Eckhart Mines, it is situated in a basin between two mountains. Coal was mined here early, the first openings being made in the Big Vein in 1820, when coal was hauled to Cumberland in wagons for transfer to barges on the Potomac. Later a branch railway line was put in from Eckhart Junction, two miles northwest of Cumberland.

EDEN MILL (Harford)

11 miles northwest of Bel Air on Eden Mill Rd. and 2 miles south of Harkins. The mill, formerly known as Stansbury's Mill, was built in 1907 and converted in 1914 to a power-plant to supply the town of Fawn Grove. The manor house opposite the mill was built in 1801.

57 acres of the site have been made into a Harford County park, with a skating pond, picnic area, nature trails and ski run. The mill now acts as the park office and a restaurant is planned.

EDESVILLE (Kent)

9 miles southwest of Chestertown. Until recently there was an interesting old blacksmith's shop on route 20, owned and operated by the Wagner family since 1899. The smithy closed in 1980 but the buildings remain.

EDGEMERE (Baltimore County) Pop. 9,078

10 miles southeast of downtown Baltimore, adjacent to Sparrows Point.

EDGEMONT (Washington)

9 miles northeast of Hagerstown at the western foot of South Mountain. In 1881 the 33.5 mile Cumberland Valley Railroad branched off here for Waynesboro and Shippensburg, Pennsylvania. Hardly a trace of the roadbed remains.

EDGEWOOD (Harford) Pop. 19,455

9 miles southeast of Bel Air, it is best known for Edgewood Arsenal, a U.S.Government facility occupying the neck of land between the Gunpowder and Bush Rivers called Gunpowder Neck. In Building E 4310, at the intersection of Douglas and Otto Roads, is the headquarters of an HO model railroad club, which is open Oct.-May, Tues. and Thurs, 7-9 p.m.

EDWARDS FERRY (Montgomery)

17 miles west of Rockville. For many years this was a Potomac crossing and the slip of a ferry which operated until 1936 can still be seen. Several troop crossings took place here during the Civil War and it was heavily guarded during the years 1861-2. There is a derelict lock and lockhouse on the C.& O. Canal.

EKLO (Baltimore County)

28 miles northwest of downtown Baltimore. The locality was once called Scrabble and later Middletown, since it was in the middle of District No. 6. The old name remains in Middletown Rd. and Church.

ELDERSBURG (Carroll) Pop. with Flohrville 4,959

12 miles southeast of Westminster on Liberty Road. The records of Holy Trinity Protestant Episcopal Church, which was built in 1771 but no longer stands, are in St. Barnabas, Sykesville. Much development is taking place here with population increases every year.

ELDORADO (Dorchester) Pop. 99. Incorp. 1947

16 miles east of Cambridge. It was formerly called The Ferry, as it was connected by ferry to Brookview (q.v.) across Marshyhope Creek. The present name was derived from a farm (which must at one time have produced a pot of gold.)

ELK LANDING (Cecil

This suburb of Elkton, south of route 40 was once the estate of the Hollingsworths and an important shipping point during colonial times.   Both the Revolutionary War and the War of 1812 saw many embarkations and debarkations of troops here;   the British were repulsed here in 1813.   The area is private. (See **GRAY'S HILL**)

ELK MILLS (Cecil)

3 miles north of Elkton. An old factory which once produced tapestries and tweeds now houses a number of small businesses.   By the railroad tracks is a modern establishment which builds railroad cars.

ELK NECK STATE FOREST (Cecil)

3,000 acres of forest and swampland southwest of Elkton between the Northeast and Elk Rivers.   Many white-tailed deer inhabit the forest;   wildlife food plots are maintained throughout the forest and there is a fishing pond.

ELK NECK STATE PARK (Cecil)

15 miles southwest of Elkton at the tip of the peninsula between Northeast and Elk Rivers, which is known as Elk Neck.   The park consists of 1575 acres, with sandy beaches, marshlands, wooded bluffs and facilities for swimming, fishing, boating and wildlife study.   The southernmost tip of the neck is called Turkey Point, and a mile off shore is the Turkey Point Light, an important navigation signal.

ELK RIDGE (Washington)

Elk Ridge is the northernmost end of the Blue Ridge, a mountain chain separated from the main area of the Appalachians by the Great Valley.   The southern end of Elk Ridge is called Maryland Heights (q.v.) which affords a nice view of Harper's Ferry across the Potomac.   The northern end is near Rohrersville about 8 miles away.   Elk Ridge is said to be an important area for botanical study.

ELKRIDGE (Howard)

7 miles southwest of Baltimore. It was originally a port named Elkridge Landing which in 1746 was Maryland's second port after Annapolis.   Cargoes were mainly tobacco, which was rolled in hogsheads down the rolling roads to this point,

and iron ore, found along the river banks. Nothing remains of the old town, and the river is so silted up that it could hardly be navigated by a rowing boat.

There are various stages of residential and industrial development in the area and some historical remnants. At the junction of Montgomery Rd. and route 103 is the great house called Belmont, once the home of the Dorseys, but from 1964 until recently, owned by the Smithsonian Institute and used for overnight conferences. It stands in 340 acres and can accomodate 20 visitors overnight.

The B. & O. Railroad crosses the river at this point by the historic Thomas Viaduct (q.v.)

ELKTON County Seat of Cecil County. Pop. 6,468. Incorp. 1787.

Elkton is situated near the head of the Chesapeake Bay on the Elk River at what was once the furthest point of navigation. It was formerly called Head of Elk and became the county seat in 1786. As the river began to silt up, ships began to dock further downstream at Frenchtown (q.v.)

At least two important troop movements took place here during the Revolutionary War. The British troops passed through in August, 1777 on their way to Philadelphia, after burning the courthouse at Courthouse Point (q.v.) and it is said that General Howe occupied a room in Hollingsworth Tavern the night after George Washington vacated it. Rochambeau and Lafayette started from here on their way to Yorktown in 1781.

The Hollingsworth Tavern at 207 Main St. still stands and is occupied by a real-estate office. Hollingsworth was a prominent landowner in the area who was later active in Washington and on local committees. His home was Partridge Hill on Main St., now belonging to the American Legion.

Another interesting house on Main St. is No. 131 East, which was built in 1769 and turned into a hospital during the Revolutionary War by its owner, Dr. Abraham Mitchell. The Maryland alcove in the chapel at Valley Forge is dedicated to him

Prior to 1938 Elkton had a reputation for ease in obtaining marriage licenses and was known as the Gretna Green of the East. In those days Maryland law did not require a waiting period between the license and the nuptials; and since Elkton was the closest town in Maryland to the centers of population further north, it received a large part of the elopement business. One wedding chapel remains for tradition's sake, and is still popular.

A number of industries are located in and around Elkton, including clothing, plastics, concrete, lumber, chemicals, electric motors, rocket fuel, luggage, mobile homes and several factories making fireworks. Spitz Laboratories, founded by Armand N. Spitz of the Franklin Institute, Philadelphia, who invented and produced the planetarium in the 1940's, had an establishment here for some years.

ELLERSLIE (Allegany)
6 miles northwest of Cumberland in the valley of Wills Creek, almost on the Pennsylvania border. The town was established in 1860, and in spite of its small size, once had four railroads passing through it.

ELLICOTT CITY County Seat of Howard County. Pop. 21,784
10 miles west of Baltimore. It was named for the Ellicott brothers, John, Joseph and Andrew, who came from Bucks County, Pennsylvania, and built a mill here in the Patapsco Valley in 1774; at that time the place was known as Ellicott Mills. The Ellicotts encouraged local farmers to turn to wheat growing, and they designed their own mill machinery, which was manufactured elsewhere and shipped to Elkridge Landing, where it was unloaded into wagons to be brought to the mills. The mills were on the east side of the river on a site now occupied by silos.

The Ellicotts were Quakers and founded the Meeting House on Columbia Pike. They were also talented surveyors -- Andrew Ellicott was associated with the laying out of Washington, D.C. assisted by his protegé, Benjamin Banneker. (See **OELLA**) The Meeting House is now a private residence, but the adjacent cemetery, where many of the Ellicotts are buried, is open.

Like other towns in the Patapsco Valley, Ellicott City has been plagued by floods. Tiber Creek, normally an insignificant stream, becomes a raging torrent after heavy rain, pouring into the Patapsco more water than it can handle. The mills were ruined by the great flood of 1868 and several buildings suffered in the flood of 1972. Under the railroad bridge the high water marks of the various floods are marked on a post.

Ellicott City. Main St. with railroad bridge at far end.

The railroad station was the first terminus of the first passenger line to be built in the country. Starting from Baltimore, the B.& O. Railroad followed the Patapsco Valley and arrived at Ellicott City and built the station in 1831. The rails were used by horse-drawn vehicles at first, and there is a famous anecdote of how a horse competing with a tiny steam engine named Tom Thumb won a race from here to Baltimore, owing to a mechanical mishap in the steam engine. Steam eventually prevailed, of course, and the first trip ever made by a steam locomotive pulling passengers on a regularly scheduled service arrived in Ellicott City. The station has some exhibits of railroad interest and is open as a museum weekend afternoons all year, Wed.-Sun afternoons April 1 - Dec. 31. The old turntable site and engine house reveal the small size of the early locomotives.

The large granite building near the bridge was once a hotel and could be approached directly from the railway platform, which early passengers considered to be the height of convenience. Another large hotel, the former Howard House, above the rock on Main St. is now apartments. The little cliff-side branch library was once a firehouse, which explains the weathervane.

At the top of Church Hill, the classical ruins were once the Patapsco Female Seminary, the only school in the South, before the Civil War, where a woman could get a quality liberal arts education. Its renown lasted until the 1890's, and it is believed that Baltimore's Vagabond Players started their theater group here. Nearby is Mount Ida, one of the Ellicott family mansions, now law offices.

A little further down the hill is the county courthouse and the Presbyterian Church, now housing the Howard County Historical Society, which is open Tues. afternoons and the 1st and 3d Sunday of every month. The houses which have their front doors on this hill have their back doors two floors below on Main St.

Also overlooking the town and the river is a castle-like edifice with wooden battlements, known as Castle Angelo, which was built in 1831 by a French artist named Samuel Vaughan and is still a private dwelling. The newly-arrived railroad would advertise special excursion to view and admire the so-called castle.

The residents of Howard County have recently realized that their county seat is something of a gem, with its steep, winding main street bordered by buildings of dark local granite. An organization called Historic Ellicott City has been formed, several new restaurants and antique shops have opened on Main St. and the railroad station has been designated an Historic Landmark. A walking tour pamphlet is available.

In 1958 the town served as the location for a Hollywood film entitled *The Goddess*.

ELLIOTT ISLAND (Dorchester)

18 miles south of Cambridge, fronting on Fishing Bay, one of the numerous inlets of this low, marshy region. It is not a true island, but the landward side is mostly marsh. Fishing, crabbing and muskrat trapping are the main occupations.

EMMITSBURG (Frederick) Pop. 1,552. Incorp. 1824

20 miles northeast of Frederick. Samuel Emmit from Ireland obtained land in 1757 and the town was laid out by William Emmit under its present name in 1785. Previously the area had been known as Poplar Fields, and then Carrollsburg. It is an interesting small town, built around a square which once held a well, later replaced by a pump and later still by a tiered fountain. The local historical society

has published an excellent walking tour describing most of the buildings.

The town is most widely known by two Catholic Institutions nearby: Mount St. Mary's College for Boys (q.v.) and St. Joseph's Institute, a former college for girls. St. Joseph's Institute was founded by Mother Elizabeth Seton as a nunnery for the Daughters of Charity and an academy for young ladies; the academy closed its doors a few years ago, but from this foundation sprung the entire Catholic Parochial School system of America. Mother Seton became the first American-born saint when she was canonized in 1975.

St. Joseph's is open to visitors, who are shown a slide lecture followed by visits to the Stone House where Mother Seton began her mission in 1809, the White House, where she died, the cemetery, and finally, the new chapel, where her remains now rest.

In addition to the pilgrim industry, Emmitsburg has some small industries making shoes, mens' trousers and leather novelties.

EMORY (Baltimore County)

21 miles northwest of downtown Baltimore. This was the only place to be bisected when Carroll County was formed from Baltimore County.

EMORY GROVE (Montgomery)

5 miles north of Rockville. This was a small run-down black community until urban development began changing the landscape. A grant from H.U.D. in 1970 helped with renewal and a new county playground was opened in 1974. (For Emory Grove in Baltimore County see **GLYNDON**)

ENGLISH CONSUL (Baltimore County)

4 miles southeast of downtown Baltimore just beyond the city line. The locality is mostly merged with Lansdowne and Baltimore Highlands, but it once had an identity of its own when William Dawson, the English consul of the day, built a mansion here on 300 acres of land around the year 1818. It was known in those days as the Dawson Manor. Since then the estate has been whittled away by developments and English Consul Elementary School has been built on the last remnant.

A strange story is told about the house. William Dawson's

brother Frederick was convicted in England for crimes unknown; through influence in high places, his punishment was limited to transportation for life and he was allowed to come to Maryland and live with his brother, the Consul, but only on condition that he receive a certain number of lashes each year. Until recently, inhabitants could point to the stump of an oak tree, to which they said Frederick was tied for punishment.

ESSEX (Baltimore County) Pop. 39,614

8 miles northeast of downtown Baltimore between Back and Middle Rivers. The area began to take shape about 1914, when the Glenn Martin plant opened, and has grown steadily ever since. The original center was at Eastern Boulevard and Mace Avenue, now swamped by modern developments of median income houses and apartments. At 516 Eastern Ave. is a small museum, open Sats. and Suns. 1-4.

EVITTS MOUNTAIN (Allegany)

A mountain northeast of Cumberland. It is said to have been named after an Englishman named Evart, who built a cabin on the summit and lived the life of a hermit. Later exploration of the mountain has yielded some evidence of early occupation of the wilderness. Evitts Creek village, 2.5 miles to the southeast, was also named for him. Rocky Gap State Park, (q.v.) 7 miles east of Cumberland, occupies part of the mountain.

EYLER VALLEY CHAPEL (Frederick)

19 miles north of Frederick. This small stone church nestled between hills, is noted for its candlelight services at holiday times. The road leading west from here has a fine view.

FAIRHAVEN (Anne Arundel)
16 miles south of Annapolis. A community on Herring Bay, where an outcrop of low cliffs provides a good view for some homeowners. The private beach is greatly diminished from the time when steam boat excursions used to run to Fairhaven from Baltimore.

FAIR HILL (Cecil)
6 miles northwest of Elkton. The village is small, consisting of but a few houses, but the Du Pont estate here is over 5,000 acres, devoted largely to racing and fox-hunting activities. The three overpasses across route 273 connect the estate on both sides of the road.

The Fox Catchers' Hunt Cup Meet has been held here annually since 1933 on the 1st and 2d Saturdays after Labor Day, the proceeds going to the Union Hospital of Cecil County. In June sheepdog trials are held and also a Highland Gathering, with bagpipers and highland dancing. The estate also boasts a race-course which is an exact replica of the course at Aintree, where England's Grand National is run.

FAIRLAND (Montgomery)   Pop. 5,154
10 miles east of Rockville. Until recently this was only a crossroads village, but a large community surrounding a golf course is now under construction.

FAIRLEE (Kent)
6 miles west of Chestertown. It was previously called Bel Air, but changed its name out of deference to the more important Bel Air in Harford County. In 1814 the Kent Volunteers were encamped here when a small force of British under Sir Peter Parker landed at Tolchester (q.v.) and a skirmish took place.

FAIRMOUNT (Somerset)

10 miles southwest of Princess Anne. The church here was transported to its present location from Holland Island (q.v.) at the time when the island was abandoned.

FAIRMOUNT HEIGHTS (Prince George's) Pop. 1,616. Incorp.1927

5 miles northeast of the U.S.Capitol. One of the older suburbs of Washington.

FAIR VIEW (Cecil)

8 miles northwest of Elkton close to the Pennsylvania border. It was once known as Kansas and then Blake, but the post office decided to change the name back to the one it was known by in 1838.

FAIRVIEW (Anne Arundel)

12 miles southeast of Baltimore on a point jutting into Rock Creek, a tributary of the Patapsco estuary. It was a resort served by a steamer from Baltimore, 1892-1941, but it is no longer open to the public; the Maryland Yacht Club owns the site and the old hotel is a clubhouse.

FAIRVIEW (Washington)

8 miles northeast of Hagerstown close to the Pennsylvania border; Fairview Mill is on a small stream to the southeast. The area was settled by the Kreight and Fiery families; John Fiery, the last of the line, was drowned in Conococheague Creek in 1868.

FAIRVIEW MOUNTAIN (Washington)

12 miles west of Hagerstown, the first ascent of the Ridge and Valley Province. Below the summit there was once an inn called Mountain Inn where travellers rested before tackling the final ascent.

FARMINGTON (Cecil)

12 miles northwest of Elkton. In earlier times it was known as Brickleytown, after Andrew Brickley, who opened a blacksmith's business here in 1819. It was one of the towns which lay in the disputed territory between Maryland and Pennsylvania.

FATHER WHITE MEMORIAL (St. Mary's)

A short distance north of St. Mary's City (q.v.) in a 2.5 acre garden. The memorial is in the shape of an altar and contains some of the original bricks from Old St. Mary's. Father White was the Jesuit priest who accompanied Maryland's first colonists on the Ark and the Dove.

FEDERALSBURG (Caroline) Pop. 1952. Incorp. 1823.

14 miles south of Denton. It is the largest town in Caroline County. When it was founded in 1789, it was known as Northwest Fork Bridge, or simply The Bridge; but tradition states that its name was changed in 1812 after a meeting of the Federalist Party was held here.

Shipbuilding was carried on here in the early days and the completed vessels were conveyed to Brown's Wharf, four miles downstream, for launching. Marshyhope Creek, which runs near the town, was called the Northwest Fork of the Nanticoke in those days.

Federalsburg has a certain amount of industry. Apart from some smaller enterprises there are two canneries, a large poultry processing plant and the nearby factory of Maryland Plastics, which employs a large number of people in the manufacture of buttons, cutlery, etc.

FENWICK ISLAND (Worcester)

Fenwick Island is the name given to part of the Barrier Beach north of Ocean City and extending to the Delaware boundary. Fenwick Island lighthouse is a tower standing somewhat inland from the beach, and at its base is the old boundary stone between Maryland and Delaware, which was placed here in 1751. The coats of arms on the stone were re-cut in 1952.

This boundary position was much disputed in colonial times, until the location of Cape Henlopen was agreed upon. The point known as Cape Henlopen today is 25 miles to the north, so that either by negligence on the part of Lord Baltimore, or by craft on the part of William Penn, Maryland lost a 25 miles strip of territory. This occurrence is known to historians as The Affair of the False Cape.

FERNDALE (Anne Arundel) Pop. 14,314

A residential area 8 miles south of Baltimore.

FINKSBURG (Carroll)

8 miles southeast of Westminster. It was named for Adam Fink who laid out the town and built the first house in 1813. Cedarhurst, one mile to the northeast, is its railroad station and the Congoleum Plant at Cedarhurst is its chief employer.

FIVE FORKS (Harford)

12 miles northwest of Bel Air. Five roads indeed meet here but there are very few habitations. Nearby, on Falling Branch, a tributary of Deer Creek, is Kilgore Rocks. This pretty spot is now private, but it was a popular spot for outings in the horse and carriage days.

FLINTSTONE (Allegany)

12 miles northeast of Cumberland, where route 40 crosses Warrior Mountain (q.v.) Some say that the town got its name from a land marker set by Mr. Flint, who was mentioned in Washington's diary. Others say the name came from a huge stone from which the Indians used to chip flints as they travelled the Warriors' Path, which followed the summit of the mountain.

In 1958, when sections of route 40 were re-aligned, the stone was bulldozed away, and the single street of old houses was by-passed. Many travellers of the Cumberland Road, including Lafayette, Henry Clay, Theodore Roosevelt and Meshack Browning stayed at the 22 room Flintstone Hotel, which was built of hand-made brick in 1807. The hotel is now an apartment house.

Iron ore was found here in 1881 by a travelling mineralogist and watch-maker named Hoster. Within a few miles there were, and perhaps still are, many warm and sulphur springs, which once attracted hundreds of visitors to the area.

FLYING POINT PARK (Harford)

9 miles southeast of Bel Air. Land was purchased for this county park in 1966 on Bush River, 2 miles east of Edgewood. There is boating, swimming, fishing, etc. and also the "Showboat," a floating theater which offers entertainment by local talent in the summer months.

FOREST GLEN (Montgomery)

9 miles north of the U.S. Capitol on the grounds of the

Walter Reed Army Hospital. This community started life as a summer resort on the B.& O. Railroad. In 1894 the Forest Inn was converted to a Ladies' Seminary and many fanciful dormitory buildings and statues were erected on the grounds, some of which remain.

FOREST HEIGHTS (Prince George's)   Pop. 2,999.   Incorp. 1949.
6 miles south of the U.S.Capitol. One of the more recent suburbs of Washington along Indian Head Highway.

FOREST HILL (Harford)
4 miles northwest of Bel Air, and probably named for its setting. The village became a milk shipping center when the old Maryland and Pennsylvania Railroad reached here in 1885. Although the railroad is defunct, the station is still in a good state of preservation and has been used for several commercial enterprises.

FORESTVILLE (Prince George's) Pop. 16,401
8 miles southeast of the U.S.Capitol. One of the newer mushrooming suburbs of Washington.

FORT ARMISTEAD (Baltimore County)
8 miles southwest of downtown Baltimore, on a promontory called Hawkins Point projecting into the harbor. It was named for George Armistead (1780-1818) who commanded Fort McHenry (where his statue can be seen) during the bombardment of 1814.
Fort Armistead is of sunken design, built during the Spanish American War, and completed in 1898 to protect the approaches to Baltimore, but never used in battle. It was manned for a while in World War I, bought by the City of Baltimore in the 1920's, used as an ammunition dump in World War II, and occupied briefly in 1952 by an anti-aircraft battery.
The surrounding area is now a park, as yet undeveloped. The fort is choked with weeds, and nearby factories create dust; but there is a nice view of the water and of the new Francis Scott Key Bridge, which spans the outer harbor at this point.

FORT CARROLL (Baltimore County)
7 miles southeast of downtown Baltimore. This round

structure of 3.4 acres in the water of Baltimore harbor between Hawkins Point and Sparrows Point was designed and
built by Robert E. Lee in 1848 as part of Baltimore's
defenses. It was never used, and soon became obsolete; for
a while it was used as a lighthouse, a pistol range and a
prison. Plans have often been suggested for its use as a restaurant or recreation area, but nothing is done and it remains isolated except for the seagulls, accessible only by
water. The new outer harbor bridge gives travellers a bird's
eye view of the island.

FORT DETRICK (Frederick)

On the northwest outskirts of Frederick, this 1,300 acre
facility was named for Major Frederick L.Detrick, a squadron
flight surgeon of the 1930's. It began life as a landing
ground and received the title of Fort in World War II, when
it became engaged in bacterial warfare research, to the fear
and horror of local residents. In 1972 the research was
abolished and Fort Detrick became a center for cancer
research, although locals believe that research in defense
against bacterial warfare is still carried on. Recently it has
become a center for government research in genetic engineering.

FORT FOOTE (Prince George's)

8 miles south of the U.S.Capitol. It was named after
Rear Admiral Andrew Hull Foote, d.1862 and built in 1863 on
a bluff overlooking the Potomac; it was one of the chain of
forts built around Washington during the Civil War. The spot
is occupied by a small park at the present time, and the
remains of earthworks and gun emplacements can be seen by
following an unmarked trail before the car park is reached.

FORT FREDERICK (Washington)

20 miles west of Hagerstown close to the Potomac River
and Big Pool (q.v.) Fort Frederick was built by the colony of
Maryland between 1756 and 1758 as a frontier defense. No
military engagement was ever fought here but it served as
an important supply depot during the French and Indian War.
During the Revolution it housed some British and German
prisoners and during the Civil War it was once occupied
briefly by Union troops.

The state purchased the fort and surrounding acreage in

1922 and began developing it as a state park. Some restoration work was done in the 1930's and much more was done in the 1970's. In the summer months, the re-created First Maryland Regiment, clothed in authentic uniforms, holds drills and shooting contests.

FORT GARRISON (Baltimore County)

9 miles northwest of downtown Baltimore. It is the oldest standing fort in Maryland and was built in 1695 as a refuge against Indian attacks when the area was a sparsely populated wilderness. In those days it was manned by nine rangers and a captain, who spent their time marking out trails and patrolling roads between the Susquehanna and Patapsco Rivers. Buildings have crept ever further into the countryside, and the fort now stands on a lot amid a suburban development of newish houses on Garrison Farms Road.

Fort Garrison.

FORT GEORGE MEADE (Anne Arundel) Pop. 14,083

14 miles southwest of Baltimore. This government installation covers 13,000 acres, bounded on one side by the Patuxent River. It was erected during World War I, at which time it was called Camp, instead of Fort Meade, and named after the Commander of the Army of the Potomac during

the Civil War. During World War II the buildings were greatly expanded and the place became a reception center for draftees. It is now the headquarters of the 2d Army, while the Army Corps of Engineers maintains its Bay Area office here.

FORT HOWARD (Baltimore County)

11 miles southeast of downtown Baltimore at North Point (q.v.) which is the southern tip of Patapsco Neck and marks the entrance of the Patapsco River. It was named for John Eager Howard, Revolutionary War hero and Baltimore landowner. The area is historic, since the British landed here in 1814 and were defeated in the Battle of North Point.

Fort Howard was established in 1896 as part of Baltimore's coastal defenses, which were never used; the old canon emplacements and bunkers can still be seen. During the Vietnam War it was used as a secret training ground and a simulated Vietnamese village was built here.

For many years Fort Howard veterans' hospital has stood here amid extensive grounds. Also on the grounds is a house on the spot previously occupied by a farmhouse where dwelt a man named Todd, who spotted the arrival of the British, tried to raise the alarm, was killed and his house burnt down.

In 1972, 62 acres of the grounds were acquired by the county as a park to be developed for swimming, fishing, boating, etc.

FORT McHENRY. See BALTIMORE - BUILDINGS.

FORT RITCHIE (Frederick) Pop. 1,745

12 miles northeast of Hagerstown. It was named for Governor Ritchie of Maryland, who was also immortalized in the name of the highway from Baltimore to Annapolis. Its 618 acres started life as Camp, rather than Fort Ritchie, a training ground for the National Guard. After changing hands several times between the State and Federal Governments it became a training ground for Intelligence personnel during World War II and has remained federal property ever since. It is a self-contained town.

FORT SMALLWOOD (Anne Arundel)

11 miles southeast of downtown Baltimore. This 100 acre park was bought from the government in 1926 by the City of

Baltimore for recreation purposes and it was a popular beach
for many years.   The fort itself was one of several which
were constructed to protect the mouth of the Patapsco but
which were never used in action.   The beach and cement
walk are less popular today but the place is still quite
pleasant to visit any time of year.

FORT SUMNER (Montgomery)

7 miles northwest of the U.S. Capitol.   Three forts were
originally built here in 1861 to protect the Washington water
works.   They were connected by earthworks in 1863 and
re-named in honor of Major General Edwin V.Sumner, hero of
Antietam.   Nothing now remains of the fort, or the 28
cannon which defended it, but an historical marker stands at
the intersection of Sangamore Road and Westpath Way, not
far from Massachusetts Ave.

FORT TONOLOWAY STATE PARK (Washington)

One mile west of Hancock.   It is known that a frontier
fort, built during the French and Indian War, stood on Little
Tonoloway Creek, but the exact location is unknown.   The 26
acre state park has been closed indefinitely.

FORT WASHINGTON (Prince George's)

12 miles south of the U.S. Capitol on a piece of land
between the Potomac River and the mouth of Piscataway
Creek.   There has been a fort on this site since 1808, as the
promontory overlooking the Potomac was a splendid vantage
point from which to bombard a prospective enemy ascending
the river.   However, no enemy has ever ascended the
Potomac and the fort has never seen action.

The present building was completed in 1824 and is
entered by a drawbridge across a moat, now filled in.   The
fort and the surrounding acreage are a national park, open to
the public 7.30 - 5 (5.30 in summer) daily, June thru Labor
Day; weekends and holidays only at other times.   The fort is
impressive and there is a fine view of the Potomac and the
Virginia shore.   Keepers dressed as Union soldiers bring the
place to life, and there are demonstrations every Sunday.

FOUNTAIN GREEN (Harford)

3 miles east of Bel Air.   On Tudor Lane is a house
called Tudor Hall, which once belonged to the Booth family,

"The mad Booths of Maryland." The estate was purchased by Junius Brutus Booth in 1821 and his sons, Edwin and John Wilkes, were born in 1833 and 1839 in a small house which is said to be still standing in the garden of the main house. The present Tudor Hall was built in 1846 and the family grew up in it; Edwin became a renowned actor and John Wilkes became an assassin. The family burial plot is in Greenmount Cemetery in Baltimore.

The house has recently changed hands and is undergoing restoration. Most of the farm has been sold off and modern houses have been erected on it.

FOUNTAIN ROCK (Frederick)

5 miles northeast of Frederick. The old county histories say that the largest natural spring in Frederick County is here; and it would seem so, for there is a spring with force enough to create fountains feeding a series of private trout-rearing pools where one may fish for a fee, or just watch, or spend time around an open fire in the lodge. Also on the grounds are a large water-filled limestone quarry and a huge derelict stone lime kiln.

FOUR LOCKS (Washington)

12 miles southwest of Hagerstown. At this point the C.& O. Canal took a half mile short cut across a 4 mile bend of the Potomac River. Four locks, Nos. 47-50, were needed to raise the canal 32 ft.

FOWBLESBURG (Baltimore County)

24 miles northwest of downtown Baltimore on the old Hanover Pike, mostly by-passed by route 30. It was named for Frederick Fowble, 1807-1898. A house at the southeast corner of the crossroads is said to have been an old toll house.

FOX GAP (Washington)

13 miles southeast of Hagerstown. It is a wind-gap on South Mountain, which played a part in the Battle of South Mountain during the Civil War. The monument on the hill, enclosed by iron railing, is to General Reno, who was killed here.

FRANKLINVILLE (Baltimore County)

17 miles northeast of downtown Baltimore. One

tortuous street of decrepit houses on the rim of the Little Gunpowder valley.

FREDERICK. County Seat of Frederick County. Pop. 28,286. Incorp. 1786.

Frederick lies in a valley between the hills of Piedmont and the wall of the Blue Ridge at what was once an important intersection of trails. It was named before the county and it is not certain whether it was named for Prince Frederick, son of George I, or Frederick Calvert, sixth Lord Baltimore. The town was laid out by Patrick Dulaney in 1745 and settled primarily by German stock; the main street is called Patrick St. after the founder.

Over the years Frederick has played a small part in most historical events since its foundation. The first official protest against the British Stamp Act took place in the Frederick courthouse and Repudiation Day is still celebrated here. On the north wall inside the present courthouse is a tablet commemorating the "Twelve immortal justices of the Frederick County Court who repudiated the Stamp Act, Nov. 23rd, 1765." Another reminder of the War for Independence is the Old Stone Barracks on the grounds of the School for the Deaf. Hessian prisoners were housed here during the war and the barracks were afterwards used as a munitions storage depot, and later still as a hospital.

Maryland's first elected governor, Thomas Johnson, lived in the vicinity of Frederick. His retirement home, Rose Hill Manor, 1611 Market St., which was built by his daughter in the 1790's, is now a museum, open daily 10-12 and 1-3 weekdays, and 1-3 weekends.

Francis Scott Key, author of the words to the U.S. National Anthem, is buried in Mount Olivet Cemetery; his monument faces the main entrance with the U.S. flag flying beside it day and night. Mount Olivet is well worth a visit, for in addition to Key's grave it contains the graves of Thomas Johnson (mentioned above,) Barbara Fritchie (of whom more anon,) Hessian soldiers and, along the west border, graves of 400 Confederate soldiers killed in the battles of Antietam and Monocacy.

The Civil War was very real in Frederick. The public buildings served as hospitals for the wounded of the various battles fought in its vicinity and in 1864 Jubal Early arrived in town and forced the mayor to pay a ransom of $200,000 if he did not want the town to be blown apart. The money could only be raised by borrowing from the banks, and the final interest on the loan was not repaid by the city until 1951.

Barbara Fritchie, made famous by Whittier's poem, lived in an old house where W. Patrick St. crosses Carroll Creek. The original house was razed soon after the event described in the poem and the pieces carried off as souvenirs; but a replica of the house re-creates the scene, believed to be fictitious, but nevertheless inspiring, where she flaunted the U.S. flag before Stonewall Jackson. A plaque marks Sir Winston Churchill's visit to the spot during his visit to Camp David; he recited aloud most of the poem of "Barbara Fritchie" which had lain dormant in his memory until now.

Up from the meadows rich with corn,
Clear in the cool September morn,
The clustered spires of Frederick stand
Green-walled by the hills of Maryland.

a   b   c

The clustered spires of Frederick: a. St. John the Evangelist. b. Trinity Chapel of Evangelical Reformed. c. Evangelical Lutheran.

President Lincoln arrived in Frederick at the B. & O. Station where he made a speech and visited the wounded at Ramsey House on Record St. The red brick station is still there on Allhallows St., now painted a strange mustard color, and is still used, although not for its original purpose. An earlier station, which was of greater historic interest, could be seen on Carroll St. until 1974, when it burnt down. One small, rickety freight pulls out of Frederick each day.

The curious piece of masonry by route 70 near the Monocacy Bridge once stood at the east end of an earlier bridge, washed away in the 1930's, which was called the "Old Jug Bridge" from the shape of this ornament.

Hood College is a well-known educational establishment which began life as the Frederick Female Seminary in the stately buildings on East Church St., which now house the county offices. Frederick County Community College has its campus in Frederick also. The once-famous hotel named for Francis Scott Key closed down in 1975.

Frederick is a town to be enjoyed on foot, and the Chamber of Commerce of Frederick County has published an excellent little guide to a walking tour of the town, beginning at Courthouse Square, which is surrounded by mellowed homes and churches; the guide can be obtained at the Public Library or the Visitors' Center. The Historical Society on East Church St. is open by appointment only.

The local industries are lime, stone and cement products and the manufacture of electric parts, and men's clothing, in addition to numerous smaller enterprises. One of the largest employers was, until recently, Fort Detrick (q.v.) There is much suburban growth on the fringes of town.

FREDERICK COUNTY. County Seat: Frederick. Pop.114,792. Area: 660 square miles.

Frederick County was formed in 1748. It was originally much larger, but is still the largest county in Maryland, embracing part of the Piedmont Region, the Frederick Valley and the eastern slopes of the Blue Ridge. It is uncertain whether it was named for Prince Frederick, son of Geo. I or Frederick Calvert, 6th Lord Baltimore.

It is bounded on the southwest by the Potomac River; on the southeast by a line from the source of the Patapsco to the mouth of the Monocacy; on the west by the crest of South Mountain and on the east by various stream valleys and part of Parr's Ridge. The population is descended largely from German and Irish settlers.

Frederick is one of Maryland's top agricultural counties, and with Carroll leads the state in the production of corn, wheat, hay and dairy products. Tree fruit is also important.

There is some manufacturing, but the industries are mostly small and diversified.

FREDERICK JUNCTION (Frederick)

3 miles southeast of Frederick, close to the Monocacy River. The junction is between a spur line from Frederick and the old main line of the B.& O. Railroad. Frederick was originally on the main line, but when the railroad continued its progress to the west, Frederick was by-passed. Passenger service on the spur has long been discontinued and only one small rickety freight train shuffles in and out of Frederick daily.

The area of the junction and the railroad bridge over the Monocacy were part of the setting for the Battle of the Monocacy, and Civil War monuments dot the surrounding fields.

FREDERICKTOWN (Cecil)

17 miles south of Elkton at a bend on the Sassafrass River. The town was laid out in 1736, the same year as the town on the opposite shore of the river named Georgetown; the two towns were probably named after the King of England and his son. Both were in Kent County until the land north of the river was laid off as Cecil County. Previously the village on this site had been known as Pennington's Point or Happy Harbor.

Both Fredericktown and Georgetown were almost destroyed by the British in 1813 but Fredericktown managed to recover and remains today as a popular center for boating.

FREEDOM (Carroll)

Insignificant village 12 miles south of Westminster. When the place was laid out, the landowner, Mr. O'Donald, gave away alternate lots free. This, rather than more lofty sentiments, inspired the town's name.

FREELAND (Baltimore County)

30 miles north of downtown Baltimore. It was named for John Freeland and there is little here except a few houses and a junk shop. Trains of the Northern Central Line once stopped here, but after the line was destroyed by the flood of 1972, the station was moved away to another site.

FRENCHTOWN (Cecil)

14 miles west of Elkton on the east bank of the Susquehanna. In earlier years the place was called Gurleytown and Frenchtown was the station on the B.& O. now called Aiken. Quarries here produced the same kind of granite as the more famous ones of Port Deposit, but no quarrying takes place here now. Another Frenchtown, near Elkton, is now called Old Frenchtown (q.v.)

FRIENDSHIP (Anne Arundel)

17 miles southwest of Annapolis. It was founded as Greenhead by Isaac Simmons in 1804. Tradition states that in 1807 a visiting Methodist preacher was taken ill here and received great kindness from the inhabitants, so he suggested the new name. The present Methodist church dates from 1834.. Another village called Friendship lay in the northern part of the county before the Baltimore-Washington International Airport was built (q.v.)

FRIENDSVILLE (Garrett) Pop. 566. Incorp. 1902

In the northwest corner of the state, 4 miles from the Pennsylvania border and 4 miles from the West Virginia border. It is thought to be the oldest town in Garrett County, and is named for the Friend family, whose name appears frequently in the history of the locality. Records show that John Friend bought the land from the Indians in 1765. Selbysport, three miles down the Youghiogheny River, is thought to have been an older settlement, but most of that town was obliterated by the Youghiogheny River Reser-Reservoir.

There was once a railroad station here on the Confluence and Oakland Railroad, but in 1942 the station was sold and the rails removed. The road bed of an old logging raillroad beside the river makes a fine hiking trail amid unspoilt (but constantly threatened) scenery. There is still some lumbering and wood products industry in the region.

Friendsville was a peaceful backwater until the 1970's when the National Freeway came soaring over the river which made it no longer remote. An annual old-time fiddlers' contest is held on the second Saturday in July each year.

FRIZZELBURG (Carroll)

Named for Nimrod Frizzell, a blacksmith who settled here in 1814.

FROSTBURG (Allegany) Pop. 7,715. Incorp. 1839

9 miles west of Cumberland, Frostburg is situated on the Appalachian Plateau between Savage and Dans Mountains, near the source of George's Creek, about 2000 ft. above sea level. The town was laid out by Meshach Frost under the name of Frost Town in 1812 when the National Road came through; previously it had been called Mount Pleasant. Frost and his brother pioneered the Cumberland coal trade; he and his wife Catharine are buried in St. Michael's Catholic Church Yard on Main St., while the Frost mansion, which was built in 1846, with a third story added in 1890, is now a funeral home.

The town developed along with the surrounding coalfields and we are told that it is undermined by coal excavations, only columns being left as supports in places. The mining gradually declined after the 1900's but Frostburg does not have the aspect of an ex-mining town, perhaps owing to the presence of Frostburg State College, the only 4 year state college in Maryland west of College Park. Founded as a teachers' Normal School in 1898, it now covers 200 acres, with nearly 3,000 students and offers majors in liberal arts.

Frostburg. Frostburg State College.

In the park along Midlothian Rd. is the spot where General Braddock is supposed to have camped on his way to Fort Necessity. An old milestone which once stood there is now in the grounds of the State College (See **BRADDOCK'S ROAD**) Ripley's Believe it Not once said that Frostburg had more churches and more bars per capita than any other town in the U.S.

FRUITLAND (Wicomico) Pop. 2,694. Incorp. 1947
3 miles south of Salisbury, of which it is almost a suburb. It was originally a cross roads settlement called Forktown, which only came to life when the railroad arrived in 1867. In 1873, Phoenix was suggested for the name of the town, but the residents chose the name Fruitland by a poll. A factory produces men's and women's shirts, while Crown Cork and Seal manufactures cans. The town is a center for holly and evergreens in December.

FULTON (Howard)

11 miles southwest of Ellicott City. A postoffice was opened under the name of Waters Store in 1874. The name was changed to Fulton in 1882, after Charles C. Fulton, who published the Baltimore Sun, but nobody seems to know why.

FUNKSTOWN (Washington) Pop. 1,103. Incorp. 1840.

2.5 miles southeast of Hagerstown on old route 40 within a meander of Antietam Creek. The site was originally called Jerusalem, but land was granted in 1754 by Frederick Calvert to Henry Funk, who is said to have introduced the cultivation of the vine to the area. According to tradition, he was the same individual who established Funkstown, or Hamburg, on the present site of Washington, D.C.

Much Civil War activity took place in the vicinity, and there are several historical markers around the town. John Brown spent the night at a hotel here in 1859 on his way to Harper's Ferry.

GAITHERSBURG (Montgomery) Pop. 26,424. Incorp. 1878

5 miles northwest of Rockville. Benjamin Gaither built the first house here in 1802 and the town was named for him. In 1850 the name was changed to Forest Grove, but the railroad restored the original name in 1873. The town was once a popular resort for Washingtonians, and a hotel was erected in 1881.

Today the area is one of spectacular population growth. Some federal agencies are located here, and research and development firms abound, although 20-30% of the population commute to Washington.

Southwest of the town on Quince Orchard Rd. at Clopper Rd. is the huge National Bureau of Standards. There are free exhibits concerning the metric system and historical documents, open to the public 8.30 - 5 Mon. thru Fri; also tours on Tuesdays at 1.30 p.m. and Fridays at 9.30 a.m. On route 28 is the headquarters of the National Geographic Soc. where there are exhibits and sales of books and maps Mon. thru Fri. 9-4.

In 1899 Gaithersburg was one of six sites around the world located on latitude 30° 8', where observatories were erected to study the wobble of the earth.

GALENA (Kent)   Pop. 361. Incorp. 1904

14 miles northeast of Chestertown. Originally called Down's Cross Roads, after William Downs's tavern, which burnt down in 1893, it later became Georgetown Cross Roads before receiving its present name. A little to the east, off the Galena-Sassafras Road, is the Shorewood Estate belonging to the heirs of an aircraft tycoon. The gardens, fronting on the Sassafras River, are known for their statuary, and although private, may be visited by the public May thru October.

GALESTOWN (Dorchester) Pop. 123. Incorp. 1951

19 miles east of Cambridge, close to the Delaware border. Named after a Dr. Gale, it was settled about 1833. Several ships were built here in the 19th century, although Gales Creek seems hardly big enough to handle them. The creek is now dammed to form a lake.

GALESVILLE (Anne Arundel)

10 miles south of Annapolis on the estuary of West River. It was once called Browntown and then West River Landing, until the postoffice named it Galloways in 1879, after John Galloway, a local landowner who is said to have been the first person to import clover and timothy grass to the U.S. The name was changed to Galesville in 1924, some people think after Richard Gale, a Quaker planter, although others think it was after a later Gale. The area was an early Quaker stronghold, and William Penn is thought to have embarked here, after a boundary conference with Lord Baltimore in 1652.

Galesville has been spruced up in recent years and the West River Sailing Club has its headquarters here. There are several restaurants and boating facilities and it compares favorably with most Bay-side communities.

GAMBER (Carroll)

8 miles southeast of Westminster. Formerly Mechanicsville, it was re-named for an early postmaster, William Snyder Gamber (1829-1916) who drifted here from Lancaster County, Pennsylvania after a varied career.

GAMBRILL STATE PARK (Frederick)

6 miles northwest of Frederick on the summit of Catoctin Mountain. There are hiking trails and picnic pavilions, a small museum and two overlooks with views.

GAMBRILLS (Anne Arundel)

11 miles northwest of Annapolis. The town was known as Sappington from 1869 to 1885, and a nearby development has taken that name. The present name is for Dr. Steven Gambrill, whose house stood at the intersection of Gambrills and Maple Roads, near where the new postoffice stands. Dr. Gambrill's father lived in what is now the parsonage of the Cross Roads Church. The Naval Academy Dairy Farm, which

supplies dairy produce to the Naval Academy in Annapolis, is located nearby.

GAPLAND (Washington)

17 miles southeast of Hagerstown at the foot of South Mountain.   This small village was the address of George Alfred Townsend, poet, novelist and Civil War correspondent, who built his home on top of South Mountain at Crampton Gap.   Since he wrote under the name of Gath, his home on the mountain became Gathland (q.v.)

GARRETT COUNTY.   County Seat: Oakland.   Pop. 26,498. Area 681 sq. miles.

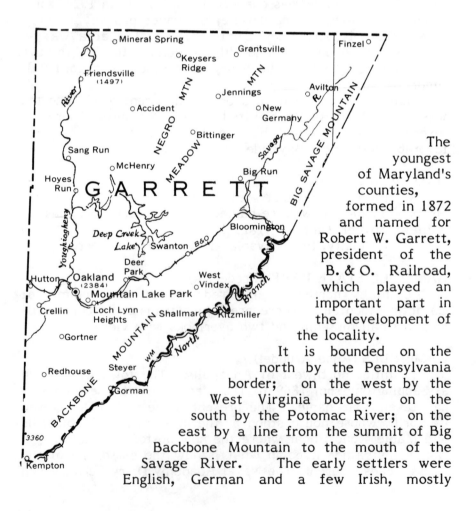

The youngest of Maryland's counties, formed in 1872 and named for Robert W. Garrett, president of the B. & O. Railroad, which played an important part in the development of the locality.

It is bounded on the north by the Pennsylvania border;   on the west by the West Virginia border;   on the south by the Potomac River;   on the east by a line from the summit of Big Backbone Mountain to the mouth of the Savage River.   The early settlers were English, German and a few Irish, mostly

migrants from Pennsylvania. There is an Amish settlement
in the Grantsville area.

The entire county is mountainous, although the southwest corner is part of the relatively level Appalachian
Plateau. There are fertile agricultural areas in the valleys
and on some of the level mountain tops, where corn, grains,
potatoes and hay are raised, with some dairying and livestock
farming. The county leads the state in oats and buckwheat
and produces most of the state's maple syrup. There is more
state-owned land here than in any of the other counties.

Garrett County has very little manufacturing, but lumbering, coal, stone, sand and gravel are important industries.
Deep Creek Lake is a thriving summer and winter resort.

GARRETT ISLAND (Cecil)

A large island in the Susquehanna River about two miles
from its mouth. It was previously known as Palmer's Island,
and later, Watson's Island, but when the B. & O. Railroad
acquired it in 1884 and placed the piers of their Susquehanna
Bridge upon it, they re-named it after Robert Garrett, the
company's president. The bridge collapsed in 1907 and the
present one was completed in 1910.

A very early settlement of the English took place on
Garrett Island, when William Claiborne, of Kent Island fame,
had a trading post here. Edward Palmer obtained it in 1622
and dreamed of planting the first American University here,
but his plans did not materialize. The island's 200 acres are
wooded and uninhabited.

GARRETT PARK (Montgomery) Pop. 1,178. Incorp. 1898.

11 miles northwest of the U. S. Capitol. It received its
name, like Garrett County, from Robert W.Garrett, president
of the B. & O. Railroad, which has always played a part in
the town's history. Garrett Park was laid out in 1887 on the
plan of an English village, with irregular lots and winding
streets, which were named after the Waverly Novels; for
the inhabitants it was an escape from the hubub of
Washington. The town is registered as an Historic District
on the National Register of Historic Places.

GARRISON (Baltimore County)

11 miles northwest of downtown Baltimore. A vaguely
defined area reminiscent of the days when the area was a

wilderness and a fort was erected for security purposes (See **FORT GARRISON.**) In the vicinity are The Stone Chapel, a Methodist Church dating from 1786, and St. Thomas's Episcopalian Church, founded in 1742 and still in a rural setting (See **OWINGS MILLS)** On Valley Road is the expensive Green Spring Valley Hunt and Golf Club; on Reisterstown Rd. the Baltimore Spice Co. employs many.

GATHLAND STATE PARK (Washington)

17 miles southeast of Hagerstown where Gapland Road crosses South Mountain by way of Crampton Gap. George Alfred Townsend, poet, novelist and Civil War correspondent, who wrote under the pseudonymn of "Gath," first saw this spot when he was covering the Battle of South Mountain. After the war he returned and bought 100 acres on the mountain top, where he built a flamboyant collection of buildings to his own design. His hospitality was lavish until his fortunes changed and he fell upon hard times, after which the buildings fell into ruins, except a large stone arch, which he built and dedicated to war correspondents. He died in 1914 and is buried in Philadelphia, while the stone tomb, which he prepared at Gathland, stands empty in the woods.

The tract is now Gathland State Park and offers an historical walking tour; some of Gath's writings and papers are housed in the visitors' center. At various times a "Newspaper Hall of Fame" has been suggested here, to complement the War Correspondents' Arch.

GEORGE'S CREEK REGION (Allegany)

George's Creek rises near Frostburg and follows the valley between Savage and Dans Mountains until it meets the Potomac at Westernport. It was named for "Indian George" who worked for the Cresaps, a family of Western Maryland pioneers. George's father, Nemacolin, marked the road from Cumberland to Brownsville, which forms the path of route 40 to this day.

The valley was settled by Germans and Scotch Irish, but the first permanent settler was William Shaw, and the first building was an old log mill, built in 1725 at the village of Moscow, where the Shaws had their family house. When coal was found in the region, the valley was mined from end to end, and a railroad was built from the Potomac as far as National. The coal was a high-grade steam coal and was worked by tunnelling into the sides of the mountains. Deep mining is over, but strip mining has taken its place to some extent in the surrounding area.

Towns in the valley are: Borden, National, Midland, Lonaconing, Moscow, Barton and some smaller places. The village of George's Creek is some distance north of the valley, a mile east of Mount Savage.

GEORGETOWN (Kent)

15 miles northeast of Chestertown on the south bank of the Sassafras River. Georgetown ws an active port in the 18th century but little remains here now, except the Kitty Knight House, which is used as a restaurant, open only for dinners. Kitty Knight made herself immortal by defying the British soldiers who sailed up the Sassafras River in 1813, bent on destruction; as fast as they ignited her house, she beat out the flames with a broom, and admiral Cockburn was so impressed by her resistance that her house was spared. This story may well be true, since we are told that her lover deserted her owing to the vileness of her language. Additions have since been made to the house. Kitty is buried in St. Francis Xavier churchyard near Warwick, although she was a Protestant, the reason being that the road to the Protestant churchyard was impassable at the time of her death.

Georgetown. The Kitty Knight House.

There is a marina on the Sassafras and the place is very popular with boaters. A second Georgetown in Kent County lies 7 miles west of Chestertown. (See also **FREDERICK-TOWN.**)

GERMANTOWN (Montgomery) 9,721

9 miles northwest of Rockville.   It was so called because the first settlement was made by German families on a site one mile to the southwest. When the railroad was completed in the 1870's, the commercial center was moved to the vicinity of the railroad tracks and the former settlement became Old Germantown.

Frenzied development is taking place in what is supposed to be a new planned community surrounded by parks and lakes and stressing local amenities and transportation. Nearby are the buildings of the Atomic Energy Commission, engaged in developing peaceful uses of atomic energy. Also the Sherman Fairchild Technology Center on a 165 acre site, the largest corporation based in Maryland, although not the largest employer.

GIBSON ISLAND (Anne Arundel)

8 miles northeast of Annapolis, but much further by road, at the tip of the neck between the Patapsco and Magothy Rivers. It is an exclusive yachting center and an area of expensive, secluded homes, guarded by a gate keeper at the only road entrance. There is supposed to be buried treasure on the island, but those who live here have no need to dig for it.

GILBERT RUN PARK (Charles)

10 miles east of La Plata. A county park covering 180 acres, with a 60-acre lake stocked with fish. There is boating, picnicking, hiking and fishing, and each June there is an art festival with entertainment.

GILPIN POINT (Caroline)

6 miles southwest of Denton, a point projecting into the Choptank River opposite the mouth of Tuckahoe Creek. Here lived Col. William Richardson (1735-1825,) revolutionary soldier, member of the Maryland General Assembly, treasurer of the Eastern Shore and presidential elector of the college that elected Washington. Of his large estate, a small dairy and his tomb remain. A nearby school bears his name.

GIRDLETREE (Worcester)

6 miles south of Snow Hill. The name is taken from a farmhouse which stood on the spot -- girdling was a common method of removing a large tree. Near here is the Ernest A. Vaughn Wildlife Management area. The village has a small seafood industry and a canning plant.

GLENARDEN (Prince George's) Pop. 4,993. Incorp. 1939.

9 miles northeast of the U.S. Capitol. Originally this was a slum, but in 1939 it was incorporated by a group of black Washingtonians with urban renewal in mind. Such has been its progress that it received an award by H.U.D. for its urban renewal efforts.

GLEN ARM (Baltimore County)

13 miles northeast of downtown Baltimore. It was named for the first syllable of his name by Thomas Armstrong, who was once the treasurer of the Maryland and Pennsylvania Railroad. Their little station here still stands and has been converted into a restaurant. Although the area remains rural, there are several industries here, the largest being Koppers Co. producing container machinery.

GLEN BURNIE (Anne Arundel) Pop. 37,263.

10 miles south of downtown Baltimore. In its early days it was known as Tracey's Station, although the postoffice changed that to Myrtle, after Mr. Tracey's wife. It became Glen Burnie in 1888, taking the name from the suburban estate of Judge Elias Glenn. The Glenns had bought land here and taken over the Curtis Creek Mining, Furnace and Manufacturing Co. which flourished here for many years, finally closing down in 1851.

The town was located at the spot where the Baltimore and Annapolis Railroad (now defunct) crossed Light St. (now route 2) leading out of Baltimore. In 1895 a tile factory opened here, using the local clay, but it was not until the 1960's that the town mushroomed into its present sprawling size, as a Baltimore suburb and the hub of northern Anne Arundel County. The Maryland Department of Motor Vehicles is located here and also many of the county offices, close to the main center of population of the county. Numerous industries are in the area, the largest being the Alco-Gravure Division of Publication Corporation, and a bindery.

GLENCOE (Baltimore County)

18 miles north of downtown Baltimore.   Perhaps its founders thought that the valley of the Gunpowder Falls here resembled Glen Coe in Scotland.   Like several other places which had a station on the Northern Central Railroad, it was a resort at one time, and a spacious hotel stood on the summit of the ridge.

Nearby is Oldfields school, formerly Oldfields Girls School, established in 1869 by Mrs. John Sears McCulloch. One of its more notable pupils was Wallis Warfield, who became Mrs. Simpson and married King Edward VIII of Britain.

GLEN ECHO (Montgomery)   Pop. 297.   Incorp. 1904

9 miles northwest of the U.S.Capitol.   The population figure applies to the small incorporated area, but residential streets surrounding it have a much larger population.

Older residents vividly remember the amusement park which functioned here for many years on what was earlier a Chautauqua Meeting Ground.   The site now belongs to the National Park Service, who have preserved a bell tower and many of the old buildings, and who organize all kinds of creative classes all the year round, and outdoor entertainment on summer weekends.

Nearby, at 5801 Oxford Rd. and visible from McArthur Boulevard, is the Clara Barton House, home of the founder of the American Red Cross and where she died, in her 91st year, in 1912.   It is built from wood taken from the Red Cross barracks at Johnstown, Pennsylvania, used to house refugees after the terrible flood of 1889, and it is designed in the style of a Mississippi River boat.   Personal items are displayed in the house, which is open to visitors Thurs. thru Sat. 10-5 and Sun. 1-5.   It was declared a National Historical Landmark in 1965.

GLENELG (Howard)

12 miles west of Ellicott City.   The name is a palindrome, reading the same backwards as forwards, and was formerly applied to a large estate owned by General Tyson. The original estate was 585 acres, with a manor house begun in the early 1700's but much added to around 1845.   The boxwood gardens were famous, and summer concerts were held in the grounds for the public in the 1930's.

Glenelg is an indeterminate place today, since much of the land has been sold off for developments.   What remains

of the estate is now the Glenelg Country School, which opened in 1942.   Nearby is the home of the Howard Hunt Club,
organized in 1930.

GLEN ELLEN (Baltimore County)
10 miles northeast of Baltimore. It is a vaguely defined
community in the Loch Raven area on Providence Rd. named
for a house which was built here in 1832 by Robert Gilmor.
The house was named after Gilmor's wife and constructed in
the style of Sir Walter Scott's Abbotsford; but although the
mansion was occupied, it was never completed, and fell into
ruins by the 1920's. The foundations can still be seen in the
reservoir area near the lake.

GLENN DALE (Prince George's) Pop. 5,106
12 miles northeast of the U.S.Capitol.   John Glenn of
Baltimore bought property here in 1872, and the town was
first called Glennville, then Glendale. On the property was
an earlier manorhouse belonging to the Du Val family, built
in the 1780's and called "Marietta." The house still stands
and belongs to the National Capital Park and Planning Commission.   At 10400 Good Luck Rd. is the Winchester Public
Shooting Center, a trap and skeet range, which is said to be
the largest public shooting center on the east coast, open
day and night, with rental equipment and instructors.

GLENWOOD (Howard)
12 miles west of Ellicott City on route 97. Near this
insignificant spot lived Charles Alexander Warfield, a chief
character in the Peggy Stewart drama at Annapolis. He is
buried at Bushey Park Farm.

GLYNDON (Baltimore County)
16 miles northwest of downtown Baltimore. The town
was founded because the railroad came through here, by-
passing Reisterstown, whose residents did not want it; the
name was picked out of a hat. The first Glyndon station was
built of local marble and was considered to be the most
beautiful on the entire Western Maryland line. Alas, it was
destroyed by fire in 1903 and the present station, now a
postoffice, was erected in 1904 and closed to passenger
traffic in 1966. The old homes surrounding it were built
1880-1815.

Nearby Emory Grove was opened as a Methodist Episcopal campground in 1868; most of the cottages are now owner-occupied. Camp Glyndon is a center for diabetic children, built in 1968 on 44 acres.

GNEGY CHURCH (Garrett)

A tiny settlement close to the West Virginia border, five miles north of the Potomac River. Named for the Gnegy family, whose name has many spelling variations.

GODDARD SPACE FLIGHT CENTER (Prince George's)

11 miles northeast of the U.S.Capitol, near Greenbelt. Close to 2,000 people are employed on the 550 acre center and the Census Designated Place of Goddard has a population of 6,147. The center was named in honor of Dr. Robert H.Goddard, father of American rocketry. A visitors' center is open Wed. thru Sun. 10-4, except Thanksgiving, Christmas and New Year's Day. There is no charge.

GOD'S GRACE POINT (Calvert)

4.5 miles west of Prince Frederick. The wide estuary of that name is all that remains of what was, in the 18th century, the largest estate in Calvert County.

GOLDSBORO (Caroline) Pop. 231. Incorp. 1906.

11 miles east of Denton. It was named after a local landowner when the railroad reached here in 1867. Previously it had been called Oldtown. There is a small seafood packer and a small cannery here.

GOOD LUCK (Prince George's) Pop. 10,584

12 miles northeast of the U.S. Capitol. One of Washington's newer suburbs, outside the beltway.

GORMAN (Garrett)

8 miles south of Oakland on the Potomac River. Named after Senator Gorman of Maryland, it was once called North Branch, then Elkins, then Gormania. It was evidently altered to Gorman to distinguish it from Gormania across the river in West Virginia. Fort Pendleton was built on a hill overlooking the town in 1861 by the Federal Army to protect the turnpike (route 50) which crosses the mountains here. Little remains and there is no road to the top. The bridge across the river was burnt by the Confederates in 1864.

GORSUCH MILLS (Baltimore County)

29 miles north of downtown Baltimore. It was named after Stephen or Steven Gorsuch, who owned several mills here, although it is now little more than a name on the map. Another Gorsuch, Edward, owned the homestead and barn on York Rd. near Glencoe, which seems to have been a meeting place for slave-owners chasing their runaway slaves along the road to Pennsylvania and freedom.

GOVERNOR RUN (Calvert)

6 miles southeast of Prince Frederick. There is a good view of the Calvert Cliffs from here, but the beach is now private and visitors cannot enjoy it. There is a small exhibit of the Calvert Cliffs fossils here.

GRACEHAM (Frederick)

14 miles north of Frederick. It was once called Moravian Town, since it was settled by a group of Moravians about 1746. The first Moravian Church in Maryland is here, with a churchyard of uniformly arranged stones: the women on one side and the men on the other. The village made the news in 1975 owing to an invasion by large numbers of starlings.

GRAHAMTOWN (Allegany)

A southeastern suburb of Frostburg, named for Curtin Graham, one of the early settlers of Frostburg and one of its largest landholders.

GRANITE (Baltimore County)

14 miles northwest of downtown Baltimore. It was formerly Waltersville, named after the Walters family who were large landowners. The present name comes from the granite quarries which were opened in the vicinity around 1820 and which supplied building stone for more than a century. Some of the buildings made from this granite are the Treasury Building and part of the interior of the Washington Monument in Washington, and the old postoffice and court house in Baltimore. A spur line operated from the B. & O. Railroad to the quarries, but all trace of it has vanished and the quarries are water-filled. One can be seen in the grounds of Woodstock College, now a state park.

GRANTSVILLE (Garrett)   Pop. 517.   Incorp. 1864.

24 miles northeast of Oakland. It was founded by a native of Baltimore nearly half a mile southeast of this location, the present village having been founded in 1832 when the National Road crossed the Casselman River at this point. Originally it was named Tomlinsons, after a local land-owning family, then Little Crossings in 1834 and Grantsville in 1846. When Garrett County was formed in 1872 and a vote was taken for the location of the county seat, Grantsville trailed Oakland by only 63 votes. In 1875 certain factions sought to divide the county, with Grantsville as the capital of the eastern portion.

Some fire clay products are made here and there is an old grist mill, dating from 1798, electric powered since the 1940's, named Stanton's Mill. The old mill stones can be seen built into the wall. There are a number of Amish settlements in the neighborhood and they run a large food store nearby called Yoder's Locker Plant. (See also: **CASSELMAN BRIDGE; CASSELMAN HOTEL; LITTLE MEADOWS; PENN ALPS**)

GRASONVILLE (Queen Anne's)   Pop. 1,910

10 miles southwest of Centreville. The small town survives by seafood, and there are seven seafood operations here. An annual festival is held in October, with the delicacies being caught, prepared and served by local people.

GRATITUDE (Kent)

11 miles southwest of Chestertown. This small settlement was originally called Deep Landing but the name was changed to that of the steamboat which regularly used the landing -- an odd reversal of the usual procedure where boats are named after places. From the marina one can get a view of the Chesapeake Bay Bridge to the left and the Francis Scott Key Bridge and the stacks of Sparrows Point to the right.

GRAYS HILL (Cecil)

2 miles east of Elkton, this small hill rises abruptly from the surrounding low area. It is composed of crystalline rock and is an outlier of the Piedmont. Sometimes it is spelt Grey's Hill. On Aug. 26, 1777, George Washington and other generals stood on this elevation and observed the British landings on Elk Landing (q.v.)

GREAT FALLS (Montgomery)

16 miles northwest of the U. S. Capitol on the Potomac River. These three miles of rapids and waterfalls presented a barrier to navigation until the C. & O. Canal by-passed them with a series of locks. When the government tapped the water here for Washington's water supply, it was expected that a great town would spring up; but the area by the river remains a pleasant afternoon excursion for Washingtonians.

A restored tavern and lockhouse remain, housing a museum with exhibits, programs, guided walks and a nature trail, while a film about the canal is shown every hour in summer. The museum is open daily, 9.30 until dark. The entire length of the canal and towpath, and the Great Falls area are a National Park.

GREAT MILLS (St. Mary's)

8 miles southeast of Leonardtown; it was once the second largest town in St. Mary's County. Maryland's first medical college was here, and a large water mill on St. Mary's River, which was washed away in 1817, while the Clifton Textile Mills produced woollen goods for many years. The last working water mill in the county is still here and a store selling local crafts is housed in the old postoffice and is open during the summer and Christmas seasons.

GREAT VALLEY

This name is applied in Maryland to the broad valley between South Mountain and the main body of the Appalachians. It is about 20 miles wide, mostly underlain by limestone. Northward, in Pennsylvania, it is known as the Cumberland Valley, and southward, in Virginia it is known as the Shenandoah Valley. The old Shenandoah Trail, later route 11, now superseded by I 81, ran down the valley. Hagerstown, the chief Maryland town in the valley, is located where route 11 crossed the old road from Baltimore.

GREENBELT (Prince George's) Pop. 17,332. Incorp. 1937.

10 miles east of the U.S.Capitol. The original town was a federal, low-cost housing project authorized in 1936 on a 2,000 acre tract with a community lake and park in the center, a pool and all amenities. The first residents arrived in 1937 and the community was expanded in 1941 and 1942. In 1952 the original rental properties were sold to residents

and Greenbelt is no longer a low-income project.   Much development has taken place around the original commuity.

Greenbelt Park is an extensive acreage just inside the Washington beltway, mainly between Kenilworth Avenue and route 295.   It has facilities for camping and picnicking.

GREENBRIAR STATE PARK (Washington)

The entrance to the park is about 9 miles east of Hagerstown on route 40 near the summit of South Mountain. There is a 42-acre artificial lake, with swimming and boats for hire and there is ample room for picnicking, fishing and hiking.   Nearby is a small village named Greenbriar.

GREENBURY POINT (Anne Arundel)

2 miles east of Annapolis, on the north shore of the Severn River where it meets the Chesapeake Bay.   It was named for Nicholas Greenberry, a Royal Governor of Maryland in 1693-4, and formerly spelled that way.

The point was occupied in the mid-17th century by puritans from Virginia.   Today it is occupied by the nine towers of the navy's transmitter facility, some over 300 ft. high, which is part of the ship to shore communications complex for the Atlantic Fleet.   The towers dominate the Bay landscape and are visible for many miles.

GREEN HAVEN (Anne Arundel) Pop. 6,577

11 miles south of downtown Baltimore.   It was originally named Outing Park, a community of summer homes and cottages on Stony Creek.   Although some modern buildings have been erected, many of the old houses remain, in every stage of dilapidation.

GREEN RIDGE (Allegany)

One of the ridges of the Ridge and Valley Province, stretching from the Pennsylvania border to the Potomac River.   Much of its slopes, and those of Town Hill, to the east, are part of the Green Ridge State Forest, which has facilities for camping, fishing and hunting.   According to the map, there are a number of sulphur springs in the area.

GREENSBORO (Caroline) Pop. 1,253. Incorp. 1826.

7 miles east of Denton.   The locality was once called Choptank Bridge, or Bridgetown, and being one of the oldest settlements on the Eastern Shore, made great efforts to have

the county seat established here instead of at Denton. In 1791 it gave up the struggle and became established under its present name.   Small boats can still get up the Choptank to this erstwhile port.   The Goldsboro House is a museum and the headquarters of the Caroline County Historical Society.   Two or three small factories produce electronic components and clothing.

GREEN SPRING FURNACE (Washington)

14 miles southwest of Hagerstown.   The small place is the site of an early iron furnace built about 1750 by Launcelot Jacques and abandoned by him because of the shortage of ore in the area.   It was later re-opened by Thomas Johnson, first post-revolutionary governor of Maryland, who had an interest in the more famous Catoctin Furnace.   From 1866 until about 1874 it was operated by J. B. Haines & Co. and manufactured about 1800 tons of pig iron annually, which was shipped across the Potomac at McCoy's Ferry, one mile south.

Although the furnace has long ceased to function, the Green Spring for which it is named still flows, and furnishes bottled water as it has done since the 1850's.   Most of the water is sold in Hagerstown.

GREEN SPRING VALLEY (Baltimore County)

10 miles northwest of downtown Baltimore.   It is the valley of the upper reaches of the Jones Falls and has always been the setting for the estates of those whose fortunes were made along the lower reaches of Jones Falls.   It still retains something of its rural and prosperous aspect, although developers are nibbling greedily at its fringes.

GROVE (Caroline)

10 miles southwest of Denton on route 16.   The Dickinson family were prominent in the neighborhood, and one of its scions, Charles, was killed in a duel with Andrew Jackson. He is buried at Harmony (q.v.)

GUILFORD (Howard)

7 miles south of Ellicott City.   It is a small ramshackle village which has probably already been swallowed up by the large industrial park which is mushrooming in the vicinity. There were formerly several granite quarries in the vicinity and a railroad connection for shipping the stone.   On a rise

west of route 32 is the one-time home of the naval hero, Joshua Barney. Born in Baltimore, he took this house on the occasion of his second marriage.

GUNPOWDER RIVER

The Big and Little Branches of the Gunpowder River, or Gunpowder Falls as it is often called, rise close to the Pennsylvania border and meet near their joint estuary, which enters the Chesapeake Bay 17 miles east of Baltimore. The Little Gunpowder Falls acts as the boundary between Baltimore and Harford Counties, while the Big Gunpowder Falls provides the Baltimore area with much of its water supply.

The name has been explained in different ways. Some say that the Indians buried gunpowder on the banks, thinking it would grow and multiply. Others say that an early miller named Winter ground charcoal for gunpowder in the vicinity.

Gunpowder State Park now occupies 10,000 acres of the stream valleys at 18 locations. The Hammerman Area is at the mouth of the river and has beaches for swimming and two marinas. Loch Raven Reservoir (q.v.) is the principal water supply for Baltimore City and County. Prettyboy Reservoir (q.v.) located several miles nearer the source, is a feeder reservoir.

HAGERSTOWN.   Seat of Washington County.   Pop. 35,862. Incorp. 1791.

Situated in the Great Valley at the crossing point of routes 11 and 40.   Captain Jonathan Hager, who came from Germany about 1730 and laid out the town in 1762, first named it Elizabeth Town, after his wife;   it later became Elizabeth Hagers Town and finally just Hagerstown.   Their House, Hager's Fancy, which was constructed in 1739, still stands, opposite City Park.   Constructed, frontier fashion, over springs, it has been restored and opened to the public, while a museum behind the house exhibits artifacts and Hager memorabilia.   House and museum are open June 1 - Oct. 1, Tues. thru Sat., 10-12 and 2-4;   also Sunday afternoons.

Across in City Park is the Washington Museum of Fine Arts, the only Maryland art museum outside of Baltimore, and one of the few county art museums in the country.   It was given to the city by Anna Brugh Singer in 1930 and enlarged by her in 1949;   it contains an interesting collection of paintings and some sculpture and artifacts.   Another feature of City Park is the Valley Store Museum, an 1840 home containing an authentic re-creation of the fabled country store.   This is closed in winter but the art museum is open all year Tues. thru Sat. 10-5 and Suns. and holidays 1-6.   There is also a lake in the park with waterfowl.

The Historical Society of Washington County is located at the Miller House, 135 Washington St. and has a museum including some relics of the C.& O. Canal, a collection of clocks, and the total remains of the Bell Pottery.   It is open Tues. thru Fri. 11-4, weekends 2-5.

The Washington County Library was opened in 1965 to replace an older building and has an excellent Western Maryland Room upstairs, open Fri. evening and Sat. afternoon.   Notice the little figure on top of City Hall - this is Little Heiskell, the symbol of the city, a metal sculpture of obscure origin which was first placed there around 1769. The present figure is a replica; the original reposes safely in the Hager Museum.

Hagerstown.   Washington County Museum of Fine Arts.

Four railroads used to meet in Hagerstown, dominated by the Western Maryland, which was headquartered here; but traffic has been largely re-routed and the imposing W.M. station is used as offices.   Note the 1912 Baldwin steam engine on display nearby. At one time, the largest industry in town was the Steam Engine and Machine Works.

A variety of manufacturing is carried on today, including womens' clothes and shoes, machinery for blast cleaning and dust control and musical organs.   Until recently the two largest industries were Mack Trucks and Fairchild Aircraft.

The name of Hagerstown is most well-known not for any of the above matters of interest, but for the *Hagerstown Almanac,* which has been published regularly every year since 1797, first in German, then in German and English, and finally in English only. It has been more widely read and its predictions have been more credited than any other almanac in America.

HALETHORPE (Baltimore County)
5 miles southwest of downtown Baltimore.   This old-

established neighborhood of individual homes seems to have had a long association with the B. & O. Railroad -- in fact railroad officials named it.   The name means healthy town. In 1927 the Fair of the Iron Horse was held here to celebrate the centennial of the B.& O. and today the railroad has its computerized car tracking station here.   There are a number of industries in the vicinity including a brewery, Kaiser Aluminum, bedding and plastic containers.

HALLOWING POINT (Calvert)

5 miles southwest of Prince Frederick, at the eastern end of the Patuxent River Bridge.   From earliest times there was a ferry at this point, and the shouting to call the ferry from the other side of the river gave the spot its name.

HALPINE (Montgomery)

A recent development 3 miles southeast of Rockville.

HAMBLETON (Talbot)

6 miles southeast of Easton.   The town was once called Hole-in-the Wall and is still called that by older local inhabitants.   Some say the name is from an inn, others say that smuggled goods were exchanged anonymously through a hole in a wall.   Near here are the ruins of Whitemarsh Church, one of the oldest in Talbot County.   The grave of Robert Morris is here (See **OXFORD**) but some of the furnishings are preserved in St. Paul's Church in Trappe.

HAMPSTEAD (Carroll) Pop. 1293. Incorp. 1888.

8 miles northeast of Westminster, Hampstead borders route 30 on both sides for nearly 2 miles. It was founded in 1786 by Christopher Vaughan, brother-in-law to Richard Richards, who founded Manchester, four miles to the north, and also to William Winchester, who founded Westminster. Originally it was called Spring Gardens, later it was called Coxville for over 50 years owing to the numerous members of the Cox family who settled here.   The present name is from Hampstead in England.

The oldest building in town, a grain store house, built in 1793, is incorporated into another building.   The largest employer for miles around is in Hampstead -- Black and Decker, whose plant employs nearly 3,000 and is said to be the largest portable power tool manufacturing plant in the world.

HAMPTON (Baltimore County) Pop. 5,220

9 miles northeast of downtown Baltimore and 2 miles northeast of Towson.   The area is named for a great post-Revolutionary mansion built 1783-90, which belonged for 158 years to the Ridgely family.   It is now owned by the National Park Service and administered by the Society for the Preservation of Maryland Antiquities.   The Ridgelys were associated with most aspects of Maryland life, but particularly with the early iron industry, using local ores. The house is open Tue. thru Sat. 11-5 and Sun. 1-5. A small restaurant provides lunch.

HANCOCK (Washington) Pop. 1,887. Incorp. 1853

24 miles west of Hagerstown at a point where the Potomac makes its most northerly bend, trimming the width of the state to two miles.   It is thought to have been named for Joseph Hancock, who settled here in 1749.   The old route from Baltimore to Cumberland, now designated route 144, is the main street and most of the traffic by-passes the town on route 40.   In the days of passenger trains, Western Maryland trains stopped in the town, while B. & O. trains stopped one mile away, across the river.

Packing houses serve the area's apple and peach orchards; there is also a factory making travel trailers.   Formerly there was a cement industry here, connected by a cable across the Potomac to the B. & O. Railroad.   On the north side of Main St. at the western end is a museum of the C. & O. Canal.

Hancock saw some action in the Civil War, when St. Thomas's Church was used as a hospital for Union troops. A thick marble slab in the cemetery marks the grave of a certain John Johnson, who died unexpectedly while surveying the boundary between Maryland and Virginia.

HANOVER (Howard)

7 miles southeast of Ellicott City.   This small village was once a railroad community known as Hanoversville. Recently it has been struggling for survival against a projected highway.

HARDESTY (Prince George's)

7 miles northeast of Upper Marlboro, close to the Patuxent River.   It was formerly known as Queen Anne and

was established in 1706 when the river was navigable to this point. The first bridge was built in 1747; the present bridge and road leading to it still bear the Queen's name. In its heyday it was a coaching stop on the road from Annapolis to Upper Marlboro; there was a tobacco inspection warehouse, inns, and a race-course. Nothing now remains of the original town.

HARFORD COUNTY. County Seat: Bel Air. Pop. 145,930. Area: 439 square miles.

The county was formed in 1773 and named after Henry Harford, the last Proprietory of Maryland and son of Frederick Calvert, last Lord Baltimore. It is bounded on the north by the Pennsylvania state line; on the east by the Susquehanna River; on the southeast by the Chesapeake Bay; on the west by the Little Gunpowder River and a line due north from its source. The northern four fifths of the county lies on the rolling Piedmont Plateau and the southern one fifth on the Coastal Plain.

Dairying and stock raising are carried on in the county and the crops are mainly corn, grains and hay, with some vegetables. Race horse breeding is also important. There is some diversified industry in the southern portion. Two federal installations, Aberdeen Proving Ground and Edgewood Arsenal, cover a total of 70,000 prime waterfront acres, and serve to make Aberdeen the largest town in the county. There are interesting historical sites at Joppa, Bush and Havre de Grace, among other places.

HARFORD GLEN (Harford)

A county park of 385 acres 5 miles south of Bel Air below the Atkisson Reservoir (q.v.) Boating, nature study and tree planting are conducted here by the County Board of Education.

HARMANS (Anne Arundel)

10 miles southwest of Baltimore. A fairly non-descript place except that the Koppers Co. has a large factory here employing 400 people and producing power transmission couplings.

HARMONY (Frederick)

8 miles northwest of Frederick between South and Catoctin Mountains. It was once called Bealsville and had a woollen mill, weaving factory and distillery. During the Revolution it is said to have been a Tory stronghold. Harmony is but a few houses among fields and streams, but it would be nice to be able to say one lived in Harmony.

HARMONY (Caroline)

8 miles southwest of Denton. At the junction of route 16 and the Grove-Agner Rd. is the tomb of Charles Dickinson, a prominent colonial figure, who was killed by Andrew Jackson in a duel in the Red Valley, Tennessee in 1806 (See **GROVE**)

HARNEY (Carroll)

15 miles northwest of Westminster. It was once called Monocacyville, owing to its proximity to that river, but the name was changed in honor of General Harney of the U.S.Army, who passed this way in 1863.

HARRISONVILLE (Baltimore County)

13 miles northwest of downtown Baltimore on Liberty Road. Some say it was named for Thomas Harrison who purchased land here in 1754; others say that it was named after President William Henry Harrison, who is said to have stopped here on his inaugural journey from Ohio to Washington. The New Tavern, marked by an historical sign, was actually a tavern 1802-1895, after which it was used for church services for some years by both Methodists and Catholics. It has been remodelled and is now apartments.

HARRISVILLE (Cecil)

16 miles northwest of Elkton. It is said that a man named Leonard Krauss, who was once a tailor to George Washington, kept a popular inn here called the Rising Sun, which gave rise to the name of the nearby town.

HART AND MILLER ISLANDS (Baltimore County)

13 miles southeast of downtown Baltimore. Two low, uninhabited islands in the Chesapeake Bay, one to three miles off shore and approachable only by water. A third island, called Pleasure Island was closer to shore and once connected to the mainland by a bridge; it was the site of a popular beach resort called Bay Shore from 1947 to 1964. A previous resort of the same name had existed on the mainland from 1907 until 1947. These properties have since been acquired by Bethlehem Steel.

It has been proposed to dump the spoil from dredging Baltimore Harbor on Hart and Miller Islands, with suitable retaining walls to enlarge the islands and prevent erosion, but there has been much controversy on this point. There is said to be buried treasure on Miller Island, which belonged to the original owner, Joseph Hart.

HARUNDALE (Anne Arundel)

12 miles south of downtown Baltimore and south of Glen Burnie. It was part of the same tract, belonging to the Glenn family, from which Glen Burnie was formed, and the name means "Dale of the Swallows."

In the early part of the century the area was used by the state as a rifle range and military installation. Housing development began in 1946-7 and grew rapidly, the houses being small, all identical, and made from semi-prefabricated components.   The streets, named for English villages, are laid out in alphabetical order.   The development has now matured, and almost every house has been given its own individual modification. The shopping mall opened in 1958. It was one of the very first suburban shopping malls and won several awards for its architecture.

HARWOOD PARK (Howard)
12 miles southwest of Baltimore. This is one of the new industrial parks which have sprung up along the Baltimore-Washington corridor between routes 1 and 95.

HAVRE DE GRACE (Harford) Pop. 8,763. Incorp. 1785.
24 miles east of Bel Air on a point between the south bank of the Susquehanna River and the Chesapeake Bay, well known to shipping as Concord Point. The town was founded in 1785 on the site of an older settlement and was originally known as Susquehanna Lower Ferry, a ferry link in the old Philadelphia Road.   The present name is said to have been sugggested by Lafayette and is a French phrase meaning harbor of mercy.

Railroad cars also were ferried across the river here before the railroad bridges were built upstream from the town. The first road bridge was not acquired until 1906, when road traffic began to use the abandoned Pennsylvania Railroad bridge, which had been built in 1866.   This was finally abandoned when the route 40 bridge was built in 1939, but its piers can still be seen.   Later still, in 1963, came the Kennedy Highway Bridge.

Concord Point was once the site of a small battery, which fired its single gun in May, 1813 when British vessels arrived and began shelling the town.   The gun was soon silenced, and the only officer present, John O'Neill, was captured and taken aboard the *Maidstone*.   He was later released owing to the courageous petition of his daughter to Admiral Sir George Cockburn, who gave her a gold and tortoiseshell snuff box.   When the Concord Point battery was replaced by a lighthouse in 1829, John O'Neill was given the job of keeper, and the post descended to his grandson until the light was converted to an automatic one. The lighthouse is still there, but no longer used for shipping. Close by it is a cannon on a granite base, on which is inscribed the story of John O'Neill.

Havre de Grace.   Concord Point Lighthouse.

Tydings Park, overlooking the Chesapeake Bay, has facilities for fishing and boat docking.   A shad fishing tournament is held in the park each May and a hydroplane regatta is held on the Susquehanna each June.

At the other end of town from the lighthouse is the lockhouse.   This was the house of the keeper of the entrance lock of the Susquehanna and Tidewater Canal, an enterprise which was completed in 1839 and followed the river from here to Wrightsville, Pennsylvania, a distance of about 45 miles.   The house has been acquired by an historical group and made into a museum, while parts of the canal and entrance lock can still be discerned.   Another remnant of bygone days is the large stone Bayou Hotel, now the Bayou apartments.

The town shows little of the industrial surge predicted for it, although there are some nearby factories producing cleaning materials and metal and plastic containers.

HEBBVILLE (Baltimore County)

9 miles northwest of downtown Baltimore.   It was once called Whitegrounds, because a pocket of white clay was found here.   De Kalb's pottery was founded here because of the clay, but later moved to Catonsville.   The village was renamed in the 1880's after Dr. Hebb, Baltimore County's Register of Wills.

HEBRON (Wicomico) Pop. 705. Incorp. 1931.
     6 miles northwest of Salisbury. Hebron lies exactly half way between the Atlantic coast and the Chesapeake Bay, since it is in line with the boundary stone placed on the middle point in 1760. The stone remains in place three miles north of Hebron on Barren Creek Road, just east of Old Railroad Road. Next to it is a stone placed there in 1763 by Mason and Dixon.

HENDERSON (Caroline) Pop. 135. Incorp. 1949.
     14 miles northeast of Denton.   It was earlier called Meredith's Crossing, or River Bridges, but in 1868, when the railroad reached it, it was named for one of the railroad's directors.   In 1891 the railroad depot was moved down to Chapel, in Talbot County, now non-existant and in 1903 Henderson got a new station, which was moved down from Greenspring, Delaware.

HENRYTON (Carroll)
     16   miles southeast of Westminster.   Henryton State Hospital was built in 1918 on 175 acres as a T.B. sanatarium for blacks, and the buildings were enlarged in 1941.   Since 1963 it has been a training school for retarded adults.

HERALD HARBOR (Ann Arundel) Pop. 1,255
     16 miles south of downtown Baltimore. It started as a summer resort on the Severn River, but like many similar communities it evolved into a year round place, at first without proper water and sanitation. County services have now been laid on and improvements made.

HEREFORD (Baltimore County)
     21 miles north of downtown Baltimore.   It takes its name from Hereford farmhouse on York Road.   The Merryman family of Hereford, England, acquired the land in the early 17th century; the house, built in 1714, is now deserted.

HERNWOOD (Baltimore County)
     14 miles northwest of Baltimore.   In the neighborhood of Hernwood are to be found the county dump and a Nike missile site.

HICKMAN (Caroline)

7 miles southeast of Denton; it is barely in Maryland. Named after a local landowner, it was originally Hickmantown, but the post office abbreviated the name. It is difficult to believe that in the 1920's there was a church, school, mills, post office and a station on the Baltimore and Eastern Railroad.

HIGHFIELD (Washington)

The two branches of the Western Maryland Railroad, which divided at Glyndon, near Reisterstown, meet again here after crossing South Mountain. The "old main line" has meandered across Maryland, following river valleys and making its horseshoe curve over South Mountain, while the newer line has traversed Pennsylvania, taking in Gettysburg and Hanover before returning to its native state. There is little freight traffic on either branch now; the old line goes no further than Westminster since the floods of 1972.

HIGHLAND (Frederick)

9 miles northwest of Frederick. Near here is Catoctin, or Crow Rock Falls; but it is on private land, hidden amid foliage, and there are no parking places, so visitors are not encouraged.

HIGHLAND BEACH (Anne Arundel) Pop. 8. Incorp. 1922.

4 miles south of Annapolis. The town was founded in 1893 by Charles R. Douglass, son of black abolitionist Frederick Douglass (See **TUCKAHOE**.) It is the only incorporated town in Anne Arundel County apart from Annapolis, the state capital. It was started as a summer placed for black intellectuals and is still a private community, with private beaches, still totally owned and governed by blacks. The founder's house still stands on Bay Ave. Although the census gives the population as only 8, its summer seasonal population is about 500.

HIGH ROCK (Washington)

A point on South Mountain near Penmar, 11 miles northeast of Hagerstown. A fine view of the Great Valley is obtained from here and the Appalachian trail passes nearby. High Rock has always been a popular overlook and wagon loads of tourists would make the trip here from Penmar (q.v.) in its palmy days. Nowadays the road to the top tends to become crowded with vehicles on summer weekends and a hang-gliding club has discovered that the awesome precipice makes a fine jumping-off spot. There is another High Rock on Savage Mountain (q.v.)

HILLANDALE (Montgomery) Pop. with Avenel 9,686.

10 miles north of the U.S.Capitol. This residential suburb, which is adjacent to Avenel in Prince George's County was started by a developer in 1933 and expanded rapidly in the 1950's and 60's. The Naval Ordnance Laboratory which designs weapons, has been located here on 875 acres since 1946.

HILLCREST HEIGHTS (Prince George's) Pop. 17,021

5 miles southeast of the U.S.Capitol. Another of Washington's spreading southeastern suburbs.

HILLSBORO (Caroline) Pop. 177. Incorp. 1822.

7 miles northwest of Denton. It received its present name in honor of Lord Hillsboro, a relation of Lord Baltimore; previously it had been called Tuckahoe Bridge, for the river had been spanned by a bridge at this point since before 1750. Charles Wilson Peale, a notable Maryland artist, resided near here for a time. A mile to the south, on the west side of Tuckahoe Road, a stone monument marks the site of an early Methodist chapel. Since the village is situated at a point where three counties meet, a tri-county fair used to be held here.

HOFFMANVILLE (Baltimore County)

29 miles northwest of downtown Baltimore near the headwaters of Gunpowder Falls. It was named for William Hoffman just before his death in 1786. Hoffman was born in Frankfort in 1740, came to Maryland and built the first paper mill in the state at this spot in 1776. He and his family are buried in the Gunpowder Cemetery of Mount Tabor Church.

The mill was a quarter of a mile upstream from the present Hoffmanville Bridge. Two hundred people were once employed in it, furnishing much of the paper for the money of the Continental Congress. The entire property was purchased in 1924 by Baltimore City for the Prettyboy Reservoir projects and it has reverted to a rural area once more.

HOLLAND ISLAND (Dorchester)

31 miles south of Cambridge. Only a vestige of this island now remains, near the shore of the larger Bloodsworth Island; but before 1912 it was an island three miles long by a mile wide with a population of about 300. After several severe storms, the people began to leave it in 1914, and by 1922 it was deserted. Some took the materials of their homes and re-erected them elsewhere; the church was transported to Fairmount, Somerset County.

HOLLOFIELD (Howard)

3.5 miles north of Ellicott City in the Patapsco Valley. This was a town in former times, but floods have taken their toll over the years and little remains. Two people were drowned here in the flood of 1868 and two more in the flood of 1972 when the bar beside the river was swept away. The town is now separated from the Hollofield Area of the state park by route 70.

HOLLYWOOD (St. Mary's)

5.5 miles northeast of Leonardtown. 3.5 miles from Hollywood, near the end of route 245 and fronting on the Patuxent River, lies the plantation of Sotterly, a working plantation, owned since 1961 by the Sotterly Mansion Foundation, and open to the public June - Sept. 11-6. The house ws built in 1730 and has the typical long, low frame structure of plantation homes in the area. Sotterly was also a port on the Patuxent River at the end of a "rolling road" where hogsheads of tobacco were rolled down to the water.

View from Sotterly towards the Patuxent River.

HOODS MILLS (Carroll)

15 miles south of Westminster. Now a small decrepit place on the South Branch of the Patapsco, it was a thriving place when James Hood and John Grimes built their mills here. It saw some activity in the Civil War when the Confederate Cavalry under Jeb Stuart crossed the river and railroad tracks at this point on their way northwards.

HOOPER ISLAND (Dorchester)

Route 335 enters Hooper Island about 15 miles southwest of Cambridge. The island is in turn connected to Upper and Middle Hooper Islands, which were once connected to Lower Hooper Island, before a storm washed away the bridge; the four islands form a chain about 14 miles long. The name is from Henry Hooper, who owned much of the land on the upper island.

Several small towns are on the islands: Hoopersville, on the Middle Island, which has two small seafood packing houses; Fishing Creek and Honga, on the Upper Island, both with dock facilities. The lower island once had a village called Apple-garth but since it lost its connection with the other island, this low marshy portion is uninhabited.

The islands were settled about 1660 by colonists from St. Mary's County across the Bay, and a Catholic church was built before 1692 called St. Mary, Star of the Sea. A church built in 1872 now stands on the site.

Captain John Smith was caught in a storm around these parts in 1608, when a gale blew away the vessel's sails and the crew were forced to turn their shirts into makeshift sails. He named the area "Limbo."

HORN POINT (Anne Arundel)

2 miles from downtown Annapolis across Spa Creek. It was named after Congressman Van Horn and was fortified in 1808. An historical marker tells that when British ships blocked the harbor, the Maryland militia was joined by French troops for the defense of Annapolis. The Maryland Capital Yacht Club is headquartered here. (See **EASTPORT**.)

HORN POINT (Dorchester)

4 miles northwest of Cambridge. On a point projecting into the Choptank River is the Center for Environmental and Estuarine Studies. Scientists study marsh ecology and shellfish aquaculture.

HORSEHEAD (Prince George's)

12 miles south of Upper Marlboro. A crossroads location named after the Horsehead Tavern, which still stands. John Wilkes Booth is said to have visited the tavern twice before the assassination, and according to a descendant of the landlady, he ate his lunch outside under a mulberry tree while examining maps.

HOUCKSVILLE (Carroll)

6 miles east of Westminster on the East Branch of the Patapsco River. There was once a paper factory near here owned by Geo. W. Keller.

HOWARD COUNTY.   County Seat: Ellicott City.   Pop. 118,572 . Area: 249 square miles.

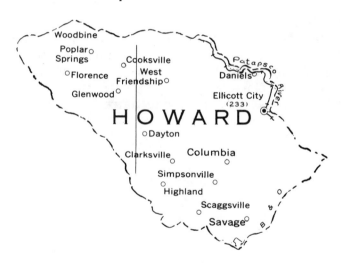

Howard County was formed in 1851. It was named after John Eager Howard the elder, who commanded Maryland troops in several Revolutionary War battles and owned land in the vicinity of Baltimore. It is bounded on the north by the Patapsco River from Mount Airy to Deep Creek; on the south and west by the Patuxent River from near Mount Airy to the B. & O. Railroad tracks near Laurel; on the southeast by the B. & O. Railroad tracks and Deep Creek. It is the only Maryland county that borders on neither the Bay nor the state boundaries.

Howard County lies totally on the rolling countryside of

the Piedmont Plateau.   Until the advent of Columbia (q.v.)
the county was almost entirely mixed farming country
containing no towns of any size apart from Ellicott City, but
with several large historic estates, notably Doughoregan
(q.v.) The building of Columbia, which is now by far the
largest town in the county, changed all that, and many
smaller new developments, both residential and commercial,
have sprung up around the old estates, although the county
still contains no incorporated towns.

HOYES (Garrett)

A small village 14 miles northeast of Oakland on route
219.   It is notable for the fact that in St. Dominic's
graveyard are buried Meshack Browning, author of *Forty four
years of the life of a hunter,* and both of his wives.

HOYES CREST (Garrett)

The highest point in Maryland, elevation 3,360 ft. It is
located in the extreme southwest corner of the state on
Backbone Mountain, and it was named for Charles E. Hoye,
founder of the Garrett County Historical Society.   It is
accessible only by foot, following a trail which begins from
route 219, two miles south of Silver Lake, West Virginia.
There is supposed to be a plaque marking the spot (if you
can find it.)

HUCKLEBERRY (Charles)

8 miles south of La Plata. It was near this point on the
Potomac that John Wilkes Booth and his companion rowed
across the river to Virginia in a boat belonging to Tom
Jones, who owned a house nearby.   The house is now the
gatehouse of the Loyola Retreat House.

HUDSON'S CORNER (Somerset)

12 miles south of Princess Anne.   There is a museum
here called the Eastern Shore Early American Museum,
crammed with tools and furnishings of the 19th century.
Housed in a large corrugated iron shed, it is open Thurs. thru
Sun.

HUGHESVILLE (Charles) Pop. 1,208.

11 miles east of La Plata. The town was founded in the
18th century and has always been an important marketing

center for Southern Maryland. It is still an important tobacco center and there are tobacco auctions here every weekday from mid-April to July.

Hughesville. Tobacco warhouses.

Three miles south of here is the Amish Farmers' Market, originally serving the Amish colony which settled in the vicinity. It is on a seven acre tract beside route 5, selling goods both old and new and a great deal of junk. Wednesday is auction day -- 2 p.m. produce and 6 p.m. livestock.

HUNTINGTOWN (Calvert)

5 miles north of Prince Frederick, a crossroads village on route 4. The original town was located several miles to the south at the highest navigable point on Hunting Creek and was a prosperous tobacco port, which was even proposed for county seat at one time. It was destroyed by the British in 1814 and never rebuilt, as the creek was becoming silted up even then.

HURLOCK (Dorchester) Pop. 1,690. Incorp. 1892.

13 miles northeast of Cambridge. John M. Hurlock, who built a warehouse near the railroad station, is said to have won a tree-felling contest over another land owner, in order to have the town named after him. The railroad stations, the first store and the first dwelling were erected between 1867 and 1890.

Two railroads cross here: the Maryland and Delaware railroad running east and west and the Baltimore and Eastern running north and south. Freight trains still run eastward from Cambridge and very occasionally northward to Preston. The town has some industries in canning, pickling, poultry processing and the manufacture of metal containers.

HUTTON (Garrett)

4 miles west of Oakland. The village was originally known as Hutton Switch, since a branch line ran from here to Crelling when it was an important lumbering center. The Hutton family of New York, who owned land here, donated some acreage to the B. & O. Railroad on condition that the name Hutton would always remain as the name of the station. There was once a large and fairly important tannery here.

HYATTSTOWN (Montgomery)

17 miles northwest of Rockville. The first house was erected here about 1800 by Seth Hyatt, a relative of the founder of Hyattsville in Prince George's County; another relative, Jesse (1763-1813) kept a hotel here behind the Methodist Church. His grave can be seen in the Christian Church cemetery just east of town.

There was a skirmish here in 1862, for it lay directly on the route from Washington to Frederick. Today route I 70 from Washington to the west passes close by and the town is becoming a commuter area. There is an abandoned grist mill on Hyattsville Mill Road.

HYATTSVILLE (Prince George's) Pop. 12,709. Incorp. 1886.

6 miles northeast of the U.S.Capitol. The town was named after Christopher Hyatt who settled here in 1860, a near relative of Seth Hyatt who founded Hyattstown in Montgomery County. Previously the settlement was called Hart.

The town has grown into a suburb of Washington. Since it is closer than Upper Marlboro to the county's centers of population, the County Library is here and also many of Prince George's County offices, housed in the County Service Building and other buildings.

James Harrison Rogers, inventor, lived here for some years. Lafayette stayed at Bothwick Hall, 3901 48th Ave., in 1824. There are numerous industries here, including a company that makes iron railings and two publishing companies.

I

IDYLWILD WILDLIFE DEMONSTATION AREA (Caroline)

12 miles southeast of Denton, near Federalsburg. The name is from the Idlewild Mills, which operated here until 1916. The Department of Game and Inland Fish has 520 acres here on both sides of Marshyhope Creek.

IJAMSVILLE (Frederick)

6 miles southwest of Frederick. An insignificant village named for Plummer Ijams, a local landowner; it was once called Ijam's Mills.

A slate quarry was opened here about 1800, employing up to 40 men, half of them Welsh miners; the slate was used for roofing and also ground into purple paint. The quarries have long been closed, but there is said to be a house in the village which is slate-covered on its sides as well as its roof. The same house is thought to have some of the early railroad rails built into it. The B. & O. station here was razed in 1950.

There was also a pottery in the village at one time; also the Glenellen Academy, which was opened by Professor Herbert Thompson in the 1870's. The academy was named after the professor's wife, who claimed to be the true author of Lorna Doone.

ILCHESTER (Howard)

9 miles south of Baltimore and 2 miles downstream from Ellicott City in the Patapsco valley. Two brothers, George and William Morris, from Scotland, living at Thistle across the river in Baltimore County, set up Thistle Factory here, turning out cotton printed cloth. Some of the stone houses of the workers and the big stone factory still stand; it was recently turning out recycled paper products.

On a hill overlooking the valley is St. Mary's College, built in 1868, which belongs to the Redemptionist Fathers, and has been vacant since 1972. The state is seeking to acquire the 170 acres of grounds.

INDIANHEAD (Charles)   Pop. of plant 1,154.   Pop. of town 1,381.   Incorp. 1920.

12 miles northwest of La Plata and 22 miles southwest of Washington, D.C. on a pensinula between the Potomac and Mattawoman Creek.   This was a desolate place before 1890, when the U.S.Navy moved its proving grounds here -- some might say it still is.   For a time it was called the U.S. Naval Propellant Plant, producing solid rocket fuel, but it is now called the U.S. Naval Ordnance Station.   The facility covers 2,072 acres and has 1,347 buildings; it is the largest employer in Charles County, employing 2,200 civilians, many of whom commute from the newer developments of Potomac Heights and other more distant places.

The town's main street is spacious, if a little down-at-heel, ending at the gates of the plant.   Some of the houses were built by the navy in its early days to house the workers, but have since been sold.   A branch railway line connects the plant with the Conrail tracks four miles away at a spot called Indian Head Junction.

Across Mattawoman Creek at Stump Neck (q.v.) is the Navy's Explosive Ordnance Disposal School, an annex of the Indian Head Plant, created in the 1940's.

INDIAN SPRINGS (Washington)

15 miles west of Hagerstown.   This crossroads village was named in 1819 when the turnpike road came through and the postoffice was established.   The name is also given to a large State Wildlife Management Area about six miles to the north, which consists of 93,844 acres of forested land clothing several mountain ridges.   Included in the area is the 40 acre Blair Valley Lake for fishing.

INDIANTOWN (Worcester)

2 miles northwest of Snow Hill.   In 1671 this was the site of the largest Indian settlement in Maryland;   five different tribes lived here.   In 1686 it was laid out as a reservation and called Askiminokonson.   Only a few mounds remain today and there is only a scattered population.

INGLESIDE (Queen Anne's)

11 miles northeast of Centreville.   Before the area was drained and re-named in 1812, this was a marshy spot called Beaver Dam or Long Marsh, after the two creeks of those names which run through the area.

IRONSIDES (Charles)

10 miles southwest of La Plata. Two miles southwest of this crossroads village is Old Durham Church, which dates from 1732 and was visited several times by George Washington. A grave in the churchyard dates back to 1692. There is a brick wall here said to be made from bricks which came from Old Port Tobacco (q.v.)

ISSUE (Charles)

18 miles southeast of La Plata. The village was settled about 1880 and the name commemorates the controversy about where in the town the postoffice should be located.

JACKSON (Cecil)

12 miles southwest of Elkton. A group of large holly trees here caught the attention of B.& O. Railroad officials and the tallest of the group became "The tree beside the tracks" illuminated at Christmas time with hundreds of lights. With passenger service ended, and a power crisis, the company gave up the practice in 1970. The local people re-started the custom in 1972 and kept it up for a few years, but there were no passengers to view the sight from train windows, so it was abandoned.

JANES ISLAND (Somerset)

17 miles southwest of Princess Anne. The island, lying between Crisfield and the open waters of the Chesapeake Bay, is low-lying, marshy and uninhabited, and since there is no bridge, it can be reached only by boat. Fertile farms were here in the last century, mostly growing garden crops, while in the 1900's it was a resort, with beautiful beaches. A tall chimney, a landmark, is the remains of a once thriving fish-fertilizer factory. The island was purchased as a state park in 1962; the park also includes a small acreage on the mainland.

JARRETTSVILLE (Harford) Pop. 1,485

8 miles northwest of Bel Air. It was named in 1838 for Luther Jarrett, who bought 300 acres here in 1835, and who served several terms in the state legislature. In 1842, Jarrett built a house at the northeast corner of the crossroads; it was of brick, with doors said to be of an unusual design, but it was pulled down in 1976 or 7 and replaced by stores. Another old house is incorporated in an unusual way into a row of stores on route 165.

JEFFERSON (Frederick)

7 miles southwest of Frederick. The village was one of the first settlements west of Catoctin Mountain. Originally it was two separate villages named New Town and New Freedom; it was later known as The Trap, then Newton's or Newtown Trap, either because it was a rough and dangerous settlement for a traveller to pass through, or because there was a tavern at each end. After much controversy, it was re-named after Jefferson in 1832.

The old Jefferson Pike, on which it is situated, was a much-travelled road, which crossed the Potomac near Harper's Ferry. Like so many of Maryland's roads it has been replaced in the last twenty years by a brand new road which crosses the Potomac at the Sandy Hook Bridge, and Jefferson has resigned itself, like so many other villages, to being by-passed.

JENNINGS (Garrett)

21 miles northeast of Oakland and south of Grantsville. On route 495 is a large firebrick manufacturing company; it is one of the few industries in the county and tours can be arranged.

JERICHO (Baltimore County)

It is difficult to pinpoint the exact location of this former village about 17 miles northeast of downtown Baltimore. It was founded by the Tyson family after the Revolution, and in their store was once employed Moses Sheppard, who later became a millionaire and founded the Sheppard-Pratt hospital in Baltimore. Jericho covered bridge is a picturesque reminder of former days and still carries traffic over the Little Gunpowder Falls.

JERUSALEM (Frederick)

12 miles northwest of Frederick. There are only a few houses in this rural, sheltered location, but the village claims to be the oldest settlement in the Middletown Valley. Within a stone's throw of the route 40 traffic is an ancient graveyard, with a monument stating that the first churches of Western Maryland were built nearby. Many of the humble stones are of the local greenstone and some date from the 1700's.

JERUSALEM (Harford)

6 miles southwest of Bel Air. Near the Gunpowder River stands a mill which was established in 1772 by David Lee, a Quaker from Pennsylvania, and which has only recently ceased operating, but is being preserved. The first story is of stone, the second story of frame. A small establishment in the rear of the mill produced guns for the Revolution in 1776. The small house on the opposite side of the road was once a blacksmith's shop.

JESSUP (Anne Arundel) Pop. 4,288

15 miles southwest of downtown Baltimore. The town started out in the early 1800's as Andersonville, then it became Pierceland, then Hooversville, then Jessup's Cut, to coincide with the name of the railroad station (which has previously been called Bridewell.) For many years it was known as Jessups, but finally, in 1963, the postmaster had it shortened to Jessup. Jessup was the name of the engineer in charge of building the railroad through here.

The name is well-known because of the fact that the Maryland House of Correction is here, a medium security prison established in 1878. It operates a farm of 1268 acres and supplies farm products to other state institutions. On the same tract is the Maryland State Reformatory for Women, started in 1939, and nearby is the Perkins Hospital, where male patients are held on a maximum security basis.

A recent addition to the town is a large industrial park where many industries have re-located, many from Baltimore, the largest being Aircoil Co., which makes cooling apparatus. Other plants produce concrete products and baking machinery.

In 1975 the name became even more well-known when the Baltimore Produce Terminal opened here, bringing all the produce markets of Baltimore under one roof. The fish markets followed suit in 1984.

JOHNSVILLE (Frederick)

13 miles northeast of Frederick. It is said that the village was named for a group of early settlers, most of whom were named John.

JONESVILLE (Montgomery)

14 miles northwest of Rockville. A small black com-

munity which is due for either extinction or renewal. There are several other similar settlements in the county, such as Mount Zion, Stewarttown and Lyttonsville.

JOPPA (Harford)
The traveller cannot help but notice how often the name of Joppa appears in names of streets, developments and businesses in Harford County. The name is also inherited by a tiny village eight miles south of Bel Air on the Old Philadelphia Post Road (route 7)

Joppa was once a town three miles south of the present village, close to the Gunpowder River. It was a thriving tobacco port, and the seat of Baltimore County, which was far more extensive then than now; the Baltimore County courthouse and prison were here from 1713 until 1768, when the county seat was moved to Baltimore. The river is so silted up today tha it is hard to believe that Joppa was ever a port. Benjamin Rumsey, a signer of the Bush Declaration (q.v.) bought the courthouse and prison and built a mansion in Joppa in 1773. The brick house and a couple of gravestones are all that remain of the town. (See **JOPPATOWNE**)

JOPPATOWNE (Harford) Pop. 11,348
8 miles south of Bel Air. This large modern development, takes its name from the old town of Joppa. The tide of dwellings has swept up almost to the door of the old Rumsey mansion, which now has a modern address: 600 Church Rd. It has been restored and is the home of the Harford County Executive. A new church nearby protects the old gravestones and several other humps, possibly old foundations. The church also has a small display of artifacts discovered during the construction of the new homes. (See **JOPPA**)

JUMPTOWN (Caroline)
7 miles northwest of Denton. This insignificant village is named after the Jump family. It was previously called Bradleysburg, after the Bradley family.

KEEDYSVILLE (Washington) Pop. 431. Incorp. 1872

8 miles south of Hagerstown. The village was settled by John and Samuel Keedy and was previously called Centerville, being half way between Boonsboro and Sharpsburg. When the postoffice established a branch here, they insisted on a name change as there were several other Centervilles in the state already. Keedysville was once a vital link on the B. & O. branch line from Weverton to Hagerstown.

KEMP MILL (Montgomery) Pop. 10,037

11 miles north of the U. S. Capitol. A new residential suburb.

KEMPTON (Garrett)

In the extreme southwest corner of Maryland, 15 miles southwest of Oakland, near the source of the Potomac River. This out-of-the-way village was once a coal mining center, but only a few dilapidated houses remain.

Since the source of the Potomac (North Branch) is the corner boundary of Maryland, one would expect to find a boundary marker here, and sure enough, in a swampy field opposite the houses, almost hidden by foliage, a boundary stone designates the spot where three counties meet: Garrett County, Maryland and Preston and Grant Counties, West Virginia.

KENDALL (Garrett)

3 miles south of Friendsville. Little or nothing remains of this old logging village on the Youghiogheny River. It can be approached only by hiking along an old railroad bed from Friendsville, along the scenic, unspoilt river valley.

KEN-GAR (Montgomery)

11 miles north of the U.S. Capitol between Kensington

and Garrett Park; its name is a combination of the two. This area of individual, partly dilapidated homes was settled in the early 1900's when it was on a main road. A new road has isolated the settlement and it is marked for urban renewal.

KENNEDYVILLE (Kent)

7 miles northeast of Chestertown. It was named for a Pennsylvania booster who purchased land on the main north-south road where he knew the railroad would cross it.. Near the town is Shrewsbury Church, founded in 1682 and named for the Earl of Shrewsbury. The present church was erected in the 19th century on the same spot as the old one, and there are some graves in the churchyard older than the church, the most notable being that of General John Cadwalader, bearing an epitaph that was written by Thomas Paine. The wording is illegible, but is printed in a booklet sold inside the church.

Kennedyville. Cadwallader's tomb in Shrewsbury churchyard

KENSINGTON (Montgomery) Pop. 1,822. Incorp. 1894

10 miles north of the U. S. Capitol. An older residential suburb, originally known as Knowles Station. It was renamed in the 1890's by an influential property holder named Brainard H. Warner, who admired the Kensington district of London. The town has spread out in recent years and its suburbs of South Kensington and North Kensington now exceed it, with populations of 9,344 and 9,039 respectively.

KENT COUNTY. County Seat: Chestertown. Pop. 16,695. Area: 281 square miles.

Kent County was formed in 1642 and named after the English county of the same name. Once Kent County was the whole of Maryland's Eastern Shore; now, after the other counties have been formed from it, Kent is the Eastern Shore's smallest county.

It is bounded on the north by the Sassafras River; on the east by the Delaware boundary; on the south by the Chester River; and on the west by the Chesapeake Bay. It lies entirely in the Coastal Plain Province and the terrain is flat, with 200 miles of tidewater shoreline, owing to its indented coast.

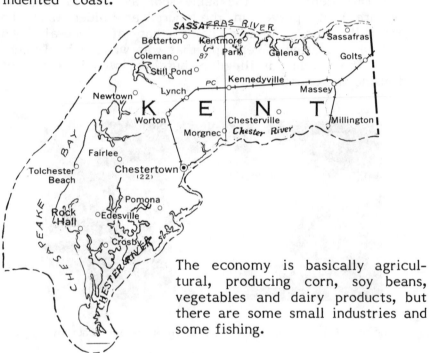

The economy is basically agricultural, producing corn, soy beans, vegetables and dairy products, but there are some small industries and some fishing.

KENT ISLAND (Quenn Anne's)

Kent Island is the largest island in the Chesapeake Bay, separated from the Eastern Shore by Kent Narrows and connected to it by a drawbridge across the Narrows. It is also connected to the western shore of the Chesapeake Bay by the Chesapeake Bay Bridge (q.v.)

Although Kent Island is now in Queen Anne's County, it

was once an important part of Kent County, whose area was originally the whole of Maryland's Eastern Shore. A court began to function on the island around 1639, although Kent County was not created until 1642. The meeting place was Kent Fort, near the southern tip of the island, where an historical marker describes Kent Fort Manor. Later, the court was removed to Broad Creek and then Eastern Neck Island.

Some years before Lord Baltimore's colonists arrived, the area had been claimed by William Claiborne of Virginia, who built a trading post here. This led to disputes, long legal battles, and even a maritime engagement before Maryland could finally claim the territory as her own.

Kent Narrows is lined with a complex of marinas, wharves, boat rentals and seafood restaurants. The drawbridge, when raised to allow the passage of small sailing vessels, causes traffic backups for several miles on summer weekends. Several new housing developments and businesses are springing up on the island and changing its rural aspect. See also: **LOVE POINT. STEVENSVILLE, CHESTER, MATAPEAKE, KENTMORR, ROMANCOKE.**

KENTLAND (Prince George's) Pop. 8,596
8 miles northeast of the U.S. Capitol. A relatively new suburban development inside the Capitol Beltway.

KENTMORE PARK (Kent)
12 miles northeast of Chestertown. Although the settlement is fairly new, the site is old, for a ferry was established in 1650 between this point and Ordinary Point across the Sassafras River. The shoreline is all privately owned and inaccessable.

KENTMORR (Queen Anne's)
A newish settlement on Kent Island five miles south of route 50. A number of boats are based here and there is a marina and restaurant.

KENWOOD (Montgomery)
8 miles northwest of the U. S. Capitol; it is considered as a part of Bethesda. The curving suburban streets are bright with cherry blossom in springtime.

KEYMAR (Carroll)

14 miles west of Westminster. It was once called York Road, but since the area has associations with the Key family, the name Key was combined with Maryland to produce Keymar. The Maryland Midland Railroad, a short rejuvenated track, crosses the tracks of the Western Maryland Railroad nearby.

KEYSVILLE (Carroll)

15 miles northwest of Westminster. It was named for the Key family, whose family home, Terra Rubra, was one mile to the southwest. The house, named for the red earth, was built in the 1770's and Francis Scott Key was born there on Aug. 1, 1779.. The house was wrecked by a storm in the 1850's and a new house, the present Terra Rubra, was built on the foundations in 1915. It is private, but the United States flag flies above it night and day. The Keys donated land for the church and school at Keysville, and Francis Scott Key is said to have conducted the first Sunday School for black children in the U.S. near the site of the present school.

KINGSTON (Somerset)

9 miles southwest of Princess Anne. The village is notable because nearby stands Kingston Hall, where one of the most remarkable women of her day was born in 1815. This was Anna Ella Carroll, a knowledgeable lawyer, pamphleteer for the Union and an important advisor to President Lincoln. She proposed a military strategy which was successful in breaking the Confederate grip in the Vicksburg area. It is said the the President died before he could reveal her contribution and give her just credit, and she received only a small pension for her services. She died in 1893 and is buried in Old Trinity Graveyard at Church Creek (q.v.) Her father was Governor Thomas King Carroll.

KINGS TOWN (Queen Annes') Pop. 1,192

It was a small town on the Chester River opposite Chestertown, laid out in 1732 under the name of Kingston. The town became extinct, but recent development has brought it to life again.

KINGSVILLE (Baltimore County) Pop. 2,824

16 miles northeast of Baltimore. Abraham King came

from Pennsylvania in 1814 and named the estate, taking up his residence in a house which later became the Kingsville Inn, the oldest part of which was built in 1710.   The inn still stands on the west side of route 1, and for some years after 1915 it served as a restaurant, but it is now incorporated into a funeral home.   Washington and Lafayette are both said to have stayed at the inn.

KITZMILLER (Garrett) Pop. 443. Incorp. 1906
14 miles east of Oakland on the North Branch of the Potomac.   This small town was named for the pioneer family of Kitzmiller after formerly being called Blaine.   It was the chief mining center of the area and in the early 1900's boasted a population of 1,500 residents.   Although there is increased interest in the area's remaining coal today, Kitzmiller does not expect to increase its population, partly owing to its situation in the river valley, hemmed in by towering mountains.   Bloomington Dam and reservoir have recently been constructed here.

KLEJ GRANGE (Worcester)
7 miles southwest of Snow Hill. The town has had several odd names in the past but this is perhaps the oddest. The first word of the name was formed from the initials of the four daughters of a local landowner.

KLONDIKE (Allegany)
A mile west of the George's Creek Valley. This small mining town is also known as Lord.

KNOXVILLE (Frederick)
15 miles southwest of Frederick. The town was founded in 1856 at the base of South Mountain and from 1864 to 1879 boasted a select boarding school for young ladies. Knoxville also boasts that in the election of 1904 it was the only place in the local election district where the sale of liquor was permitted.

LADEW TOPIARY GARDENS (Harford)

9 miles northwest of Bel Air and 5 miles northeast of Jacksonville. The house and gardens were owned by Harvey Ladew, a bachelor millionaire whose wealth derived from the leather tanning industry and whose hobby was fox-hunting. The house and gardens are administered by a trust fund since the death of Ladew in 1976 and are open to the public for a fee, April 19 to October 31. Hours are Tues. - Sat. 10-4, Sun. 12-5; house Wed. and Sun. only.

The gardens cover about 22 acres and consist of a number of individual gardens, each with its special characteristics, all grouped around a central open space with a pool, where outdoor entertainments are held in the summer. The most notable of the individual gardens is the topiary garden, where bushes are trained and clipped to represent all manner of birds and beasts.

LADIESBURG (Frederick)

14 miles northeast of Frederick. According to tradition, around the year 1800 the population consisted of seven ladies and one man.

LAKELAND (Prince George's)

8 miles northeast of the U.S. Capitol. This community was laid out in 1892, and shortly afterwards the Baltimore Goldfish Co. built a number of lakes for fish-raising. The area is now absorbed by College Park, but they say one can still see the remains of the lake walls along the B. & O. Railroad tracks.

LAKE ROLAND (Baltimore County)

7 miles north of downtown Baltimore. The lake was formed as a water supply for the city of Baltimore around 1861 by damming Jones Falls. It is somewhat silted up today

and other larger reservoirs have long since replaced it as a water supply. But the lake and a large surrounding area still belong to the City of Baltimore, although outside its limits. They have been re-designated Robert E. Lee Park and there are pleasant walks, boating in season and picnicking.

LAKESVILLE (Dorchester)
16 miles southwest of Cambridge. It was named for the Lake family who were early settlers. There were mills and a certain amount of activity here around 1800 but the area is uneventful now and habitation is sparse.

LANDER (Frederick)
11 miles southwest of Frederick. Although a somewhat nondescript place near the Potomac River today, it once had a postoffice and was a stopping place on the B. & O. Railroad named Catoctin. A union schoolhouse nearby, built in 1824, was said to have been one of the finest in the county.

LANDOVER (Prince George's) Pop. 5,374
7 miles northeast of the U. S. Capitol. In addition to residential development, there is a meat products factory here and several food distributing points, such as the coffee division of A. & P. and the milk department of Safeway Stores.

LANDOVER HILLS (Prince George's_ Pop. 1,428. Incorp. 1945
8 miles northeast of the U.S.Capitol. The population has been outstripped by Landover.

LANGLEY PARK (Prince George's) Pop. 14,038
7 miles north of the U.S.Capitol. Another of Washington's rapidly growing residential suburbs.

LANHAM (Prince George's) Pop. with Seabrook 15,814
10 miles northeast of the U. S. Capitol. Named for the family who held land in the area. Lanham and Seabrook, just outside the Capital Beltway, are two suburban communities of rapid growth. The Capital Beltway Station, Washington's suburban stop for the eastern corridor Amtrak trains, is at

Lanham. Next to the Washington Bible College is a private estate named Azalea Acres, where the public may view thousands of azaleas in season.

LANSDOWNE (Baltimore County)   Pop. with Baltimore Highlands 16,759

4 miles southwest of downtown Baltimore. One of Baltimore's early suburbs, first settled by an Irishman named McGrath, who named it after the Marquis of Lansdowne, another Irishman, who was postmaster of England in 1782. Many of the residents once worked for the B. & O. Railroad. In earlier times much iron ore was dug in the vicinity. The Lansdowne Christian Church has a small museum dedicated to the Union soldiers of the Civil War. For information call 242-4281.

LAPIDUM (Harford)

13 miles northeast of Bel Air on the banks of the Susquehanna. A ferry operated here in the days of early settlement. In the 18th century it was a thriving fishing center, the main fishing places being upstream on Robert, Spencer and Wood Islands. In 1800 the catch was so huge that the surplus fish were made into fertilizer, a practise which continued until 1800 when it was prohibited on account of the foul smell.

LA PLATA. County Seat of Charles County. Pop. 2,484. Incorp. 1888.

The name is a corruption of the French Le Plateau, meaning a flat area, and is usually pronounced La Playta. The town has no ancient connections, as it did not take shape until the coming of the railroad in 1872 and did not become the county seat until 1895. The courthouse was remodelled in 1956 and again in 1974.

Port Tobacco (q.v.) had been the county seat until the railroad completed its line from Bowie to Pope's Creek, taking a direct line through the La Plata area. The completion of the Potomac Bridge in 1940 and the widening and re-aligning of route 301 led to some growth in La Plata, but the town is still farily bucolic. The only historical building is Christ Episcopal Church, which was moved here from Port Tobacco in 1904.

There is little industry apart from two tobacco warehouses. The U. S. Army Radio Receiving Station is two miles to the northeast on 500 acres of land. Constructed in 1943 it is the principal receiving station for the army, and can receive signals from all over the world.

LARGO (Prince George's) Pop. 5,557
    10 miles due east of the U.S.Capitol. The name comes from the name of an early mansion, now called "Mount Lubentia" which was built before 1770. The house, which is on route 202 just east of 214, was once rented by Rev. Jonathan Boucher (See Leeland.) Largo has recently sprung into prominence owing to the fact that the Capital Center opened here in 1973. It is the home of the Washington basket ball and hockey teams, where games and other entertainments on various scales are held. The Watkins Regional Park (q.v.) is within two miles of Largo.

LAUREL (Prince George's) Pop. 12,103. Incorp. 1870. Pop. of North Laurel: 6,093. Pop. of South Laurel: 18,034.
    17 miles northeast of the U. S. Capitol. The area was settled by the Snowden family of emigrants, Richard Snowden being the first to arrive in 1658. Mills sprang up on the Patuxent and the place became known as Laurel Factory. The Snowden family prospered, putting their efforts into iron smelting also, and their great mansions dot the surrounding countryside: Montpelier (q.v.) on a knoll three miles to the south; Walnut Grange on the grounds of Beltsville Agricultural Station, and Snowden Hall in the Patuxent Wildlife Preserve, five miles downstream from Laurel.
    Some traces of the mill town remain. The Avondale Flour Mill, now used by the Laurel Department of Parks, still stands at the river's edge on Avondale St. and there are a few mill homes left at the west end of Main St. The main mill, however, burnt in 1855, was rebuilt but finally razed in the mid 1940's.
    The B. & O. Railroad has a station here at the east end of town, near route 1 and still picks up commuters to Washington and a few to Baltimore. The station is in a good state of preservation and is on the National Register of Historic Places. A building on Main St. at 6th St. is said to be the original electric car station.
    Laurel Race Track, a one mile track, opened here in 1911 and the name has been associated with horse racing ever since. Laurel Raceway is also nearby, holding harness races every June and July.

LA VALE (Allegany) Pop. with Narrows Park 5,523

4 miles west of Cumberland but spreading far along both sides of route 40.   La Vale's chief claim to fame is the old seven-sided toll house, erected 1835-6 and the first toll house to be erected on the National Pike.   It is the only toll house on the Pike remaining in Maryland and was purchased in 1958 by the State and placed in the custody of the Allegany County Historical Society.   The La Vale Century Club maintains the building, and it is on the National Register of Historic Places.

There is much recent development in the area, including some industries, among them ready-mix concrete, concrete burial vaults and precision drilling machines.

La Vale.   Old toll house on route 40

LAYHILL (Montgomery)

14 miles north of the U. S. Capitol. A village which is undergoing suburban development, although partially saved by the presence of the Northwest Branch Regional Park (q.v.) The National Capital Trolley Museum is situated east of here on Bonifant Road, within the park. It is open free to the public on weekend afternoons; also on Wed. Thur. and Fri. afternoons in summer.

LAYTONSVILLE (Montgomery) Pop. 293. Incorp. 1892.

9 miles north of Rockville. The area was originally settled by the Layton family and it is thought that the first house was built by John Layton in 1780, although when the postoffice was established in 1826 it took the name of Goshen Mills. In 1848 the name was changed to Cracklintown, after a nearby tavern, which made cracklin bread, but changed again to the present name in the same year. The sources of Rock Creek are near here. But although the area is still fairly rural, development is creeping to its doors.

LEEDS (Cecil)

4 miles northwest of Elkton. It was settled around 1804 by John Wilson, a cloth manufacturer from Leeds, England, who originally called it New Leeds, when he built a factory here. The Wilsons are buried in the Old Stone Church, but the exact location is not known.

LEELAND (Prince George's)

4 miles due north of Upper Marlboro. A mile west of the village is St. Barnabas Church, built in 1774 and replacing an earlier church established in 1705. George Washington and Sir Robert Eden, Maryland's last colonial governor, attended services at the original church in 1772. The rector here in the 1770's was a fiery tory named Jonathan Boucher. He tells in his diary that his political views were so unpopular that when the revolution was imminent he delivered his sermons with a brace of pistols beside him. Eventually he went to England for the duration of the war.

LEITERSBURG (Washington)

6.5 miles northeast of Hagerstown, close to the Pennsylvania border. It was named for the Leiter family. According to "Gath" in one of his novels, it was once a famous kidnappers' settlement. There is a small plastic works here.

LEONARDTOWN. County Seat of St. Mary's County. Pop. 1,448. Incorp. 1858.

Leonardtown was founded in 1660, when it was called "Sheppard's Old Fields." In 1706 its name was changed to Seymour Town, after Governor John Seymour, and two years later it became the seat of St. Mary's County. It received its present name in 1728 when it was decided to name the town in honor of Leonard Calvert, Maryland's first colonial governor.   The first courthouse was built in 1710 but the present courthouse was built in 1910 and rebuilt in 1957.

The Old Jail, built in 1896, has found a new use as the St. Mary's County Historical Society Museum, which houses artifacts and is open Tues. thru Sat. 10-4.   The old canon outside is thought to be from the *Ark*, one of the ships that brought the colonists to Maryland.

Leonardtown.   Old Jail and canon.

Another interesting building is Tudor Hall, built 1750 and enlarged 1796, which once belonged to the ancestors of Francis Scott Key.   The building faces a fine view of Breton Bay and is now empty, although until recently it housed the county library.

There is very little industry in Leonardtown.   Visitors who stop here are usually on their way to the shrines around St. Mary's City, although many come for the Annual Maryland Oyster Festival at the fairgrounds here in the second week in October.   In addition to oyster eating and entertainment, the National Oyster Shucking Contest is held.

LEVEL (Harford)
9 miles northeast of Bel Air.   The village lies just off the main road, and until recently Foard's blacksmith shop

was in business, repairing farm machinery rather than shoeing horses.   Mr. Foard kept the place just as it had always been, and when he was too old to hammer, sat by the door in warm weather and allowed visitors to step over his threshold into a bygone world.

At the junction of Green Spring Road and route 161, a mile north of Level, is a small hexagonal school house, dating from the 1860's. It belongs to the elderly couple on whose property it stands, and who both attended school here in their youth.

LEWISTOWN (Frederick)

8 miles north of Frederick. The town was laid out by Daniel Fundenberg in 1815 and there was a woollen factory on Fishing Creek, a tributary of the Monocacy. In 1936 the W.P.A. constructed a number of pools here for a state fish hatchery, which was a successful operation until recently, when a dwindling water supply caused the state to move all its trout-raising operations to the Beaver Creek hatcheries (q.v.) on the west side of South Mountain.

LEXINGTON PARK (St. Mary's) Pop. 10,361

10 miles southeast of Leonardtown. An area of rapid residential development, owing to its proximity to the Patuxent Naval Air Test Center (q.v.) It was formerly a small crossroads village named Jarboesville, after its first postmaster.

LIBERTY DAM AND RESERVOIR

Liberty Dam holds back the waters of the North Branch of the Patapsco River, about 3 miles above its confluence with the South Branch and 16 miles from downtown Baltimore. It was built in 1954 and the resulting lake holds 43 billion gallons of water to serve the Greater Baltimore area and supplement the older reservoirs on Gunpowder Falls. There is a fine observation area with a parking lot and a flight of steps leading down to the level of the dam.

LIBERTYTOWN (Frederick)

10 miles northeast of Frederick. A prominent family of the town was the Clemson family, whose name is borne by Clemsonville, four miles to the northeast and several country roads in the area. Clemsons are also in the burial ground on

route 26. A little east of town is an interesting Catholic cemetery containing several grottoes.

LICKSVILLE (Frederick)
12 miles south of Frederick. This tiny village was on the Carrollton estate (q.v.) and was formerly larger and more important since it was located on the Monocacy Trail, which ran down the Frederick Valley and crossed the Potomac near here. There were taverns, several racetracks and a thriving slave market on the north side of the Point of Rocks Road.

LILY PONS FISH PONDS (Frederick)
8 miles south of Frederick. It was named for the opera singer. Tropical fish breeding ponds here are said to be the country's largest producer of commercial gold fish.

LIME KILN (Frederick)
5 miles south of Frederick. This small village has always been associated with limestone operations and in earlier times was called Slabtown, since a number of houses and walls were built of limestone slabs. Freight trains of the B. & O. still serve the lime industry, which is now engaged in producing Portland cement and employs 125 people. Crushed limestone for roads is also produced.

The village was one of the settlements on the Carrollton estate (q.v.) It furnished large quantities of lime for building the Capitol in Washington, D. C. and in addition was a flour milling center.

LINCHESTER MILL (Caroline)
14 miles south of Denton and a mile southeast of Preston on Hunting Creek, a tributary of the Choptank. The mill, known in colonial times as Murray's Mill, is named for its location on the borders of Caroline and Dorchester Counties. It has been said to date from 1681, although the present building was probably constructed in the early 18th century; it is a three-story frame structure with several additions tacked on. Like any other functioning mill of the time, it produced flour that was shipped to Washington's troops at Valley Forge. It is a disappointing sight today.

LINEBORO (Carroll)
13 miles northeast of Westminster. It received its name

because the railroad station, at the north end of town, was almost on the Mason-Dixon line.

LINGANORE (Frederick)

11 miles east of Frederick. In bygone days this part of the Piedmont was called the Hills of Linganore and a resort called the Linganore Hills Inn overlooked the valley. Some years ago a developer bought 3,400 acres here and began to plan a community which would consist of seven villages and a golf course around a lake. An artificial lake was created with a 9½ mile shoreline, but in 1974 the company went broke and most of the lots remain unsold.

LINKWOOD (Dorchester)

7 miles southeast of Cambridge. It was so named because it once linked two patches of woodland, before it moved to its present location.

LINTHICUM (Anne Arundel) Pop. 7,457

7 miles southwest of downtown Baltimore. Land was sold here to Abner Linthicum in 1801; he and his descendants farmed it until 1908 when it was decided to break up the estate. The town has grown and a number of industries have located here, including a sand and gravel operation and companies making mattresses and elevators.

LINWOOD (Carroll)

8 miles west of Westminster. The Western Maryland Railroad named the town after a farm on which it built its station; the farm was named after a giant linden tree planted in 1760's. The place was originally centered around a warehouse and grain elevator.

LISBON (Howard)

16 miles west of Ellicott City. The village was formerly called New Lisbon and was one of several stage coach stops on the road westward, now route 144. The first house was built by Caleb Pancoast around 1810 and is said to be still standing. Two inns can be identified on the main street, one a private home, the other unoccupied and decaying.

LITTLE BENNETT REGIONAL PARK (Montgomery)

In the northern part of Montgomery County along three branches of Little Bennett Creek near Hyattstown. This recently acquired park of 3,100 acres will be developed to offer boating, fishing, hiking, biking, camping and horse riding.

LITTLE MEADOWS (Garrett)

3 miles east of Grantsville. Although little remains here but a name on the map, this was an important spot in colonial history, a natural clearing in the wilderness where the Tomlinson family had their large estate. Braddock's army camped here on their way to do battle with the French in Ohio. Some say that the first coal mine in Garrett County was started just north of here as early as 1800.

LITTLE ORLEANS (Allegany)

20 miles east of Cumberland. This insignificant spot is at the point where Fifteen Mile Creek enters the Potomac. The creek is 15 miles from Oldtown and 15 miles from Hancock, a fact which had some significance in the days of the old trails. There is a boat launching ramp on the Potomac.

LLOYDS (Dorchester)

6 miles northwest of Cambridge. A boatyard on the Little Choptank here has recently finished building a replica *The Dove*.

LOCK LYNN HEIGHTS (Garrett) Pop. 507. Incorp. 1896.

2 miles east of Oakland. This settlement originated as a rival resort to Mountain Lake Park, being built on the opposite or south side of the B. & O. tracks. It was named for Captain David Lynn who owned pasture land here. Today it is mainly residential and the only industry is a small cannery.

LOCH RAVEN DAM AND RESERVOIR (Baltimore County)

10 miles northeast of Baltimore. The dam holds back the waters of the Gunpowder River and the resulting reservoir is Baltimore's main water supply. It was named after Abraham Raven, who formerly owned the land, and the Loch was added by the president of the water board, who thought the lake amid the rolling hills of the Piedmont resembled a Scottish Loch.

The dam was built in 1912 and heightened in 1922. It is 240 ft. high and the lake is ten miles long. The surrounding acreage is owned by Baltimore City and is a popular recreation area for hiking, picnicking and fishing.

LONACONING (Allegany) Pop. 1,572. Incorp. 1880.

Half way between Frostburg and Westernport, in the heart of the   George's Creek coal region, where the creek makes a sharp bend and the valley closes in between high mountains.   The name has several different explanations: some think it is derived from an Indian word meaning either "the great right hand pass" or "where many waters meet;" others think it was named for Nemacolin, the Indian scout employed by the Cresaps (See **OLDTOWN.**) Whatever its meaning, the town is known to the local inhabitants as "Coney."

The coal mines were first worked here in 1835 and most of the company houses were built by the George's Creek Coal Co. in 1852-4. Iron smelting began soon after mining, and there remains an old iron furnace built in 1837, said to be the first smelting furnace to use coke in the U.S. and now on the National Register of Historic Places. Machinery in the valley was brought from New York by ship, railroad, canal boat and wagon.

Several Lonaconing citizens have made names for themselves and in World War I the town furnished more soldiers than any other town its size in the U.S. In 1861 the first speech in Maryland in favor of the Union was made by one named Dr. G. E. Porter, while Robert Moses (Lefty) Grove of the baseball Hall of Fame also lived here.

LONDONTOWNE (Anne Arundel) Pop. 6,052

4 miles southwest of Annapolis. A new development which takes its name from an early settlement on the south bank of the South River, of which only one building remains, and which was spelled without the final e. The name first appeared in records in 1684. From 1689 to 1695 the Anne Arundel County Court met here, and the place was probably busy. A ferry operated across the river for many years, and the point on the opposite shore is still known as Ferry Point.

The single remaining building stands on a knoll overlooking the river and is thought to have been built in 1744-50. There is some disagreement over what purpose it served; some think an inn, others a ferry house, or perhaps the town hall. The building has belonged to the county for many years and served as the county alms house between 1828 and 1966. It has recently been restored and is open to the public for a small fee.

LONG BEACH (Calvert) Pop. with Calvert Beach 1,203
The beach is private, but is used by the local inhabitants.

LONGWOODS (Talbot)
6 miles north of Easton. Talbot County's last remaining little red schoolhouse is here. It has been restored and is open by request.

LOVE POINT (Queen Anne's)
The northern tip of Kent Island. Until World War II a ferry from Baltimore used to dock here. The lighthouse is two miles offshore. There are no public beaches here now.

LOVERS' LEAP (Allegany)
An overlook on Wills Mountain approached from the western suburbs of Cumberland. It is private territory belonging to a garment factory, but they do not seem to object to visitors. The climb is steep, the hairpin bends daunting, and the ledges harrowing if you have young children, but the view of Cumberland Narrows from the over-look is well worth the effort. The name comes from a legend of an Indian brave who went up here with his sweet-heart before a battle. In order to avoid a separation, she threw both him and herself over the edge to their deaths.

LOVEVILLE (St. Mary's)
5 miles northwest of Leonardtown. This town was named for the postmaster in 1895, but a large number of people believe the town was named for Cupid; they send their valentines to the post office here to be mailed out bearing the Loveville postmark. The postoffice is on the west side of route 5 and the grocery next door sells postcards.
In 1938 a colony of Amish moved from Pennsylvania and settled not far from here. They can be seen working in their fields, or driving their horses and buggies along the back roads.

LOWER MARLBORO (Calvert)
10 miles northwest of Prince Frederick. The town was established in 1683 with the name of Coxtown, when the Patuxent River was navigable as far as this point; it was an important port with the usual warehouses, stores, taverns

and miscellaneous homes; a very early ferry was here. The town was re-named after the Duke of Marlborough, and the Lower was added to it around 1706 to distinguish it from Upper Marlboro, now the capital of Prince George's County. The spelling was abbreviated in the 19th century. A few 18th century homes remain and one or two other 18th and 19th century buildings have been moved to here from other locations. There was an important school here in colonial times named Marlborough Academy.

Lower Marlboro. Former postoffice and general store.

LUKE (Allegany) Pop. 424. Incorp. 1922

One mile west of Westernport, pinched between high cliffs and the Potomac River. It was named for the Luke family who started the paper mill here in 1888. The mill was America's first commercially successful sulphite pulp mill; it is now one of the world's largest paper mills and belongs to the Westvaco Corporation. It can be seen for miles, and often smelled, in spite of expensive pollution control installations. Over 2,000 people are employed at the factory, which is in operation 24 hours a day, seven days a week, turning out 1,000 tons of high quality paper each day and drawing 60 million gallons of water daily from the Potomac. Mostly local coal and local wood pulp are used for this oldest of Allegany County's manufacturers.

LUSBY (Calvert)

11 miles southeast of Prince Frederick. Lusby has considerably increased its importance since the Baltimore Gas and Electric Co. built its large nuclear Calvert Cliffs Electric Power Station nearby. The company has a small museum exhibiting marine fossils found in the cliffs, open Tues. thru Sun. 10-3, and an overlook for visitors.

Middleham Episcopal Church, built in 1748 is the oldest cruciform church in Maryland, although an addition obscures its shape. It stands on a bank beside the road and is open to visitors. A company in the vicinity builds motor yachts.

LUTHERVILLE (Baltimore County)   Pop. with Timonium 17,854.

10 miles north of downtown Baltimore. It was named after Martin Luther by its founder, John G.Morris, whose home, Oak Grove, still stands. New developments surround the old community, which, with its old homes and railroad station, has been designated an Historical District. Among the earlier buildings is the former Lutherville Female Seminary and an interesting octagonal house, built in 1855. The original seminary burnt down in 1911 and its new buildings are now a nursing home for the aged.

On York Road, at No. 1301, is the Fire Museum of Maryland, which displays over 40 pieces of fire-fighting equipment, dating back to 1800. It is open April 1 thru Nov. 1, Sats. 10-4, Suns. 1-4. Admission is charged.

LUX MANOR (Montgomery)

4 miles southeast of Rockville. There is an old farmhouse here, which, in the 1820's belonged to the master of a slave named Josiah Henson. Henson, who was born near Port Tobacco, later escaped to Canada and wrote his life story, which was published in 1849 and was the book which inspired *Uncle Tom's Cabin*. The farmhouse still stands on the west side of Old Georgetown Road, near Tilden Lane, among trees and difficult to glimpse. During re-modelling, one of the old slave cabins was saved, moved, and attached to the house, where it still remains, perhaps the original "Uncle Tom's Cabin."

LYTTONSVILLE (Montgomery)

8 miles north of the U. S. Capitol. It was a community inhabited by blacks, probably a land grant made to some families after the Civil War. New homes have been built and it is now integrated.

McCOOLE (Allegany)
    18 miles southwest of Cumberland.   The B. & O.
Railroad crosses the Potomac River to Keyser, W.Virginia, at
this point.

McCOYS FERRY (Washington)
    14 miles southwest of Hagerstown.   The first action of
the Civil War in Maryland took place here in May, 1861,
when some Confederates tried to seize the ferry boat.

McCULLOUGH'S PATH (Garrett)
    Originally an animal trace, this is the oldest of all the
Garrett County trails. It was named for Samuel McCullough,
a fur trader, who is supposed to have ridden his horse over a
cliff and survived. A monument beside route 40 in Wheeling,
West Virginia, commemorates this occurrence.
    Little trace of the path remains, but it is known that it
entered Maryland about 11 miles northwest of Oakland and
following a southeasterly direction, crossed the Youghiogheny
River near Oakland, crossed Backbone Mountain at Allegany
Heights, which is almost due south of Oakland, and left
Maryland by crossing the Potomac River into West Virginia
one mile west of Steyer. Part of the path is marked in
Herrington Manor State Park.

McHENRY (Garrett)
    11 miles northeast of Oakland on the northern inlet, or
cove, of Deep Creek Lake, 3 miles above the bridge on route
219. It was named for Dr. James McHenry (1753-1816) who
served as Secretary of War in Washington's cabinet, and who
bought the tract here for his son. It is now the center for
resort activities; the Wisp ski area is close by, and summer
cottages abound near Deep Creek Lake. It is also the
address of Garrett Community College and the Garrett
County Fair Grounds.

McKINSTREY'S MILL (Carroll)

9 miles south of Westminster. Samuel McKinstrey arrived in the area in 1814 and was the postmaster for a time. He operated the mill, which was built in 1797, but the present building dates from 1844 and bears the name "Zubrun" on its side.

Not far from here was born William Rinehart, the sculptor (1825-1874) some of whose works are in the Peabody Institute in Baltimore, the Corcoran Gallery in Washington, and the Metropolitan Museum in New York, while his statue of Roger B. Taney stands in front of the Statehouse in Annapolis. The quarry from which he obtained his marble has now been obliterated by the Lehigh cement works at Union Bridge. Rinehart settled in Rome in 1858, where his studio became a Mecca for rich American tourists, and he devoted most of his time to portrait sculpture. His estate was bequeathed to the Maryland Institute in Baltimore and their school of sculpture is named after him.

MACTON (Harford)

11 miles northeast of Bel Air. Here, on Macton Rd., near route 136, is the Steppingstone Museum, devoted to rural life in the 19th century. It was founded in 1969, and the displays of tools and implements of the old time rural craftsmen and farmers are housed in five buildings. It is open May thru Oct. Sats. and Suns. 1-5.

MADISON (Dorchester)

9 miles southwest of Cambridge. A village has been on the site since 1760, although its earlier name was Tobacco Stick. The name was changed to that of the fourth president of the U. S. In 1814 the doughty inhabitants of Tobacco Stick distinguished themselves by capturing a bargeload of British soldiers under Captain Phipps, when their barge ran aground. The sole industry here is an oyster packing plant.

MADONNA (Harford)

10 miles northwest of Bel Air. The village was first called King's Corner, then Briar Ridge, but was named Madonna in 1898, after the postmaster's daughter. Later it became Cathcart, after the name of the store owner, but after 1907 resumed its previous name. There is some development in the neighborhood, and a forest ranger station with a lookout tower.

MAGO VISTA (Anne Arundel)

7 miles north of Annapolis on the Magothy River. The beach is still open to the public for a small fee and a yacht basin is being put in, while the pavilion is being made into a restaurant.

MAIDEN CHOICE (Baltimore County)

6 miles west of Baltimore. A new neighborhood of single and group homes and garden apartments.

MANCHESTER (Carroll) Pop. 1,830. Incorp. 1833

8.5 miles northeast of Westminster. It was laid out in the 18th century by Captain Richard Richards from the nearby town of Hampstead, and named after the town in England from which he emigrated. The first Lutheran Church was erected in 1760 and was the first place of worship in Carroll County; its direct descendant is the Immanuel Lutheran, founded in 1862. A large white oak, older than the church, stands beside it.

A college was founded here in 1858 by Dr. F. Dieffenbach and named Irving College, after Washington Irving, but it has long since gone. Industries in the town are a meat products factory and a factory making men's pants.

MANOKIN (Somerset)

6 miles southwest of Princess Anne. It would seem that there has long been a settlement of this name in the vicinity, although it has no importance now. The Manokin River flows through Princess Anne and gives its name to an important Presbyterian church there.

MANRESA (Anne Arundel)

2 miles northeast of Annapolis on the opposite side of the Severn River. This building, in a most beautiful setting, fronting on the river, was erected in 1926 as a retreat house for catholic men. Recently, however, it has been converted to accomodate groups of both sexes and all religions for the purpose of conferences as well as retreats.

MARDELA SPRINGS (Wicomico) Pop. 356. Incorp. 1906.

10 miles northwest of Salisbury. It was originally called Barren Creek, a name which remains on a nearby road, but changed to the present combination of Maryland and Delaware in 1906. A natural spring at the end of the town,

now enclosed in a brick pavilion, is supposed to have health-giving qualities, but is now polluted. There was a hotel on the slope above the spring when the water attracted frequent visitors. A small company here makes paper boxes.

MARION (Somerset)

12 miles southwest of Princess Anne. Although there had been a town here previously, it was not named until the railroad to Crisfield passed through the area. Then it took the name of the daughter of John C. Horsey, who donated land for the railroad. In its early days, Marion was located closer to Colbourn Creek; it was the chief agricultural center for the area and had a busy port, with stores and wharves. For years it had the reputation of being the largest shipper of strawberries in the world, and buyers came from far and wide. Strawberry farming started its collapse here in the 1920's when the growing centers shifted to California, Washington and Oregon.

MARRIOTSVILLE (Howard)

9 miles northwest of Ellicott City. A small Patapsco Valley village named for General William Marriott of Revolutionary War fame. It was in the news during the 1950's as "a town owned by one woman." It is said that John Eager Howard owned a house here.

MARSHALL HALL (Charles)

13 miles northwest of La Plata fronting on the Potomac River almost opposite Mount Vernon in Virginia. It was the home of the Marshall family from 1690 to 1866, and George Washington was a frequent visitor to the Marshall Plantation, only a short boat ride from his home. The Marshalls were forced to part with most of their land after the Civil War, but the mansion and a small cemetery still exist.

During the years 1949-1968 when gambling was legal in Southern Maryland, this was a close gambling spot for Washingtonians, and a casino here housed hundreds of slot machines. Today there is an amusement park by the waterfront, and boats still make cruises from Washington. A jousting tournament is held here each August, in which knights on horseback try to spear small rings suspended from an arch. This colorful pastime is Maryland's state sport.

MARTINAK STATE PARK (Caroline)

2 miles south of Denton. It consists of 100 acres near route 404 at the confluence of the Choptank River and Watts Creek, and is named for a former owner who donated the site. It contains a replica of George Martinak's original log cabin, and it is thought that the area may have been the site of an Indian village. Facilities include picnicking and there is a boat-launching ramp. On the first Saturday in May is held a "day-in-the-park" with fish fry, games, contests, etc. The remains of a pungy, an extinct type of Chesapeake Bay sailing craft, are on view.

MARTINSBURG (Montgomery)

19 miles northwest of Rockville. A small town whose residents are mostly black owner-occupiers.

MARYDEL (Caroline) Pop. 176. Incorp. 1929.

17 miles northeast of Denton. Once it was called Halltown, but changed to the present name, which is a combination of Maryland and Delaware. The Choptank River rises in a number of springs around this area, while nearby, beside the road can be seen a crown stone marker of the north-south section of the Mason-Dixon line.

MARYLAND CANAL (Cecil)

One of the first works of its kind, this project was begun in 1783 on the east bank of the Susquehanna River. It ran parallel to the river from the highest point of navigation, near Port Deposit, to the Pennsylvania line. It is thought to have been completed in 1805 and widened in 1810. Later it was purchased by a Pennsylvania company, who built a continuation to Columbia, Pennsylvania. Rafts of goods were floated down to Port Deposit to be transferred to ships. The canal closed in 1890 and the Conowingo Dam finished it off in 1910, but remnants of the canal can still be seen along route 222 between Port Deposit and route 1.

MARYLAND CITY (Anne Arundel) Pop. 6,949

17 miles southwest of downtown Baltimore near Laurel. A new development lying between routes 1 and 295.

MARYLAND HEIGHTS (Washington)

A summit of Elk Ridge (q.v.) overlooking Harper's Ferry and the Potomac River. There is an historic fort here, built during the Civil War to protect the B. & O. Railroad and the C. & O. Canal. The overgrown ruins are still there approachable only by foot along the steep blazed trail which begins near Sandy Hook. From 1862 to the end of the war, about 6,000 men were stationed here at various times.

MARYLAND LINE (Baltimore County)

30 miles north of downtown Baltimore. It was once called Newmarket but the postoffice insisted on a change of name as there was a more important Newmarket in Maryland. The present name was chosen owing to the town's proximity to Pennsylvania.

MASON-DIXON LINE

The Mason-Dixon Line is the boundary which separates Maryland from Pennsylvania and Delaware. It was known before the Civil War as the line dividing the slave from the non-slave states and has long been regarded, although inaccurately, as the division between north and south.

The line was agreed upon to settle once and for all the conflicting territorial claims of Maryland and Pennsylvania. Charles Mason and Jeremiah Dixon, two English surveyors, were sent out to mark the boundary in 1763. It was to run from Cape Henlopen (q.v.) on the Atlantic coast, due west to the middle point of the Delmarva Peninsula, then due north, tangent to a circle of twelve miles radius, based on the courthouse at Newcastle, then due west on a line fifteen miles south of the southernmost part of Philadelphia. The task of following these complicated instructions took four years.

Boundary stones were brought over from the famous Portland quarries, and placed at one mile intervals. Each had a P on the northern side and an M on the southern side, but each fifth stone, known as a crown stone, bore the coat of arms of the Penn family on the northern side and that of Lord Baltimore on the southern side. Most of the stones are still in place, including the middle point stone and the tangent stone. One has found its way into the Maryland Historical Society in Baltimore. A fairly visible one is number 103 near route 63, 6 miles northwest of Hagerstown.

MATAPEAKE (Queen Anne's)

On Kent Island, south of route 50. A ferry terminal was

here for the boats which used to carry passengers across the Chesapeake Bay before the Bay Bridge was opened. The slips can still be seen and the site is now a public fishing pier where an annual Chesapeake Bay Fishing Fair is held.

The Maryland Department of Natural Resources has its Police Academy at Matapeake. This force is responsible for enforcing laws and regulations regarding protection and preservation of wildlife.

Until recently visitors could study the Chesapeake Bay model, constructed by the U.S.Army Corps of Engineers here, and view a short film about it. The model, if it still exists, covers nine acres under a large shed; it can simulate many natural phenomena and was supposed to allow scientists to study the effects of storms, dams, sewage, erosion etc. on the Bay.

MAUGANSVILLE (Washington) Pop. 1,069

4 miles northwest of Hagerstown. Although it was named after Jonathan and Abraham Maugan, who settled here in the 1800's, most of the town is of fairly recent vintage.

MAYO (Anne Arundel) Pop. 2,795

11 miles south of Annapolis. The name is from Isaac Mayo, U.S.N., who bought land here in 1835. Mayo is an indeterminate area along Mayo Rd. between South and Rhode Rivers; there are a number of private beaches and much suburban growth. A company manufactures cabin cruisers.

MECHANICSVILLE (St. Mary's)

12 miles northwest of Leonardtown. Several Maryland towns have borne this name in the past, notably Thurmont; but this is the only remaining town of the name in the state. An annual jousting tournament with exhibits and home-cooked food is held at Horse Range Farm near here each August.

MERRITT POINT (Baltimore County)

6 miles southeast of downtown Baltimore. A point between two creeks in a highly industrialized area adjoining Baltimore City. A county park has been made here with shade trees and picnic tables, while the tip of the point has a small beach which would be charming but for beer bottles, tainted water and massive electric lines overhead.

MEXICO (Carroll)

4 miles northeast of Westminster. According to an old resident it was named for an early settler from Mexico.

MIAMI BEACH (Baltimore County)

13 miles east of downtown Baltimore, fronting on the Chesapeake Bay. It is an area of former summer cottages, with much expansion, but the county has acquired a small beach, which is open for a small fee in summer.

MIDDLEBURG (Carroll)

12 miles west of Westminster. The name indicates that it is half way between Westminster and Thurmont. There was once a large pottery here. Historical markers show that there were Union troop movements in the area in 1863 when the Army of the Potomac moved through here on its way to Gettysburg. Nearby Bowling Brook Farm was named for raising race horses and produced seven Preakness winners in a period of 14 years before horse breeding stopped in 1955. The mementoes went to the Maryland Historical Society and the farmhouse is now a home for homeless boys.

MIDDLE RIVER (Baltimore County) Pop. 26,756

10 miles east of downtown Baltimore. This densely populated area was formerly dominated by the Martin-Marietta Co. which was previously the Glenn Martin Aircraft Co. Glenn L. Martin purchased 1,260 acres here in 1929, when Middle River was a small rural town just outside Baltimore City. He pioneered the aircraft industry, and his plant was visited by Lindbergh, Orville Wright, Douglas Corrigan and Amelia Earhart among others. When the Martin plant turned to manufacturing war planes, it became the largest aircraft company in the country and was visited by President Roosevelt and Vice-President Truman. The State of Maryland has purchased the former Martin-Marietta airport.

The river for which Middle River is named is an inlet between the Back and Gunpowder River estuaries. Middle River Neck is a portion of deeply indented land between Middle and Gunpowder Rivers.

MIDDLETOWN (Frederick) Pop. 1,748. Incorp. 1833

7 miles west of Frederick on old route 40 between

Catoctin and South Mountains, in the Middletown Valley (q.v.) of which it is the hub. The town was laid out soon after the Revolution by Margaret Crone. It was once called Smithfield but the present name is appropriate since, besides being in the middle of the valley, it is nearly midway between the north and south boundaries of Maryland at this point. The single street of houses retains all its original charm, in spite of the fact that its surroundings are fast becoming a dormitory town for Washington, D.C.

Middletown played a part in the Civil War. Skirmishes took place in its streets and many of its buildings became hospitals for the wounded, one of whom was Rutherford B. Hayes, wounded in the Battle of South Mountain in 1862. A certain Miss Nancy Crouse was involved in a flag incident with Confederate troops, somewhat resembling the more famous Barbara Fritchie incident in Frederick.

In the graveyard of the Methodist Church is a monument to a veteran of the Revolution, Lawrence Everhart.

MIDDLETOWN VALLEY (Frederick)

The valley between Catoctin and South Mountains, running from the vicinity of Jerusalem in the north to Brunswick on the Potomac River, a distance of about 16 miles. It is about eight miles wide in the south tapering to almost nothing in the north. Catoctin Creek meanders down the valley, emptying into the Potomac near Lander. Jerusalem is said to have been the first settlement in the valley, founded in 1710-11. Other towns in the valley are: Myerstown, Middletown, Burkittsville, Petersville and Brunswick.

MIDLAND (Allegany) Pop. 665. Incorp. 1900

In the George's Creek Valley about midway between Frostburg and Barton. It was once called Koontz for an early settler. Its economy has always been based on coal and the railway line to National runs down the middle of one of its main streets. The Thrasher Museum, housed in a former school building, displays carriages and wagons and other horse transport articles. An appointment to tour the museum can be made by phoning J.R.Thrasher at (301) 463-2242.

Midland. Railroad Avenue.

MIDLOTHIAN (Allegany)

A mile west of George's Creek Valley and half a mile south of route 48. This small mining town was named after the Scottish county but little remains of it today.

MILBURN LANDING (Worcester)

6 miles southwest of Snow Hill. A 350 acre state park beside the Pocomoke River in Pocomoke State Forest. There are picnicking and camping facilities, public boat ramp and nature trails. Formerly it was one of the numerous points on the river where boats stopped for cargo, and was also a stopping place on the underground railroad for escaping slaves fleeing to the north.

MILES RIVER

An Eastern Shore River that lies entirely within Talbot County. It was called St. Michael's River, but various settlers along its banks objected to the Saint; so it became abbreviated and apocopated. The town by its banks remained St. Michael's.

MILESTOWN (St. Mary's)

7 miles west of Leonardtown. Beside the road near here stood a large willow oak, the largest of the species in

Maryland, over 400 years old, 105 ft. tall and 22 feet around (they say.) Alas, it was felled in 1981.

MILFORD MILL (Baltimore County)   Pop. 20,354
7 miles northwest of downtown Baltimore. This portion of Greater Baltimore has only recently become a census designated place. The mill was on the Gwynn's Falls but the name is better known for the quarry which was opened here to excavate metagabbro rock for road surfacing. The quarry has long been water-filled and converted into a popular swimming pool.

MILLER'S SAWMILL (Washington)
15 miles south of Hagerstown. It was named for a sawmill operated by Mr. Miller! There is some kind of a summer community here. A little to the west a limestone cement factory operated for 40 years in the last half of the 18th century. The huge stone furnace can still be seen from the road but it is on private land with forbidding signs.

MILLERSVILLE (Anne Arundel)
10 miles northwest of Annapolis. It was known as Head of Severn until George Miller opened a store and postoffice in 1841. Although there is little else here, the town is the location of the Anne Arundel fire headquarters and the Anne Arundel Police headquarters.

MILL GREEN (Harford)
9 miles northeast of Bel Air. It is but a few houses in a pretty rural setting; and the mill still stands although it has not operated for many years.

MILLINGTON (Kent) Pop. 474. Incorp. 1824
13 miles northeast of Chestertown. It was originally two settlements called Head of Chester, for several small streams meet in the area to become the Chester River. The town is still divided, since a small part lies south of the river in Queen Anne's County. The present name was chosen in 1827 because of the numerous mills operating here at the time. Higman's Mill, a grist mill built in 1764 is still standing. There are several manufacturing industries in the area.

MILLTOWN LANDING (Prince George's)

12 miles southeast of Upper Marlboro on the west bank of the Patuxent River. This is the site of a mill town established in 1706, which failed to develop. Nothing remains.

MITCHELLVILLE (Prince George's)

15 miles east of the U. S. Capitol. The railroad and the postoffice could never agree about the name; although the postoffice uses Mitchellville, the railroad seems to prefer Mullikin. At 13710 Central Ave. (Route 214) is Wild World, where shows, games and water slides, etc. are open Memorial Day thru Labor Day.

MONKTON (Baltimore County)

20 miles north of downtown Baltimore. It was named after a former mill, which was named after Monkton Priory in Wales. Previously the town had been called Charlotte Town after Charlotte Calvert, grand-daughter of Charles Calvert, third Lord Baltimore. Miss C. had once owned My Lady's Manor, a large tract of which Monkton is the center. When she gave the tract to her father-in-law as payment for a debt, he obligingly named the town after her. (See **MY LADY'S MANOR**)

Near St. James's Church is the My Lady's Manor Race Course, where a four mile race is held each April. The local pack of hounds is blessed at the church each Thanksgiving Day.

MONOCACY RIVER

The Monocacy enters Maryland from Pennsylvania near Harney, $6\frac{1}{2}$ miles east of Emmitsburg, and follows a meandering course down the Frederick Valley, entering the Potomac two miles west of Dickerson. Near its mouth it is crossed by the C. & O. Canal (q.v.) carried by a splendid aqueduct built in 1833 of sandstone hauled from the foot of Sugarloaf Mountain. In former times boats went up the Monocacy as far as Double Pipe Creek, its main tributary, but it is only navigable by canoes today.

The Monocacy Trail was a network of trails down the Frederick Valley, used by Indians, and there was a village named Monocacy settled by Germans about a mile east of Creagerstown, although the exact site is uncertain.

MONTGOMERY COUNTY. County Seat: Rockville. Pop. 579,053. Area: 517 square miles.

Montgomery County was formed in 1776 and named after General Richard Montgomery, an Irish officer who was killed leading the attack on Quebec, Dec. 31, 1775. It is bounded on the northwest by a straight line from the source of the Patapsco near Mount Airy to the mouth of the Monocacy; on the northeast by the Patuxent River from its source, also near Mount Airy; on the southeast by a straight line from a point on the Patuxent River, formerly to the mouth of Rock Creek; on the southwest by the Potomac. In 1790 Montgomery County ceded 60 square miles to the Federal Government for the National Capital.

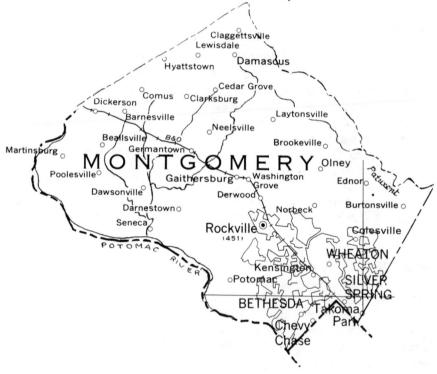

The county lies entirely on the Piedmont and the land is typically rolling. The northern part remains relatively rural and agricultural, but the southern portion, adjacent to Washington, D.C. is densely populated, with new suburbs continually growing and spreading. These suburbs are affluent and house a population with median income greater than any other part of Maryland and almost the entire nation. The residents are mostly well-educated professional people and government employees, large numbers of whom were not born locally.

A large proportion of the county's industries are concerned with research and development. There are also a number of large government departments. Between and beyond the centers of population, agriculture is still carried on, mostly dairying and livestock with some corn, grains, hay and nursery products. In spite of its rapid urbanization, Montgomery County has a most extensive and varied park system, operating 168 county parks of various kinds, many in lengthy stream valleys, with a total area of 19,000 acres.

MONTPELIER (Prince George's)

Montpelier is a colonial mansion standing on a knoll beside the Laurel-Bowie Road, three miles south of Laurel and 16 miles northeast of the U. S. Capitol. It was built around 1740 and was the home of the Snowdens, a great land-owning and iron-smelting family. (See **LAUREL**.) Numerous historical personalities have stayed at Montpelier, including, naturally, George Washington.

The house and grounds are now the property of the Maryland National Capital Parks and Planning Commission and are used for community activities. Most of the estate has long since been sold off for housing developments but the boxwood gardens remain and are open to visitors.

MONTROSE (Montgomery) Pop. 6,140

An area of recent growth 3 miles southeast of Rockville.

MORGANTOWN (Charles)

13 miles south of La Plata. It is situated on Lower Cedar Point, a place well-known for its excellent fishing and oystering since it was founded in the 18th century. Even George Washington must have known about this, for it was near here that he ran his schooner aground while fishing. A ferry used to operate from here to Potomac Beach, Virginia, before the Potomac River Bridge (q.v.) was built two miles upstream.

MORNINGSIDE (Prince George's) Pop. 1,395. Incorp. 1945.
7 miles southeast of the U. S. Capitol. One of Washington's innumerable southeastern suburbs; many of the residents work at government departments in Suitland or Andrews Airforce Base.

MOSCOW (Allegany)
One mile north of Barton in the George's Creek Valley. The town was laid out by Andrew Bruce Shaw, who laid out Barton and also Pekin, a mile further north. Shaw is thought to have been the first permanent settler of the region, and his old log mill, built here in 1725, to have been the first building. The Shaw family mansion still stands on the west side of the road.

MOUNT AETNA (Washington)
6 miles southeast of Hagerstown. The village was founded in 1761 and an iron furnace, recently discovered behind the fire station, must have illuminated the hilltop, giving the village its fanciful name. The Seventh Day Adventists own an estate called Highland View Academy. In the vicnity is a privately-owned limestone cavern, which was opened to the public for a short time in 1932.

MOUNTAINDALE (Frederick)
8 miles northwest of Frederick. A village of black and white log houses built by the C. C. C. in the nineteen thirties, but now privately owned. Above the village the road follows Fishing Creek to the dam and reservoir which supply the town of Frederick. It is a picturesque spot and there are picnic and camping facilities, but permits must be obtained from the caretaker's house. The small earlier reservoir and building remain nearby and are of some historical interest.

MOUNTAIN LAKE PARK (Garrett) Pop. 1,597. Incorp. 1931
2 miles east of Oakland. This was a summer resort owned by the Methodist Church and founded in the 1880's. It consisted of nearly 800 acres, fronting three quarters of a mile on the B. & O. Railroad tracks. The gardens were laid out by M. E. Faul, who designed Druid Hill Park in Baltimore, and there was a large amphitheater where camp meetings and lectures were held from 1882 until 1964. At

the foot of the hill was a spring and lake, and surmounting the hill a large hotel, which burnt down in 1955. New homes dot the area now, mingled with the remains of the original buildings. There are several lumber companies and a tennis club, where the Western Maryland champion tournaments are held each August.

MOUNT AIRY (Carroll) Pop. 2,450. Incorp. 1894.

16 miles southwest of Westminster. The town is situated on Parr's Ridge (q.v.) mostly in Carroll County, but part of it spills over into Frederick County. Its relatively high situation accounts for its name, and the fact that its water tower, and that of its close neighbor, Ridgeville, are outstanding landmarks for miles.

The town was settled in 1814 by Henry Bussard. It annexed neighboring Ridgeville in 1966. The early B. & O. Railroad, closely following the valley of the South Branch of the Patapsco, found that its early engines could not negotiate Parr's Ridge, so a series of inclined planes was constructed on either side. A later line passed through the town, and remains there, unused. Parr's Ridge is now negotiated by the Mount Airy tunnel, built in 1890.

The Mary Garrett Childrens' Hospital, named for a benefactor of Johns Hopkins University, was a sanitarium located here because of the high situation. It was famous for some years, but has now been converted into apartments. Mount Airy is still a center for shipping of farm products and it also has one or two small industries.

MOUNT CARMEL MONASTERY (Charles)

2 miles northwest of La Plata. This was originally a convent, the first in the United States, when a Carmelite order of nuns moved into the completed building in 1790. A farm, operated by slave labor, also belonged to the convent. The seven buildings were vacated and fell into ruins when the nuns moved to Baltimore in 1831 but recently two of them have been restored and the place is maintained as a religious shrine.

MOUNT HARMONY (Calvert)

11 miles north of Prince Frederick. Its name is from the fact that it lies close to the highest point in Calvert County -- 186 ft. above sea level!

MOUNT PLEASANT (Frederick)
6 miles northeast of Frederick. The famous race horse, Dancer's Image, lived at Glade Valley Farms near here.

MOUNT NEBO WILDLIFE MANAGEMENT AREA (Garrett)
1,791 acres about 3 miles north of Oakland on Hoop Pole Mountain. The land is owned by the state and there is a five acre lake for fishing.

MOUNT RAINIER (Prince George's) Pop. 7,361. Inc. 1910.
4 miles northeast of the U.S.Capitol. The land in the area had once belonged to some army officers from Seattle who gave the estate its name. Land was purchased to found the town in 1902.

MOUNT SAINT MARY'S COLLEGE (Frederick)
19 miles northeast of Frederick, near the foot of Garrick's Knob, which is part of Catoctin Mountain. The land on which the college stands was donated by William Elder, who came to this locality from St. Mary's County in 1734 and named the estate after his previous home. He was born in Lancashire England, and is buried in the old Catholic cemetery, half a mile below St. Mary's College. His home here was a favorite gathering place for Catholics.

The college, which is a Catholic institute for men, was founded in 1808 by Father John Dubois, afterwards Bishop of New York. An imposing monument surmounted by a gilt statue of the Virgin Mary stands on the site of the Old Church on the Hill, which preceded the college. A circular walk, flanked by pieces of statuary and the stations of the cross, leads to the Grotto of Lourdes, a prominent Catholic shrine further up the mountain, which is visited by thousands of pilgrims. The setting is one of great beauty. The sons and grandsons of Mother Seton (See **EMMITSBURG)** are buried on the grounds.

MOUNT SAVAGE (Allegany) Pop. 1,640.
7 miles northwest of Cumberland. The area was settled by Archibald Arnold in 1793 and called Arnold's settlement. At another period it was called Luthworth. Arnold did not foresee the possibilities offered by the local iron ore, fire clay and coal; but in 1839 a company of English entrepreneurs erected a rolling mill and two blast furnaces.

The company was later sold out to an American group and became the Mount Savage Iron Company, which made the first iron rails in America, for which they were awarded a medal by the Franklin Institute in Philadelphia. The brass and iron foundries later gave rise to the locomotive shops of the Cumberland and Pennsylvania Railroad; locomotives were built here from the 1880's until 1917. The Union Mining Co. was also here, headed in the 1880's by President Roosevelt's father.

Mount Savage still retains something of the appearance of a company town, although it is hard to believe that it was once the center of frenzied activity and the leading industrial town of Western Maryland. It is mainly residential, except for the company which still manufactures firebrick from the local clay and owns much of the land in the area, including part of Savage Mountain.

MUDDY CREEK FALLS (Garrett)

Maryland's highest waterfall. It is near the point where Muddy Creek enters the Youghiogheny, in Swallow Falls State Park. The water of Muddy Creek is crystal clear. Henry Ford, Thomas Edison and Harvey Firestone once camped near this spot surrounded by giant hemlocks; the trees still form one of Maryland's tiny pockets of virgin forest.

MUTUAL (Calvert)

5 miles south of Prince Frederick. This is another place which features a jousting tournament each summer. It is held on the last Saturday in August at the Mutual Homecoming

MYERSVILLE (Frederick) Pop. 450. Incorp. 1904.

10 miles northwest of Frederick. It was founded by James Stottlemyer in 1742, which makes it one of the oldest towns in the Middletown Valley -- only Jerusalem is thought to have preceded it. Although the village is situated between route 40 and 70, it has escaped the influence of either, and unlike Middletown, seems to have evaded the notice of the developers so far.

MY LADY'S MANOR (Baltimore County)

A 10,000 acre tract in northern Baltimore County which

Charles Calvert, third Lord Baltimore, held in reserve for his own use. It came to his grand-daughter, Charlotte, who lost it to her father-in-law as payment for a debt and he named the village in the center of the tract after her (See **MONKTON.**) The manor was sold off in lots after the Revolution and today some new houses are being built, although a residents' association guards the preservation of the area as far as possible.   At Shepperd, three miles northeast of Monkton, is said to be the oldest remaining house on the former estate, while the village of Manor, three miles south of Monkton preserves the name.

MYRTLE GROVE (Charles)
    7 miles northwest of La Plata.   An 800 acre wildlife refuge on route 225 near Indian Head.

NANJEMOY (Charles)

14 miles southwest of La Plata. A creek of the same name meanders nearby and enters the Potomac as a mile wide estuary. This part of the state is somewhat remote and little visited. Purse State Park, fronting on the Potomac, is being constructed nearby.

Two celebrities were born near here: Matthew Henson, who accompanied Peary to the North Pole in 1909, and Raphael Semmes, author and mariner, who was born in 1790. The site of Henson's cabin is known; the cabin itself no longer exists, but a gavel made from the wood is in the Maryland State House at Annapolis.   Semmes was in command of the Confederate ship *Alabama,* which did more damage to Union shipping than any other single ship. His best-known book is *Captains and Mariners of Early Maryland.*

Nanticoke. Evening.

NANTICOKE (Wicomico)

18 miles southwest of Salisbury. It is near the mouth of the Nanticoke River, for which it is named and has a little harbor with a little oyster fleet and a little marina. There are also two sea food packing houses. The Nanticoke River rises in Delaware and forms the boundary between Wicomico and Dorchester Counties before entering the Chesapeake Bay; it is named for a tribe of Indians whose name is said to mean "tide-water people."

THE NARROWS (Allegany)

Often called the Cumberland Narrows, this scenic and historic spot is a mile northwest of Cumberland, where Wills Creek flows through the narrow defile between Haystack Mountain and Wills Mountain. Route 40 and two railroad tracks also find room in the valley and it is easy to see why this route has always been known as "The Gateway to the West," since it penetrates the formidable wall of the Appalachian Plateau. A flood control project and the demolition of the picturesque bridge over the creek have somewhat marred the beauty of the spot. A fine view of the Narrows can be obtained from Lovers' Leap (q.v.)

NASSAWANGO (Worcester)

5 miles northwest of Snow Hill. There was once a community here and an important iron furnace on Nassawango Creek from 1832 to 1847. The remains of the furnace are being restored, the foundations of the old village uncovered and a small museum is being prepared. Much of the plot of *The Entailed Hat* by George A. Townsend (See **GATHLAND**) is laid here.

NATIONAL ROAD

The National Road started at Cumberland in Maryland and ended at Wheeling, West Virginia. When $30,000 was approved for its construction in 1806, it was the first road ever to be built with government funds, and except for its avoidance of Haystack Mountain, it largely followed the road built by General Braddock. In 1925 it was designated route 40. Historical markers are plentiful along its length. See **BRADDOCK'S ROAD, NEMACOLIN'S PATH)**

NEGRO MOUNTAIN (Garrett)

The spot where route 40 crosses Negro Mountain, west

of Grantsville, is the highest point on the National Road. The mountain was named for a negro named Nemesis who accompanied Colonel Cresap, an active frontiersman, on an expedition, and was the only member of the party killed. He is said to have predicted his own death beforehand.

NEWARK (Worcester)

7 miles northeast of Snow Hill. It is said that a house built near the cross roads, just before the Civil War, was dubbed The New Ark. However that may be, the railroad called there station here Queponco, to avoid confusion with other Newarks. Tomatoes and tomato puree are canned here in season.

NEW CARROLLTON (Pr. George's) Pop. 12,632. Incorp. 1953.

9 miles northeast of the U. S. Capitol. The developer, Albert Turner, named it in 1953 after Charles Carroll of Carrollton. When a post office was opened here in 1965, another Carrollton in Carroll County complained about receiving so much of the wrong mail; so the name was changed to New Carrollton.

NEW GERMANY (Garrett)

A state park 5 miles south of Grantsville in the Savage River State Forest. A small stream has been dammed to form a 13 acre lake. Camp sites and cabins are available and there are hiking trails and vistas.

NEWMARKET (Frederick) Pop. 339. Incorp. 1878

8 miles east of Frederick. The town was laid out by Nicholas Hall in 1793 and once boasted a metal and bone button factory. Today it is an important stop on the antique collectors' circuit and boasts 31 antique shops. Interstate 70 bypasses the town and it has retained much of its charm.

NEW MIDWAY (Frederick)

12 miles northeast of Frederick. This otherwise undistinguished village is the location of Cookerly's Tavern, where George Washington stayed on July 1, 1791.

NEWTON (Caroline)

10 miles southwest of Denton. It was first called Hog Creek, and later Smithson, after the Rev. R. Smithson who

was the first minister in the town. When the postoffice was established in 1895, the name was changed to that of the first postmaster, although there seems to be some disagreement as to whether it should be Newton or Newtown.

NEWTOWN NECK (St. Mary's)

4 miles southwest of St. Leonards. A neck of land between St. Clements Bay and Breton Bay. Newtown Neck Manor House, patented in 1640, was one of the antecedents of Georgetown University, started here about 1677 by Father White, the Jesuit priest who accompanied Maryland's first colonists. Next to the house, amid rich open farmlands, stands St. Francis Xavier's Church, founded 1640. The present building was erected in 1731 and restored in 1984. The tip of the neck, like so many of the choicest locations, is government property and cannot be reached.

Newtown Neck. St. Xavier's Church.

NEW WINDSOR (Carroll) Pop. 799. Incorp. 1843

$6\frac{1}{2}$ miles southwest of Westminster. The town was founded by Isaac Atlee and called Sulphur Springs until 1816. The building which housed the springs later became Dielman's Inn. The present name comes from Windsor, England. Troops of the Army of the Potomac marched through here towards Gettysburg in June, 1883.

An establishment known as Blue Ridge College was founded here quite early but changed its identity when it was purchased in 1913 by the Church of the Brethren. Modern buildings were added and today, this this small rustic town we find The Church World Service of the National Council of the Church of Christ in the U. S. A., the largest of four such centers in the U. S. and many more throughout the world. Here are trained a body of dedicated young people who work without pay in disaster areas, leper settlements, among itinerant harvesters, etc. In addition to the training courses, the center prepares used garments and makes new clothing. An international gift shop stems from the organization's encouragement of native crafts in far-off places. There is also a cafeteria catering, they say, to 10,000 visitors a year.

The town has issued a small tour guide to the vicinity.

NICHOLS (Caroline)

11 miles south of Denton. It was once called Midway but was re-named in 1896 after a local landowner.

NOLANDS ISLAND (Frederick)

An island in the Potomac River 12 miles southwest of Frederick, one of several islands in this stretch of the river where it passes through the Frederick Valley. The Monocacy Trail, an early north-south route, crossed the Potomac at this point, making use of Nolands Island, until a bridge at Point of Rocks caused the old crossing to be forgotten.

NORRISVILLE (Harford)

16 miles northwest of Bel Air, near the Pennsylvania border. The first house was erected by Edward Norris in 1770 and many of his large family settled here. The town was not named until 1856, and the postoffice not until 1870, when a Norris was the first post master.

NORTH BEACH (Calvert) Pop. 1,504. Incorp. 1910.

12 miles northeast of Prince Frederick. Named because it was a northward extension of the earlier resort, Chesapeake Beach. Before the Bay Bridge lured holiday-makers to the Atlantic beaches, North Beach on the Chesapeake Bay was a popular resort; it had a boardwalk, a pavilion and two piers with a restaurant and dancing. Man and nature have

conspired to destroy it as a resort. Fires have wrecked the piers and the boardwalk, and hurricanes have eroded the beaches. The town retains its inhabitants and what is left of the beach is still public, but it has little attraction for visitors today.

NORTH BEACH PARK (Anne Arundel)

Fronting on the Chesapeake Bay at the very southern tip of the county; the county line seems to have been bent to accomodate the town. It is a non-descript area of former summer homes extending along the shore for a mile. Each street leading to the shore is named for a variety of tree.

NORTH BRANCH PARK (Allegany)

Beside the Potomac River near Cumberland. There is a replica of a C. & O. canal barge here, open to visitors.

NORTH BRENTWOOD (Prince George's) See BRENTWOOD.

NORTHEAST (Cecil) Pop. 1,469

6 miles west of Elkton; the name is sometimes spelled as two words. This small town on the Northeast River at the head of the Chesapeake Bay has always been water oriented. Herring fishing was so important here, that it once had the nickname of Herringtown. Boat building is still carried on here to some extent and marinas and tackle shops abound. A water festival is held here annually with sailing races, boat parade, fish fry, etc.

St. Mary Anne's Episcopal Church, built in 1742, has its main door facing the river, reminding us that it was erected for a congregation that mostly arrived by boat. The churchyard is older than the church and contains graves dating from the 1600's and also a number of Indian graves, marked with plain stones. The parents of Richard Brooking, founder of the Brookings Institute, are buried here. The first Protestant Episcopal clergyman ordained in America was rector here.

There are a few other enterprises in town: several small factories produce explosive, fuses and fireworks among other things.

NORTH POINT (Baltimore County)

11 miles southeast of downtown Baltimore. The point

marks the entrance to the Patapsco River on the north bank; the equivalent point on the south bank is considered to be Bodkin Point.   The name is intimately associated with the Battle of North Point, which took place Sept. 12, 1814, immediately before the bombardment of Fort McHenry.   The Americans scored a minor victory when a sharpshooter killed the leader of the British raiding party, General Ross, during a rain storm, and the British retreated to their ships anchored in the harbor.   A small monument was erected in 1817 to commemorate the event.   Early engravings show a rural setting, but today the area is in the midst of nondescript urban sprawl. (See also **FORT HOWARD**)

NORTHWEST BRANCH REGIONAL PARK (Montgomery)

A stream valley park along the Northwest Branch of the Anacostia River.   It stretches for some miles through the county and among its attractions are a golf course, model railroad, and the National Capital Trolley Museum near Layhill (q.v.)

NOTTINGHAM (Prince George's)

8 miles southeast of Upper Marlboro.   Established in 1706, it was an active port by 1747 and had a tobacco inspection warehouse, several inns, fairs, a racecourse and a

Nottingham.   Decaying village store.

population of 1500. The British encamped here in August, 1814. Like several other towns along the Patuxent, little but the name remains, apart from a few houses, a ruined store and a pleasant view of the Patuxent River from a dead-end street.

OAKLAND.   Seat of Garrett County.   Pop. 1,994.   Incorp.
1862.

Oakland sits atop the Appalachian Plateau on Hoop Pole
Ridge, not far from the West Virginia border at an elevation
of 2,650.   The height is not apparent until one senses the
morning and evening chill in September and sees the early
snow falls.

Founded in 1849 by the McCarty family, the town was
called Yough Glades, after the nearby Youghiogheny River
and the glades of Garrett County.   The present name commemorates the splendid oak timber which originally covered
the area.

The town grew with the B. & O. Railroad, whose station
here, erected in 1851, is a National Historical Landmark and
boasts about its situation on top of a mountain.   With the
railroad came the lumber industry and also the Oakland
Hotel, (now gone,) a commodious resort surrounded by
handsome grounds.   The town is still resort oriented, being
the headquarters for Deep Creek Lake and the nearby
Herrington Manor and Swallow Falls State Parks.   After the
summer season is over, the Autumn Glory Festival, held each
year in October since 1968, brings crowds of visitors to enjoy
the beauty of the autumn colors, enlivened by a parade and
other activities and culminating in the state fiddlers' and
banjo players' contest.

Oakland has not been entirely neglected by celebrities.
The Church of the Presidents at the corner of Second and
Liberty Streets saw Presidents Grant, Harrison and Cleveland
attend services there.   The town also remembers when
Albert Einstein was seen in town before World War II.   A
classic botany book, *Wildflowers of the Alleghenies,* was
written by Joseph E. Harned, a former owner of the drug-
store which is now Proudfoot's.   The oldest house in town is

a small store at the northeast corner of Water and First Streets.   The Garrett County Historical Museum is open every Saturday morning, and daily during the summer.

A few industries support the town: some wood related manufacturing, a poultry-packing plant and a factory making ophthalmic lenses on route 560.

Oakland. The historic B. & O. Railroad station.

OAKLAND (Carroll) Pop. 2,242
12 miles southeast of Westminster. It is a spread out community of individual homes on the west bank of Liberty Reservoir. The Bureau of Water Supply has an office here.

Apart from the more famous Oakland in Garrett County, several other places in Maryland commemorate the oak tree. A small town in Baltimore County, 28 miles north of downtown Baltimore, is the next Oakland in size and there are other small places with the name in Anne Arundel, Caroline and Prince George's Counties.

OAKLAND MILLS (Howard)
Now part of the new town of Columbia. The developers have retained and sanitized the old farm buildings and used them for community purposes.

OAKMONT (Montgomery)

9 miles northwest of the U. S. Capitol. A tiny enclave of Bethesda covering only 18½ acres, with 46 large, tree-shaded houses.

OAK ORCHARD (Frederick)

15 miles northeast of Frederick. A locality whose only claim to fame is that one of its residents authored the inscription on the block which Maryland contributed to the Washington Monument. His name was David W. Naill, a miller. The inscription reads: "Maryland - the memorial of her regard for the Father of His County, and of his cordial, habitual and immovable attachment for the American Union."

OAKWOOD (Cecil)

19 miles southwest of Elkton. It is an innocuous cross-roads village now, but it is said to have been a notorious place during the two years that the Conowingo Dam was being built.

OCEAN (Allegany)

4 miles south of Frostburg. This village in the George's Creek Valley was so named because the coal mines in the area belonged to the Ocean Steam Co. in the 1880's, a company which used most of the coal mined here to fire ocean-going steamers.

OCEAN CITY (Worcester) Pop. 4,946. Incorp. 1880.

20 miles northeast of Snow Hill and the only town on Maryland's Atlantic coast. It is one of the best-known communities in the state, famous for its sandy beaches and deep sea fishing, which has given it the nickname of The White Marlin Capital of the World.

Ocean City is built on a quarter mile wide strip of sandy, treeless, coastal barrier reef, separated from the mainland by a narrow arm of Sinepuxent Bay and connected to it by two bridges. The first hotel was built here in 1875 and a railroad brought ever-increasing numbers of visitors across the bay. Today, thousands of visitors are attracted annually from Baltimore, Washington and other urban centers to the ten miles of beach and three miles of boardwalk and the many amusements that go with them. In addition to the fine swimming and sunbathing, there are boats for hire, deep-sea fishing, the nearby Ocean Downs raceway, convention hall, golf course and a theme park called Frontier Town within driving distance. The number of motels, hotels, rooms and cottages for rent and condominiums for sale increases each year.

Ocean City inlet was opened by a storm in 1933, the same storm that washed out the railroad bridge. It separates the resort from Assateague Island to the south and prevents development in that direction.

The comparatively small year-round population finds some employment at a manufacturer of concrete products and a seafood packing house.

OCEAN PINES (Worcester)

North of Ocean City across Assawoman Bay. This community of homes and condominiums, which was founded in 1969, has a golf course, country club, yacht, tennis and swim clubs. Many residents live here all year.

ODENTON (Anne Arundel) Pop. 13,270.

15 miles southwest of Baltimore. It originated at the crossing point of two railroads: the Baltimore and Potomac (now part of Conrail) and the Washington, Baltimore and Annapolis (long defunct.) The station was named for Governor Oden Bowie, who became governor in 1869. A daily commuter train from Baltimore to Washington still stops here, but the Amtrak trains ignore it.

The town caters mainly to Fort Meade (q.v.) and the road bordering the installation is lined with fast food establishments. A number of factories have located here, including companies which make plastics, corrugated boxes and furniture.

OELLA (Baltimore County)

$9\frac{1}{2}$ miles southwest of downtown Baltimore and a mile upstream from Ellicott City on the opposite bank of the Patapsco River. The town was built to accomodate the workers of the large stone cotton mill, which still dominates the town, and is said to have been named for the first woman in America to spin cotton. The mill was built by the Union Manufacturing Co. in the early 1800's and underwent periodical expansion. In 1870 both mill and town were sold to W. J. Dickey Co. and underwent some modernization, turning out cotton duck, and later, woollen sport coats.   It finally closed in 1972.

The houses cluster in the Patapsco Valley and climb the hillside, picturesque but not completely sanitary.   Most of the rents are very low and the houses are in danger of being either condemned or gentrified.   The trend seems to be towards gentrification and the inhabitants fear that they will find themselves unable to pay the higher rents.

Mount Gilboa Church at the intersection of Oella Rd. and Westchester Ave. is associated with Benjamin Banneker (1731-1806) who was born near here, a "free man of color." He was a gifted scholar and self-taught mathematician, astronomer and surveyor, who came to the attention of Thomas Jefferson, and was called upon to assist in the laying out of Washington, D.C.   There is an historical marker on the west side of Westchester Ave. one block south of Oella Ave.

OLD BALTIMORE (Harford)

11 miles southeast of Bel Air.   The first seat of Baltimore County, before it was divided, was on the east bank of the Bush River, three miles south of the Present Pennsylvania Railroad bridge, and it was called Baltimore.   A courthouse was erected by 1676.   The town was abandoned between 1691 and 1693 and re-located twice before settling in this position.   There is very little to see at the site today, apart from a few old graves of the Phillips family.   It lies within the bounds of the Aberdeen Proving Ground (q.v.) and it is only possible to view it on Armed Forces Day, when the Proving Ground holds open house and runs bus tours to the site.

OLDFIELD POINT (Cecil)

7 miles southwest of Elkton.   The point marks the location of an early ferry, which ran from here to Courthouse Point across the Elk River, a very busy and important crossing.   The British fleet sailed up the Elk River in 1777 and landed near here;   General Howe's headquarters were established just north of the ferry house and three days later the troops continued on to Elkton. Bishop Asbury, one of the founders of American Methodism, spent Christmas here in 1782.

Nothing remains of the early settlement and the point is

private, but a nearby house bearing the date 1768 is built with bricks from a house at Oldfield Point.

OLD FRENCHTOWN (Cecil)

3 miles south of Elkton on the east bank of the Elk River. It was originally called Transtown, a Swedish name meaning crane, but became Frenchtown when a group of Arcadians moved here in 1755.

In earlier times Frenchtown was an important shipping point; ships out of Baltimore with cargoes for Delaware and Pennsylvania were unloaded here and the freight was carried in wagons to Newcastle, Delaware. The first steamboat out of Baltimore, "The Chesapeake" docked at Frenchtown.

In 1813 the British destroyed a number of small wooden vessels and the wharves and warehouse, but the town continued as before and by 1831 a railroad was constructed from here to Newcastle across the narrow neck of land which separates the Chesapeake Bay from Delaware Bay. It had wooden rails and stone ties and the cars were pulled by horses until the company acquired a steam engine in 1832. Some of the ties can be seen at the Elkton Public Library, while at Newcastle, the station and some of the rails are preserved in place.

The railroad ran until 1853 or 4, when the Philadelphia, Wilmington and Baltimore Railroad (later the Pennsylvania) opened a route directly from Baltimore to Wilmington. There is nothing to see at Frenchtown today. The area is private property and inaccessible, although Lewis Shore Road is obviously laid on the old railroad bed.

OLDTOWN (Allegany)

12 miles southeast of Cumberland near the Potomac River at an historic crossing point. This small settlement is well named, since it was for many years a true frontier outpost, preceding other settlements of the area, and even before that it was an Indian settlement.

Colonel Thomas Cresap established a frontier house and fort here in 1741 at a spot then called Shawnee Old Town. He was the first settler of Allegany County, and he called the place Skipton, after his home town in Yorkshire, England. The name was changed to Oldtown in 1844. For years it was a well-known stopping place, trading post, stockade and home, and most travellers to the west, including George

Washington on more than one occasion, stopped here. Only the chimney remains of the fort, but a house, built by Michael Cresap, the youngest son, still stands, and is the oldest house in the county. It is open to the public by request.

A toll bridge crosses the Potomac River on the site of the old ford. Privately owned by a local Maryland landowner, and sometimes flooded, it is the only crossing for many miles in either direction. Where the toll house stands, Thomas Cresap built his mill.

This historic spot once aspired to be the seat of Allegany County. Its former importance is commemorated in the names of Town Hill and Town Creek, and an old road named Oldtown Road that can be traced for many miles. The confluence of the North and South Branches of the Potomac is two miles downstream.

OLNEY (Montgomery) Pop. 13,026
7 miles northeast of Rockville. The first house here was called Fair Hill, and the village took the same name for a time; later it was called Machanicsville. The present name is said to have been bestowed by a former postmaster who named it for a town in England, which was the home of the poet William Cowper, whom he admired.

Washingtonians have been coming out here to dine and visit the summer theater for many years. The theater is still flourishing, but the Olney Inn, which was built around a residence dating from 1875 has succumbed to fire. The area was pleasantly rural until recently, but is fast becoming just one more Washington suburb.

ORCHARD BEACH (Anne Arundel)
10 miles southeast of Baltimore. A small community on Stony Creek, with a private beach.

ORCHARD HILLS (Washington) Pop. 1,589.
A suburb 3 miles north of Hagerstown. East of here was Long Meadows, where Col. Thomas Cresap resided and built a fortified home before pushing on to Oldtown. Only the name remains, borne by a church and a road.

ORDINARY POINT (Cecil)
19 miles southwest of Elkton. On this curious peninsula

jutting out into the Sassafras River, the first courthouse in Cecil County was erected at a point called Jamestown, later changed to Oldtown, and now called Cassidy Wharf. The date of its erection is thought to have been 1792, although the county was formed in 1674. There was probably an ordinary, or inn, nearby where travellers could refresh themselves at a common table.

Since the point was at the extremity of the county, it was decided to move the courthouse to Courthouse Point in 1717, a location which was not much better.

OVERLEA (Baltimore County) Pop. 12,965. (See PARKVILLE)

OWENS CREEK (Frederick)

A mountain stream which rises near the Pennsylvania border and flows into the Monocacy. Its steep valley down the mountainside provides a passage for the Western Maryland Railroad in its climb over the Blue Ridge. The stream boasts two covered bridges along its length: Loys, four miles east of Thurmont, where there is a parking lot and picnic tables; and Roddy, one mile east of Thurmont on Roddy Bridge Rd., built in 1856.

OWINGS (Calvert)

13 miles north of Prince Frederick, almost on the Anne Arundel County line. A small company here produced fiberglass boats.

OWINGS MILLS (Baltimore County) Pop. 9,526

13 miles northwest of downtown Baltimore. The name comes from Samuel Owings, who set up three grist mills here in the mid-eighteenth century. He called the mills Upper, Lower and Middle; the trademark on his flour sacks - ULM - was their initials. The Upper mill still stands, near Reisterstown Rd. and his house on Painter's Mill Rd, also called Ulm, where he lived 1765-83, has been restored and is now a restaurant.

In the vicinity is Rosewood State Hospital (q.v.) and also St. Thomas Church, built 1742 (See GARRISON) which is a chapel of St. Paul's Church in Baltimore, and where some of the Owings family are buried. The Painter's Mill Music Fair, which puts on a season of entertainment each summer, is also on Painter's Mill Rd.

Grave of Samuel Owings in St. Thomas Church, Garrison.

The largest industry is the Maryland Cup Corporation on Reisterstown Rd. employing 2,000 people. A number of industries are moving into the Owings Mills Industrial Park.

OXFORD (Talbot) Pop. 750. Incorp. 1706

8 miles southwest of Easton on a peninsula jutting out into the Tred Avon River near its confluence with the Choptank. The town was established over 300 years ago; it became a registered port of entry in 1694 and branches of London and Liverpool commercial houses were established here. Oxford's trade declined after 1750 but it has remained water-oriented to this day, its harbor crowded with pleasure craft. There are several small boat building and repairing companies, the well-known Tred-Avon Yacht Club, and establishments catering to sport fishermen. The U. S. Government maintains a bureau of Commercial Fisheries Biological Lab. here, studying cultivation of the oyster. But the most fascinating feature of the town is the Tred Avon Ferry.

The ferry boat continues a service which began in 1683 with a rowed scow, when the rates were paid in tobacco. The present boat, which is called the Southside, was built in 1923, and runs every fifteen minutes or so until dusk; it can accomodate several cars, the fare for car and driver being $2.50 (probably more by now.) The ferry conveys its passengers to Bellevue, a nondescript collection of houses, that would probably never be visited but for the ferry.

A noteworthy inhabitant of Oxford was Robert Morris, a successful tobacco merchant who became known as "The Financier of the Revolution." He was killed accidentally by a wad from a saluting cannon on a ship in Oxford harbor, but his house remains here, incorporated into the Robert Morris Inn. The building became an inn after the Civil War and is still in use as a hotel and restaurant, attracting many visitors. Robert Morris was buried in Whitemarsh cemetery, six miles southeast of Easton.

Another resident of the neighborhood was Tench Tilghman who was Washington's aide-de-camp and confidential secretary throughout the Revolution. His widow is buried in Oxford cemetery, outside the town limits and near the grave is an obelisk inscribed with Washington's tribute to Tench and a description of his historic ride to Philadelphia, with the news of the surrender at Yorktown. Tench himself is buried in Old St. Paul's cemetery in Baltimore.

Just off the main street is a small town museum, which is open Fri., Sat. and Sun., 2-5.

OXON HILL (Prince George's) Pop. 36,267.
6 miles due south of the U. S. Capitol. This Washington suburb is fast losing all its rural aspect, but it is saved by the presence of Oxon Hill Childrens' Farm, which is an authentic late 19th century farm, administered by the National Park Service. Here one can stroll through a country setting and watch hand milking, horse plowing, etc. It is open 8-5 throughout the year.

Also on the grounds of the farm is Oxon Hill Manor, a farmhouse which replaced the original manor house which was burnt down in 1783. John Hanson (1721-83,) president of the Continental Congress in 1781, died here, and is thought to be buried on the grounds, but the site of the grave is unknown. Hanson was born in Maryland at a house called Mulberry Grove, near Chapel Point.

Hanson Junior High School on route 414 has some Hanson memorabilia on display, which can be viewed during school hours. Rosecroft Raceway, which is open for trotting for 20 nights in May and June, is close by.

PAINT BRANCH PARK (Montgomery)
A stream valley park owned by the county along Paint Branch, which is a tributary of the Northwest Branch of the Anacostia River.   The valley is a botanical and wild life haven and there are some intersting rock outcrops.

PALMER (Harford)
7 miles northeast of Bel Air.   This is a 462 acre estate on Deer Creek, donated to the state by Mrs. Gerald C. Palmer.   It will eventually be developed for recreational purposes.

PALMER PARK (Prince George's) Pop. 7,986.
8 miles northeast of the U. S. Capitol.   One of the many suburbs surrounding Washington, D. C.

PARKER CREEK (Calvert)
3 miles southeast of Prince Frederick.   Its name is from the small stream meandering eastward into the Chesapeake Bay, which is considered to be one of the most scenic and unspoilt stream valleys in Maryland.   However, the area is private and inaccessible.

PARK MILLS (Frederick)
8 miles south of Frederick.   Once known as Fleecy Dale, it became New Bremen in 1789 when John F. Amelung from Bremen, Germany, came here and started the first glass works in America.   It traded under the name of "The American Glass Manufactory" and the products were sold in Frederick and Baltimore.   A few pieces of this glass remain in collections;   for instance there are some in the Masonic Lodge of Alexandria, Virginia, and some in the Metropolitan Museum of Art in New York.   The old mansion, Amelung House, still stands and is occupied.

PARKTON (Baltimore County)

24 miles north of Baltimore. It was named for the Parke family who were local landowners. Commuter trains ran from Parkton to Baltimore until the flood of 1972 put a stop to rail traffic on this line. The same flood washed out the road bridge, so that Parkton became a town separated into two parts. There was an unsuccessful attempt to build a railroad from here to Manchester in bygone days. The stone building on Bush Cabin Branch was once Foster's Mill.

PARKVILLE (Baltimore County) Pop. 35,159

8 miles northeast of downtown Baltimore, just over the city line. It was originally called Lavender Hill, and is, with Overlea, one of Baltimore's earlier suburbs, consisting mainly of row houses.

PAROLE (Anne Arundel) Pop. 3,377

$2\frac{1}{2}$ miles west of Annapolis on route 2. The name comes from the fact that a camp for paroled Federal prisoners was established here about 1862; at one period 30,000 prisoners were encamped here.

A mile to the west, at the intersection of routes 178 and 450 is "The Three Mile Oak." Under this oak, General Washington was greeted by a welcoming committee from Annapolis in 1783, when he came to resign his commission. A pitiful black stump anchored to a cement block opposite the Equitable Trust Bank is supposed to be the remnants of the tree, and an historical marker outside the bank describes the occasion. Other markers commemorating the event have been moved down route 450 to a spot near the route 50 bridge by a "No stopping any time" sign.

PARRS RIDGE

The highest ridge of the Piedmont Plateau in Maryland, and the divide from which stream flow eastward into the Chesapeake Bay and westward into the Monocacy. It runs from the vicinity of Westminster, southwesterly to the Potomac and reaches about 900 ft. at its highest point, diminishing to almost nothing at the Potomac. The northeasterly continuation from Westminster is called Dug Hill Ridge. The most prominent towns situated on the ridge are: Westminster, Mount Airy and Ridgeville.

PARRS SPRING (Montgomery)

19 miles north of Rockville and a mile south of Ridgeville. It is an insignificant village but has some importance since the source of the South Branch of the Patapsco River is here. The spring is the common boundary point of four counties: Carroll, Frederick, Howard and Montgomery. The actual marker is on private land, under a farm pond, but is said to be visible through the planks of a pier.

PARSONBURG (Wicomico)

16 miles northeast of Salisbury. It was named after the Parson family when the railroad came into the locality. A small hill nearby has yielded many Indian relics and is thought to be a burial mound. There is a large poultry processing company here.

PARSON ISLAND (Queen Anne's)

13 miles southwest of Centreville. A small island in Eastern Bay between Kent Island and the Eastern Shore, possibly named for Joshua Thomas "the Parson of the Islands." (See Deale Island) McCormick & Co. bought it in 1944; they have experimental plots of spices here, and also use the island for holding sales and management meetings.

PASADENA (Anne Arundel) Pop. 7,439

13 miles southeast of downtown Baltimore. It was first settled in 1890 when a silk company bought land and attempted to raise silkworms here, without success. The silk-grower's wife was from Pasadena, California, hence the name. The word is supposed to be from an Indian language, meaning "between two hills," scarcely an appropriate name for this flat area. Pasadena began to develop as a commuter town in the 1950's and many residents drive to work in Baltimore.

PATAPSCO (Carroll)

6 miles south of Westminster. It is named for its situation at the confluence of the East and West Branches of the North Branch of the Patapsco River! New suburbs are springing up nearby and the village center, although still recognizable, is diminished.

PATAPSCO NECK (Baltimore County)

The area between the estuaries of the Patapsco River

and Back River, sometimes referred to as The Neck. Land
was deeded to Thomas Todd here as early as 1664. The
Neck contains the heavily industrialized communities of
Dundalk and Sparrows Point, which, although outside the
Baltimore City limits are vital to the city's economy. North
Point (q.v.) is at the tip of The Neck.

PATAPSCO RIVER

The South Branch of the Patapsco River rises near
Parr's Spring, just south of Ridgeville, and the source forms
the boundary point of four counties. The North Branch is
divided into the East and West Branches, which rise at
springs between Westminster and Manchester and meet at
the village of Patapsco. The North and South Branches meet
in the McKeldin area of the Patapsco State Park, off of
Marriottsville Road. The Patapsco enters Baltimore Harbor
in southwest Baltimore, where it expands suddenly into an
estuary, which can be described as either the mouth of the
river or an inlet of the Chesapeake Bay.

The name is an Indian one and has been variously
interpreted as "jutting ledge of rock" from the White Rocks
(q.v.) or "black water, white-capped waves."

The valley of the Patapsco was once Maryland's greatest
industrial center and drove numerous power wheels for
furnaces and mills until floods destroyed them one by one.
The valley also provided the location for America's first
practical railroad, the Baltimore and Ohio, from Baltimore to
Mount Airy. The track is still used today, although
re-located in several spots, shortened by tunnels and rebuilt
several times after being washed out by floods.

Much of the stream valley is a park today. The park
begins about seven miles from the mouth and extends to
Liberty Dam on the North Branch and to Sykesville on the
South Branch. Acquisition started in 1912, and the park now
has 8,000 acres with six main recreation areas.

PATUXENT (Charles)

Village between Benedict and Hughesville on the road to
the Patuxent River Bridge.

PATUXENT NAVAL AIR TEST CENTER (St. Mary's)

A 6,400 acre tract on the south side of the mouth of
the Patuxent River on a peninsula two miles wide and three

miles long. It is on the site of the Mattapany Estate, named after the Indians who once resided here. The estate once belonged to Charles Calvert, Third Lord Baltimore, and several scenes of Maryland's early history were played out on it. A colonial house is used by the Center, and there are some foundations of early buildings.

The Air Test Center was commissioned in 1943 and has facilities for testing naval planes and weapons. There is also a U. S. Naval Test Pilot School. 6,000 people are employed, most of whom are housed in developments along route 235, such as Lexington Park (q.v.) The Center is not open to the public, except when air displays are held occasionally; however, there is a museum, which is open Tues. thru Sat. 11-5 and Sun. 12-5. (See also **PINEY POINT**)

PATUXENT RIVER

This is the longest of Maryland's rivers (not counting the Potomac) -- 110 miles long and totally within the state. The main branch rises on Parr's Ridge, near Parr's Spring, close to the source of the Patapsco, meets the Little Patuxent just above the route 3 bridge, and enters the Chesapeake Bay sixteen miles above the mouth of the Potomac, in an estuary two miles wide. It is spanned by a new bridge near the estuary at Solomons and an earlier bridge on route 231 near Prince Frederick.

Two reservoirs supplying the Washington, D. C. area are located along the upper reaches: Tridelphia Reservoir formed by Brighton Dam and the Rocky Gorge Reservoir, formed by the Howard T. Duckett Dam. Mink Hollow pumping station, three miles below Brighton Dam, pumps water over the divide at the rate of 12 million gallons per day.

Along its lower reaches the Patuxent flows due south, paralleling the Chesapeake Bay, and large areas of its banks are marshy and inaccessible. Much of the upper valley is being acquired by the state for a park, and development is planned to include camping, golf, hiking, canoeing and a natural zoo.

PATUXENT RIVER BRIDGES

The bridge which connects Benedict in Charles County with Hallowing Point in Calvert County, was completed as a toll bridge in 1951. The toll was lifted in 1956. The length of the bridge is 3,343 ft. and a drawbridge provides passage for vessels under 50 ft. wide. Near the mouth of the river is the 1.37 mile Thomas Johnson Bridge, opened in 1982, which connects the southernmost tip of Calvert County with St. Mary's County.

The Thomas Johnson Bridge across the Patuxent River.

PATUXENT WILDIFE REFUGE (Prince George's)

17 miles northeast of the U. S. Capitol and midway between Laurel and Bowie, fronting on the Patuxent River; the entrance is on Bowie Road. The refuge was established in 1939 by the U. S. Dept. of the Interior, who recognized that the varied conditions of the tract make it a good place to study birds, mammals and fish. The National Bird Banding Office is here, and Wildlife Review is published here. There are numerous laboratories, and a small museum of Indian artifacts. Nothing is open to the public.

PAW PAW TUNNEL (Allegany)

The only tunnel on the Chesapeake and Ohio Canal. Its three quarters of a mile length cuts off a bend of the Potomac River, which the canal follows. Completed in 1850, the tunnel was considered an engineering marvel at the time. The entrance can be reached from route 51 on the Maryland side of the bridge which connects with Paw Paw, West Virginia.

PECKTONVILLE (Washington)

18 miles west of Hagerstown and a mile north of route 40. Camp Harding Park, a small county park bordering

Licking Creek, is named for President Harding, who often camped here.

PEKIN (Allegany)

In the George's Creek Valley, north of Moscow. An ex-coal town consisting of a few houses close to the road.

PEN MAR (Washington)

Located on South Mountain at the Pennsylvania border, this community consists mainly of the left-overs of a once popular resort created by the Western Maryland Railroad in 1878; the name, of course, is a combination of Maryland and Pennsylvania. By the early 1900's there were about 100 buildings, including seven hotels and numerous cottages. Then came a fun fair, miniature railway, restaurant, theater, dance hall, etc. The mountain playground attracted families and organized outings, all hauled there by the Western Maryland Railroad.

In the 1920's the resort began to decline and the Railroad sub-leased it. It was finally closed down and most of the buildings removed in 1942, although some of the cottages remain. Recently, Washington County has acquired the site and has opened it as a park, with a reconstruction of the scenic overlook following the original plan, and a small museum containing memorabilia. Signs mark the locations of the former attractions.

PENN ALPS (Garrett)

On route 40 east of Grantsville, beside the historic Casselman bridge. The complex is a non-profit organization in the heart of Western Maryland's Amish country, devoted to Amish interests. There is a house, dating from 1818, a guesthouse and restaurant with spacious dining rooms serving Pennsylvania Dutch food, and a gift shop. On the grounds are a number of workshops manned by craftsmen, many of whom are retired, widowed, unemployed or handicapped. One of the major purposes of these workshops is the revival, preservation and teaching of early American crafts; demonstrations are given in the summer of pottery making, cabinet making, weaving, carving, etc.

PERRY HALL (Baltimore County) Pop. 13,455

11 miles northeast of downtown Baltimore. It was once called Germantown. In 1774 a tract of land was acquired by

Harry Dorsey Gough who completed a large dwelling and called it Perry Hall after a castle belonging to one of his English ancestors. It was one of the largest and most lavish mansions in Maryland, but it was partly destroyed by fire in 1824. The estate has since been whittled away, and the much diminished mansion now stands on a tract of about five acres north of route 1 at the east end of town. The town itself is today a suburb of Baltimore with many new housing developments.

PERRYMAN (Harford) Pop. 1,819

9 miles southeast of Bel Air. It was named Perrymansville by the railroad, who bought the land from the Perryman family in the 1830's. The village which developed near the station shortened the name to its present length in 1880.

Half a mile to the north is old Spesutie Church, thought to have been organized in 1671 as one of the original Anglican parishes of Maryland. The present building dates from 1851, although it is on the same foundations as an earlier church built in 1760, and contains some of its bricks. A small brick vestry house, built in 1766 remains in the churchyard. (See **SPESUTIE ISLAND**.)

PERRY POINT (Cecil)

12 miles southwest of Elkton. The name originally was applied to the point jutting out into the Chesapeake Bay opposite Havre de Grace, which was once owned by Captain Richard Perry. Today the name is applied to the U. S. Veterans' Hospital and the complex of buildings and dwellings which support it, while the point itself is named Stump Point, after the family who purchased it around 1800. The Stump family moved to Havre de Grace when the government bought the land in Feb. 1918, leaving behind them their mansion, which was converted into an officers' headquarters. It is thought, however, that the government had operations here much earlier, training cavalry mules and horses during the Civil War.

At the end of World War I, a plant at Perry Point was turning out ammonium nitrate for high explosives and employing over 5,000 people. After the armistice the area was turned over to the U. S. Public Health Service and since that time has been continually enlarged and modernized. It is now a well-known veterans' hospital, where the emphasis is on psychiatry.

PERRYVILLE (Cecil) Pop. 2,018. Incorp. 1882
  14 miles southwest of Elkton on the east bank of the Susquehanna River, opposite Havre de Grace. This has always been an important crossing point, long before the nearby rail and road bridge were built. At various times the spot was called Chesapeake, Lower Ferry, or Susquehanna, and lay on the Old Post Road (MD route 7) which now ends at the water on either side of the river. When the railroad first arrived in 1835, the cars were ferried across the river, except in the winter of 1852-3, when tracks were laid directly on the ice. The Pennsylvania Railroad opened its bridge in 1866 and replaced it with the present one in 1906. The old bridge then acquired a second deck and was used by road vehicles until it was demolished in 1943. (See **HAVRE DE GRACE**) An important freight line branches off the main line at Perryville, to follow the bank of the Susquehanna into Pennsylvania.
  A surviving relic of ferry days is the Rogers Tavern, built in 1771 and named for John Rogers (1726-91) who operated the ferry and the inn. It now belongs to the Society for the Preservation of Maryland Antiquities, who are restoring it. Many greats are known to have stayed here: Washington, of course, several times, Martha Washington, Lafayette, Rochambeau, and no doubt nearly everybody who ever crossed the river at this point.

PETERSVILLE (Frederick)
  12 miles southwest of Frederick on old route 340. In the cemetery of St. Mark's Episcopal Church (a small, somewhat derelict edifice) is a stone to the memory of Francis Thomas, governor of Maryland 1842 - 5 , bearing an inscription to the effect that he signed the decree that freed 90,000 human beings. Governor Thomas had a home nearby. There are also Claggetts in the cemetery; Bishop Claggett also lived nearby for a time.

PHOENIX (Baltimore County)
  16 miles north of downtown Baltimore in the valley of the Gunpowder Falls. Today it is just a group of older houses, but it once had a flourishing cotton factory, built in 1847. When Baltimore City purchased the town in 1914 at the time

of building the Loch Raven dam and reservoir, the factory was producing cotton duck and employed 200 people. The name of Phoenix has been given to surrounding developments and the Phoenix postoffice is at Jacksonville.

PIEDMONT
The Piedmont Province is an area of low, rolling hills running in a northeast, southwest direction, intersected by deep, narrow stream valleys, lying west of the coastal plain. The hills are composed of a complex variety of metamorphic rocks and are the roots of a much older mountain chain. In Maryland the Piedmont is about 65 miles wide near the northern border and about 40 miles wide near the southern border. The hills rise gradually to their highest point of about 900 ft. at Parr's Ridge (q.v.)

PIKESVILLE (Baltimore County) Pop. 22,545.
9 miles northwest of downtown Baltimore. The town's founder, Dr. James Smith, named it after his friend, Zebulon Pike, veteran of the War of 1812 and discoverer of Pike's Peak. Dr. Smith introduced vaccination into America and was granted the title of U. S. Agent of Vaccination.

A U. S. Arsenal was established here in 1819. The building became a Confederate soldiers' home in 1888, the only state-supported such institution outside the original Confederate States. It closed in 1933 when the last veteran died and now houses the offices of the Maryland State Police. Numerous housing development sprang up in Pikesville after World War II and the suburb is completely urbanized. Nearby Milford Industrial Park has a number of small industries.

PINDELL (Anne Arundel)
18 miles southwest of Annapolis. It was once a station on the old railroad between Washington and Chesapeake Beach but it is insignificant now.

PINECLIFF PARK (Frederick)
3 miles southeast of Frederick. This park fronting on the Monocacy River covers 95 acres, with picnicking, a boat ramp and skating and sledding in season.

PINEHURST (Anne Arundel)
16 miles southeast of downtown Baltimore on Bodkin

Neck.   One of the many former, and formless, summer resorts along the Bay shore, now a year round community with private beach.

PINEY GROVE (Allegany)
Small village on old (or scenic) route 40, three miles west of Sideling Hill Creek. A state wildlife management center is here.

PINEY POINT (St. Mary's)
12 miles southeast of Leonardtown.   The point itself projects into the Potomac River and is the spot where pilots were taken up in the days when the river was a shipping highway.   The village of Piney Point is a mile to the northwest on route 249.

The area has been a resort for many years and many eminent Washingtonians have found relaxation here in the past, including President Monroe, who had a cottage at Piney Point.   This residence was the first to acquire the title of "Summer White House."   It was swept away in a gale in 1933.

There is still a resort here, but marred by the fact that the Steuart Petroleum Co. also found Piney Point an attractive spot and erected a large marine terminal and oil storage plant here in 1950 and are planning a large new refinery, which is meeting with local opposition.

Also near here is the Harry Lundeberg School for Sea-men.   Its interest to the public lies in its collection of restored boats, including the yacht which President Kennedy used to sail, and a ferry boat which used to ply from Mount Vernon to Marshall Hall and which now houses the school library.   There is open house the first Sun. of every month, 9-4.   Piney Point lighthouse was acquired by St. Mary's County in 1980.

PINEY RUN RESERVOIR (Carroll)
12 miles south of Westminster.   This 775 acre tract contains the fairly new reservoir to supply Eldersburg and other growing communities.   Surrounding the lake is an attractive park with picnic facilities, rustic walks and other activities, and a small museum.

PINEY RUN RESERVOIR (Garrett)
Piney Dam forms the reservoir for the Frostburg water

supply which is pumped over Savage Mountain. Although the lake is at 2,400 ft. and Frostburg is at 2,200 ft. pumping is required as Savage Mountain lies between them at an elevation of 2,900 ft. There is a nature trail here.

Piney Run Reservoir, Garrett County.

PINTO (Allegany)

7 miles southwest of Cumberland. The town is really Potomac, Pinto being across the river in West Virginia, but the Pinto postoffice is here. The name is supposed to have been taken from the fact that the rider who delivered mail to the Mail Drop rode a pinto pony for many years. Nearby, beside the B. & O. tracks is a famous geologic exposure of rock.

PIONEER POINT (Queen Anne's)

5 miles northwest of Centreville. A large estate here, fronting on the Chester and Corsica Rivers, belonged to the Raskob family, who were pioneers in farm mechanization, which is how the point got its name. The 1,800 acre estate has been broken up and sold off. United Nuclear has a research facility here, and 45 acres of prime waterfront, including the two mansions, has been purchased by the Russian Embassy.

PIPE CREEK (Carroll)

Big Pipe Creek rises on Dug Hill Ridge and Little Pipe Creek rises on Parrs Ridge. They meet at the village of Detour, where they become Double Pipe Creek and enter the Monocacy a mile further down. Big Pipe Creek is notable for the number of abandoned flour mills along its length: Bachmans Mills, Union Mills, Arters Mill, Pipe Creek Mill, Wolfs Mill, Otterdale Mill, Crouse Mill and Wiley Mill, among them.

In 1863 Pipe Creek almost became another Antietam Creek, for General Meade's preliminary plan was to oppose the enemy on a line extending along Pipe Creek from Manchester to the Monocacy.

PISCATAWAY (Prince George's)

14 miles south of the U. S. Capitol. Only a few old houses remain at the junction of route 223 and Floral Rd. and the place has little significance; but it once gave its name to a wide area when Piscataway Creek was navigable to this point.

The name is Indian, and in early times Piscataway was the principal community of Indians along the Potomac; the local chief had his seat here. Leonard Calvert, leader of the Maryland colonists, visited the chief in 1634, and Piscataway was among the sites considered for a landing place. It is believed that Indians had lived in the vicinity for 14 to 18 centuries before the colonists founded the town in 1707.

Piscataway became an important stop on the post road from Annapolis to St. Mary's County and quite a social center, but its importance diminished when the river silted up and today it is an area of scattered developments.

Piscataway Park fronts along the Potomac River, on land that George Washington was very interested in preserving since it was the view he saw from Mount Vernon. He would be relieved to know that 1091 acres has been acquired between Mockley Point and Marshall Hall in order to preserve the view forever.

PITTSVILLE (Wicomico) Pop. 477. Incorp. 1945

10 miles northeast of Salisbury. It was named for William Pitts, who was president of the Wicomico and Pocomoke Railroad, when it built its line through here. The town was a strawberry center in the days when strawberry growing was important on the Eastern Shore, but its only

occupations now are small enterprises in pine bark products and ornamental iron work, and the collection of holly and evergreens in December.

PLANE NO. 4 (Frederick)

11 miles east of Frederick. Even the name has now been erased from the map, but the village was at a point where the railroad negotiated Parr's Ridge by a series of inclined planes in the early 1830's. In those days engines were not powerful enough to climb the hill; today there is a tunnel.

PLEASANT HILLS (Harford) Pop. 2,790

5 miles southwest of Bel Air. A area of new development.

PLEASANT VALLEY

There are several locations of this name in Maryland. From west to east they are: Between Hoop Pole and Backbone Mountains, southwest of Oakland, where an Amish community settled in 1864. Between Negro and Meadow Mountains, northeast of Oakland, where there is a lake, a recreation area and the forest management section of the University of Maryland. Between Evitts and Martin Mountains, 8 miles northeast of Cumberland. Between South Mountain and Elk Ridge, 20 miles southeast of Hagerstown. A tiny village on route 77, east of Smithburg. A village in Carroll County five miles northwest of Westminster.

PLUMMERS ISLAND (Montgomery)

10 miles northwest of the U. S. Capitol, in the Potomac River. Since 1901 it has been the home of the Washington Biologists' Field Club.

PLUM POINT (Calvert)

6 miles northeast of Prince Frederick. At the Point there is a small beach and a few genuine summer cottages, a breed which has almost vanished from the shores of the Chesapeake. A small fee is charged for beach and parking lot.

POCOMOKE CITY (Worcester) Pop. 3,558. Incorp. 1865.

12 miles southest of Snow Hill. This settlement beside the deep Pocomoke River was first called Stevens Landing,

then Warehouse Landing, then Meeting-House Landing, then New Town, until the present name was adopted in 1878. Since it is only five miles from the Virginia border, it was once a minor Gretna Green for eloping couples from the South, until Maryland adopted the 48 hour waiting period before the marriage ceremony in 1938.

Pocomoke City has a wide main street but few older buildings, since the business section was destroyed by fire in 1922. Several small companies make wood products and there is also a tomato cannery and a Campbell's soup factory. A 50 acre park contains a small zoo and a floating fishing pier. The town is the headquarters for the bass roundup each year.

POCOMOKE RIVER

An Eastern Shore river bordered by picturesque cypress swamps and wetland areas, very deep for its width. It starts as a narrow, meandering stream near the Delaware border and enters the Chesapeake Bay at the southern boundary of Maryland. The only two major urbanized areas along its length are Pocomoke City and Snow Hill; points of access are Pocomoke State Forest and Milburn Landing and Shad Landing State Parks. Above Pocomoke City the river is not very accessible and remains fairly undisturbed and a sanctuary for much wildlife.

POCOMOKE STATE FOREST

The forest, which extends over about 13,000 acres of swamp, forests, open meadows and tributaries, was acquired in the 1930's after it had been extensively cut over. It is being scientifically managed by the state, and its famous stands of loblolly pine, a tree which is very important in Maryland timber production, are being rejuvenated.

POCOMOKE SWAMP

The swamp borders the Pocomoke River for 30 miles, merging with salt marsh near Rehobeth, and varies from a half to two miles in width. From earliest colonial days the chief industry of the area was cutting shingles from its cypress trees. Most of the virgin timber was exhausted by 1860 and a forest fire of 1930 destroyed the remainder, including the buried peat, although a few stands of bald cypress, white cedar, sweetbay and other trees remain. Rare plants can also be found.

The swamp is a legendary place. It is said to have concealed Tories during the Revolution, slaves prior to the Civil War and hundreds of deserters and southern sympathizers during the Civil War. It supported its refugees with game and fish and supplied timber for their crude shacks.

POINT LOOKOUT (St. Mary's)

The southernmost tip of Maryland west of the Chesapeake Bay on a peninsula between the Bay and the mouth of the Potomac River. It was originally named St. Michael's Point by Leonard Calvert, Maryland's first governor.

A large hospital was erected here in 1862, which became a notorious prison for captured Confederates after the Battle of Gettysburg. Of the over 20,000 prisoners held here, it is estimated that 3,384 died. A monument three miles north of the point on route 5, erected jointly by the Federal Government and the State of Maryland, commemorates the dead. One of the prisoners was the poet Sidney Lanier, who survived the ordeal.

After the Civil War the prison buildings were dismantled. The tip of Point Lookout is still a government facility, but now it is a U. S. Coastguard Reservation, and an important lighthouse marks the mouth of the Potomac. There are also 700 acres of State Park fronting on the Potomac and on the Bay, where visitors can picnic, fish and swim.

Four miles to the north, Point Look-In projects into the Bay and three miles above that is Point No Point, so called because it appears to be a point until you reach it, when it seems to disappear.

POINT NO POINT (Dorchester)

In addition to the above, there is a marsh of this name in a bend of the Nanticoke River 16 miles southeast of Cambridge. Another Point No Point is a projection into Fishing Bay on an unapproachable marsh 16 miles south of Cambridge. The land is so low that one can understand that the points would disappear.

POINT OF ROCKS (Frederick)

12 miles south of Frederick where Catoctin Mountain reaches the Potomac. The first house was built here by George Snouffer in the early 1700's; the village, called Trummelstown in its early days, was about a mile from its present location. The rock point for which the town is

named was destroyed during the building of the present road bridge over the Potomac.

The most notable building in Point of Rocks is the railroad station, a gem described by the National Register of Historic Places as Gothic Revival, and still used by a single weekday commuter train in each direction. Just east of the station is Washington Junction, where the two lines of the B. & O. Railroad, which diverge at Glyndon, meet again. East of the station Catoctin Mountain is penetrated by a tunnel.

It is said that more Civil War skirmishes took place around here than in any other place in Maryland. It is also said that General Meade received his command of the Army of the Potomac from Lincoln at the railroad telegraph office here.

There are several exposures of the unusual "calico marble" in the vicinity and also a fine exposure of the Catoctin greenstone. There is said to be a warehouse made of the original B. & O. rails.

POINT PATIENCE (Calvert)

15 miles southeast of Prince Frederick and 2 miles from the tip of Calvert County. It is a hook of land protruding into the Patuxent River, which narrows the channel and causes the river to be very deep here, with a strong current. Some think the name was given to the point as sailing vessels required patience to round it.

The point is part of a naval reservation. Mines were tested here and in 1942 landing craft practised here, as the cliff area was thought to resemble the Normandy beaches. The new Patuxent River bridge took advantage of this projection and of Town Point in St. Mary's County

POMFRET (Charles)

4 miles northwest of La Plata. At this place lived Maurice James McDonough, an itinerant peddler, who made enough money to leave a bequest for founding a school for children at La Plata. It was the only high school in Charles County until 1924. McDonough would have liked to know that the Charles County Community College is now located at Pomfret.

Pomfret Siding is two miles to the northwest on the U. S. Government Railroad leading to Indian Head.

POMONKEY (Charles)

8 miles northwest of La Plata. Until recently a small industry produced small wooden objects from the local gum trees. Nearby is the Maryland Airport, which serves Southern Maryland, with private planes for transport or crop dusting. Pomonkey Landing is a deserted spot two miles to the northwest, where Pomonkey Creek enters the Potomac.

POOLESVILLE (Montgomery) Pop. 3,428. Incorp. 1867.

18 miles west of Rockville. The first house was erected here in 1793 by John Poole; built of logs, it is still standing on Fisher Ave., renovated and protected by a local preservation group and used as a store selling old-time commodoities.

In spite of three serious fires, several houses dating from the late 1700's and early 1800's still stand, together with the picturesque old town hall on the village square. Poolesville saw a great deal of Civil War activity, perhaps more than any other town in Maryland, except Sharpsburg. It was frequently occupied by Federal troops and occasionally by Confederates; skirmishes, raids, advances and retreats took place in its neighborhood.

Extensive development is taking place in the region, but the village itself is on the National Register of Historic Places and has the attention of conservationists. A leaflet describing a walking tour is available locally, or from Sugarloaf Regional Trails, Box 87, Stronghold, Dickerson, MD

Poolesville.   John Poole's house.

POPE'S CREEK (Charles)

9 miles south of La Plata. The "Pope's Creek Branch" of the Baltimore and Potomac Railroad reached here in 1872. Since the railroad company was prohibited from entering Washington, D. C. with a main line, they built the "main line" to Pope's Creek, and entered Washington on a branch line. There was some talk of continuing the line across the Potomac, but it was never done. A derelict power house near the water and a broken railroad wharf are all that remain, apart from the three "Crab Houses" that keep Pope's Creek on the map. These restaurants are built on piles over the water and specialize in steamed crabs, a delicacy for which Maryland is famous. In the summer they attract hoards of visitors, mainly from the Washington area. Three miles downstream is the Potomac River Bridge (q.v.) which can be clearly seen from here.

POPE'S FREEHOLD (St. Mary's)

A scenic overlook just north of St., Mary's City. There is a small garden of local interest, where excavations have been carried out.

POPLAR ISLANDS (Talbot)

Three small islands in the Chesapeake Bay, two miles west of the Tilghman Island peninsula. Once they were a single island named Poplin's or Popeley's Island, but owing to the general subsidence of the area, it became divided by the encroaching waters and is now three small islands named Poplar, Jefferson and Coaches.

The first settlers, Richard Thompson and his family, were murdered by Indians. There is a story that in 1847, Charles Carroll, grandson of Charles Carroll of Carrollton, began to raise black cats here, in order to sell their pelts to China. However, the cold winter of that year caused an ice bridge to form to the mainland, along which the cats all escaped.

More recently there was a club on Jefferson Island, which was visited by Presidents Roosevelt and Truman. It burned in 1950 and was not replaced. Today the islands belong to the Smithsonian Institute whose members conduct bird watches to study osprey and the great blue heron. They are uninhabited and still shrinking.

POPLAR SPRINGS (Howard)

18 miles northwest of Ellicott City. The spring still exists on Watersville Road near the town, and is marked; the poplars, however, have fallen. A roadside tavern was opened when the turnpike road was completed through here and the village became a summer resort of a kind. It is now a backwater on route 144, by-passed by the main road.

PORT DEPOSIT (Cecil) Pop. 906. Incorp. 1824.

15 miles west of Elkton. The town consists mainly of one long, picturesque street squeezed between the Susquehanna River and the high granite bluff which borders it. The name was adopted around 1813 in the days when this was the highest navigable point on the river and goods were deposited here from boats to be transferred to wagons and canal rafts, or vice versa. Previously the area had been called The Upper Ferry, or Creswell's Ferry, for it was an important crossing point to Lapidum on the other side of the Susquehanna.

Port Deposit remains largely unspoilt -- there is no room for development. The houses lining the main street, the little square and the single side street are of different sizes, shapes and materials. The bluffs have been terraced and stairways lead to the top. Adams Hall of the old Tome Institute is now the Town Hall but the Institute's Washington Hall, which used to add dignity to the street, has been razed (except for its granite doorway) and is a cinder-covered parking lot. The school continued at Bainbridge until 1971 when the remnant was moved to Northeast, where some of the relics from the school on the hill found a new home. (See **BAINBRIDGE NAVAL CENTER.**)

The main industry of the town today is Wiley's Manufacturing, which employs 350-400 people and makes heavy steel products, including tunnel tubes, much of it for overseas. Some other small fatories produce explosives, while nearby Mount Ararat Farms employs 45 in dairying.

Adjoining the town to the north is the village of Rock Run (q.v.) Also at this point is a large granite quarry, which was first opened in 1829 by the proprietors of the Maryland Canal (q.v.) The stone's distinctive appearance -- grey with short parallel black lines -- can be easily recognized in buildings in Baltimore and elsewhere, but it has been little used since 1942.

Port Deposit. The Town Hall.

PORT REPUBLIC (Calvert)

4 miles southeast of Prince Frederick. A mile to the southwest is Christ Protestant Episcopal Church, where Maryland's oldest jousting tournament is held on the last Saturday in August. The present church was erected in 1769 on an older site, and has a biblical garden.

PORT TOBACCO (Charles)

3 miles southwest of La Plata. This romantic spot is the remnant of a once thriving deep water tobacco port on the Port Tobacco River, five miles from its junction with the Potomac. It was originally called Chandler's Town, after its first white settler, Job Chandler; the name was changed to Charles Town in 1729 and to Port Tobacco in 1821. The name is doubly apt, for an Indian village of Potobac had been inhabited here for many years, as Captain John Smith found when he visited the vicinity in 1608. Father Andrew White, the Jesuit priest who accompanied the Maryland colonists in the 1630's lived among these Indians for some years, convert- ed the Indian Queen to Christianity and compiled the first dictionary, catechism and grammar of the Indian language.

Soon after its founding, Port Tobacco became a very

busy tobacco seaport, able to accomodate deep water vessels serving distant ports.   It became the county seat when Charles County was created in 1658 and a new courthouse, the one of which a remnant remains, was built in 1821.   The town was a principal stop on the stage route between Philadelphia and the South and the center of social and commercial life of Southern Maryland.   George Washington visited here many times.

With the siltation of the river, the town's importance declined, and the coming of the railroad in 1872 sealed its doom by taking a route through La Plata and by-passing the old port.   A fire destroyed the courthouse in 1895, the same year in which the county seat was moved to La Plata.

Port Tobacco was re-discovered in the 1960's when a group of citizens became interested in salvaging the few remains.   The town originally had a public square around which were the courthouse, Christ Episcopal Church (which was removed to La Plata,) stores, hotels, etc.   Nothing remains except one wing of the courthouse, built 1819-21, and two 18th century houses, all of which have been acquired by the Society for the Restoration of Port Tobacco.

POTOMAC (Montgomery)
5 miles southwest of Rockville.   Although the village is several miles from the banks of the Potomac River, it was probably the nearest village to the river when the numerous locks around the Great Falls of the Potomac were being constructed on the C. & O. Canal.   The area is undergoing rapid residential development, particularly with the type of dwelling that goes with the Hunt Club and the Polo Club, which flourish here.   Its   suburb, North Potomac, has a population of 12,546

POTOMAC HEIGHTS (Charles) Pop. 2,456
10 miles northwest of La Plata.   A residential town close to Indian Head.

POTOMAC PARK (Allegany)   Pop. with Bowling Green, 2,275.   3 and 4 miles southwest of Cumberland.   Two fairly large housing developments on route 220.

POTOMAC RIVER
The Potomac River's two branches, the North Branch

and the South Branch, unite eighteen miles below Cumberland. To this point the South Branch is 133 miles long and the North Branch is 97 miles long; together they continue another 285 miles to the Chesapeake Bay. The low water mark of the southern bank of the Potomac and its North Branch marks Maryland's southern boundary. The source of the North Branch marks the southwest corner of the state, although the original marker, the Fairfax Stone, now lies in West Virginia and the accepted boundary marker is a short distance away. (See **KEMPTON**)

Continuing a winding course eastwards and southeastwards, the North Branch cuts deep gorges through the ridges, picking up acid drainage from old worked-out coal mines and untreated sewage from small mining villages. After its junction with the South Branch, it continues its course across the Great Valley and through the Blue Ridge and becomes sufficiently cleansed by the time it reaches Great Falls to serve as Washington's drinking water. Below the Capital it becomes polluted again, but plans are under way to improve the treatment of Washington's sewage and purify the water sufficiently to make it safe for swimming near the city. Below Washington the river turns sharply south and gradually broadens until at its mouth it is over two miles wide.

POTOMAC RIVER BRIDGE

11 miles south of La Plata. Its correct name is the Governor Harry W. Nice Memorial Bridge; Mr. Nice was governor of Maryland 1935-39. The bridge was opened in 1940 at the approximate site of one of the eighteenth century ferries across the Potomac called Ludlow's Ferry. At the same time improvements were made to route 301, making north-south travel possible directly from Baltimore. The bridge has no drawbridge, but the 135 ft. clearance is ample for navigation.

The Morgantown Generating Station with its huge twin chimneys is nearby. Its ash collectors are said to be 99.5% efficient.

POTOMAC STATE FOREST (Garrett)

12,400 acres of rugged mountainous forest with numerous streams; it borders on the Potomac and reaches up the valley of the South Prong of Lostland Run. There are some hunting areas and primitive camping.

POTOMAC VALLEY (Montgomery)　Pop. 5,094
A new development near Potomac.

PRESTON (Caroline) Pop. 509. Incorp. 1892.
13 miles southwest of Denton. The town was called Snow Hill when it was founded in 1845, but owing to the presence of a more important Snow Hill in Worcester County, the name was changed in 1856 to that of Preston, a Baltimore lawyer. The railroad reached here in 1890, but has been abandoned for many years. There is a tomato processing plant here and also a brokerage house for canners for the whole Eastern Shore district, although canning is a diminishing industry.

PRETTYBOY DAM AND RESERVOIR (Baltimore County)
The dam is on the Gunpowder Falls 23 miles north of downtown Baltimore. It is 140 ft. high, creating a reservoir which stretches for about five miles and acts as a feeder for Loch Raven Reservoir further down stream (q.v.) Steps lead from the parking area to the vicinity of the dam and there are trails through the state park on either side of the valley below the dam. The name is said to come from that of a horse.

PRICEVILLE (Baltimore County)
18 miles northwest of downtown Baltimore. The name of Quaker Bottom Road reveals that the area was settled by Quakers, who built the village and named it after Mordecai Price, a landowner. Little remains of any early habitation here, but it is believed that many of the surrounding farmers are still Quakers.

PRINCE FREDERICK. (County seat of Calvert County. Pop. 1,805
The town was originally called Old Fields and its site was chosen because it connected the north-south road with the road from the old county seat at Calverton (See **PRISON POINT**) Prince Frederick became the seat of Calvert County in 1722 and was named for the eldest son of George I. It was burnt by the British in 1812 and the whole town was destroyed again by fire in 1882. The present courthouse, the fifth on the site, was erected in 1916 and remodelled in 1948.

The construction of the Calvert Cliffs Nuclear Power Station at Lusby, the improvement of route 4 and the opening of the new Patuxent River Bridge at the southern tip of the Calvert County peninsula have all contributed to some population increase.   But in spite of its increased accessibility, the town retains much of the conservatism that it acquired when the county was isolated from the rest of the state.   A small shopping center and some new homes surround the nucleus of the town but there is no industry to speak of.

PRINCE GEORGE'S COUNTY. County seat: Upper Marlboro. Pop. 665,071. Area: 479 square miles.

Prince George's County was formed in 1695 and named after Prince George of Denmark, husband of Queen Anne. It is bounded on the east by the Patuxent River; on the west by the Potomac River; on the northwest by a line from Rocky Gorge Reservoir on the Patuxent to the mouth of Rock Creek on the Potomac (except for the portion cut off by the District of Columbia; and on the south by an irregular line from a point on the Patuxent to a point on the Potomac opposite Mount Vernon.

Over 90% of the residents live in the district of Columbia Metropolitan Area; there are large residential developments adjacent to Washington, which have given Prince George's County by far the largest recent population growth of any Maryland county.

Geographically, the county is almost entirely on the coastal plain. Manufacturing is important and there are several large federal installations, including Andrew's Air Force Base, and the National Agricultural Center at Beltsville. But the eastern and southern parts of the county are still basically rural, tobacco, corn, grains and nursery stock being the main crops.

The University of Maryland is located at College Park (q.v.) which is also an area of dense population. The county seat of Upper Marlboro, however, is a small town somewhat removed from the centers of population. For this reason, the county library and a number of county offices are situated in Hyattsville, near College Park.

PRINCESS ANNE.   County seat of Somerset County. Pop. 1,499. Incorp. 1867.

The town was named after the daughter of King George II of England and laid out on the Manokin River in 1733. It became the seat of Somerset County in 1742 after Worcester County was established, making the old courthouse at Dividing Creek (q.v.) too far from the center of the county. In those days the Manokin River was navigable for ocean-going vessels and Princess Anne was an active port.

The town lies in the center of what has always been a conservatively minded area. There was strong opposition to Independence, and in the early days of the Revolution, Tory groups were active here, until Brigadier Wm. Smallwood arrived in 1777 to put an end to such matters and to arrest the ringleaders.

The present courthouse dates from 1904 and is the third on the site, but there are a number of older buildings in the town. Manokin Presbyterian Church, founded by Francis Makemie, a Scotch-Irishman, was built in 1765 on the site of a church erected before 1692 (See **REHOBETH.**) St. Andrews Episcopal Church was built in 1770, evidently to cater to Scots who were not Presbyterians.

The Teackle Mansion was designed after a Scottish house in 1801 by Littleton Dennis Teackle, an associate of Thomas Jefferson, and now belongs to the Somerset County Historical Society; it is open Sundays, 2-4. The mansion, the town, and the surrounding countryside were the locales for *The Entailed Hat* by George A. Townsend, which gives excellent descriptions of the physical features and romantic aspects of the Eastern Shore.

The Washington Hotel on Somerset Ave. two doors from the courthouse, was built in the late 18th century and has been in continuous use as an inn. George Washington and several Maryland governors have stayed here.

Princess Anne.   The Washington Hotel.

Across the railroad tracks stands the University of Maryland, Eastern Shore (UMES.) Founded by Methodists in 1886, it has over 1,000 students, predominantly black; but some integration has taken place and the University at College Park is considering re-organization of this campus.

There are a few industries in town including a tomato cannery and a small oyster packing house. "Old Princess Anne Days" have been held in October for the last twenty years or so, and thousands of visitors are attracted for touring the old town and its homes.

PRINCIPIO FURNACE (Cecil)

11 miles southwest of Elkton on the Old Post Rd. from Baltimore to Philadelphia (route 7) Although there is little to see, the furnace was one of the foremost in production of pig iron from 1724 to 1780. Among the many who had a financial interest in the company at different times were George Washington's father and half brother.

The first iron furnace in colonial Maryland was built on this site in 1722 by Joseph Farmer, an iron-master from England, and production was started two years later by John England. Ore was at first obtained from local ore banks and later from the ore banks in the Baltimore region and even further afield.

The Principio Company came to an end in 1780, but the furnace was soon re-built and continued its production of cannons, cannonballs and guns until destroyed by the British in May, 1813. Once again it arose and in 1836 was sold to George P. Whitaker and others. After Whitaker's death in 1890, it became part of the Whitaker Iron Co. of Wheeling, West Va. and continued to operate in melting scrap until shortly after World War I. The present furnace remnant, which is on private land, is the third or fourth on the site and is listed on the National Register of Historic Places. The Whitaker lands are 4,500 acres on both sides of I 95, still owned by the company, but managed by the state. Five miles to the north, on Principio Creek, is a village of the same name.

PRISON POINT (Calvert)

7 miles southwest of Prince Frederick on a point of land where Battle Creek enters the Patuxent. Although there is nothing to be seen here now, a town was laid out on this spot in the mid-17th century, which became the seat of Calvert County, and remained as such until 1725, when the county seat was moved to Prince Frederick. Robert Brooke, who laid out the town, called it Battle Town (See **BATTLE CREEK;**) later it was named Calvert Town, or Calverton.

By 1814 there was very little left of the place, and what remained was destroyed by the British and never re-built. During the Civil War, the Union forces established a military camp, arsenal and prison for Confederates here, which may be the reason for its present name. Roger B. Taney was born at an estate on a nearby hill overlooking the site.

PROVIDENCE (Cecil)

6 miles northwest of Elkton. Providence must have abandoned the town, for recently a high proportion of the inhabitants discovered that they were suffering from a chemical related illness, owing to the dumping of chemical wastes in a disused quarry nearby.

PUMPHREY (Anne Arundel) Pop. 5,666

5 miles southwest of Baltimore. A community of individual homes on both sides of Old Annapolis Road, inhabited by black residents. Their ancestors were brought here to work the strawberry plantation, and much of the land on which they had their shacks was later deeded to them.

PURSE (Charles)

16 miles southwest of La Plata.   148 acres fronting on the Potomac River and undergoing development for public boating, fishing, etc.

QUAKER NECK (Kent)

5 miles south of Chestertown on the Chester River. The county has a public beach here and there are boats for hire at the old steamboat landing.

QUANTICO (Wicomico)

7 miles west of Salisbury. The town was established before the Revolution and took its name from Quantico Creek, which is supposed to be Indian for Dancing Place. There is a cannery near here.

QUEEN ANNE (Queen Anne's) Pop. 292. Incorp. 1953.

10 miles southeast of Centreville. Although it is considered to be in Queen Anne's County, the village lies partly in Talbot County and is close to the border of Caroline County. It was named after the Queen of England and must have been an important spot at one time, as many roads radiate from it. There is a cannery in the vicinity.

Queen Anne. Statue outside the courthouse at Centreville.

QUEEN ANNE'S COUNTY County seat: Centreville. Pop. 25,508. Area: 363 square miles.

Queen Anne's County was formed in 1706 and named after the Queen of England. It is bounded on the north by the Chester River; on the east by the Delaware boundary; on the south and southeast by various streams and inlets; and on the west by the Chesapeake Bay.

The terrain is flat and sandy and the shoreline greatly indented. Although the Chesapeake Bay Bridge now disgorges large numbers of people into the county, which has given rise to a number of housing developments and businesses near the bridge approaches, the county is still basically agricultural. Corn, grains and soybeans are grown, cattle and hogs are raised and there are numerous centers for crabbing, fishing and oystering.

QUEENSTOWN (Queen Anne's) Pop. 387. Incorp. 1892.

6 miles southwest of Centreville. It was named for the Queen of England and became the first county seat of Queen Anne's County until the seat was moved to Centreville in

1782.   A court house was erected in 1710, enlarged in 1749, and is now being restored.   Queenstown is beside an inlet of the Chester River and once had a harbor, which the British thought was a sufficiently important shipping point to be worth harrassing in 1813.   Later the town became a junction for the Eastern Shore railroads.   A cannery here employs 400.

QUIRAUK MOUNTAIN (Washington)

A knob of South Mountain 2 miles below the Pennsylvania border, whose rocky top interests geologists.   There is an army transmission tower and also a microwave relay tower on its summit.

RANDALLSTOWN (Baltimore County) Pop. 25,927
11 miles northwest of downtown Baltimore. It was named for Thomas and Christopher Randall from England, who purchased land here in the early 18th century. It is an area of rapid suburban growth.

RAVEN ROCK (Washington)
11 miles northeast of Hagerstown on the summit of South Mountain. It was formerly a tourist resort and in 1841 a monument to President Harding was started on the summit, but it was never completed.

RAWLINGS (Allegany)
11 miles southwest of Cumberland. This place at the foot of Fort Hill was named for Col. Moses Rawlings (d.1809) who commanded a Maryland rifle regiment in 1776 and was later in charge of Fort Frederick. His children were among the first to settle in this part of the county. Daniel Cresap also lived here for a time.

RAYVILLE (Baltimore County)
25 miles north of downtown Baltimore and named for the Rays, who were early landowners. It is said that this used to be orchard country and there were a number of cider presses here.

RECKORD (Baltimore County)
17 miles northeast of downtown Baltimore, where Harford Road crosses Little Gunpowder Falls. It was named after Henry Reckord, born in Maine in 1825, who is said to have opened the first nail factory in his home state. When he came to Baltimore County in 1860, he erected grist and saw mills here, and a mill which ground bones for fertilizer. No trace of these operations remains today.

REDHOUSE (Garrett)

8 miles southwest of Oakland, where route 50 makes a brief appearance in the extreme southwest corner of the state. It was named for a red-painted inn, built in the early 1830's by Joseph Tomlinson, a member of a prominent local land-owning family. When the inn was taken down after 1877, the timber was used in building a dwelling, which was dismantled in 1939 - 40. The material may be incorporated into another house in the area. There is a rustic restaurant at the cross roads.

REHOBETH (Somerset)

11 miles south of Princess Anne along the banks of the Pocomoke River. It was named after the plantation on which it was built and is the only survivor in Somerset County of a number of towns which were directed to be laid out in 1668.

Historians generally regard the area as the cradle of American Presbyterianism, since the father of American Presbyterianism, Francis Makemie, built the first Presbyterian Church in America here in 1705-6; the church still stands, its exterior unaltered. Makemie was a Scotch-Irish immigrant who stayed in Maryland several times during his wanderings, in 1683, 1690 and from 1698 until his death.

Two hundred yards away are the ruins of Coventry Episcopal Church, which was built in the mid-18th century. Near the ruins can be traced the foundations of an earlier church, and some early gravestones.

REISTERSTOWN (Baltimore County)   Pop. 19,385.

17 miles northwest of downtown Baltimore. It was named for John Reister (c.1715) who came to Pennsylvania from Germany and settled at this spot in 1758. Two years later he bought land at the fork in the road, which even then was an important junction, and built an inn. Several old homes along the main road date from this period, notably nos. 234, 202 and 410, which belonged to the Reister family and their descendants. Today some of the old dwellings house antique dealers.

In the old cemetery on Cockey's Mill Road are buried a son, Philip Reister, and other early settlers. Also on Cockey's Mill Road is a brick building which was once the Franklin Academy, founded 1820 by act of the General Assembly. It became a public school in 1849 and has housed the Reisterstown Public Library since 1961.

RELAY (Baltimore County)

7 miles southwest of downtown Baltimore. The name was given in the days when the Baltimore and Ohio Railroad changed their teams of horses at this point, before the introduction of steam locomotives.

When the Thomas Viaduct (q.v.) was opened in 1835, Relay became an important railroad junction at the point where the old line led to the west and the new line led to Washington. A large station and hotel were erected at the junction, but nothing whatever remains of either, except a densely weeded patch of ground and an historical marker. The junction was guarded by Federal troops in 1861 and a cannon was stationed on the heights overlooking it.

The surrounding area is one of older individual homes and little recent development. Samuel Morse lived here briefly while the telegraph wires were being strung along the B.& O tracks. On Washington Boulevard is a large distillery, once the home of a local brand of rye but now owned by Seagram.

RELIANCE (Caroline)

18 miles south of Denton at a point where the boundaries of Caroline and Dorchester Counties meet at the Delaware border. Formerly it was called Johnson's Crossroads, but it was renamed in 1882, because the name Johnson had become notorious.

Joe Johnson, for whom the crossroads was named, was the son-in-law of a sinister character named Patty Cannon, kidnapper, robber, murderess and slave trader, who owned a house and inn here. Her main occupation was kidnapping free negroes whom, with Johnson's aid, she collected in the attic of her steep-roofed house while awaiting shipment to the South. Her name is immortalized in *The Entailed Hat* by George A. Townsend. Since the state line ran through Patty Cannon's house, the combined efforts of the Maryland and Delaware authorities were needed to arrest here.

Her dwelling is gone, but the inn still stands, although there seems to be a difference of opinion as to whether it is the original or one built to the same design in 1885 from the original materials. Patty Cannon committed suicide in the jail at Georgetown, Delaware, after confessing to at least nine murders. The inn today houses an interior decorator.

REMINGTON FARMS (Kent County)

10 miles west of Chestertown off route 20. This 3,000

acre estate formerly belonged to the aviator Glenn Martin. It is now operated by the Remington Arms Co. in co-operation with the Maryland Game and Inland Fish Commission. Common and rare waterfowl are protected and the estate is open to visitors Feb. 1 to Oct. 10.

RHODESDALE (Dorchester)

13 miles northeast of Cambridge. When the railroad built a station here they named it for the largest land holder, Richard E. Rhodes. There are two tomato canneries here.

RICHARDS OAK (Cecil)

16 miles northwest of Elkton. The oak tree stands beside route 1 and has been preserved because it is believed to be the tree under which Lafayette and his troops camped in 1781 during their march from Elkton to the Susquehanna River crossing at Bald Friar. It is sometimes called Lafayette Oak. A marker near the tree states the the age of the tree is believed to be over 500 years. It is now cared for by the Cecil County Historical Society.

RIDGE AND VALLEY PROVINCE

The series of northeasterly, southwesterly trending ridges which lie between The Great Valley and the Appalachian Plateau. Travelling westward on route I 70, one traverses the ridges of Sideling Hill, Town Hill, Green Ridge, Warrior Mountain, Martin Mountain and Wills Mountain. They are all of a fairly consistent height and the valleys between them carry streams which run southward into the Potomac.

Ridge and Valley Province.

RIDGEVILLE (Carroll)

17 miles southwest of Westminster. It is named for its elevated position on Parrs Ridge. In 1966 it was assimilated into Mount Airy, and like that town it lies partly in Carroll and partly in Frederick Counties. A unit of the Army of the Potomac assembled here in 1863.

RINGGOLD (Washington)

9 miles northeast of Hagerstown and a mile south of the Pennsylvania border. The village was settled in 1825 by John Creager, and originally called Ridgeville, as it sits on a small ridge.   In 1850 it was re-named for Major Samuel Ringgold, who was killed in battle in 1846; Major Ringgold was the inventor of the McClellan saddle, which was later used by the army during World War I.   In the village is the only church in Maryland of the River brethren, or Brethren in Christ, built in 1871.

RISING SUN (Cecil) Pop. 1160

15 miles northwest of Elkton. It was formerly named Summerhill or Summer Hill but the present name is taken from a popular hotel which once stood by the road. (See **HARRISVILLE**.) Most of the town was built after 1866 when a small railroad line was constructed through the town, branching from the line which runs along the Susquehanna Valley. This branch line has long been defunct. Small factories produce men's work clothes and meat products. Nearby is Richards Oak (q.v.)

RIVERDALE (Prince George's)   Pop. 4,748.   Incorp. 1920. Pop. of East Riverdale: 14,117.

6 miles northeast of the U. S. Capitol. This is an older suburb of Washington, but it has a point of interest in the Calvert Mansion at 4811 Riverdale Rd.   This imposing mansion named Riversdale (confusing) was built in 1799 for the wife of George Calvert, a relative of the last Lord Baltimore, by her Belgian father. George Calvert founded the University of Maryland on part of his estate nearby.

From this mansion the first successful telegraph message was sent -- the B. & O. Railroad tracks are only a short distance from the house. Behind the house stands a cannon which is thought to have been brought over in the Ark and the Dove, the ships that brought the first colonists to

Maryland. The Calvert house now belongs to Prince George's County and houses the County Legislative Offices. Some of the Calverts are buried in the graveyard of Riverdale Presbyterian Church.

RIVERDALE HEIGHTS. Pop. with EAST PINES 8,941.

6 miles northeast of the U. S. Capitol. It is a more recent development than Riverdale and is separated from it by the Northeast Branch of the Anacostia River.

RIVERSIDE (Charles)

13 miles southwest of La Plata. A desolate spot on the Potomac River in a seldom-visited corner of Maryland. There is a small seafood industry here.

RIVIERA BEACH (Anne Arundel) Pop. 8,812

11 miles southeast of downtown Baltimore. It fronts on the Patapsco estuary and like so many other waterfront colonies started as a summer vacation spot. Since the Bay Bridge made access to the Atlantic beaches easier, the houses have become permanent dwellings and the beaches private.

ROCKAWALKIN (Wicomico)

4 miles northwest of Salisbury. Nothing much is at this location except the name, which is surely enough. Interpretations have ranged from the utterance of a town drunk, to the name of a sacred Indian stone.

ROCK CREEK

Rock Creek has its sources near Laytonsville; it flows through the north suburbs of Washington and enters the Potomac at Georgetown. Its mouth was formerly a boundary point between Montgomery and Prince George's Counties before Washington, D. C. was laid out. The valley of Rock Creek is a park for most of its length, very popular with Washingtonians.

ROCK HALL (Kent) Pop. 1,511. Incorp. 1908.

10 miles southwest of Chestertown. Rock Hall once enjoyed a position of far more importance than it does today, for an important ferry plied from here to Annapolis, providing a link in a main post road from north to south. The ferry lasted well into the steamboat age, and ships from

Baltimore continued to call here until the 1930's.

Many historical figures crossed the ferry, some of the more notable being George Washington, many times, and Tench Tilghman, in October, 1781, as he was taking the news of the surrender at Yorktown to the Continental Congress in Philadelphia. In the cemetery of St. Paul's Episcopal Church nearby is buried Tilghman's father; he and several of his brothers were staunch loyalists.

Rock Hall today is a popular boating and fishing center. It has a genuine harbor and a bona fide seafood trade with picturesque wharves with wholesale and retail seafood houses. The watermen fear for its future however; since the Army Corps of Engineers rebuilt the jetties and upgraded the harbor in 1981, more and larger pleasure craft have been docking in this convenient location, and new marinas are crowding out the boats of those who fish for a livelihood.

There is a small museum in the Municipal Building on S. Main St., open Fri. to Sun. 2 - 4 p.m. See also (**EASTERN NECK.**)

Rock Hall waterfront.

ROCK HALL (Frederick)
12 miles southwest of Frederick. A tiny settlement near Point of Rocks, once called Wood Land.

ROCKLAND (Baltimore County)
8 miles northwest of downtown Baltimore. The group of stone houses was originally built to house workers from

Rockland Mill on the southwest corner of the intersection of Falls Road and Old Court Road. Rockland Farm, which owns the village, is on the west side of Old Court Road. The houses have recently been refurbished.

ROCK POINT (Charles)

19 miles southwest of La Plata, fronting on the Wicomico River near its junction with the Potomac. It is said to be named for the rockfish, or striped bass, Maryland's state fish, now becoming dangerously depleted. The town was founded in the 18th century and was once a seafood industry center and had a large hotel. During the Civil War it was always occupied by Union troops.

ROCK RUN (Cecil)

16 miles west of Elkton. It adjoins the north end of Port Deposit and faces a stream and mill of the same name on the opposite bank of the Susquehanna. The area was once called the Upper Ferry before a bridge was built across the river at this point in 1818. The bridge was destroyed by fire five years later, ignited, it was thought, by sparks from an iron shod sleigh. Another bridge was built in 1829-30 and suffered another mishap in 1854 when a span was broken by a drove of cattle. It was never repaired and a flood finished it off in 1857; the massive stone piers can still be seen. Rock Run Mill, built about 1725 is here, open to visitors on weekend afternoons in summer.

Rock Run Mill, Cecil County.

..JN (Harford)

..ock Run is a stream that enters the Susquehanna six ..iiles from its mouth opposite the village of Rock Run on the Cecil County side (see above.) The state acquired a stretch of land beside the river in 1965, including the old bridge toll house, and the remains of a mill, built in 1794, with a large, impressive wheel. The mill has been put into working order and is open to visitors.

ROCK SPRINGS (Cecil)

19 miles northwest of Elkton. An old inn remains here dating from the time when route 22 was a wagon road from Pennsylvania to Port Deposit.

ROCKS STATE PARK (Harford)

8 miles northwest of Bel Air where Deer Creek cuts its way through rocky outcrops. A unique rock formation known as King and Queen Seat provides a fine view of the stream valley but is quite dangerous for children. The name of this point is supposed to come from an Indian legend.

The old Maryland and Pennsylvania Railroad once had a stop here, but nothing remains except traces of the bridge. There are picnic tables at several locations, hiking and fishing, and a museum called Stoneywood Nature Center, which has a display of Indian artifacts and other specimens found in the area.

ROCKVILLE. County Seat of Montgomery County. Pop. 43,811. Incorp. 1860.

Rockville started life as a tavern on the road between Georgetown and Frederick. It achieved some fame as Hungerford's Tavern, when a group of local citizens met at the tavern, then kept by Charles Hungerford, on June 11, 1774, in order to issue resolves to break off commerce with Britain. The tavern was demolished in 1913, but the site is marked on South Washington St.

The little town of Hungerford's Tavern was chosen as the county seat when Montgomery County was formed in 1776, and the name was changed to Montgomery Courthouse. Ten years later it was re-named Williamsburg, after a local developer; the present name, of uncertain origin, was bestowed in 1803.

Union and Confederate forces both occupied the town

during the Civil War. In 1873 the B. & O. Railroad put the town within easy train travel from Washington; many vacation homes were built and several large hotels, one of which, the former Woodlawn, still stands at 500 W. Montgomery Ave. It has been used as a private sanitarium since 1908.

In 1930 the population was still under 2,000. Now it is growing so rapidly that statistics are soon out of date. The U. S. Department of Health, Education and Welfare has a large office complex here, and in all, 40% of Rockville's population are estimated to work for the Federal Government. Another large section works for the numerous research and development industries in the area, or the companies involved in communications equipment, printing and publishing.

The commercial center of Rockville was nearly all demolished in the early 1970's to make way for a large new shopping center, which, when last heard of, was a failure. What remains of the older streets has been declared an Historic Preservation District by the City Council. Interesting buildings are: The third courthouse of 1891, which still stands near the present courthouse of 1931; the B. & O. Railroad station, which has been placed on the National Register of Historic Places; the Beall-Dawson House, headquarters of the Montgomery County Historical Society, open Tues. thru Sat. 12-4. In the Catholic cemetery is the grave of the author F. Scott Fitzgerald and his wife, who were recently re-interred here.

An organization called Peerless Rockville Historic Preservation Ltd. has issued a walking guide of the town.

ROCKY GAP STATE PARK (Allegany)

The main entrance is on route 40, 7 miles east of Cumberland. The park consists of 3,500 acres on Evitt's Mountain. Rocky Gap Run has been dammed to form a 240 acre lake, and there are hiking trail, and sledding and skating in winter.

ROCKY GORGE RESERVOIR. See DUCKET, HOWARD T. DAM.

ROCKY POINT PARK (Baltimore County)

11 miles southeast of downtown Baltimore fronting on the Chesapeake Bay. It is owned by Baltimore County and contains a large public golf course with club house, picnic

and swimming facilities. Also in the park is Ballestone Mansion, built before 1744 and recently restored by the county.

ROCKY RIDGE (Frederick)

15 miles northeast of Frederick. The village was first settled by the Krise family around 1757. It became Emmitsburg Junction in 1875 when the Western Maryland Railroad constructed a branch line from here to Emmitsburg; the branch has long been defunct.

ROE (Queen Anne's)

8 miles northeast of Centreville. It was Roe's Crossroads when James Roe had a store here, and later Roesville, until it became plain Roe.

RODGERS FORGE (Baltimore County)

6 miles north of downtown Baltimore. It is a vaguely defined suburb of well-kept, mostly row houses. The forge for which it is named was operated by the Rodgers brothers at the southeast corner of York Rd. and Stevenson Lane until 1934. Part of the original equipment was rescued during demolition and is now displayed in the foyer of the Rodgers Forge Elementary School.

Relic of Rodgers Forge in the
Rodgers Forge Elementary School.

ROHRERSVILLE (Washington)

15 miles south of Hagerstown. It is named for David Rohr, who had a sawmill nearby. His father, Frederick Rohr, emigrated from France, and is said to have taken the first

wheat over the mountains to Pittsburgh in 1767. This enterprising gentleman also discovered springs of salt water, boiled the water down, and traded the salt to the Indians.

ROMANCOKE (Queen Anne's)

7 miles south of Stevensville on Kent Island. It was a former ferry terminal, but now there is a small park and a fishing pier here.

ROSARYVILLE (Prince George's)

6 miles southwest of Upper Marlboro. It is an insignificant spot on route 301 but the countryside round about has had connections with Maryland's early landowning families. The Dower House, marked by a pond of that name a mile from town, was the center of a large estate and a hunting lodge of the Calverts, Maryland's proprietory family. On route 223 stands "His Lordship's Kindness," a five part brick colonial mansion. To the east and northeast are Mount Calvert and Croom (q.v.)

ROSEDALE (Baltimore County) Pop. 19,956.

6 miles northeast of downtown Baltimore. An area of industrial and residential development adjacent to Baltimore City along route 40.

ROSE HAVEN (Anne Arundel)

19 miles south of Annapolis fronting on the Chesapeake Bay. The community was founded by Joe Rose in 1947 as a yachting center and resort, when a harbor was dredged out and a marina built. There is also a motel, open all year (the sign says.) The motel is rather dilapidated, but, if it is still there, it faces the water and has a small private beach and is one of the few places where a visitor without a shore home can spend a night beside the Chesapeake Bay.

ROSE HILL (Charles)

3 miles southwest of La Plata. Although Rose Hill is only a house, it is mentioned because it once housed a colorful figure of the Civil War named Anne Olivia Floyd, a crippled woman who was a link in the Confederate communications chain. She is supposed to have carried messages to Pope's Creek, where they were signalled across the Potomac to Virginia. On one occasion her house was searched by Union Soldiers but the material was hidden in

the andirons and remained undiscovered. She is buried at St. Ignatius Church at Chapel Point (q.v.)

ROSEWOOD STATE HOSPITAL (Baltimore County)
A psychiatric hospital near Owings Mills. Opened in 1887 on 790 acres, it was formerly called Rosewood Training School and catered only to ages 7 - 17. Today there are no age limits, and 2000 people live in the cottage-type accomodations.

ROSEMONT (Frederick) Pop. 250. Incorp. 1953.
A development 13 miles southwest of Frederick.

ROUND TOP HILL (Washington)
$3\frac{1}{2}$ miles southwest of Hancock. Close to the Potomac River, this is a geologically interesting location, since it is sliced through by the Western Maryland Railroad. A cement plant began operating here in 1837 and the chimney still stands beside the C. & O. Canal.

ROWLAND ISLAND (Harford)
The island in the Susquehanna River below the Conowingo Dam(q.v.) Five flashing lights on the island act as a warning signal to fishermen when a rise in water level can be expected.

ROWLANDSVILLE (Cecil)
17 miles northwest of Elkton, in the steep valley of Octororo Creek. From 1828 to 1893 an iron-rolling mill was here, and later a paper mill.

ROXBURY MILLS (Howard)
14 miles west of Ellicott City. There has been a mill here on Cattail Creek, a tributary of the Patuxent, since the middle 1700's. The last operating mill closed in 1958 and is still there, just off route 97, in dilapidated condition.

ROYAL OAK (Talbot)
6 miles southwest of Easton. Some think the village is named for a large oak tree, in which a British cannon ball lodged during the bombardment of St. Michaels in 1813. Others think it was named earlier, when some oak seedlings were imported. There is another Royal Oak in Wicomico County, 12 miles west of Salisbury.

RUSHVILLE (Montgomery)

10 miles west of Rockville near the Potomac River at the mouth of Seneca Creek. The area was previously called Seneca, and still seems to be part of the village of Seneca; but it is marked Rushville on the map, and was named after Richard Rush, secretary of the Treasury, when the C. & O. Canal reached here in 1830.

RUXTON (Baltimore County)

8 miles northwest of downtown Baltimore. The area is one of Baltimore's wealthier suburbs covering approximately five square miles. The individual homes on large sites were erected when this was a rural area beyond the city limits.

SABILLASVILLE (Frederick)

20 miles north of Frederick. The town stands on route 550, which is one of the earliest roads built over the mountain ridge, sharing the valley of Owens Creek with the Western Maryland Railroad, which almost encircles Sabillasville in a horseshoe curve. The village was first called Zollingers Town, after the founder, but upon the death of his wife, Servilla, Mr. Zollinger named the town after her. Time altered the pronunciation. A stone marker on the corner of Harbaugh Valley Rd. commemorates the three Harbaugh brothers from Switzerland who settled in the Harbaugh Valley in 1760.

The village is known for the former Maryland T. B. Hospital, which was built in this airy spot in 1908 on 310 acres. It is now the Victor Cullen School for rehabilitation of delinquent boys, named after the founder of the hospital. Cullen was a pioneer in Maryland's sanatoria program and directed the founding of the institution in what was, in 1908, a very remote spot.

SAGAMORE FARMS (Baltimore County)

16 miles northwest of downtown Baltimore, the entrance being on Tuft Avenue. The farms are owned by members of the Vanderbilt family and are conspicuous by their white fences. Racing fans are interested to know that this has been the home of many great race horses; the great stallion, Native Dancer, is buried here. The farms are open for visitors daily 1-3 except Sundays.

ST. AUGUSTINE (Cecil)

8 miles south of Elkton. St. Augustine Episcopal Church once ministered to all the region between the Elk and Bohemia Rivers, and was the place of worship of the Protestant settlers of Bohemia Manor (q.v.) In those days it was

called The Manor Chapel. Its records date back to 1692, but the present building was erected in 1838 on the old foundations, and restored in 1962. On the northwest corner of the village cross roads stands a brick pre-Revolutionary house that once served as a temporary court house. There was a skirmish here during the Revolutionary War.

ST. CHARLES (Charles) Pop. 13,921

6 miles northeast of La Plata. This community was started in 1968 with a grant from H. U. D. and was the first industrial park in Southern Maryland. Housing estates now complement the industries and it is planned to erect five separate villages. The entire area is 8,000 acres. It is said that the place attracts many police officers from Washington D. C. as residents.

ST. CLEMENT ISLAND (St. Mary's)

9 miles southwest of Leonardtown. An island in the Potomac River near Colton (q.v.) This is a revered spot in Maryland, for it was here that the Ark and the Dove dropped anchor for two days on March 25, 1634, while the colonists debated the location of what would later become St. Mary's City. According to Father White's history, one of their small boats overturned while the women were taking out the clothes to be washed, and much of the linen was lost. In those days the island was 400 acres in size, but at the present time it has been reduced to 40 acres by erosion.

The name of the island was changed by a later proprietor to Blakistone Island, and during the Revolution it was used as a base of operations by the British, who are said to have burned Mr. Blakistone's house and carried him away. In 1934, to commemorate the 300th anniversary of the arrival of the Maryland colonists, a 40 ft. cross was erected on the island. At the time it belonged to the U. S. Navy, but in 1961 it was handed back to the state and soon thereafter its name was changed back to St. Clement. An erosion project was completed in 1970 to preserve the remnant that remains.

The island is accessible only by boat. Each year, on the last Sunday in September, a ceremony of the Blessing of the Fleet is held, to commemorate the landing; free boat rides to the island are a feature of the celebrations.

ST. DENIS (Baltimore County)

7 miles southwest of downtown Baltimore. The name is from an early landowner named Denis A. Smith, once the state treasurer. He was nicknamed St. Denis by his associates. It is a commuter stop on the railroad between Baltimore and Washington, even although the railroad station has recently been demolished.

ST. GEORGE ISLAND (St. Mary's)

16 miles southeast of Leonardtown, close to the mouth of the Potomac. It is nearly three miles long and less than a mile wide at its widest point, and connected to the mainland by a road bridge. In July 1776, the British fleet, under Lord Dunsmore, captured the island and used it as a base for attacking the mainland; the first naval action of the Revolution took place not far away. There are now a number of homes and private beaches on the island.

ST. INIGOES (St. Mary's)

17 miles southeast of Leonardtown and 4 miles southeast of St. Mary's City. It is named for an extensive colonial estate of the same name, now occupied by Webster Field, a U. S. Naval installation. Nearby is St. Ignatius Catholic Church, which was erected in 1785 on the site of an earlier church which dated from the 1630's; this church was the successor to the church founded at St. Mary's City, the oldest Catholic parish in English-speaking America.

ST. JAMES (Washington)

St. James is a station on the Norfolk and Western Railroad, 5 miles southwest of Hagerstown. It once served the village 2 miles to the northeast and St. James School, one mile to the north. The school was founded about 1850 on the old estate of Fountain Rock, as a Diocesan School of the Episcopal Church in Maryland. It was said to be a center of contention during the Civil War, with faculty and students adhering to different sides. It is now a prep school, and the spring from which the estate got its name is still on the grounds behind the building.

ST. LEONARD (Calvert)

6 miles southeast of Prince Frederick. St. Leonard was founded in 1683 at the mouth of the St. Leonard River and re-established in the late 17th century at the head of

navigation of St. Leonards Creek, one of the main tributaries of the Patuxent River. It never gained much population, and in 1900 moved away from the creek, which is now nothing but a trickle, while the town itself has somewhat gone to seed.

The mouth of St. Leonards Creek was the scene of a naval encounter in 1814. British war ships bottled up Joshua Barney's "barges" here; the barges were burnt to prevent their falling into the enemy's hands.

ST. MARGARETS (Anne Arundel)

3 miles northeast of Annapolis. The area takes its name from St. Margaret's Church, which is said to have been named after St. Margaret's, Westminster in London. The church has been located at several different sites since its founding in 1696 when it was the parish church for the whole of Broad Neck. It is now located at a cross roads south of route 50 between Ritchie Highway and the Bay Bridge.

ST. MARYS CITY (St. Marys)

14 miles southeast of Leonardtown. Although nothing of the original town remains above ground at this historic site, it is the most hallowed ground in Maryland, for here, on March 27, 1634, Lord Baltimore's band of colonists first set foot on the American mainland and gathered under a mulberry tree to give thanks for their safe arrival. An obelisk, erected in 1890, marks the spot of the mulberry tree.

St. Marys City became the first state capital and a courthouse was erected in 1676, a building which was considered to be one of the finest in the English colonies. When the state government was moved to Annapolis in 1695, the old state house served as the courthouse for St. Mary's County; when the county seat moved to Leonardtown in 1708, the building was used as a chapel. In 1829 it was dismantled and the bricks were used to construct nearby Trinity Church. An authentic reproduction was erected on the site in 1934, the year of Maryland's tricentennial. It is open daily 10-5 except on Thanksgiving, Christmas and New Year's Day.

Also in 1934 was erected the Freedom of Conscience Monument, a rugged piece of statuary which commemorates "The Act Concerning Religion." which was passed by the Maryland Colonial Legislature in 1649.

Each year, on Maryland Day, the last Sunday in March, a symbolic legislative session is held at the courthouse; this opens the "living history season," which continues until the last Sunday in November. In the summer months there is colonial pageantry and historical drama.

ST. MARY'S COUNTY. County Seat: Leonardtown. Pop. 59,895. Area: 269 square miles.

St. Mary's County was formed in 1637 and named in honor of the Virgin Mary, the first colonists having landed on the feast of the Assumption in 1634. It consists of a peninsula between the Patuxent and the Potomac estuaries, cut off in the north by an irregular line from Budds Creek on the Wicomico River to Indian Creek on the Patuxent. The ground is mostly level.

St. Mary's County is considered to be the cradle of Maryland, since Leonard Calvert and his little band of colonists landed from the Ark and the Dove, first at St. Clement Island, and then at St. Mary's City in 1634, establishing it as the colonial capital until 1694.

The county is basically agricultural, growing tobacco, grains and soybeans, with some livestock, fishing and oystering. It has the least industry of any Maryland county, and the only area of growth is in the vicinity of the Naval Air Test Center, near Lexington Park.

ST. MICHAELS (Talbot) Pop. 1,301. Incorp. 1804.

8 miles west of Easton beside the wide Miles River (q.v.) It was named for St. Michaels Protestant Episcopal Church which was built in the late 1600's near the site of the present church. The town was settled in the 1670's and became a busy shipbuilding center, reaching its height in the 1800's, after which it began to decline, as timber became scarce, and Baltimore increased in importance.

The town struck several small blows for independence. In 1781 the citizens outfitted the armed barge "Experiment" to protect Eastern Bay and the Miles River. In 1813, when British ships were approaching, lights were extinguished in the houses and placed on tree tops and mastheads as decoys, so that most of the cannon balls passed harmlessly over the town. This earned St. Michaels the nickname of "The town that fooled the British."

St. Michaels is still geared to water activities; there is fishing and yachting, packers of fresh seafood, several seafood restaurants and a maritime museum, which includes a number of Chesapeake Bay craft, models, a lighthouse, a light ship and much more. It is open daily, 10-5 in summer, closed Mondays in winter.

In St. Mary's Square is another museum which has a collection relating to the history of St. Michaels. A map of the town and a walking tour guide is available locally. St. Michaels figured as the background in a Hollywood movie.

SALEM (Dorchester)

10 miles southeast of Cambridge. The name is a biblical one, meaning peace. A Methodist church was built here in 1800 and the village became a Methodist settlement. A preacher by the name of Freeborn Garrettson, well known in his day, was arrested at Salem and jailed in Salisbury.

SALISBURY.   Seat of Wicomico County.   Pop. 16,429.
Incorp. 1811.

Salisbury is located on the upper reaches of the Wicomico River, half way between the east and west shores of the Delmarva Peninsula. It has always been an important social and industrial center for the Eastern Shore and is the sixth largest incorporated town in Maryland. The population of Greater Salisbury is in the region of 40,000 people, 20% of whom are black, and still growing.

The town began in 1732, when Isaac Handy established a boat landing for fishermen and woodcutters at the head of the Wicomico River. He built himself a house, Pemberton Hall in 1741, and this still stands, five miles west of Salisbury, on Pemberton Drive, overlooking the Wicomico River. The house is being restored and there is an open house each year on the last Sunday in October. Poplar Hill Mansion, a pre-fire relic built in 1795 by Major Levin Handy, an officer of the Maryland Line during the Revolution, is at 117 Elizabeth St. and has recently been purchased by the Maryland Historical Trust. The spot where the Salisbury Times now stands was occupied during the Civil War by Camp Upton, which was the control center for the entire Eastern Shore.

Division Street marks the old county line in the days when Salisbury was half in Somerset County and half in Worcester County; parts of both counties were split off in 1867 to form Wicomico County, with Salisbury as the county seat. Much of the city was destroyed by fire in 1869 and again in 1886, so that few of the older buildings remain.

Industry has expanded mainly to the north, where there is an industrial park. The largest employer of labor is Perdue, a poultry packer, with over 2,000 employees, said to supply New York City with almost all its chickens. Next comes Campbell's Soup and frozen foods, followed by manufacturers of gasoline pumps, shirts, sawn lumber, steel products and business forms. The Wicomico River has been dredged and barge traffic is carried on, with cargoes of oil, fertilizer and road materials.

Salisbury has been called a mini-city, since it has industrial and cultural resources usually found only in larger communities; it was the recipient of the first Federally financed urban renewal program in Maryland, outside Baltimore City, and is the shopping and cultural center for a wide area of Maryland, Virginia and Delaware. There is a pleasant shopping plaza along Main St., closed to traffic since 1967 and adorned by shrubbery and a modern sculpture with an inspiring inscription. In addition there is a large shopping mall a mile from the town center. Cultural resources include a municipal park along a branch of the Wicomico River, an interesting zoo, and, until it was burnt down, a Civic Center where the National Indoor Tennis Championships were held. The center is being rebuilt. The old City Hall was opened as a museum in 1977 and there are art classes and lectures as well as exhibits. Opening hours are Mon. - Fri. 10-4 and Sat. 10-2.

In October, the Atlantic Flyway water fowl carving and art exhibition is held. The University of Maryland has a poultry and vegetable research farm nearby.

SAMS CREEK (Carroll)

8½ miles southwest of Westminster on the stream of the same name. The area surrounding the small village has several Methodist shrines, since Robert Strawbridge, the first preacher of Methodism in America, came from Ireland to this vicinity in 1760 and lived here for 17 years. His house is still standing beside a narrow stoney road near Marston. Built in 1772, it is a log structure, covered with clapboard and well marked with Methodist Historical Markers. It has belonged to the Strawbridge Shrine Association since 1973.

During his lifetime Strawbridge built the Strawbridge Meeting House, the first Methodist Church in America. It was a log structure on the road between Marston and New Windsor and the site is marked. Its direct descendant is The Stone Chapel, about half way between Sam's Creek and Westminster at the junction of Stone Chapel Road and Bowersox Road. It has been rebuilt several times. Strawbridge is buried in Mount Olivet Cemetery in Baltimore.

SANG RUN (Garrett)

7 miles south of Friendsville near the confluence of Sang Run and the Youghiogheny River. The name is a corruption of "ginseng," a medicinal plant which once grew in great profusion in this area but is now hard to find. The roots were collected by the early settlers and sold to the Chinese, who valued them highly; the name is from the Chinese language, meaning "shape of a man." The plant is commemorated in the names of Ginseng Run and Ginseng Hill nearby.

Meshack Browning (1781-1859) author of the classic *Forty*

Four Years of the Life of a Hunter settled here in 1807, and the foundations of his cabin still stand on the banks of Sang Run, although there is nothing to identify them. Little else remains, but anyone who has read the old bear-hunter's reminiscences cannot but enjoy standing on the spot. Browning's name still lives on in Browning Dam on Muddy Creek, 4 miles to the southwest, Browning Run, a tributary of Muddy Creek, and Browning Bear Hill, 12 miles east in the Savage River State Forest. Browning is buried at Hoyes (q.v.)

SASSAFRAS (Kent)

The village is at the head of Sassafras River, where several streams meet. Sassafras River is short, rising near the Delaware border and reaching the Bay in less than twenty miles. It divides Cecil County from Kent County.

SAVAGE (Howard) Pop. with Guilford 2,928.

9 miles south of Ellicott City. The town was named after the individual who financed the mill that was built here in 1750, although he did not live nearby. The mill evolved into a factory which dominated the town for 130 years, producing cotton products such as duck, belting, laundry nets, tents, tank covers, tarpaulins, etc. The factory closed in 1947, had a brief resurgence in 1948-51 making Christmas ornaments, and has stood more or less idle since. The row of identical, well-preserved homes built by the company still stands, making this a town of unusual aspect.

A branch line formerly served the factory, carried across the Middle Patuxent River by an iron truss bridge, designed by Wendel Bollman (1814-1884) a Baltimore engineer, whose few remaining structures are considered to be museum pieces. A quarry further upstream produces gabbro rock (and dust)

SAVAGE RIVER (Garrett)

The Savage River is fed by a number of tributaries arising on Savage and Meadow Mountains and flows in a southwesterly direction until stopped by the wall of Backbone Mountain, after which it makes a right angled turn through a steep valley and enters the Potomac River at Bloomington. Six miles from its mouth it is dammed to form an extensive lake.

The name may have been given to it by a surveyor called Major William May, on account of its rapidity and fierceness; or it may have been named after another surveyor called John Savage. However, the sad trickle of water below the dam belies its name, except on some Spring weekends when the river comes to life again because the Army Corps of Engineers releases water from the dam. On these occasions it becomes the scene of Olympic kayak racing trials and competitors come from far and wide.

The Savage River Valley provides a route for the B. & O. Railroad to begin its climb over Backbone Mountain. The mouth of the river marks the south end of the boundary between Allegany and Garrett Counties.

SAVAGE RIVER DAM (Garrett)

The dam, about six miles above where the Savage River joins the Potomac, was begun in 1939, suspended in 1942 and finished in 1951. It is 1,050 ft. long and 184 ft. high; the lake behind it, as well as supplying water to nearby communities, provides year round fishing. A motor road skirts the western side of the lake.

SCARBORO (Harford)

8 miles northeast of Bel Air. An outcropping of soapstone near here has been worked for many years, but is now nearly exhausted. Although products are still made at this location, most of the soapstone is imported from elsewhere. The soft stone from this locality had the unusual characteristic of hardening when heated.

SCOTLAND (Montgomery)

3 miles south of Rockville. This was a dilapidated black community until recently, when loans were secured from H. U. D. to build new townhouses.

SEAT PLEASANT (Prince George's)   Pop. 5,217.   Incorp. 1924.

$5\frac{1}{2}$ miles east of the U. S. Capitol. One of Washington's many residential suburbs. At one time it was called Chesapeake Junction, as a railroad ran from here to Chesapeake Beach from 1900 to 1935, but the name was changed in 1906.

Of historical interest is the Addison Chapel of St. Matthews Episcopal Church at North Addison Rd. and 62d Place. This small square brick building, built in 1809 on the site of two earlier churches, was named for the Addison family, and has associations with some of Maryland's early leading families, including the Calverts. There are some interesting graves in the churchyard.

SECRETARY (Dorchester) Pop. 352. Incorp. 1900.

7 miles northeast of Cambridge. It was named for Henry Sewell, who was Secretary of Maryland under Governor Charles Calvert. Part of a brick house called "My Lady Sewell's Manor" is thought to be the house that was erected by The Secretary himself, in 1662. It originally contained some fine panelling which is now in the possession of the Brooklyn Museum of Fine Arts. After Sewell's death his widow married Charles Calvert, who became Third Lord Baltimore. The house is located next to the car park of the Catholic Church, the only brick building on the main street.

Secretary remains remote and undeveloped and is somewhat photogenic. Secretary Creek, which was once a regular port of call for ships, is now called Warwick Creek. An oyster packing plant employs some residents.

SECURITY (Washington)

2 miles northeast of Hagerstown. There has been an important cement works here for many years. Until recently a rickety branch of the B. & O. Railroad from Weverton joined the Western Maryland Railroad here.

SELBY ON THE BAY (Anne Arundel) Pop. 3,125

7 miles south of Annapolis. A non-descript residential area fronting on Selby Bay, which is an inlet of the South River, which is an inlet of the Bay.

SELBYSPORT (Garrett)

It was 22 miles north of Oakland before it was obliterated by the Youghiogheny River Reservoir in 1947; if it had survived, it is thought that it would have been the oldest town in the county. The name is from Captain Evan Shelby; the port was added because it was anticipated that the river would eventually be made navigable up to this point. The Methodist Church and a public school situated on higher ground escaped inundation.

SELLMAN (Montgomery)

15 miles northwest of Rockville. It was named for its post master and sprang up around the B. & O. station, now demolished.

SENECA (Montgomery)

10 miles west of Rockville. The village, once called Newport, was laid out by John Garrett, on the west bank of Seneca Creek in 1787, but never realized the hopes of its founder. Between the village and the Potomac River a few summer homes line the creek, and the mouth of the creek is spanned by a picturesque aqueduct, partly collapsed, which carried the C. & O. Canal. There is also a lock house, dating from 1836.

The name of the village has been preserved in the name of the local red sandstone, "Seneca Red." The aqueduct is built of this stone, as are many well-known buildings in Baltimore and Washington, the most famous being the original Smithsonian building. The quarries were a short distance west along the Potomac and can still be seen; there are also the ruins of an old stone cutting mill, which operated 1850 - 90 and is listed on the National Register of Historic Places.

At 16800 River Road is the Seneca School House Museum, open March 15 - Dec. 15, Suns. 12-4. School classes may book an eighteenth century school day here. The upper part of the valley of Seneca Creek has been acquired by the state and is under development as a park. One of its attractions will be a large peony collection assembled by a former owner.

SETH DEMONSTRATION FOREST (Talbot)

3 miles southeast of Easton. 125 acres of state-owned forest which is used for research and demonstration in loblolly pine and hardwoods. One can hike through it but not camp.

SEVEN OAKS (Montgomery)

9 miles southeast of Rockville. Another new suburb close to the Washngton area.

SEVERN (Anne Arundel)

12 miles southwest of downtown Baltimore. A number of small springs in the area give rise to the Severn River. A company here makes paper boxes and another makes electrical switches.

SEVERN RIVER

The Severn begins as Severn Run, an insignificant stream

in Anne Arundel County. East of route 3 it widens into a tidal estuary for 13 miles and empties into the Chesapeake Bay just below Annapolis. Homes, beaches, boat ramps and marinas dot the shoreline for most of its length.

SEVERNA PARK (Anne Arundel) Pop. 21,253

$7\frac{1}{2}$ miles northwest of Annapolis off route 2. It started as a resort area on the Severn River in 1910, when it was only a collection of summer homes served by the Baltimore and Annapolis Railroad. Earlier it was known as Boone. Suburban growth has been rapid in Severna Park, although it remains mainly residential. The railroad station has survived and now belongs to the Severna Park model railroad club who have a fine layout. It is open Thursdays 8-11 p.m. and has open house for one week in the Spring.

In nearby Round Bay lies St. Helena Island, which was used as a prison camp called Mount Misery during the Civil War.

SHAD LANDING (Worcester)

4 miles southwest of Snow Hill. The state park here is one of the few places from which the scenic Pocomoke River can be viewed from its forested banks. There is a marina, camping facilities, a large swimming pool and a natural science display in a building on the picnic grounds.

SHAD POINT (Wicomico)

A southwestern suburb of Salisbury on the Wicomico River, where there are a number of slips for boats and boat repairs. The menhaden fleet operates out of here. Menhaden are fish that are used for fertilizer and not for food, and a fleet of boats, each 140 ft. long, operated by a crew of 17, winters here Oct. 15 to May 15. They fish from Cape Hatteras to Boston in season.

SHADYSIDE (Anne Arundel) Pop. 2,877.

10 miles south of Annapolis. A village on the peninsula between West River and the Chesapeake Bay, consisting of individual homes and private beaches. It was once called The Swamp but the postoffice considered this indelicate when it opened a branch here about 1888.

On Woods Wharf Road there is a small wharf operated by the county. Boating here is mainly for pleasure, but a few oyster boats, mostly owned by blacks, tie up here. A company builds and rents boats. In earlier times Shadyside was a public resort with hotels and cottages, with cruise ships calling from Baltimore.

SHALLMAR (Garrett)
2 miles west of Kitzmiller beside the Potomac River and 11 miles southeast of Oakland. This insignificant spot is not easily accessible, although it was once a fair sized coal mining town. The name is the reverse of Marshall, the name of the New Yorker who founded the town.

SHARON (Harford)
5 miles northwest of Bel Air. Many railroad buffs remember the intricate wooden tressle which carried the Maryland and Pennsylvania Railroad over the valley here. It was demolished in the 1960's.

SHARPSBURG (Washington)
12 miles south of Hagerstown. The town was laid out in 1763 by Joseph Chapline, who also owned Antietam Furnace (q.v.) and who is buried in Mountain View Cemetery. A house at the end of Chapline St. is the first stone house, and was built by J. Chapline II in 1769. The name of the town commemorates Governor Horatio Sharpe, who arrived in the Colony in 1753 and remained Governor until August, 1768. Sharpsburg wanted to be the seat of Washington County, but Hagerstown defeated it by one vote. George Washington is said to have visited here twice.

The name of the town is known nation wide on account of the Civil War Battle of Antietam, known in the South as the Battle of Sharpsburg. The Battle of Antietam, named for the stream which flows down the valley, the bloodiest battle of the Civil War, was fought in and around the town on Sept. 14, 1862. Neither side gained a decisive victory, but it brought to an end the first of Lee's two attempts to carry the war into the North. The dead numbered 12,410 Federals and 10,700 Confederates.

About 5,000 Federal dead are buried in the National Cemetery at Sharpsburg, 1,836 of them unidentified, while the Confederate dead lie in the churchyards at Hagerstown and other towns in the vicinity. No civilians were killed, and after the battle most of the buildings in the town were turned into hospitals for the wounded soldiers. President Lincoln visited the town on Oct. 3, about three weeks after the battle.

In 1962, a hundred years after the event, the battle was re-enacted, and every house which was standing at the time of the battle was marked with a small black iron plaque. Since 1933 the area has been a National Park of 810 acres. A visitors' center north of the town was opened in 1963 by the National Park Service, and there is a self-drive auto tour laid out with numerous markers and nine stopping places. It is recommended that visitors view the 18 minute slide program at the center before taking the auto tour, in order better to understand the significance of Bloody Lane, Burnside Bridge, the Dunker Church (reconstructed) and other locations, whose peaceful, rural aspect gives no indication whatever of events long past.

SHARP'S ISLAND (Talbot)

A small uninhabited island in the Chesapeake Bay 4 miles south of the point of Tilghman Island. Within living memory it was an island of several hundred acres and a resort with pier and a large hotel.

SHARPTOWN (Wicomico) Pop. 660. Incorp. 1874.

14 miles northwest of Salisbury. It was named for Horatio Sharpe, who was governor Maryland, 1753-1769. There is a small park beside the Nanticoke River for fishing and swimming. A factory nearby makes childrens' dresses.

SHEPPERD (Baltimore County)

22 miles northeast of downtown Baltimore. The village was named for an early family of settlers. A stone house here is thought to be the oldest building still standing on the tract called "My Lady's Manor." (q.v.)

SHOWELL (Worcester)

19 miles northeast of Snow Hill. It was named for a local family of landowners; an old two-story frame house is thought to be part of a much larger Showell House. There is a large poultry packing plant here.

SIDELING HILL (Washington)

One of the long, narrow ridges of the Ridge and Valley Province, which runs from the Pennsylvania border to the Potomac River, which are only 6½ miles apart at this point. Travellers on route 40 west always recognize it by the violent hairpin bend on the summit. Sideling Hill Wildlife Management Area is on the west slope of the mountain and also in the valley between it and Town Ridge. Down this valley runs Sideling Hill Creek, forming the boundary between Washington and Allegany Counties. There is trout fishing in the creek.

SILVER RUN (Carroll)

8 miles northwest of Westminster. The small village was founded by Germans in 1729 on a stream of the same name. St. Mary's Church, built in 1763 of wood, and rebuilt in 1822 of brick, was originally both Lutheran and Reformed. Later it separated into St. Mary's Lutheran and St. Mark's Reformed.

SILVER SPRING (Montgomery) Pop. 72,893

7 miles north of the U. S. Capitol, just beyond the District of Columbia line. The spring from which it takes its name was on the estate purchased by Francis Preston Blair, friend of President Lincoln and father of Montgomery Blair, Postmaster General under Lincoln. Its silvery appearance was due to the white sand and mica below the clear water.

The spring still exists, although it no longer retains the remotest aspect of silver. It was acquired by a citizens group in 1942 and restored in 1955. A small park has been constructed around it on Newell Rd. at the intersection of the East West Highway and Blair Mill Rd. one block south of Georgia Ave; beside the spring there is a small acorn-shaped shelter.

In 1897 Silver Spring was a cross roads, without inhabitants. In 1918, in addition to the railroad station there were 75 dwellings, 10 stores, a mill and a bank. Today it is a busy suburb of Washington, with huge apartment and office blocks, most of which have sprung up within the last 25 years. If the town were incorporated, it would be the second largest in Maryland, after Baltimore. In the churchyard of Grace Church, on Georgia Ave. is a marker to unknown Confederate troops buried there.

SKIPTON (Talbot)

8 miles north of Easton. It is named after a town in Yorkshire, England. The village is tiny and unimportant but the area was a notable one when the court of Talbot County was held here at a very early date. At that time there

was a point on the Wye East River called York.

SMALLWOOD STATE PARK (Charles)
11 miles west of La Plata fronting on Mattawoman Creek near its confluence with the Potomac. The 333 acre park surrounds the home of General Smallwood, hero of the Battle of Brooklyn in 1776, and Governor of Maryland, 1785 - 1788. Only the foundations of the home remain, but in 1938 a restoration project was begun and a brick home, closely resembling the original, was erected on the foundations. Smallwood's grave stands in an open space 150 yards from the house.

During the first weekend in May, Revolutionary War Days take place here, with marching units, colonial music, seafood stalls and craft shows. The park is open daily June thru Sept, 10-6; April, May, Oct. and Nov. weekends only, 10-5, closed other times.

SMITH ISLAND (Somerset)
Situated in the Chesapeake Bay 8 miles from Crisfield, it is the only inhabited island in Maryland approachable only by water. The origin of the name is unknown -- it is not thought to be named for Captain John Smith. The whole island is only two feet above sea level and the northern half, being marshy and uninhabited, is reserved as a National Wildlife Refuge and a feeding ground for migratory birds.

The island was first settled in 1657. It measures today about 4 miles by 8 miles, but the inhabited part is only 3 square miles and the population is about 700. There is no jail, no police force and no city government. The streets of its three small towns, Ewell, Tylerton and Rhodes (or Rogues) Point are narrow and tree-lined.

A school boat carries pupils daily to and from Crisfield High School, and a ferry leaves Crisfield at 12.30 p.m. and returns at 5.15 p.m. every day between Memorial Day and September. The only occupation is fishing for crabs and oysters and every island family has a boat. There is a small seafood packing house at Ewell.

SMITHSBURG (Washington) Pop. 671. Incorp. 1841.
8 miles east of Hagerstown. The founder, Christopher Smith (1750-1821,) commonly known as "Stuffle" Smith, is buried in the Lutheran Churchyard in an unknown grave. The publishing firm of Doubleday has a printing plant near the town.

Smithsburg saw some Civil War activity on two occasions. Soldiers from the Battles of South Mountain and Antietam were hospitalized in the town; and after the Battle of Gettysburg, the town was occupied by Kilpatrick's cavalry and was shelled from South Mountain by General Stuart.

SMITHVILLE (Caroline)

10 miles southeast of Denton. In 1840 Samuel G. Smith put up a sawmill here and the village took his name, although there had been earlier mills here. A dammed stream nearby produces a narrow lake over a mile long.

SMOKETOWN (Washington)

8 miles southeast of Hagerstown. It was probably named for the blue haze which sometimes lingers in the valleys of South Mountain. The place figured in George A. Townsend's novel *Katy of Catoctin* as the home of a female abolitionist and fortune-teller and as the center of Dunkard activities. There is nothing but the name today.

SNOW HILL. Seat of Worcester County. Pop. 2,192. Incorp. 1812.

Snow Hill was founded in 1642 by a group of settlers from the Snow Hill district of London, and laid out in 1686 on the southeast side of the Pocomoke River. It became the seat of Worcester County, and the first courthouse was erected in 1742. Fires destroyed the town, including both the first and second courthouses, in 1834 and 1893; the present red brick courthouse dates from 1894.

Snow Hill was a commercial center for the lower Eastern Shore and the deep, narrow river could accomodate ocean-going ships. On July 26, 1775, it made a small contribution to history when about 60 men from Worcester County met here to sign the Declaration of the Association of Freemen.

All Hallows Church, built on the site of an earlier church, dates from 1748-54. There are some late 19th century houses which escaped destruction, some with Victorian gingerbread adornments and some with tall cupolas from which ships could be sighted coming up the river. The Julia A. Purnell Museum exhibits local memorabilia, 1-5 daily in summer, Sundays only in winter. There are two or three lumber companies, two small clothing companies, a poultry packing plant and a company producing business forms.

SNOW HILL LANDING (Worcester)

6 miles east of Snow Hill on Chincoteague Bay. It was called Public Landing until fairly recently and the inhabitants still prefer that name. In bygone days it had a dance hall and shooting gallery in addition to a long pier and picnic tables. Many of the facilities were destoryed by the storm of 1933 and what remains has been made into a small park with 600 ft. of bay frontage, a pier and a parking lot. It is popular for swimming and crabbing, particularly for children, as the water is shallow.

SNYDER'S LANDING (Washington)

13 miles southwest of Hagerstown. This was a landing and loading point on the C. & O. Canal for goods to and from Sharpsburg, and was originally named Chapline's Landing, after the founder of Sharpsburg. Later it became Sharpsburg Landing, then Snyder's Landing around 1900. In the 1930's there was a kind of resort here with public dances and parties held in a large barn. The summer homes along the canal banks date from the turn of the century. Barron's store, which opened in 1971, serves tow path users and has a small museum of C. & O. memorabilia.

SOLDIERS DELIIGHT (Baltimore County)

15 miles northwest of downtown Baltimore, roughly bounded by Lyons Mill Road, Wards Chapel Road and Church Road. The name was once Soldiers Delight Hundred and covered a large area extending from the Patapsco River to the Pennsylvania border. In the 18th century it was subdivided several times and the name applies now to an area of about 2,000 barren, stony acres, covered with stunted evergreens. The underlying serpentine rock gives the scanty soil a greenish hue and renders it somewhat unproductive. A unique vegetation flourishes, however, particularly in the stream valleys, and the area has recently become a state park.

The first discovery of chromite in the U. S. occurred here in 1827. The discovery was made by Isaac Tyson of Baltimore, who was already working chrome mines at Bare Hills, closer to the city. This gentleman established a chrome plant in Baltimore in 1845 and acquired interests in all the chrome pits and mines for a distance of many miles. Between 1828 and 1850, most of the world's chrome came from the Baltimore region; after that time richer deposits were discovered in Asia Minor and later in Africa.

The mines at Soldiers Delight have not been worked since the 1880's except for an experimental attempt during the first world war, but some of the mine openings can still be seen.

Rare fringed gentian at Soldiers Delight.

SOLOMONS (Calvert)

17 miles southeast of Prince Frederick. The town is a picturesque cluster of dwellings on a narrow neck of land extending into the Patuxent River near its mouth. It was known as Bourne's Island in its early days, and later as Somervell's Island. Captain Solomon established the first oyster business here in 1867, and it was known as Solomon's Island henceforth. The connecting causeway disguises the fact that the place is an island, and so the second part of the name has been dropped.

A large oystering fleet has always been maintained here, although today the oyster boats are far outnumbered by the pleasure craft which tie up here. Two innovations came from Solomons: deep water oystering tongs, and the bugeye, one of the Chesapeake Bay's most distinctive work boats, wide and of shallow draft.

The Chesapeake Biological Laboratory of the University of Maryland is located in Solomons, and has been situated here since 1922, although the present building dates from 1932. Its purpose is to study marine life and the fluctuations of the local fish supply. There is an exhibit room open to visitors weekdays 9-5. The only industries in Solomons, apart from restaurants and businesses catering to boatmen, are a seafood packer and a small company building pleasure craft.

North of the town on route 4 is the Calvert County Maritime Museum, which is a small gem for a county of such small size. There is a fine display of models, paintings, tools, etc. illustrating local marine history and biology. Here can be seen the deep water oystering tongs, mentioned above and also a lighthouse removed from the Bay. The museum is open Sat. and Sun. 1-5.

SOMERSET (Montgomery) Pop. 1,101. Incorp. 1906.
7 miles northwest of the U. S. Capitol. The boundaries are those of an earlier farm named Friendship. The land was acquired and the town founded in 1890 by a group of government scientists, who evidently had feelings of nostalgia for England. The name is that of an English county and most of the streets are named after places in England.

SOMERSET COUNTY. County Seat: Princess Anne. Pop. 19,188. Area: 328 square miles.

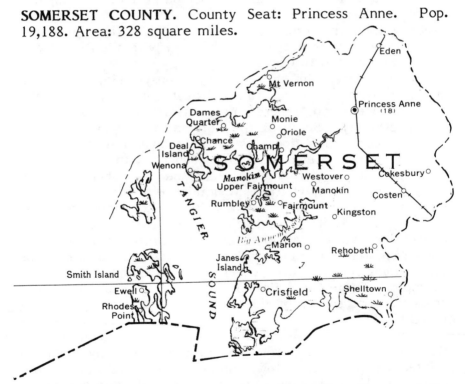

Somerset County was formed in 1666 and named for Mary Somerset, sister-in-law of Cecilius, Second Lord Baltimore. It is bounded on the north by the Wicomico River; on the east by Dividing Creek; on the south by the Pocomoke

River estuary; on the west by the Chesapeake Bay. The terrain is flat and much of the Bay coast is bordered by marshes.

The county is noted for fishing, crabbing and oystering, and the processing of seafood. The interior is agricultural, raising grains and soybeans and some strawberries and tomatoes, although not on the scale it once did. Poultry rearing is also important.

SOUTH GATE (Anne Arundel) Pop. 24,185

An area of rapid growth 12 miles south of downtown Baltimore.

SOUTH MOUNTAIN

South Mountain and its smaller eastern neighbor, Catoctin Mountain, form the easternmost outpost of the Appalachians in Maryland. Separated from the main ridges by the Great Valley, this range is called The Blue Ridge in Maryland, although it is not directly aligned with the Blue Ridge of Virginia and North Carolina.

South Mountain begins in Pennsylvania, traverses Maryland from northeast to southwest and ends in a steep bluff at Weverton, where there is a nice view of the Potomac Valley. South of the Potomac in Virginia, there is only a small continuation. Its height is consistent along most of its length, between 1,200 and 1,800 ft. with its knobs and outcrops only slightly higher than the main ridge. High Rock, Raven Rock, Quirauk Mountain, Buzzards Knob, Pine Knob and Lamb's Knoll are overlooks accessible from the Appalachian Trail (q.v.) which runs along the summit. Greenbriar, Washington Monument and Gathland State Parks are all on South Mountain. The crest of the mountain forms the dividing line between Frederick and Washington Counties. Crampton, Turners and Fox Gaps, where the east-west roads cross it, were scenes of the Battle of South Mountain during the Civil War.

For those interested in folk lore, a book by Madeleine V. Dahlgren called *South Mountain Magic* has recently been reprinted by the Hagerstown library. The Dahlgrens were owners of the South Mountain Inn, where old route 40 crosses the mountain at Turner's Gap.

SOUTH RIVER (Anne Arundel)

South River is one of the estuaries, or inlets, which

dissect the western shore of the Chesapeake Bay. It starts nine miles inland where several small streams converge, and enters the Bay south of Annapolis. A small village on route 468, 3 miles south of the river, also bears the name. South River Club is near here, founded prior to 1790 and said to be one of the oldest continually active social clubs in the U. S. The present structure was built in 1742.

SPANIARD POINT (Queen Anne's)
The point is at the tip of Spaniard Neck, which is a mile wide peninsula between the Chester and Corsica Rivers. It received the name when it came into the hands of a freed Spanish indentured servant in colonial times.

SPARKS (Baltimore County)
16 miles north of downtown Baltimore. It was named after the Sparks family, and the original location was somewhat west of the present vaguely defined area. On York Road is the Milton Inn, built in 1740, which started life as the Milton Academy, or Milton Hall, a school for boys, one of whose students was John Wilkes Booth. The Inn is now an expensive restaurant, once featured in Life Magazine as one of America's most interesting eating places.

SPARROWS POINT (Baltimore County)
9 miles southeast of downtown Baltimore, on a portion of Patapsco Neck, surrounded by water on three sides. Land was deeded to Thomas Sparrow here by Lord Baltimore in 1652. Sparrow's son, Solomon, built a house on it which he called Sparrow's Nest.

Bethlehem Steel acquired the land in 1916 and now has one of the world's largest steel-making facilities here, capable of employing 22,000 people if it ever achieves full production again; the shipyards have facilities to employ 3,500 people, building tankers, freighters, ore-carriers and other types of ships up to 265,000 tons. "The Point" as it is known locally, is an extremely important factor in the economy of the Baltimore area and of the whole of Maryland.

SPENCERVILLE (Montgomery)
10 miles east of Rockville. It was named for the postmaster, William Spencer, about 1859, but it was previously called Drayton, after the family who founded the town in 1850.

SPESUTIE ISLAND (Harford)

An island in the Chesapeake Bay 15 miles southeast of Bel Air and separated from the shore by less than half a mile. It was known before 1652 as Bearson's Island, but later named for its owner, Captain Nathaniel Utie, who came from Virginia, where his land had been confiscated. The name means Utie's Hope, and it was a well-known landmark to early shipping in the Bay. A meeting of both the Virginia and Maryland Councils was held on the island in 1661.

Today this historic spot is connected to the mainland by a small bridge at the north point, but it is within the boundaries of the Aberdeen Proving Ground and not accessible by the public. The ground is swampy and there are few buildings.

SPRINGDALE SCHOOL (Carroll)

2 miles southwest of Westminster. The interesting old school house here is open to the public on the third Sunday of each month, May until August. Its name is a combination of Avondale and Spring Mills, as it served both communities.

SPRINGFIELD HOSPITAL CENTER (Carroll)

14 miles south of Westminster, on route 32. The property was once the estate of George Patterson, the brother of Betsy Patterson, whose name is well remembered in these parts, since she married Jerome Bonaparte, brother of Napoleon (See **WOODENSBURG.**) The estate was well farmed at the time and was noted for its herds of Devon cattle. There were also iron and copper mines on the property. The estate is now a psychiatric hospital, formerly called Springfield State Hospital, and the 1,000 acre farm is still worked.

SPRING MILLS (Carroll)

2 miles southwest of Westminster. Lead and iron deposits were discovered here in 1878.

STEVENSVILLE (Queen Anne's)

On Kent Island, one mile east of the Bay Bridge. It is thought to be on the site of an earlier town called Broad Creek, which served the ferry route across the Bay. A company here produces electronic equipment.

STEWART TOWN (Montgomery)

7 miles north of Rockville. A small black community surrounded by new development.

STEYER (Garrett)

11 miles southeast of Oakland. This insignificant spot on the Potomac River has two claims to fame. McCullough's Path (q.v.) crossed the river a mile west of here; and John Steyer, the founder of the town, took part in the Boston Tea Party.

STILL POND (Kent)

8 miles north of Chestertown. The nearby creek of the same name appears on old maps as Steel Pone Creek, although the town was previously called Four Corners. In this village once lived a fighter by the name of Tom Hyer, who is said to have won, in 1841, the first American heavyweight boxing championship over Yankee Sullivan. The village also like to think of itself as being the first place in Maryland to grant women's suffrage, as women voted in the town election of 1908.

STOCKTON (Worcester)

9 miles south of Snow Hill. It was called Sandy Hill until 1872 and its present name may come from the fact that it was an assembly point for cattle to be herded to northern cities.

STONELEIGH (Baltimore County)

6 miles north of downtown Baltimore. This affluent neighborhood just beyond the city line was started by a wealthy Baltimore importer named Thomas Brown, who erected a mansion here and named it after Stoneleigh Abbey in England.

STREET (Harford)

9 miles north of Bel Air. The village was founded in 1774 by Scotch-Irish settlers and named Highland. The post office changed the name to Street, after the Street family, who were landowners in the neighborhood; but the elementary school and a church are still named Highland, while some of the older inhabitants still refer to it by that name. The general store was once the Maryland and Pennsylvania Railroad office.

STUMP NECK (Charles)

14 miles southwest of La Plata. On this neck of land protruding into the Potomac near the mouth of Mattawoman Creek is the U. S. Navy's Explosive Disposal School, a subsidiary of the Indian Head Naval Ordnance Station. The only school of its kind in the world, it deals with emergency situations throughout the western part of the world. The facility covers 1,081 acres and employs 550 military personnel. It is a desolate place and there is scarcely a habitation for two miles inland.

SUDBROOK PARK (Baltimore County)

8 miles northwest of downtown Baltimore in the vicinity of Pikesville. This area of large cottages on spacious lots was originally planned by Frederick Law Olmsted as a model suburb and summer colony, although it is now surrounded by newer developments and somewhat obscured. It was recently threatened by both the Northwest Expressway and the Baltimore subway system. Spirited opposition has triumphed in banning the expressway and routing the subway underground.

SUDLERSVILLE (Queen Anne's) Pop. 417. Incorp. 1870.

15 miles northeast of Centreville. It was named after the Sadler family, but the railroad changed it to Sudler when it put a station here in the 1860's. A plant nearby processes soy beans.

SUE ISLAND (Baltimore County)

12 miles east of downtown Baltimore. A small projection of land on Back River Neck where the Baltimore Yacht Club has its headquarters.

SUGARLOAF MOUNTAIN (Frederick)

10 miles south of Frederick. This isolated peak between the Piedmont hills and Catoctin Mountain has always been a prominent landmark. During the Civil War it was occupied by the U. S. Government as a military post and observation point; later it was used by the Coast Survey as a triangulation point. It was often eyed as a prospective resort but in the 1920's it came into the hands of Gordon Strong, who built a mansion half way up the mountain called Stronghold. Strong died in 1954 and left the estate in trust for the public. A winding road ascends to the top where

there are parking area, overlooks and picnic grounds, all beautifully landscaped. The highest point is 1281 ft.

SUITLAND (Prince George's) Pop. with **SILVER HILL** 32,164.

6 miles southeast of the U. S. Capitol. The name is from Samuel Tyler Suit, who had a distillery here in the 1800's and owned much property both here and at Oxon Hill, where he is buried. Suit also built the castle in Berkeley Springs, West Virginia.

In, 1941 the Federal Government bought land here and began work on the Federal Building Complex on 360 acres. Today the complex houses the U. S. Bureau of the Census; the Hydrographic Office; the Naval Photographic Interpretation Center; the U. S. Weather Bureau, and other federal agencies. Much population growth has been encouraged by the presence of the Federal Center.

There is said to be a unique bog near Suitland, belonging to the Park Service.

SUNDERLAND (Calvert)

9 miles north of Prince Frederick. One mile south of

Sunderland. Bishop Claggett's sundial.

the town is All Saints Episcopal Church, a brick building which was completed in 1777, replacing a former log structure. The church is notable for the fact that Thomas J. Claggett, the first Episcopal Bishop to be consecrated in America, was rector here from 1767 to 1776 and from 1788 to 1792. When he left All Saints, he presented the church with a sundial, which can still be seen in the churchyard here.

SUNSHINE (Montgomery)

11 miles northeast of Rockville. The inhabitants of this tiny settlement think that the name was bestowed by a stranger who appeared at the general store of the unnamed town one sunny day. The postoffice was opened under this name in 1874; the general store is now apartments.

SUSQUEHANNA RIVER

Only about 20 miles of the 448 mile long Susquehanna River are in Maryland, but nearly all of its water flows into the Chesapeake Bay, which can be regarded as its estuary. Eighty percent of the fresh water in the Bay above the Potomac, and fifty percent of all fresh water flowing into the Bay throughout its length comes from the Susquehanna. The stretch of the river in Maryland forms the boundary between Harford and Cecil Counties.

The Susquehanna is dammed at Conowingo (q.v.) and route 1 passes across the top of the dam. The reservoir mostly supplies towns in Pennsylvania, but there is a pipeline to Baltimore, which is tapped occasionally when the Baltimore water supply runs low. The river is also bridged by routes 40 and 95 and by the former B. & O. and Penn-Central Railroads, all in a cluster in the vicinity of Havre de Grace. (q.v.)

The earliest crossing of the river was at Bald Friar, where there was a fording place until after 1800. Ferries were established at Havre de Grace in 1695 and at Lapidum in 1727. (See also **GARRETT ISLAND, ROCK RUN, PERRYVILLE**)

SWALLOW FALLS STATE FOREST (Garrett)

The forest begins five miles northwest of Oakland and contains two state parks. Maryland's scenic forestry program began here, when the state received a gift of land. The Swallow Falls State Park is 10 miles northwest of

Oakland and embraces a part of the sparkling Youghiogheny River, including the falls which give the park its name, and the Muddy Creek Falls (q.v.) on its tributary. Also in the park are some of the state's last remaining stands of virgin hemlocks. There are self-guided and conducted nature walks. The Herrington Manor Area is five miles northwest of Oakland and has a lake for fishing and swimming.

SWANTON (Garrett)

10 miles northeast of Oakland. This point on the B. & O. Railroad at an elevation of 2296 ft. was an important shipping point for lumber for many years. On the map of 1823 it was shown as "Swan's Mill." A little wooden station remains, although no freight trains ever stop here.

SWEETAIR (Baltimore County)

16 miles northeast of downtown Baltimore. An indeterminate locality whose name was taken in 1812 from a 5,000 acre land grant made in 1704 to Charles Carroll. The area is slowly losing its rural aspect.

SYKESVILLE (Carroll)   Pop. 1,712.   Incorp. 1904.

15 miles south of Westminster. The town was named for James Sykes, who bought 1000 acres here in 1825 and founded the town on the Howard County side of the Patapsco River. Today, Sykesville is mostly in Carroll County and the part of town across the river seems doomed to decay, since the bridge which formerly connected its few buildings was washed out for the last time in the flood of 1972. Since route 32 now by-passes the town on an elevated bridge, the old bridge will probably never be replaced.

The B. & O. Railroad, pursuing its course up the valley of the Patapsco, arrived here in the 1830's and built a hotel called The Halfway House; the area became a resort for Baltimoreans many of whom stayed at neighboring farms in the summer. Later came a large flour mill, later converted to a cotton mill, but both hotel and mill were destroyed in the great flood of 1868, and presumably the station also. A railway station still remains here, but no passenger trains have passed for years except the occasional Fans' Special.

The town is still a trade center for the farmers of the surrounding country. Employment is provided by the nearby Springfield Hospital Center (q.v.) and the Westinghouse

Corporation, which opened a plant here in 1967 for the manufacture of welding equipment and ultrasonic cleaning
equipment, employing over 300 people. Patapsco State Park
and the Hugg-Thomas Wildlife Refuge extend along the river
valley.

Sykesville railroad station

TAKOMA PARK (Montgomery and partly in Prince George's)
Pop. 16,231. Incorp. 1890.

6 miles north of the U. S. Capitol, just outside the D. C.
line. The suburb was founded in 1883 by Benjamin Franklin
Gilbert. When the B. & O. Railroad put a station here, they
called it Brightwood, but later changed it to the present
name, which is supposed to be an Indian word for "High up --
near Heaven;"   they spelled it with a k to avoid confusion
with Tacoma, Washington. Mr. Gilbert died in 1907 and is
buried in Cedar Hill Cemetery. There is a memorial to him
in Gilbert Memorial Park, at Takoma and Eastern Avenues,
which was dedicated in 1939.

At Elm and Poplar Streets there was once a spring
which supplied water that was bottled and shipped all over
the East. At Maple Ave. and Sligo Creek Parkway stands a
tree on which Union soldiers in the area carved the names of
all the presidents. The tree survived and was dedicated as
the Presidents' Tree in 1948.

The Seventh Day Adventists moved here in the 1890's
and established their world headquarters, although there has
been some talk about moving it to Hagerstown.

North Takoma Park has an additional population of 7,373.

TALBOT COUNTY. County Seat: Easton. Pop. 25,604.
Area: 267 square miles.

Talbot County was formed in 1662 and named for Grace
Talbot, daughter of George, First Lord Baltimore. It is
bounded on the north by the Wye East River and Tuckahoe
Creek; on the east by Tuckahoe Creek and the Choptank
River; on the south by the Choptank River; on the west by
the Chesapeake Bay. This means that the county is bounded
by water all except for $7\frac{1}{2}$ miles of the northern boundary.

Talbot County lies entirely within the coastal plain and

the terrain is flat, although there is less marshland than in most counties of the Eastern Shore. Over 75% of the land area is arable farm land; corn, grains and soybeans are the chief crops; there is also dairying and poultry and livestock raising. The industries are mostly small and consist mainly of food processing and canning, fishing, and boat building.

TANEYTOWN (Carroll) Pop. 2,618. Incorp. 1836.

12 miles northwest of Westminster. Although it was named after the Taney family, Chief Justice Roger Brooke Taney had no part in the founding of the town. Raphael and Frederick Taney were among the first settlers, and the first land grant was issued in 1754. Taneytown is the oldest town in Carroll County.

George Washington, who called it Tawneytown, slept a night and took a bowl of mush for breakfast at the Adam Good Tavern here in 1791; legend relates that the poorly spaced sign reading A dam good tavern, drew his attention. The site of this tavern is marked by a small plaque on the second house off the main street on route 194, south of the town.   The oldest building now standing is part of an old stone building on the opposite side of Frederick St.

The name of the town is remembered for the Taneytown clock;   grandfather clocks were made here in the late 1700's and early 1800's and are now valuable collectors' items.   The most well-known maker was Eli Bentley, whose home was the fourth lot from the corner of Frederick and W. Baltimore Streets and who worked here until his death in 1822.

Many troop movements took place in and around the town in 1863 before and during the battle of Gettysburg. General Meade had his headquarters one mile north of town on route 194, and the tower of the Lutheran Church was used for signalling with flags and flares.

Among the town's industries are men's clothing, rubber footware, pumps and wooden stairs.

TANNERY (Carroll)

2½ miles due east of Westminster.   There was indeed a leather works here at one time on the West Branch of the Patapsco.

TAYLOR'S ISLAND (Dorchester)

Taylor's Island is separated from the Eastern Shore by a series of creeks, and connected to it by a bridge 14 miles southwest of Cambridge.   Although it looks like a northern continuation of Hooper Island, there is no connection.   It was named for Thomas Taylor, an early settler, and inhabited ten years before Dorchester County was laid out.

Most of the habitations are around the village of Taylor's Island, just across the bridge.   In the churchyard of Grace Church, the colonial Chapel of Ease of Old Trinity (See **CHURCH CREEK)** is a 12 ft. by 12 ft. early log school house, moved here from a plantation for preservation.   The same church has a balcony constructed from the timbers of a ship.   By the shore of Slaughter Creek is an old gun known as Beccy Phipps, which was captured in an engagement with the British in 1812 (See **MADISON.)**   Phipps was the name of the lieutenant who commanded the invaders and Beccy was a slave whom they captured.   It is said that a canal dug by slave labor, crossing the marsh to improve a nearby plantation can still be seen.

TAYLORSVILLE (Carroll)

9 miles southwest of Westminster. A crossroads village where route 26 begins its westward climb over Parr's Ridge. It was named for General Zachary Taylor, and the first house was built in 1846 by Henry D. Franklin. The Franklins are thought to have settled in the area in about 1745, and Franklinville, a mile to the west, commemorates their name. The area is fast losing its rural aspect.

T.B. (Prince George's)

11 miles southwest of Upper Marlboro. The strange name comes from the initials of Thomas Brooke, a 17th century land owner, who put his initials on the stones marking the boundaries of his property. One of the stones was discovered at the point where the village was founded, at the junction of five roads. Although the village is insignificant, five roads do actually meet here, not counting the modern routes 5 and 301. The roads were originally Indian trails.

TEMPLEVILLE (Caroline and Queen Anne's)   Pop. 102. Incorp. 1865.

18 miles north of Denton. The north side of the street is in Queen Anne's County and the south side is in Caroline County. It was named for the Temple family, one of whom was governor of Delaware; earlier it was called Bullocktown. Patty Cannon (See **RELIANCE**) is supposed to have hidden captives in the hotel here.

TENFOOT ISLAND (Montgomery)

12 miles west of Rockville in the Potomac River above Seneca. During prohibition, a moonshine still operated successsssfully here.

TEXAS (Baltimore County)

12 miles north of downtown Baltimore. It was once called Clark's Switch, after a local landowner and quarry operator. In 1830 it became Ellengowan. The name was changed to Texas in 1840, when many inhabitants went to fight in the Mexican War, they say.

Its existence has long centered around the marble, or limestone quarries, which provided lime from 1804 until the early 1900's. Today no lime is burnt but the huge workings provide mostly crushed limestone for dozens of purposes, including, we are told, the fine coating on chewing gum.

Visitors are allowed to view the quarry operations from an overlook, provided they call for permission beforehand.

THOMAS POINT (Anne Arundel)

5 miles southeast of Annapolis, projecting into the Bay at the mouth of the South River. Off shore a hexagonal wooden lighthouse on iron stilts, called a screwpile, is the last manned off-shore lighthouse in the Bay.

Forty four acres on the point was donated to the county in 1965 but continual efforts are needed to prevent its loss by erosion. Admittance to the area is by permit only to prevent overuse of this fragile resource.

THOMAS VIADUCT

When the Baltimore and Ohio Railroad constructed its line from Baltimore to Washington in the 1830's, the first obstacle was the Patapsco River. The bridge which was built over the river in the 1830's and named for Philip Thomas, the first president of the B. & O. Railroad, still stands, and carries heavy freight trains, although critics predicted it would not support even the small engines of the 1830's. Designed by Benjamin H. Latrobe II, it is 612 ft. long and stretches in a graceful four degree curve supported on eight elliptical arches. Although very little water flows under it today, there were violent floods in 1868 and 1972 but no damage was caused to the structure.

Thomas Viaduct.

THURMONT (Frederick) Pop. 2,934. Incorp. 1831.

15 miles north of Frederick, at the foot of Catoctin Mountain. It was incorporated under the name of Mechanicsville, but at the request of the Western Maryland Railroad, it changed its name to Thurmont, meaning "Gateway to the Mountains," in 1894. The railroad station, which in those days made Thurmont a resort town, has been demolished.

The town was founded by a family named Weller, who built the first house just west of town by a spring on what is now route 77. In 1800 they built a hotel at the crossroads, now a store. Joseph and John Weller manufactured the first lucifer matches in America in a little grey stone house on W. Main St. The house has been much altered and enlarged, but any resident can point it out.

Thurmont also has another first. The electric crossing bell for railroads was invented hereby Richard J. O'Toole, on Boundary Ave., although it is said that he never profited from his invention.

Thurmont is the nearest town to Camp David and has hosted many illustrious visitors in the recent past. Winston Churchill dined at the Cozy Restaurant; Kruschev was seen being whisked through town during the "Spirit of Camp David " days, and the Kennedys were occasionally seen shopping along Main St.

The town has a few small industries: business forms, printing, ladies' dresses, furniture and shoes. A monumental mason firm has produced some public monuments, among them the Alabama Monument at Gettysburg and the Boy Scout Monument on the Ellipse in Washington, D. C.

TILGHMAN ISLAND (Talbot)

It lies at the southern tip of one of the strange projections of the Eastern Shore into the Chesapeake Bay, and is separated from the shore by Knapps Narrows. It has had many names in the past, including Choptank Island; but its present name is taken from Matthew Tilghman, who owned it in 1775 and who was known as "The Patriarch of Maryland." (See **CLAIBORNE**.) The Tilghmans were numerous in Talbot County, and can still be found there.

The road approaching Tilghman Island from St. Michael's passes across the bridge over Knapps Narrows, which is Maryland's longest single span drawbridge. The town of

Tilghman is close to the bridge and the terrace of a restaurant offers a good view of the Narrows and its boating activities; the drawbridge is constantly raised and lowered to allow the passage of work boats and pleasure boats.

At the southern tip of the island is Black Walnut Point, which is inaccessible to the public since the Navy has a large radar tower here; the point was used for testing radar in its early days.

There is a small boat building operation at Tilghman and several seafood packers on the island. Each autumn Tilghman Island hosts a seafood festival with demonstrations of working boats, tours of packing plants and other activities.

TILGHMANTON (Washington)

8 miles south of Hagerstown. It was named for Colonel Frisby Tilghman, who came here before 1800 from the Eastern Shore and laid out the town in lots for poor people, although there is nothing in the small village to indicate this today.   The Tilghmans were a prominent Eastern Shore family. The village is noted for jousting tournaments.

TIMONIUM (Baltimore County)

11 miles north of downtown Baltimore. There is some disagreement over how the town got its name. Some favor the story that it was named by Mrs. Archibald Buchanan, who, after the loss of a dear friend, named it after the tower in Alexandria in Egypt to which Mark Anthony withdrew, to spend the rest of his life in sorrow after his defeat and loss of friends.   Others say that she named it after Timon of Athens, who also suffered grief. Still others say that it was named for the timothy grass which was grown abundantly on farms in the vicinity.

Today the name is associated with a different kind of turf, for there is a well-known race track here. The Maryland State Fair is held here each year at the end of August. There is much suburban and industrial development along the York Road corridor.

TOBYTOWN (Montgomery)

A tiny black community near Rockville, which was hopelessly dilapidated until H. U. D. came to the rescue of the inhabitants with an urban renewal program.

TOLCHESTER (Kent)

9 miles west of Chestertown. The name is familiar to the older generation because Tolchester was a popular resort for many years and frequent steamer excursions left Baltimore for a day on the beach here. The resort was opened in 1877 by the Tolchester Beach Improvement Co. and by 1888 the company owned and operated four steamers and 155 acres of land, with a hotel, penny arcade, ferris wheel, dance floor, etc. A race track closed in 1914 and the rest of the resort closed in 1961. The whole property is now a very private marina and route 21 ends abruptly at the water with no guard rail and no turning place.

Tolchester is notable for being the place where the only battle of the War of 1812 on Maryland's Eastern Shore took place. In 1814, a British Officer, Sir Peter Parker, landed a force near here and a skirmish took place in which Parker was mortally wounded. A granite monument, erected in 1902 beside route 21 marks the spot, known as Caulk's Battlefield.

TOMS CREEK (Frederick)

A tributary of the Monocacy, which enters Maryland near Emmitsburg. Toms Creek Presbyterian Church was organized at an early date three miles southeast of Emmitsburg.

TOWN HILL (Allegany)

One of the most easterly long narrow ridges of the Ridge and Valley Province, reaching from the Pennsylvania border to the Potomac River. It is said to have been named for Oldtown, once the dominant settlement of the area. It is densely forested and large areas belong to the Green Ridge State Forest. On its west flank is the Billmeyer Wildlife Management Area of 708 acres, and on its east flank is the Belle Grove Game Farm. An old road follows the crest of the hill.

TOWN POINT (Cecil)

10 miles southwest of Elkton. Town Point Neck is the land between the Bohemia and Elk Rivers, and Town Point is its furthest extremity. An early attempt was made to establish a town here, but without success. The land belonged to Philip Calvert, a relative of Cecilius, Lord Baltimore, and the proposed town was to have been called Ceciltown. A

town of that name was finally established some miles to the south.

TOWSON. County Seat of Baltimore County. Pop. 77,809.

8 miles north of downtown Baltimore. It was named for the Towson family, who kept a tavern here, and was formerly called Towsontown; the second part was dropped around 1900.

The Towson family are first mentioned in records in 1771. Ezekiel Towson left his mark on the town when he petitioned for the York Road to be diverted in order to pass the door of his inn, which stood where the Towson Theater now stands, and was demolished in 1929. The petition was granted, and the resulting bend in the road harrasses traffic to this day. General Nathan Towson, born 1754, distinguished himself in the War of 1812 and is buried in Oak Hill Cemetery in Georgetown, Washington, D. C.

Towsontown became the seat of Baltimore County in 1850 when Baltimore, the previous county seat, became a separate town. The present courthouse was built in 1854 and enlarged in 1925 and 1956. Towson has undergone a surge of development in the last few years and much of its original character has been lost; the views which resulted from its position on a hill have been largely obscured by high rise office blocks and shopping malls. Black and Decker, the world's largest producer of portable power tools with 125

Towson. a. Towson State University.
b. Baltimore County Courthouse.

branches throughout the world, has its headquarters and a small museum here. The Bendix Co. is also in Towson.

Towson State University started as a state teachers' college in Baltimore in 1866 and moved to Towson in 1915. In 1965 it became Towson State College and it achieved university status in 1976. The campus has an area of 326 undulating acres and the original building with the clock tower is considered to be an outstanding example of Jacobean revival architecture.

Goucher College, which opened in Baltimore in 1888 as a Methodist institution, is also in Towson. It moved into its present 300 acre campus in the 1940's. At 535 Hampton Lane is the Hampton Mansion (q.v.)

TRACY'S LANDING (Anne Arundel)

15 miles southwest of Annapolis. North of the village, beside the main road, stands St. James's Church where Thomas J. Claggett was rector from 1786 to 1792 before he became the first Episcopal bishop to be consecrated in America. The first church was completed here in 1695 but the present structure dates from 1765. In the churchyard are some 17th century graves, and the oldest known grave in Maryland, dating from 1665. A lending library started at the church in 1695 is said to be still functioning.

TRAPPE (Talbot) Pop. 426. Incorp. 1856

8 miles south of Easton. Some believe the name came from a Trappist monastery whose remains are thought to be built into a farmhouse south of the town on the main road. Others say the name is from an old tavern "The Partridge Trap." St. Paul's church here has the furnishings from the ruins of Whitemarsh Church (See Hambledon.) There are several canning and packing companies nearby. Trappe Landing is two miles west of Trappe on a deep inlet of the Choptank River.

TRED AVON RIVER

A tributary of the Choptank River which rises in the vicinity of Easton and runs for about 10 miles. The name supposedly is a corruption of Third Haven (See **EASTON.**) Near its mouth is the town of Oxford, where the river is crossed by a ferry.

TRENTON (Baltimore County)

23 miles northwest of downtown Baltimore. It was previously called Soucksville after a local landowner and was once larger than it is today and had a hotel and several small industries.

TRIDELPHIA (Howard)

Tridelphia was a village 13 miles southwest of Ellicott City before its remnants disappeared under the Tridelphia Reservoir in 1941. It was founded in 1809 and named for three Quaker brothers-in-law. There was once a large stone cotton factory and several mills in operation before half of the town was destroyed by a flood in 1868. Most of the remainder was destroyed some years later, so that it was but a ghost town when Brighton Dam was built and Patuxent Valley flooded. Tridelphia Reservoir is $5\frac{1}{2}$ miles long, was opened in 1943 and holds six billion gallons of water, serving Montgomery County. The name still lingers in a road which no longer crosses the river.

TRUMP (Baltimore County)

28 miles north of downtown Baltimore. It is named for a Mr. Van Trump who once ran the general store here.

TUCKAHOE (Caroline)

3 miles northwest of Denton. The village was only a place of minor importance when the Baltimore and Eastern Railroad was functioning and it is even more insignificant now. Tuckahoe Creek rises in Delaware and empties into the Choptank River seven miles below Denton. It is named for the Tuckahoe weed. Tuckahoe Neck is not a true peninsula, but a triangle of land between the Tuckahoe and Choptank Rivers, once noted for its fertility and well-kept farms. Tuckahoe State Park consists of 4,000 acres on both sides of Tuckahoe Creek, north of route 404; the area is still being developed and when complete there will be a dam, a large lake for recreation, a visitors' center and an arboretum.

Not far from Tuckahoe was born Frederick Douglass, the son of a slave, Harriet Bailey, and probably a white father. He became a plantation slave at Lloyd House (q.v.) until he fled in 1838. After various anti-slavery activities in Massachusetts and in England, he returned with money to buy his freedom, and founded a weekly abolitionist paper, The North Star. After the Civil War he held government positions. His statue stands on the grounds of Morgan State College in Baltimore.

Between Tuckahoe and Denton is the Caroline Sales Barn, where auctions of livestock, produce, used furniture, etc. are held each Wednesday.

TURKEY POINT (Cecil)

15 miles southwest of Elkton. Turkey Point is the southernmost tip of Elk Neck, which is the triangle of land between the Elk and Northeast Rivers at the head of the Chesapeake Bay. Turkey Point Light, one mile off shore, is an important mark for ships coming up the Bay to the C. & D. Canal. It was built in 1833 and at one time had the only female lighthouse keeper in the U. S. The modern light is automatic.

There are several other Turkey Points along the Bay shores but this is probably the most well-known.

TURNER CREEK (Kent)

A Kent County recreation area is here, stressing local education, with outdoor classrooms and a mile long nature trail. There is also a public landing and an old granary undergoing preservation. A farm museum is planned.

TURNER STATION (Baltimore County)

5 miles southeast of downtown Baltimore, near Dundalk. This old-established black community, originally built to house workers at Bethlehem Steel in the 1940's, consists of individual and group homes and apartments, mostly rented.

TUSCARORA (Frederick)

11 miles south of Frederick. In this neighborhood was the home farm of the estate of Charles Carroll of Carrollton (See **CARROLLTON.**) Tuscarora Creek was once lined with paper mills.

TYRONE (Carroll)

6 miles northwest of Westminster. It was founded by the Farmwalt family on what was once known as "The Plank Road" from Westminster to Taneytown.

UNICORN (Queen Anne's)

11 miles east of Chestertown. The name comes from the Unicorn Woollen Mills which were once established here. The 45 acre mill pond, on a tributary of the Chester River, is now a public fishing pond.

UNION BRIDGE (Carroll) Pop. 927. Incorp. 1872.

10 miles west of Westminster. Originally it was known as The Pipe Creek Settlement from its location on that river (q.v.) and before that as Buttersburg, presumably because it was the center of a flourishing dairy industry. Its present name was given when the first bridge over Little Pipe Creek was built.

The Western Maryland Railroad reached here in 1862 and for some years this was the western terminus; the company's workshops and dwellings for employees were built here, burnt and rebuilt in 1868. They were used until 1909 after which all operations were moved to Hagerstown. Although there are no longer any workshops here, and no passenger trains, the station is well preserved and serves as the headquarters and museum of the Western Maryland Railroad Historical Society, which is open to the public on Sundays 12-4, April 1 to Oct. 31. The railroad is also commemorated by the name of Canary St. which was named for a diminutive but restless yellow locomotive which came into town for the railroad construction work in the '80's.

Near the outskirts of the town is the Pipe Creek Quaker Meeting House, beautifully located near a grove of trees. Built in 1768 it was damaged by fire and the interior rebuilt in 1935.

Union Bridge is believed to have been the site of the first nail factory in the U. S. The prototype of the first modern reaper was invented by a resident of Unionbridge,

John B. Thomas and tried out in a nearby field in 1811. The machine was improved upon by Thomas's cousin, Obed Hussey and the scissors action used by this invention is used by reapers and combine harvesters to the present day. Credit was later given to a rival inventor, Cyrus B. McCormick.

Although Union Bridge has several small industries, the town is dominated by the cement works which operates in the local limestone. Cement manufacturing was first established here in 1910; the plant was bought by Lehigh in 1925 and remodelled in 1939.

UNIONTOWN (Carroll)

$6\frac{1}{2}$ miles northwest of Westminster. This small town was originally called The Forks, but it changed to the present name in 1813 and advanced claims to be the county seat of a new county, to be called Union County. It was a go-ahead place in its day and was the home of the first printing press in the area; but when the Western Maryland did it a favor by by-passing it, the town failed to grow. Frozen in time, it has been described as "one perfect street of homes and churches," and was designated as Historic Area in 1970. Pipe Creek Church, the oldest Church of the Brethren in Maryland, organized in 1758, is two miles to the south.

UNIONVILLE (Baltimore County)

14 miles northeast of downtown Baltimore. The village is insignificant but the nearby Cloverland Dairy Farm used to be a popular place to visit. One could watch the cows being milked, pet the calves and buy ice cream.

UNIONVILLE (Frederick)

13 miles northeast of Frederick. Another small village which commemorates the Union. Iron and zinc were mined nearby until 1879.

UNITY (Montgomery)

11 miles northeast of Rockville. The first house was built here in 1811 by Elisha R. Gaither. In 1827 the town consisted of six dwellings and is much the same today, although probably not for long.

UNIVERSITY PARK (Prince George's)   Pop. 2,536. Incorp. 1936.

7 miles northeast of the U. S. Capitol. It adjoins the

south side of College Park although it was actually incorporated nine years before College Park.

UPPERCO (Baltimore County)

25 miles northwest of Baltimore. This odd name does not stand for Upper County, as one might think, but was named after the Upperco Family. It was first settled before 1800. See **ARCADIA**.)

UPPER FERRY (Wicomico)

5 miles southwest of Salisbury. A free ferry crosses the Wicomico River here, 8 miles above the ferry at Whitehaven. Its hours are Mon. - Fri. 7-6 in summer, 7-5 in winter. Sats. 7-1.

UPPER MARLBORO.   County Seat of Prince George's County. Pop. 646. Incorp. 1870.

15 miles southeast of the U. S. Capitol. The town was established in 1706 and named for the first Duke of Marlborough, a famous military leader of Queen Anne's reign and ancestor of Sir Winston Churchill.   It is called Upper Marlboro to distinguish it from a small town in Calvert County called Lower Marlboro, and was spelled Marlborough until 1893.

It became the seat of Prince George's County in 1718. A new courthouse was built in 1747, but the present one dates from 1880, enlarged beyond recognition in 1940, 1947 and 1960, even although many of the county agencies and offices are located in Hyattsville, closer to the centers of population.   Upper Marlboro has remained small and surprisingly rural considering its closeness to Washington, D. C.

There are several points of historical interest in the town. The first American Catholic Bishop, John Carroll, was born on the main street, where the courthouse now stands, while Trinity Church was founded by the first American-consecrated Episcopalian Bishop, Thomas Claggett in 1810. The present building dates from 1846.

Three blocks from Main Street on a knoll opposite the county administration building, is the tomb of Dr. Beane, whose arrest by the British in 1814 indirectly caused the writing of the *Star Spangled Banner*. It was while negotiating for Dr. Beane's release on a British Man-of-War that Key saw the flag flying over Fort McHenry and was inspired to write the memorable words.

There is very little industry in or around the town except for some wood, sand and gravel products and two tobacco warehouses. Tobacco auctions are held from April 15th to July 15th and visitors are sometimes able to watch these animated and somewhat eccentric proceedings.

Upper Marlboro. Beane tomb with County Office Building in background.

URBANA (Frederick)

7 miles southeast of Frederick. Roger Johnson, brother of Maryland's first elected governor, had an elegant mansion here and it is said the window panes bore the names of many prominent guests cut into the glass with a diamond ring. The Peter Pan restaurant occupies a house built in 1849 on the site of an inn destroyed by fire the previous year, and which sheltered soldiers during the Civil War. It opened as a restaurant in 1926 and now caters to family parties in the summer months, both indoors and out.

UTICA (Frederick)

8 miles north of Frederick. On Utica Road, crossing Fishing Creek, is Utica Mills covered bridge, the largest of Frederick County's three covered bridges, which was built in 1889.

VALE SUMMIT (Allegany)

8 miles southwest of Cumberland. This small mining village in a hollow on the west side of Dans Mountain was settled early by Welsh, Scottish and Irish miners, and for many years its name was Pompey Smash. Legend relates that a driver named Pompey was bringing a loaded wagon down the mountain and it collapsed here, at the dangerous bend in the road, which has since been straightened out. In 1867 the Astor mine caught fire near here, and bas been burning ever since, underground. A glimpse of small puffs of smoke issuing from roadside banks can sometimes be seen when passing along the new route 48.

VALLEY LEE (St. Mary's)

10 miles southeast of Leonardtown. St. George's Church here was built in 1750 on the site of a predecessor dating from the 1650's.

VIENNA (Dorchester) Pop. 358. Incorp. 1833.

15 miles southeast of Cambridge. It was established by the Maryland Assembly in 1709 on land purchased from the Nanticoke Indians and may have been named for Vinnacoka-simmon, chief of the local tribes.

The first public warehouse was built in 1762 and the town was made a port of entry in 1768; it remained an important point of entry until 1860. A small frame custom house built in 1791 remains on the river bank near the intersection of Water and Church Streets.

A bridge was built across the Nanticoke River in 1828 but removed in 1860 as it was a menace to navigation. After that a ferry connected with a mile long causeway over the marshes on the east side of the river. Today, traffic thunders over the route 50 highway bridge, built in 1931, heading for the Atlantic beaches or the south.

Vienna. Old dwelling by the Nanticoke River.

The river is still navigable, principally by oil barges, which supply the Delmarva Power and Light Company, the main producer of electric power for the Eastern Shore. Vienna's only other industry is a tomato packing house.

Three miles southwest of the town is the Le Compte Wildlife Refuge, where the endangered Delmarva Fox Squirrel is protected.

VIERS MILL VILLAGE (Montgomery)

4 miles southeast of Rockville. It was named after the Veirs family who settled here in the 19th century, but the name has changed its spelling to Viers by custom. A development started here in 1948 when the Veterans' Administration backed construction of 1,105 identical small houses on a maze of winding streets between Viers Mill Road and Rock Creek Park. None have been built since, but many have been improved, while more affluent developments have sprung up adjoining the village.

VINDEX (Garrett)

East and West Vindex are 10 and 12 miles east of Oakland in mountainous terrain. A few scattered dwellings remain of West Vindex but nothing whatever remains of East Vindex. Collectively known as Vindex, the place was built as a coal company town by the Johnstown Coal and Coke Company in 1906 and razed in 1967, years after mining operations ceased. Strip mining in the area is a possibility.

WAKEFIELD (Carroll)

4½ miles southwest of Westminster. This tiny village has given its name to the Wakefield Valley, a limestone valley which was once famous for the beautiful marbles it produced. A quarry near the village is abandoned and water-filled, but there are still some working quarries in the formation, although the stone is no longer used for decorative purposes.

WALDORF (Charles) Pop. 9,782.

8 miles northeast of La Plata. The name means "Village in the Woods" but it is hardly a village now, and the woods have long since been cleared and turned into tobacco farms.

A settlement was founded here in the 18th century, but it did not develop or receive a name until the railroad came through in 1872, when it totally eclipsed neighboring Beantown, which had been the nearest postoffice. The original town is obscured by residential developments and the numerous motels and restaurants which line route 301. Since Waldorf is close to the county line, it attracted many visitors during the period 1949-1968 when the three southern counties of Maryland were the only places in the East where gambling was legal. Even after the axe fell in 1968, the town never lost its popularity with Washingtonians.

Among the local industries are tobacco auctions and a company making plastic boats.

WALKER (Baltimore County)

25 miles north of downtown Baltimore. It used to be known as Walkers Station or Walkers Switch, a stop on the Northern Central Railroad. There is no station and no switch any more, indeed no anything except an isolated house.

WALKERSVILLE (Frederick) Pop. 2,212. Incorp. 1892

6 miles northeast of Frederick. It was originally called Georgetown after an inhabitant named George Cramer, but the railroad re-named it after George Walker, the owner of the land when they built their station here. The line from here to Taneytown was abandoned in 1972 but has recently been purchased by an interested group who operate it under the name of the Maryland Midland Railroad.

WALLMAN (Garrett)

9 miles southeast of Oakland on the Potomac River. It was once the site of a large sawmill, which shut down in the 1930's, but only the name now remains at the end of a dead-end road.

WALNUT LANDING (Dorchester)

17 miles east of Cambridge on the Nanticoke River at the mouth of Marshyhope Creek. There is nothing here to-day but it is thought to be the place where, in earlier days, Patty Cannon shipped her captives. (See **RELIANCE**.)

WARDOUR (Anne Arundel)

$1\frac{1}{2}$ miles north of Annapolis fronting on the Severn River. The area was inherited by a historian named Elizabeth Giddings in 1884, and she named it for a family prominent in English history.

WARREN (Baltimore County)

12 miles north of downtown Baltimore. The place marked Warren on the map was named in 1922 when some of the inhabitants of the village of Warren, three miles north of here, lost their village below the waters of Loch Raven Reservoir.

In former times Warren was a manufacturing village with several mills on the Gunpowder River and many stone houses. In 1922, when Baltimore City bought the properties for one million dollars, one factory remained, manufacturing cotton duck, and the inhabitants numbered 900. The surviving families, although scattered, still hold reunions to remember their town, now under the lake.

WARRIOR MOUNTAIN (Allegany)

One of the steep, narrow ridges of the Ridge and Valley

Province, stretching from the Potomac River to the Pennsylvania border and beyond. Its name is supposed to commemorate the Warriors' Path, an Indian trail which ran along its crest and crossed old route 40 at Flintstone. The state owns the 2,597 acre Warrior Mountain Wildlife Management Area about eight miles southeast of Cumberland, which has only fair parking access.

WARWICK (Cecil)

14 miles south of Elkton, close to the Delaware border. Near here was born James Rumsey (1743-92) who was considered to be the inventor of the steam boat, and who demonstrated his invention on the Potomac River in 1787. He is commemorated by a tall monument beside the Potomac at Shepherdstown, West Virginia.

Two miles northwest of Warwick lies St. Francis Xavier Catholic Church, established in 1704 and the first Catholic Church on the Eastern Shore of Maryland. It is often called Old Bohemia Church, since it lies within the territory of Bohemia Manor (q.v.) Connected with it was Bohemia Academy, founded 1745, one of whose pupils was Bishop John Carroll, first Catholic Bishop of the U.S. and cousin of Charles Carroll of Carrollton. The school has disappeared, but its bricks were used in the construction of the rectory which was built in 1792, on the north side of the present church. The church and rectory, which contains a small museum, are open to the public on the third Sunday afternoon of each month during the summer.

In 1953 the Old Bohemia Historical Society was formed and the members began documenting everything that lay within the former manor territory.

WASHINGTON COUNTY. County Seat: Hagerstown. Pop. 113,086. Area: 457 square miles.

Washington County was formed in 1776 and named after George Washington in a fateful year. It is bounded on the north by the Pennsylvania border; on the south by the Potomac River; on the west by Sideling Hill Creek; on the east by the crest of South Mountain from Blue Ridge Summit to Weverton.

The county embraces the western slope of the Blue Ridge province, the Great Valley and part of the Ridge and Valley Province. The early settlers were Swiss, English, Scotch and French, followed by Scotch-Irish, German and

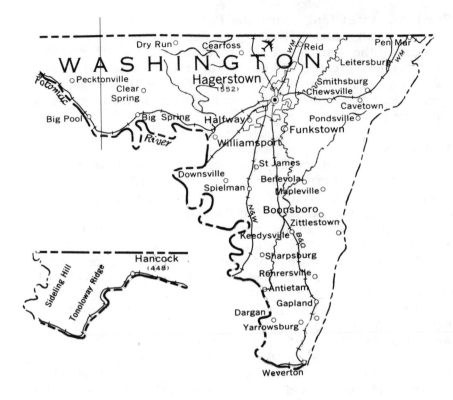

Dutch. Interstate 81, replacing older route 11, passes down
the Great Valley, just west of Hagerstown, while two tributaries of the Potomac, the Antietam and the Conococheague,
meander southwards down the valley.

The main agricultural products are tree fruits and nuts,
in which the county leads the state, followed by livestock,
grains and hay. It is the second county in the state in dairying. Manufacturing is also important in the Hagerstown
area.

WASHINGTON GROVE (Montgomery)   Pop. 688.   Incorp.
1937.   4 miles north of Rockville. The original Washington Grove was a camp meeting ground of the Methodist
Church. The residential village has been preserved in a
manner which attempts to retain the original atmosphere;
the narrow paths in front of the old houses have been retained and motor roads have been built in the rear. Modern
houses now surround the old village.

WASHINGTON MONUMENT STATE PARK (Washington)

11 miles southeast of Hagerstown on the summit of South Mountain, the park is approached from alternate, or old route 40.   In 1827 the townsfolk of Boonsboro were inspired to erect the first public monument to George Washington at a point on the steep, rock-covered hillside known as Blue Rocks.   On the fourth of July the men of Boonesboro went in a body to the summit of South Mountain and without pausing to eat or drink, erected in one day a "crock-shaped" structure 15 ft. high; a year later they raised it to 30 ft. Owing to its lack of mortar it crumbled after a few years, but was re-erected in 1882.

Today the spot is known as Monument Knob, and the monument is still there, but well-cemented and sturdy, with a stone staircase inside.   The Civilian Conservation Corps restored it in 1934 after the original design, thought uninspired by some, but which harmonizes well with the surroundings.   The view from the top across the Great Valley is well worth the short climb from the parking lot.

WATERLOO (Howard)

7 miles south of Ellicott City at the intersection of routes 1 and 175.   In coaching days this was a stop on the road from Baltimore to Washington, where Spurriers Inn provided rest and refreshment.   George Washington is said to have stopped here once or twice.

WATKINS POINT (Somerset)

A point at the mouth of the Pocomoke River at the tip of Cedar Point Wildlife Management Area, which is a low swampy peninsula.   Although the point is marked only by an iron beacon and is unapproachable by land, it marks the southernmost tip of Maryland and is of great significance since it is the first place mentioned in the Maryland Charter --- the point from which the state boundary started and to which it returned.

The charter describes it as being near the river of Wighco, which is marked on Captain John Smith's map where the Pocomoke River is today.   Rival claimants to the territory tried to prove that the point was really on Wicomico River, 22 miles to the north, regardless of the fact that a point opposite the mouth of the Potomac was obviously indicated.

WATKINS REGIONAL PARK (Prince George's)

12 miles east of the U. S. Capitol on Maryland route 556 south of 214. This was originally a model dairy farm, which was acquired by the National Capital Parks and Planning Commission in 1971. It covers about 500 acres and there is picnicking, tennis, childrens' zoo, miniature train and a farm, with vegetable gardens and animals and a nature center.

WAYSON'S CORNER (Anne Arundel)

16 miles southwest of Annapolis. At this crossroads, which has been somewhat altered by new road building, a tobacco warehouse has stood for many years, where the usual auctions are held in season.

WESTCHESTER (Baltimore County)

9 miles west of downtown Baltimore. A scattered community of individual homes near Oella.

WESTERNPORT (Allegany) Pop. 2,706. Incorp. 1858.

20 miles southwest of Cumberland at the point where George's Creek enters the Potomac. It owes its name to the fact that it was the furthest point westward that coal was loaded to be shipped down the Potomac in the days when George's Creek Valley was a great coal-producing area. It was also a point of debarkation for westward journeys and the Andrew Mullins house on Main St. hosted George Washington on his last westward expedition. Before its present dignified name, Westernport was called Hard Scrabble.

The population finds employment in the paper mill at Luke and in the small amount of mining which remains in the area.

WEST FRIENDSHIP (Howard)

9 miles northwest of Ellicott City on the old Frederick Road (route 144.) The Howard County Fairgrounds are here and a "Tractor Pull" competition is held here each June on a Saturday.

WESTMINSTER. County Seat of Carroll County. Pop. 8,808. Incorp. 1818. Pop. of Westminster South: 3,521.

Westminster is situated on Parrs Ridge (q.v.) and was originally five separate villages, which accounts for the town's unusually long main street, stretching almost two miles. It was laid out in 1764 by William Winchester and called Winchester until 1768, when the name was changed to avoid confusion with Winchester, Virginia.   The founder and his family are buried in the cemetery near City Hall, the graves easily recognized by their table-like shapes.   On a mound near the graves stood the Union Meeting House from 1760 to 1891, which was used for meetings of all Protestant denominations.   A piece of its altar rail, made into a kneeling bench, is in the Methodist Episcopal Church.

At the northwest end of the town is Western Maryland College, a liberal arts college founded by the Methodist Church in 1867 and said to have been the first co-educational college south of the Mason-Dixon Line.   Near the other end of the town is the Carroll County Historical Society, housed at 206 East Main St. in a house which dates from 1807.   It contains a museum with collections of 19th century dolls, early American flags and a hobnail glass collection which belonged to Mrs. H. L. Mencken, wife of the well-known Baltimore writer.   There is also a postal museum in the building, which commemorates the first R. F. D. service in the U. S., which was tried out in Westminster.   The museum is open 2-5 on weekdays, except Monday, and 1-4 on Sundays.   The nearby Cockey's Tavern dates from stage-coaching days and still serves as a restaurant.

The present courthouse was built in 1837.   Nearby is the City Hall, formerly the Emerald Hill Estate, standing in a pleasant garden.   Historical markers here and there tell that the town was entered three times by Confederate troops in the Civil War and that skirmishes took place.

In spite of the suburban shopping centers which have sprung up, Westminster is still very much alive and a new mini-mall has been built near the center. Among the town's industries are some manufacturers of clothing and shoes, canneries, meat packers and manufacturers of metal signs and electrical aparatus.

A mile south of the town is the Carroll County Farm Museum on a property which was formerly the grounds of the old alms-houses.   It consists of an 1850 period farm house, barn and outbuildings, with draft horses and early farm machinery.   The farm is open April to October, but several times a year there are working demonstrations of black-smithing and other farm activities and rural crafts.

WEST NOTTINGHAM (Cecil)

15 miles northwest of Elkton.   The name is a reminder of the Nottingham Lots, a territory once laid out by William

Penn when this border country was disputed between the Penns of Pennsylvania and the Calverts of Maryland.

West Nottingham Academy was established about 1744 by Samuel Finley, a young Presbyterian minister and was the forerunner of many such institutions affiliated with the Presbyterian Church in America, although it is the last remaining academy under the church's jurisdiction today. It was moved to its present 360 acre campus in 1821 although the earliest portion of the present building dates from 1865. Two signers of the Declaration of Independence were educated here: Benjamin Rush and Richard Stockton. Girls were accepted at the school for the first time in 1953.

WESTOVER (Somerset)

5 miles south of Princess Anne. In the neighborhood are a mill, erected in 1876, now closed, and the largest fresh water spring in Somerset County. A plant here cans and packs tomatoes.

WEST RIVER (Anne Arundel)

West River enters the Chesapeake Bay ten miles below Annapolis; it is one of the creeks which dissect the western shore of the Bay. At Chalk Point, which juts into the river opposite Galesville, occurred the only military action in Anne Arundel County of the War of 1812, when a party from a British ship proceeded up the West River and attacked the property of Stephen Steward.

WETIPQUIN (Wicomico)

15 miles west of Salisbury. The State Road Commissioin's hand-operated ferry over Wetipquin Creek was replaced by a bridge some years ago.

WEVERTON (Washington)

22 miles south of Hagerstown, where South Mountain meets the Potomac. It was named for Caspar Wever, an engineer connected with the B. & O. Railroad, who built the first bridge at Harper's Ferry, laid out Pennsylvania Avenue in Washington, D. C. and was secretary of the U. S. Senate for a time.

Wever purchased the water rights here and had great plans for an industrial complex. A large dam and a series of mills were built, but floods later destroyed the mills and all his plans. Nothing now remains of them, and what is left of the village is totally divorced from the river by Route 340, which slices through South Mountain at this point. The outcrop of rock revealed by the road cut is well known to geologists, and insignificant Weverton gives its name to the Weverton quartzite, which caps many of the local mountain peaks. A decrepit branch of the B. & O. from Weverton to Hagerstown is no longer used.

WHALEYSVILLE (Worcester)

16 miles northeast of Snow Hill. The locality was first called Mitchell's Store, then, about 1720, the Turn in the Road. It was named for Capt. Peter Whaley about 1850, and local historians think it should be Whaleyville, rather than Whaleysville.

Before drainage took place, the area was an island in the surrounding swamps. Mills of various kinds occupied the town at different times and it was the center of a shingle industry until the local cypress and cedar trees were exhausted. When the railroad was abandoned in 1933, the station was moved to Mitchell Avenue, where it was converted into a dwelling. Canned whole tomatoes are produced at a plant nearby.

WHEATON (Montgomery) Pop. with Glenmont 48,598.

11 miles north of the U. S. Capitol. Originally it was called Mitchell's Cross Roads after the keeper of a tavern at the intersection of Georgia Ave. and Plyer's Mill Road where a pharmacy now stands. After the Civil War, George Plyer, a Union soldier, settled here and became the post master on the spot where the Hughes Methodist Church now stands on Georgia Ave. He called the town after his commander, Captain Wheaton.

In 1906 the town was considered too small to have its own post office and it became a branch of Sandy Spring. By 1958 it regained an independent station and growth since that time has been phenomenal.

Wheaton Regional Park has boat rentals, fishing, nature trail, and a nature center. At 1500 Glenallan Ave., off Randolph Road is the interesting Brookside Gardens, covering 50 acres and devoted to various horticultural displays, with lectures and demonstrations. The staff distributes "Garden Notes" six times a year.

WHITEHALL (Anne Arundel)

4 miles northeast of Annapolis. This area of individual homes on large properties was named after the house built by Governor Horatio Sharpe, on a point of land jutting out into the Bay. Sharpe was governor of Maryland 1753-1769.

WHITE HALL (Baltimore County)

22 miles north of downtown Baltimore. There was once a large building, painted white, which served as post office, boarding house and railroad station on the Northern Central Railroad, now defunct. It is said that much pig-iron used to be loaded here.

WHITEHAVEN (Wicomico)

12 miles southwest of Salisbury. It was named after the home town in England of George Gale, who established a community here at the beginning of the 18th century. Whitehaven was once a prosperous place with a shipbuilding industry which survived until World War I and produced submarine parts. A free ferry operates across the Wicomico River, as it has done for 250 years. The present ferry can carry three cars and runs from 6 a.m. to 7.30 p.m. in summer, 7-6 in spring and 7-5.30 in winter.

Several miles upstream, on Green Hill Church Road, is Green Hill Church, previously called St. Bartholomew's Church, which was built on an earlier site in 1733, when it was intended to found a town here. However, there is no trace of a town and the church remains, isolated, shore erosion bringing it yearly closer to the water.

WHITELEYSBURG (Caroline)

7 miles northeast of Denton. It was named after the Whiteley family who were prominent landowners in the area.

WHITEMARSH (Baltimore County)

12 miles northeast of downtown Baltimore. The boundaries of this area are somewhat vague, centering on the flat land near the B. & O. Railroad. When the railroad put a station here in the 1880's they called it Cowenton, after one of their officials. There are several quarries here producing sand and gravel, but a large shopping mall has recently been constructed in anticipation of further development which will include industry, parks and homes to eventually house 10,000 people.

WHITE OAK (Montgomery) Pop. 13,700

10 miles north of the U. S. Capitol. An area of new suburban development.

WHITE PLAINS (Charles) Pop. 5,167

4 miles northeast of La Plata. On De Marr Road is the 200 acre White Plains Park. There is a golf course, lighted driving range, tennis and swimming, with skating and camping in season.

WHITE ROCK (Frederick)

5 miles northwest of Frederick. It is a white rock among the trees on Catoctin Mountain, visible only from a distance; it cannot be seen from White Rock grocery at the foot of the mountain. The rock is approachable only on foot, from Hamburg Road and was once a place of considerable notoriety and a favorite place for picnics. Legend says that Indian weddings were celebrated here. On one occasion a rejected Indian suitor hurled the maiden over the rock as she was being married to another, after which, he and the bridegroom-to-be followed her to their deaths.

WHITE ROCKS (Baltimore County)

An outcrop of white sandstone about a mile off shore near the mouth of the Patapsco. It served as a guide to shipping from earliest times, and is part of the same outcrop that can be seen at Elvaton, on Wishing Rock Road.

WHITE'S FERRY (Montgomery)

White's Ferry.

20 miles northwest of Rockville. It is the only crossing of the Potomac between Point of Rocks and Washington, D. C. and it has been in operation, with few interruptions, for 150 years. It is the last of the more than one hundred ferries which once crossed the Potomac. Originally called Conrad's Ferry, it became White's when it was owned by an operator of that name who lived on the Virginia side after the Civil War.

In 1864 Jubal Early and his troops crossed the Potomac here and at White's Ford, another formerly important crossing about three miles upsteam. The ferry boat which operates today bears Early's name. It runs daily between 6 a.m. and 11 p.m. and can carry seven cars and a limit of 40,000 lb. Cost for an auto is $2.00 one way, $3.00 round trip. and for foot passengers 50¢. There is a small store and restaurant near the dock, also a few picnic tables and canoes for rent.

WICOMICO COUNTY. County Seat: Salisbury. Pop. 64,540. Area: 368 square miles.

Wicomico County was formed in 1867. It was named after the Wicomico River which flows through it, and which is an Indian name supposedly referring to an Indian town near the banks, or meaning "A pleasant place to live."

It is bounded on the north and northeast by the Delaware boundary; on the east by the Pocomoke River; on the south by the Wicomico River, Wicomico Creek and an arbitray line; on the west by the Nanticoke River. The county lies within the Coastal Plain Province and the terrain is level.

Its capital, Salisbury, is the Eastern Shore's largest town; outside of Salisbury the main occupation is chicken-raising and Wicomico ranks as one of the largest chicken producing counties in the U. S. There is also some raising of corn, soybeans and rye, and some lumbering and fishing.

WICOMICO RIVER (Eastern Shore)
A river which rises near Delmar, flows through Salisbury and enters the Bay at the same point as the Nanticoke. It is navigable for barges as far as Salisbury.

WICOMICO RIVER (Western Shore)
It originates in Cedarville State Park and flows south through Zekiah Swamp into the Potomac, where it is two miles wide at the mouth. The tidal estuary runs for 15 miles and forms part of the boundary between Charles and St. Mary's Counties.

WICOMICO STATE FOREST (Wicomico)
8 miles east of Salisbury. The forest covers 1100 acres and is used primarily for research on the loblolly pine.

WILLARDS (Wicomico) Pop. 494. Incorp. 1906.
14 miles east of Salisbury. It was named for Willards Thompson of Baltimore, an executive of the railroad which once ran through here. He may have been a relative of Daniel Willard, a director of the B. & O. Railroad in its heyday, and whose name is borne by several railroad towns in several states.

WILLIAMSBURG (Dorchester)
The first house was built here in 1804 and it received its present name in 1840. Legend tells us that the town's original name was Bunker Hill, as so many fights took place here.

WILLIAMSPORT (Washington) Pop. 2,153. Incorp. 1823.
6 miles west of Hagerstown where Conococheague Creek

enters the Potomac. It was a town on route 11, which runs down the Great Valley and crosses the Potomac here; but Interstate 81 now takes most of the traffic away from the town.

Williamsport was founded in 1787 by Otto Holland Williams, a friend of George Washington and a Brigadier-general of the Revolution ; his monument is in the cemetery overlooking the town. Around 1790 there was an effort made to have the National Capital established here, and Washington visited the town to assess its advantages. Some years later the town became the western terminus of the Western Maryland Railroad and a port for boats coming up the C. & O. Canal, which spans the Conococheague by an aqueduct, now somewhat dilapidated. The Civil War brought troops up and down the Great Valley, crossing and re-crossing the Potomac at this point.

There are industries in tanning, crushed stone, plastic pipe and travel trailers. A brick works has been in business for many years making use of local material, while the highly visible chimneys nearby belong to a power plant of the Potomac Edison Power Co.

Williamsport was the home town of canal author George "Hooper" Wolfe, whose book *I Drove Mules on the C.& O. Canal* gives a vivid picture of canal life.

WILLISTON (Caroline)

4 miles south of Denton. The town was formerly called Potter's Landing, and the name is still on the map at the Choptank River end of the town. It was named after the Potter family which had a long association with the town from the days when the stream here turned their mill, through the days when two steamboats called at Potter's Landing daily. The property was later bought by John A. Willis and the town became Williston, while the lake formed by the mill dam became, and remains, Willison Lake.

WILLS MOUNTAIN (Allegany)

Immediately west of Cumberland, this northward extension of Dans Mountain (q.v.) was once a formidable barrier to westward migration. It forms the eastern boundary of the Allegheny Plateau and is one of the bulwarks of the Cumberland Narrows.

This mountain, and Wills Creek, which flows through the

Narrows and enters the Potomac at Cumberland, were named for an Indian named Will, who remained in the vicinity and befriended the whites in their early struggles. He is supposed to have been buried on the top of Will's Knob. Lovers' Leap (q.v.) is an overlook on Wills Mountain.

WILSON BRIDGE (Washington)

8 miles west of Hagerstown. This five-arched structure spans Conococheague Creek and it considerably improved the road to the west when it was built in 1819. It carried traffic until damaged by a flood in 1972, but is now closed to all but pedestrians and all traffic goes over the nearby route 40 bridge. Wilson Bridge was restored in 1984.

Wilson Bridge.

WINDY HILL (Talbot)

8 miles southeast of Easton. This quiet cluster of houses beside the Choptank River was once a bustling shipping point, as were Kingston Landing and Kirby's Wharf and other points along the banks.

WINFIELD (Carroll)

10 miles southwest of Westminster just north of route 26. It was named in honor of General Winfield Scott. There is some new development in the area.

WINGATE (Dorchester)

19 miles south of Cambridge. It was named for the first postmaster, Urim G. Wingate, in 1902. Near here is a small promontory called John's Point, which was the site of an early county seat of Dorchester County; later the seat moved to Harwood's Choice, which is thought to have been on Fishing Creek about 8 miles southwest of Cambridge. There are two seafood packing companies here.

WISEBURG (Baltimore County)

23 miles north of downtown Baltimore. The town was founded in the 1770's by John Weise, who changed his name to Wise. His tavern, once known as The Halfway House, is said to be still standing, although it has been used as a dwelling since 1890.

WOLF ROCK (Frederick)

1½ miles from Thurmont on the map, but considerably more by foot, which is the only way to reach this overlook in Catoctin Mountain National Park.

WOLFSVILLE (Frederick)

13 miles northwest of Frederick. It was named for Jacob D. Wolf, who also built the Black Rock Hotel, two miles west of here on South Mountain. Black Rock was formerly a favorite picnic spot, but the hotel was never very successful, and burnt down several times. Some of its ruins remain.

Each October the Catoctin Antique Gas Engine Show takes place in Wolfsville. The engines operate saws, presses, churns, etc. and there are other displays and food.

WOODBINE (Carroll)

16 miles southwest of Westminster. The village spans the Patapsco, and retains something of its rural atmosphere in spite of developments in the area. There is a pub and a few small enterprises.

WOODENSBURG (Baltimore County)

19 miles northwest of downtown Baltimore. It is named for Benjamin Wooden who received a land grant here in 1756. Toll gates once barred the Hanover Pike, and the house diagonally across from Mount Gilead Church is said to be a

former tollgate house.

Near Woodensburg is the estate of Montrose, named originally for the Marquis of Montrose, a Scottish loyalist. The estate was part of the holdings of William Patterson, a wealthy Baltimorean and father of Betsy Patterson. Betsy met Jerome Bonaparte, Napolean's youngest brother, in Baltimore when he was a guest of Joshua Barney, and later married him; but Napolean disapproved of the marriage and forced a separation. The Montrose estate descended to their son and was later purchased by the State of Maryland and in 1922 became the Montrose School for Girls. It is now the Montrose School, under the jurisdiction of the Dept. of Health and Hygiene. The film *Hearts Divided* was shot on location here.

WOODLAWN (Baltimore County) Pop. 5,306

7 miles northwest of downtown Baltimore. It began life before 1856 and was called Powhattan, after a company that owned a mill in the vicinity. In 1902, after a fire at the mill, an extensive property was bought by the Woodlawn Cemetery Company, and the village also took the name.

Woodlawn is better known, however, for the Social Security Complex, the fifth largest federal building in the U.S. It is the national administrative and record-keeping headquarters of the Social Security System and covers over two million square feet of office space. Tours can be arranged weekdays by calling 944-5000, ext. 2984.

There are extensive residential developments in the area and a number of light industries.

WOODMONT (Washington)

8 miles west of Hancock. This 6,000 acre estate close to the Potomac River is the home of the Woodmont Gun Club. A mere 80 miles from the White House, it has previously attracted six presidents, who used to arrive at Tonoloway Station on the Western Maryland Railroad in order to enjoy the club's facilities and the club house with its fireplaces built of stones from historic places. Members today arrive by car or plane (it has its own airstrip) and the Western Maryland Railroad is left mainly to geology students who come to examine the formation of Tonoloway Ridge, exposed by the railway cutting.

WOODSBORO (Frederick) Pop. 439. Incorp. 1836.

10 miles northeast of Frederick. It was laid out in 1786 byJoseph Wood, an officer of the Revolution, who had a fine brick house here before 1776. First it was called Woods Town, then Woodsberry, then Woodsborough, before it was changed to Woodsboro in 1922.

The Rosebud Perfume Co. was founded here in 1891 and is still here, although the salve is now made in Baltimore and the perfume in New York. On Tuesday mornings there is an outdoor farmers and antiques market.

WOODSIDE (Montgomery)

8 miles north of the U. S. Capitol. A Washington suburb which was promoted by Benjamin F. Leighton, when the B. & O. Railroad put in a station in the 1870's.

WOODSTOCK (Howard)

6 miles northwest of Ellicott City. Like most of the Patapsco Valley towns, it has seen better days, and nothing but a few ramshackle houses and a bar remain in the village. Across the river in Baltimore County and high on a hill stands the solid Woodstock College, built from the local granite. Founded in 1869, it was a seven year college for Jesuits, the only Jesuit seminary in the U. S. at the time. The Jesuits moved out in 1970 and part of the premises is now used by the Job Corps to train young men and women, while most of the grounds became part of the Patapsco State Park.

WOOLFORD (Dorchester)

7 miles southwest of Cambridge. If it is true, as old-timers say, that it was earlier called Loomtown, because every household had a weaver's loom, one must assume that they wove wool on their looms.

WORCESTER COUNTY.   County Seat: Snow Hill.   Pop. 30,889. Area: 491 square miles.

Worcester County (pronounced Wooster) was formed in 1742 and named after the Earl of Worcester. It is bounded on the north by the Delaware boundary; on the east by the Atlantic Ocean; on the south by the Virginia boundary; on the west by the Pocomoke River plus a sparsely inhabited triangle based on the west side of the river. It is the only Maryland county which is bordered by the ocean, and the terrain is flat and sandy.

Apart from the seasonal industry of Ocean City, the economy is primarily agricultural, chiefly poultry, followed by corn and grain and some market gardening. Holly is collected in season. Ninety percent of industrial employees are engaged either in canning or chicken processing.

WYE CHURCH (Talbot)

8 miles south of Centreville, near the village of Wye Mills. This is a very early Episcopal church, built in 1721 on the foundations of an earlier building, and restored in 1949. It has high box pews, a hanging pulpit and the royal arms of England on the gallery. The nearby vestry house was reconstructed on the old foundations.

Next to the church is the tiny Wye Oak State Park, which was developed in order to preserve a large white oak tree known as the Wye Oak. The tree, which inspired Maryland to adopt the white oak as its state tree, is 32 ft. in circumference andd 108 ft. high, and is reckoned to be 400 years old. The state has recently acquired some more acreage to enlarge the park.

WYE HOUSE (Talbot)

8 miles northwest of Easton and 2 miles north of Copperville. The estate is private but has a long history, since it has been in the Lloyd family since 1658, although the present house near the banks of the Wye East River was built about 1784. The gardens include an orangery and miles of boxwood hedges.

The founder of the Lloyd family, one of the richest families on the Eastern Shore, was a Welshman who named the estate after the River Wye in Wales. The family has included provincial and state legislators, two state governors and a U. S. Senator.

Frederick Douglass (See Tuckahoe) spent his childhood at Wye House and describes it in his book *My Bondage and My Freedom*. This estate should not be confused with Wye Plantation, which is across the river on Wye Island.

WYE INSTITUTE (Queen Anne's)

10 miles southwest of Centreville on Wye Neck. The University of Maryland has acquired 780 acres here, the former estate of Cheston-on-Wye, an historic property with an eight mile frontage on the Wye River. The Institute's primary purpose is to assist in the educational, cultural and economic development of the Eastern Shore.

WYE ISLAND (Queen Anne's)

12 miles south of Centreville. An island approximately one mile by six miles, formed by the Wye and Wye East Rivers and Wye Narrows, which was bridged in 1876. It has been called at various times Lloyd's, Chew's, Bordley's and Paca's Island. Wye Neck is the peninsula on the landward side of Wye Narrows.

WYE MILLS (Talbot)

7 miles south of Centreville. The village is little more than a store, postoffice and an old mill. Although the address is Talbot County, the boundary between Talbot and Queen Anne's Counties runs through the old mill. This mill was in operation before 1672 and is still in operation, although the present building is only about 150 years old. Like other mills of its time and place, it supplied flour for Washington's troops at Valley Forge.

The Society for the Preservation of Maryland Antiquities now owns the mill and since 1971 it has been operated by students from Chesapeake College as part of a work-study program. It is open every day in summer 9-5, and weekends all year.

The mill at Wye Mills.

WYE PLANTATION (Queen Anne's)
3 miles southeast of Carmichael and 10 miles southwest of Centreville on Wye Neck Road. It was the summer home of William Paca, one of the four Maryland "Signers" and governor of Maryland 1782-5. Nothing of the original house remains, but a large granite monument has been erected to Paca and a ceremony is held here each July 4th.

Wye Plantation recently belonged to Arthur A. Houghton and the present mansion was erected in 1972. Houghton, who was president of Wye Institute and chairman of Steuben Glass, has a library of priceless first editions and manuscripts and a famous herd of black angus cattle; until recently the herd and a visitors' center could be seen by the public, but in early 1978 Mr. Houghton donated the herd to the University of Maryland and the house and grounds to the Aspen Institute.

WYE RIVER
Named after the river in Wales, probably by the Lloyds, who were of Welsh descent and owned much of the surrounding territory. It has given its name to Wye Church, House, Institute, Island, Mills and Plantation.

YELLOW SPRINGS (Frederick)

5 miles northwest of Frederick at the foot of Catoctin Mountain. The village was once known as Brooke Hill and was something of a resort. It is said to have been a favorite spot of the Indians who thought that the streams flowing down from the mountainside had medicinal properties. Indian Springs, two miles further south, was another of their favorite spots. The area now belongs to the City of Frederick and there are groves and picnic spots beside the stream.

YOUGHIOGHENY RIVER

Although the source of the Youghiogheny is but a few miles from the Potomac, the river flows northward and westward, away from the Potomac and towards the Ohio. The name is said to be an Indian word meaning "flowing in the contrary direction."

The portion of the Youghiogheny in Maryland is the most scenic river in the state, with surroundings that are rocky and forested for most of its length. Along the gorge from near Oakland to Friendsville, there is unspoilt geology and wildlife, rapids, falls and placid stretches. Swallow Falls, and Muddy Creek Falls, on one of its tributaries, are preserved in Swallow Falls State Park.

There are few settlements along the river and access is mainly by foot along abandoned logging trails and old railroad beds. Efforts are being made, with some opposition by land holders, to preserve it in its natural condition, but threats are constant.

The river is dammed in Pennsylvania and the southern tip of the resulting lake extends into Maryland.

ZEKIAH SWAMP (Charles)

A wildlife refuge extending along both banks of a stream which rises in Cedarville State Forest, 12 miles northeast of La Plata, and opens out into the Wicomico River 9 miles south of La Plata, a distance of about 16 miles. There are few access roads, and wildlife, including beaver, is plentiful. John Wilkes Booth and his companion became lost in this swamp during their flight from Washington.

ZIHLMAN (Allegany)

A mile northeast of Frostburg. The village was once called Allegany Mines, but the present name is for Congressman Fred N. Zihlman.

ZITTLESTOWN (Washington)

12 miles southeast of Hagerstown. "Here vegetate some scores of souls, nées Zittles, married to Zittles, related to Zittles, or connected with Zittles." So wrote M. V. Dahlgren in 1882 in *South Mountain Magic.*

ALLEN'S FRESH (Charles)

8 miles south of La Plata. A locality at the point where Zekiah Swamp (q.v.) joins the salt water of the Wicomico River. Once called Allen's Mill, it is a favorite spot for anglers.

BALTIMORE   Southern Hotel   (Light and Redwood Sts.)

When the 14-story hotel opened in 1918 it had 350 rooms, a ballroom and a roof garden. In 1964 it was sold to an organization of the Methodist Church to be converted into a senior citizens' home, but three years later it was leased out as a training center for apprentice marine engineers. It is now undergoing renovations and will again become a hotel.

BALTIMORE & OHIO RAILROAD

The B & O although it exists only as a part of the CSX System today, is still a vital part of Maryland memories. Its cornerstone was laid amid much fanfare on July 4, 1828 and it became the nation's first genuine railroad as it pioneered a winding course from Baltimore along the Patapsco Valley, reaching Ellicott's Mills, now Ellicott City, in 1830. Continuing a westward course it reached the Potomac River at Point of Rocks and followed the river valley to Cumberland, finally reaching the Ohio at Wheeling in 1853. Meanwhile a connection had been made from Relay to Washington in 1835, crossing the Patapsco by the stone arches of the Thomas Viaduct.   Later, extensive yards at Locust Point and Curtis Bay connected the rails with the Port of Baltimore.

The B & O affiliated with the C & O in 1963 and gained control of the Western Maryland RR in 1968, all three eventually losing their identity in the CSX System.

BALTIMORE HARBOR TUNNEL

The tunnel under the harbor was opened in Nov. 1957 and is 1.7 miles long.   When constructed it was the first 4-lane tunnel in the U.S. to be laid in a trench.

BUSHWOOD (St. Mary's)

A crossroads village 8 miles west of Leonardtown. Bushwood Wharf, two miles to the west on the Wicomico River was once an important place, designed as a town in 1680 and first known as Port Wicomico, but all the old buildings are gone. It was occupied by Union Forces during the Civil War. Only a county pier and boat ramp remain.

EDMONSTON (Prince George's)   Pop. 1,441. Incorp. 1924.
6 miles northeast of the U.S.Capitol. An older suburb of Washington, D.C.

FORT McHENRY TUNNEL
Begun in 1980 and due for completion in 1985, this will provide an alternative link in I 95. This also consists of tubes (made by Wiley of Port Deposit) laid in a trench and will be the widest 8 lane underwater tunnel in the world.

FRANCIS SCOTT KEY BRIDGE
Completed in 1977, this bridge across the outer harbor not only completes the Baltimore Beltway but provides an excellent view of the city.

KENSINGTON (Addition)
A Morman Temple, the largest Mormon edifice east of the Mississippi, is here at 9900 Stoneybrook Road. The dramatic white building, surmounted by the golden angel Moroni, is visible from the Washington Beltway. A visitors' center is open Monday thru Saturday 9-9.

MARYLAND & PENNSYLVANIA RAILROAD
Affectionately known as the Ma and Pa, this small railroad was greatly loved by all before its demise in the 1950's. It followed the valley of the Jones Falls out of Baltimore and took a winding route through Towson and across the countryside to York, Pennsylvania, serving the farms and quarries.

MUIRKIRK (Prince George's)
14 miles northeast of the U.S. Capitol on Route 1. It was named by the Scottish founders who settled here in 1747 and built furnaces, first for iron, later for baking bricks. Brick clay was dug in the vicinity for many years and innumerable pits dot the area. The plant was unusual in that the kilns travelled on circular tracks over a circular flue.

Bricks are no longer made here but a plant employs 200 in producing "synthetic and natural iron oxides and inorganic chemical colors." Remains of early cretaceous reptiles were found here when clay was being excavated.

SANDY HOOK (Washington)

21 miles south of Hagerstown strung out along the bank of the Potomac River. There is barely sufficient room between the river and Maryland Heights for the village, the roadway, the C. & O. Canal and the B. & O. Railroad; in fact the road from here to Pleasantville borders the canal too closely for carefree driving.

Sandy Hook gives its name to the route 340 highway bridge across the Potomac. The name is said to have been taken from a quicksand pool in which a teamster once lost his team.

SANDY MOUNT (Carroll)

5 miles southeast of Westminster. There seems to be a difference of opinion whether the name should be one word or two.

SANDY POINT STATE PARK (Anne Arundel)

23 miles southeast of downtown Baltimore fronting on the Chesapeake Bay beside the Bay Bridge. The park covers 700 acres and has two bathing beaches, a large car park, fishing facilities, boats for rent, etc. There is a small fee charged for use of the park.

From here one can watch the shipping on the Bay and also get a fine view of the impressive William Preston Lane Memorial Bridge. Several events are held in the park during the summer months; Chesapeake Appreciation Days are on the 1st weekend in October, with boating competitions and other events.

Away from the shore line is an extensive wooded section and an open area containing an early 18th century farmhouse. Part of the wooded section is reserved as a wildlife study area, entered by permit only, and contains some fine trees, perhaps the only remaining virgin timber in Tidewater Maryland.

SANDY SPRING (Montgomery)   Pop. with Ashton 2659

8 miles northeast of Rockville. The spring from which it takes its name was half a mile south of town and the waters were considered especially adapted for washing and scouring.

Although an insignificant place today, it played an important part in the business and cultural activities of the area, owing to the activities of the Society of Friends who built a meeting house here in 1742; a brick building which replaced the frame structure in 1817 still stands on Meeting House Lane, and there is a Friends' School in Sandy Spring to this day.

SAVAGE MOUNTAIN (Garrett)

For years this was the retreat of the Indians beyond the range of the settlers, so it was assumed that it belonged to the so-called savages. Or perhaps it was named for a surveyor named Savage. It is flanked by the Savage River on the west and the George's Creek Valley on the east. Its northern continuation is Little Savage Mountain, traversed by route 40 and its highest point is High Rock, elevation 2991 ft. five miles west of Barton. A hiking trail has recently been opened along the mountain's crest.

SAVAGE RIVER STATE FOREST (Garrett)

The largest of Maryland's state forests, consisting of 52,770 acres on mountain slopes and valleys with numerous streams, completely surrounding the Savage River Reservoir. New Germany and Big Run State Parks (q.v.) are in the forest.

UNION MILLS (Carroll)

7 miles north of Westminster. It was named for the partnership between the owners, Andrew and David Shriver, who built the homestead and the mills in 1797. The original house was a small log and clapboard dwelling but later additions enlarged the estate to a farm with a large house, which served as an inn for stagecoach passengers, two mills, tannery, cooperage, blacksmith, etc. The village was once called Myersville, after the founder, Peter E. Myers, and was across the creek from the present mill, but nothing remains of it.

The present mill is on the National Register of Historic Places and was in actual use until 1942. Mill and house are privately owned but are open to the public at certain times, and occasional plant fairs and corn roasts are held here to raise money for charity.

During the Civil War the Shriver family was divided. The story goes that JEB Stuart was entertained on June 30th on the southwest side of the road and General James Barnes was entertained on the northeast side the following night.

WESTERN MARYLAND RAILROAD

The W. M. was chartered in 1852 and its first route paralleled the Gwynn's Falls into Baltimore and the N. Branch of the Patapsco River into Westminster and the wilds of Carroll, Frederick and Washington Counties until it reached the Potomac at Williamsport. From there it paralleled the B & O into Cumberland and beyond. Its port facilities in Baltimore were at Port Covington, now derelict. The W M became part of the Chessie System but shortly after the birth of CSX it ceased to exist, although a few freights still run over part of its tracks.

SELECTED BIBLIOGRAPHY

Numerous books, pamphlets and travel folders were scanned in addition to the following selected list of books. The local history sections of public libraries were examined in Baltimore and each of the county seats and also in a number of branch libraries, particularly in Baltimore, Montgomery and Prince George's Counties.

By far the richest sources of material were the vertical files of public libraries and historical societies, including the unique collection in the Maryland Room of the Enoch Pratt Library in Baltimore. Invariably they contain folders stuffed with newspaper clippings, programs of events, pamphlets, announcements, memoranda and reminiscences.

The task of compilation was greatly facilitated by the county maps, frequently updated, issued by the Maryland Geological Survey and by the Manual of Co-ordinates published by the Maryland Department of State Planning.

Maryland
Agle, Nan H. & Bacon, Frances A. The Lords Baltimore. 1962.
Carter, Annette. Exploring from the Chesapeake Bay to the Poconos. 1971.
Christian, Howard N. Life and Living in the Chesapeake Bay Region. 1959.
Davis, M.E. The Caves of Maryland. 1950
Di Lisio, James E. Maryland (Geographies of the U.S.) 1983.
Earle, Swepson. Chesapeake Bay Country. 1938
Footner, Hulbert. Maryland Main and the Eastern Shore. 1942.
Greenberry Series on Maryland. vols. 1-6. 1962-8.
Kaessmann, Beta, et al. My Maryland. 1955.
Martin, Oliver. From Baltimore to Wheeling on the National Pike. 1929.
Maryland Bicentennial Commission. Official Guide to Landmarks of the Revolutionary Era in Maryland.

Maryland Civil War Centennial Committee. Maryland Remembers. A guide to Historic Places and People of the Civil War in Maryland.

Maryland Department of State Planning. Scenic Rivers of Maryland. 1970.

Maryland Department of State Planning. The Counties of Maryland and Baltimore City. 1963

Maryland Department of State Planning. Maryland Manual of Co-ordinates. 3d ed. 1969. 4th ed. 1978.

Maryland Department of State Planning. Compendium of Natural Features. 1975.

Maryland Department of Economic Development. Economic Inventories of Maryland Counties. Issued 1970's.

Maryland Department of Education. Picture Portfolios. Issued 1950's.

Maryland Geological Survey. Topographic Maps of Maryland Counties. 23 maps.

Matthews, Edward B. The Counties of Maryland. 1907.

National Register of Historic Places. 1972. Supplement 1974.

Noble, Edward M. Maryland in Prose and Poetry. 1909

Papenfuse, Edward E. et al. Maryland. A New Guide to the Old Line State. 1976.

Pogue, Robert E. T. Old Maryland Landmarks.

Radoff, Morris L. The County Court Houses and Records of Maryland. 1960-63.

Reps, John W. Tidewater Towns. 1972.

Robbins, Michael W. Maryland's Iron Industry During the Revolutionary War Era. 1973.

Roberts, Mary-Carter. Historic Sites Surveys of Maryland Counties and Baltimore City. 1966-8.

Rollo, Vera F. Your Maryland. 1971.

Scharf, John T. History of Western Maryland. 1882

Shepherd, Henry E. The Representative Authors of Maryland. 1911.

Towpath Guides to the Chesapeake and Ohio Canal. 4 vols. 1971-3.

U.S.Geological Survey. Bulletin 1212. Boundaries of the United States and the Several States. 1966.

U.S. Census. 1970. 1980.

Wilstach, Paul. Tidewater Maryland. 1931.

Allegany County

Allegany County Preservation Society. Heritage Press. Nov.
    1971 - Oct. 1972.
Cumberland, Frostburg and George's Creek Almanac. 1945.
Historical-Biographical Sketch of Frostburg, Maryland. 1912.

Anne Arundel County

Riley, Elihu.   A History of Anne Arundel County in Maryland. 1905.

Baltimore County

Canton Company.   Canton Days.   1928.
Davidson, Isabel.   Real Stories from Baltimore County.   1917
Gontrum, Edwin K.   Sidelights on the History of Baltimore
    County.   1966.
Huttenhauer, Helen G.   Baltimore County in the State and
    Nation.   1973.
Jessop, Jennie E.   The origin of Names in Baltimore County.
    1967.
Marks, Lillian B.   Reister's Desire. 1975.
Martinak, George J.   A Short History of Essex and Middle
    River.   1963.
Offutt, E. Francis.   Baltimore County Landmarks.   1971.
Scharf, John T.   History of Baltimore and Baltimore County.
    1881.
Seitz, Mary A.   The history of the Hoffman Paper Mills in
    Maryland.   1946.

Calvert County

Stein, Charles F.   A History of Calvert County, Marylnd.
    1960.

Caroline County

History of Caroline County, Maryland from its Beginnings.
    By Teachers and Children of the County. 1920.
1774 - 1974. 200th Anniversary.   1974

Carroll County

Bulletin of the Historical Society of Carroll County.
Lynch, Branford G.   A hundred years of Carroll County.
    1939.

Shellman, May B. The Pioneers of the Early Days of West-
    minster. 1924.
Souvenir of Carroll County's Celebration of the 200th Anni-
    versary of the Birth of George Washington. 1932.
Stonesifer, Oliver J. History of Unionbridge, 1729-1937.
    1937.
Taneytown Bicentennial Celebration. 1954.
Warner, Nancy M. Carroll County, 1837 - 1976. 1976.

Cecil County

Gifford, George E. Cecil County, Maryland. 1608-1850.
Johnson, George. History of Cecil County. 1881.
Miller, Alice E. Cecil County, Maryland. 1949.
McNamee. Rising Sun Centennial Historical Booklet. 1960.

Charles County

Brown, Jack. Charles County, Maryland. A History. 1976.
Hinkel, John V. See Charles County. 1959.
Klapthor, Margaret B. History of Charles County. 1958.

Dorchester County

Huelle, Walter E. Footnotes to Dorchester History. 1969.
Jones, Elias. New Revised History of Dorchester County.
    1966. Original ed. 1925.
North Dorchester Heritage Festival. 1955
Souvenir Book - Dorchester Tercentenary Bay Country Festi-
    val. 1869-1969.
Stump, Brice N. It happened in Dorchester. 1969.

Eastern Shore

Clark, Charles B. The Eastern Shore of Maryland and Vir-
    ginia. 1950.
Footner, Hulbert. Rivers of the Eastern Shore. 1944.
Thurston, Walter C. The Eastern Shore of Maryland in Song
    and Story. 1938.
Wilstach, Paul. Tidewater Maryland. 1931.

Frederick County

Chapline, Harry E. Views and Sketches of Historic Fred-
    erick. 1906.
Grove, William J. History of Carrollton Manor. 1928.
Helman, James A. History of Emmittsburg. 1906.
Martin, Charles. History of Wolfsville. 1972.

Moser, Ira C. History of Myersville.   1905.
Moylan, Charles E.   Ijamsville.   1951.
Quynn, Wm. R.   Bicentennial History of Frederick City and
     County.   1975.
Rose, Thomas.   History of Myersville.   1971.
Souvenir of Historic Frederick.   1925.
Thurmont bicentennial and homecoming.   1951.
Williams, Thos. J. History of Frederick County. 1910.
Wireman, George G. Gateway to the Mountains. 1969.
Wolfe, Ralph S. Historic Sketch of Middletown Valley. 1914.
Wood, Alban M. Sketch of Braddock Heights. 1907.

Garrett County

Robinson, Felix. The Ballad of Oakland. 1949.
Tamarack. Taming of the Savage River. 1968.
Weeks, Thelma R. Oakland Centennial History.

Harford County

Mason, Samuel. Historical Sketches of Harford Co. 1940.
Preston, Walter W. History of Harford County. 1901.
Wright, C. Milton. Our Harford Heritage. 1967.

Howard County

Holland, Celia M. Ellicott City, MD, 1772-1971. 1972.
Holland, Celia M. Landmarks of Howard County. 1975.
Porter, Kent. Tour of Howard County. 1974.
Stein, Charles F. Origin and History of Howard County. 1972
Warfield, Joshua D.   The Founders of Anne Arundel and
     Howard Counties.   1905.

Kent County

Hanson, George. Old Kent. The Eastern Shore of Maryland.
     1876.
Swain. Creeks and Manors of Old Kent.

Montgomery County

Armstrong, Edith M.   A Brief History of Cabin John Park.
     1947.
Bethesda, Chevy Chase Community Guide. 1973-4.
Blair, Gist. Annals of Silver Spring. 1918.
Boyd, Thos, H. S. The History of Montgomery County, MD.
     1879. Repr. 1968.

Chevy Chase Village, MD. By the County Council. 1949.

Farquhar, Roger Brooke. Old Homes and History of Montgomery County, MD. 1962.

Filby, Vera R. Savage, Maryland. 1965.

History and Directory of Wheaton, Maryland. 1958.

MacMaster, Richard K. A Grateful Remembrance. The Story of Montgomery County. 1976.

Semi-Centennial Celebration of the Founding of Tacoma Park. 1901.

Prince George's County

Greene, Daniel M. A Brief History of Prince George's County. 1946.

Hienton, Louise J. Prince George's Heritage. 1972.

Poe, Gertrude L. Laurel, MD Centennial. 1970.

A Research Action Project Devoted to Aspects of the His- of Maryland and Prince George's County. 1959.

Watson, James D. Prince George's County Past and Present. 1964.

Queen Anne's County

Emory, Frederic. Queen Anne's County. Originally published in the Centreville Observer, 1886-7.

Somerset County

Bowen, Littleton P. Days of Makemie. 1885.

Somerset County Board of Education. Maryland's Historic Somerset. 1955.

Torrence, Clayton. Old Somerset on the Eastern Shore of Mayland. 1935.

Wilson, Woodrow T. History of Crisfield and Surrounding Areas. 1974.

Talbot County

Tilghman, Oswald. History of Talbot County, Maryland. 1967.

Washington County

Barron, Lee. The History of Sharpsburg, Maryland. 1972.

Williams, Thos. J. C. History of Washington County. 1906.

William, Thos. J. C. Hagerstown, An Illustrated Description. 1887.

Worcester County

Truitt, Reginald V.   Worcester County, Maryland's Arcadia.
     Worcester County Historical Soc.   1977.

Magazine

Chronicles of St. Mary's.
Glades Star.   1941 onward.
Maryland Magazine.   vol. 1, 1968 onward.
Tableland Trails.   1953-6.
Valleys of History.   vol. 1, 1965 onward

INDEX

A & P   199
Aberdeen Proving Fround   1, 172, 245, 320
Academy, The   91
Academy of Arts   122
Accident   99
Accokeek Foundation   60
Adam Good Tavern   328
Adams Hall   270
Adams, President   83
Adamstown   70
Addison Chapel   306
Aerospace Div. Westinghouse 37
Affair of the False Cape   134
Agner, John   3
Agricultural Co-operative Extension Service   95
Agricultural Research Center 43
Aiken   146
Aircoil Co.   190
Aireys   3
Airy, Henry   3
Al Marah horse farm   38
Alabama Monument   332
Albert Co.   109
Alberton   109
Alco-Gravure Div. oc Publications Corp.   157
Algonquin Hotel   107
Allegany County Academy   106
Allegany Hist. Soc.   107, 202
Allegany County Library   106
Allegany Mines 367
All Hallows Church   47, 314
All Saints Episcopal Church 324
Altamont   15
Amelung, John F.   251
Amelung House   251
American Glass Manufactory 251
American Presbyterianism   284

Amish Colony   210
Amish country   257
Amish Farmers' Market   183
Amish settlement   153
Amos, John   5
Anacostia Naval Air Station   5
Andersonville   190
Andrew Small Male & Female Academy   111
Andrews Air Force Base   67, 228, 276
Andrews, Frank M., Lt. Gen.   5
Anglican parish   258
Annapolis   19, 300
Anne Arundel Community Coll. 13
Anne Arundel County Court   209
Anne Arundel fire hq.   224
Anne Arundel Plice hq.   224
Anne Arundel Town   6
Antietam, Battle of   viii, 310
Antietam furnace   310
Appalachian Trail   10, 49, 318
Apple-Garth   180
Aquarium   27
Arcadians   246
Archer   91
Ark and Dove   77, 78, 134, 298
Armidstead Gdns.   19
Armistead, George   136
Armstrong, Thomas   157
Arnold, Archibald   230
Arnold's Settlement   230
Army Corps of Engineers   139, 289, 306
Army of the Potomac   267
Arters Mill   263
Asbestos   75
Asbury, Bishop   1, 245
Ashburton   29
Ashland Iron Co.   13
Askiminokonson   186
Aspen Institute   365

Assatequque Island   244
Astor mine   343
Atkisson Reservoir   172
Atlee, Isaac   236
Atlantic flyway   304
Atomic Energy Commission   156
Audubon Naturalists Soc.   89
Avenel   178
Avondale   320
Avondale flour mill   201
Azalea Acres   200

Babe Ruch   21
Bacon Hall   16
Bachman Valley R R   15, 123
Bachmans Mills   263
Backbone Mountain   182, 306
Bainbridge   270
Bailey, Harriet   337
Bald Friar   324
Ballestone Mansion   293
Baltimore   ix, 198, 335
Baltimore & Annapolis RR   37
Baltimore & Ohio RR (B & O)
    ix, 18, 106, 114, 145, 152,
    169, 201, 214, 219, 229,
    241, 254, 267, 285, 287,
    292, 306, 307, 324, 325,
    331, 352, 357
B & O RR Museum   70
B & O RR stations:
    Ellicott City   128
    Frederick   143
    Ijamsville   185
B & O trains   170
B & O RR Transportation Mus.
    27
Baltimore & Potomac RR   244,
    269
Baltimore Arts Tower   23
Baltimore Co. Courthouse and
    prison   191
Baltimore & Eastern RR   91,
    177, 184, 337
Baltimore Fire Museum   27
Baltimore Gas & Electric Co.
    212
Baltimore Goldfish Co.   198
Baltimore Highlands   130
Baltimore Maritime Museum   27
Baltimore Mus. of Art   27
Baltimore Mus. of Industry   27
Baltimore Normal School   53
Baltimore Pub. Wks. Mus.   27
Baltimore Produce Term'l   190
Baltimore Spice Co.   154
Baltimore Street Car Mus.   27

Baltimore Yacht Club   322
Baltimore Washington Intern'l
    Airport (BWI)   37, 146
Banneker, Benjamin   127, 245
Bare Hills   315
Barnes, Wm.   38
Barney, Joshua   166, 300, 361
Barren Creek   216
Barron, James   50
Barron's store   315
Barry Postoffice   59
Barton   155, 228
Basilica of the Assumption   21
Bata shoe factory   43
Battle Grove   40
Battle Monument   22
Battle of Antietam   viii, 142, 310
Battle of Bladensburg   98
Battle of Gettysburg   266
Battle of Monocacy   142, 145
Battle of N. Pt.   viii, 139, 239
Battle of South Mtn.   52, 61,
    100, 141, 154, 222
Battle Town   278
Bay Ridge Inn   39
Bay Shore   173
Bayou Hotel   175
Beacon Hill   16
Beall-Dawson House   292
Beall, Thomas   105
Beall's Cross Roads   40
Beallsville   172
Beane, Dr.   341
Beantown   345
Bear Creek Fish Rearing Sta. 2
Bearson's Island   320
Beaver Creek   56
Beaver Creek Fish Hatchery
    41, 205
Beaver Dam   186
Beaver Dam quarries   41
Beccy Phipps (gun)   329
Beckley, George   41
Bel Air   101
Belair   132
Bell, Graham   114
Bell Pottery   167
Belle Grove Game Farm   334
Bellevue   249
Belmont   14, 126
Belt, Truman   43
Beltsville   276
Beltsville Agric. Sta.   201
Belvedere Hotel   26, 86
Benedict   255
Benedict Leonard Town   44
Bennett's Creek   58
Bentley, Caleb   57

Bentley, Charles W.   44
Bentley, Eli   329
Berlin   59
Bethesda   243
Bethlehem Steel   119, 319, 338
Big Hunting Creek   72
Big Pipe Creek   263
Big View   123
Billmeyer Wildlife Management
    Area   334
Bird, Bird family   47, 48
Bishop family   48
Bishop's Cave   73
Black Ankle   109
Black & Decker   169, 335
Black & Decker plant   69
Black Horse Tavern   48
Black Rock   15
Black Rock Hotel   360
Black Walnut Point   333
Blackistone Island   298
Bladen, Thomas   49
Blaine   197
Blair, Francis Preston   312
Blair, Montgomery   312
Blair Valley Lake   186
Blake   133
Blessing of the Fleet   298
Bloodsworth family   50
Bloodsworth Island   103, 179
Bloody Lane   311
Bloomington   305
Bloomington Dam   51, 197
Bloomington Dam & Reservoir
    197
Blue Ball Tavern   51
Blue Mount quarries   51
Blue Ridge College   237
Bobinger, Rosa   63
Bobinger's Hotel   63
Bodkin Neck   261
Bodkin Point   239
Bohemia Academy   347
Bohemia Manor   297
Bohemia River   75
Bolton Hill   29
Bollman, Wendel   305
Bonaparte, Jerome   361
Boone   309
Boone, George & Wm.   52
Boonsboro   349
Booth, Edwin   141
Booth family   20, 140
Booth, John Wilkes   20, 40,
    43, 141, 181, 182, 319, 367
Booth, Junius Brutus   141
Borden   155

Borden family   53
Bordley's   364
Bothwick Hall   184
Boucher, Rev. Jon.   201, 203
Bourne's Island   316
Bowers Mills   15
Bowie, Oden   53, 244
Bowley, Daniel, Capt.   54
Bowling Brook Farm   221
Bowling Green   272
Boy Scout Monument   332
Boys' Village   82
Boyd, James A., Capt.   54
Boyd's Station   54
Bozman family   54
Bozman, John Leeds   54
Braddock, General   54, 92,
    105, 148, 234
Braddock Heights   72
Braddock (Hotel)   55
Braddock's Army   208
Braddock's Road   107
Bradley family   191
Bradleyburg   191
Brandywine People   55
Breezy Point   16
Brereton   4
Breton Bay   204
Briar Ridge   215
Brick Hotel   122
Brick Meeting House   63
Brickley, Andrew   133
Brickleytown   133
Bridewell   190
Bridgetown   164
Bridge-Tumme;   121
Brighton Dam   255
Brightwood   327
Broad Creek   57, 320
Broad Neck   300
Bromo Seltzer   58
Brooke family   57
Brooke Hill   366
Brooke, Robert   38, 278
Brooke, Thomas   330
Brookeville Academy   57
Brooking, Richard   238
Brooklandwood   58
Brooklyn   29
Brookside Gardens   353
Broome (Brome) family   58
Brown, John   110, 149
Brown, Thomas   321
Browning Dam   305
Browning, Meshack   50, 135,
    182, 304
Browning Run   305

Brown's Wharf   134
Browntown   151
Bruce, Norman   58
Brunswick   ix, 222
Buchanan, Archibald   333
Buckey, George & Michael   60
Buckeystown   70
Bull, Thomas   60
Bullocktown   330
Bunker Hill   357
Bunting, George   48
Burkitt, Henry   61
Burkittsville   222
Burleigh Inn   45
Burnside Bridge   311
Burton, Isaac   61
Bush Cabin Branch   252
Bush Declaration   61, 191
Bushey's Cavern   73
Bussard, Henry   229
Buttersburg   339
Buzzards Knob   318

C.C.C.   228
Cabin John Regional Park   63
Cadwalader, John (Gnl.)   193
Callister's Ferry   104
Calvert, Cecil   10
Calvert, Cecilius   6
Calvert, Charles   viii, 232, 255, 307
Calvert, Charles B.   95
Calvert Cliffs   161
Calvert Cliffs Electric Power Station   212
Calvert Cliffs State Park   64
Calvert family   103, 307
Calvert, George   viii, 287
Calvert, Lady Caroline   68
Calvert, Leonard 263, 266,302
Calvert Co. Maritime Mus.   317
Calvert Museum   287
Calvert, Philip   77, 334
Calverton   274
Cambridge   117
Camden Station   26
Campbell's soup   88, 265, 303
Camp David   72, 143, 332
Camp Glyndon   160
Camp Harding Park   256
Camp Springs Airforce Base   5
Cannon, Patty   56, 285, 330, 346
Canton   30
Cape St. Clair   57
Capital Beltway Station   199
Capital Center   201

Capt. John's Branch   63
Carmelite Order   229
Carmichael   365
Caroline Sales Barn   338
Carrigan, Matthew   98
Carroll, Anna Ella   90, 196
Carroll John (Bishop)   78, 347
Carroll, Charles   269, 325
Carroll, Charles of Carrollton   58, 68, 338
Carroll Co. Farm Museum   351
Carroll Co. Hist. Soc.   351
Carroll, John   341
Carroll mansion   21
Carroll Park   19
Carroll, Thomas King   90, 196
Carrollsburg   129
Carrollton estate   206
Carrollton Manor House   60
Carvel Hall cutlery   102
Castle Angelo   129
Castle Haven   90
Castle Thunder   73
Casselman bridge   257
Casselman River   71
Catawba grape cultivation   92
Cathcart   215
Catholic cemetery   206
Catoctin   199
Catoctin Antique Gas Engine Show   360
Catoctin Furnace   90, 165
Catoctin Mountain   355
Catoctin Mtn. Nat. Park   72, 360
Catoctin Recreation Demonstration Area   107
Caton, Richard   73
Catonsville Comm. College   73
Catonsville Hist. Soc.   73
Cattail Creek   295
Caulk's Battlefield   334
Cearfoss, Daniel   74
Cedar Hill Cemetery   327
Cedar Point Lighthouse   76
Cedar Point Neck   76
Cedar Point Wildlife Management Area   349
Cedarville State Forest   367
Cedarville State Park   357
Cecil Cross Roads   75
Ceciltown   334
Celanese Fiber Co.   5
Celanese plant   107
Center for Environmental & Estuarine Studies   180
Center Stage   27

Centerville 192
Centralia 10
Ceresville Estate & Mills 77
Chalk Point 352
Chalk Pt. Generating Sta. 77
Chandler, Benjamin 64
Chandler, Job 271
Chandler's Town 271
Chapel 176
Chapline, J. 11
Chapline, Joseph 310
Chapline's Landing 315
Charles Branch 81
Charles Center 30
Charles County Comm. College 267
Charles Co. Fair Grounds 43
Charles Town 271
Chales Village 30
Charlotte Hall Military Acad. 82
Charlotte Hall Veterans' Home 82
Charlton Heights 45
Charlotte Town 225
Chartwell Golf & Country Club 82
Chase, Charles 82
Chase, Samuel 9, 20
Chautauqua Meeting Ground 158
Chesapeake 259
"Chesapeake",The 246
Chesapeake & Delaware Canal 338
Chesapeake & Ohio Canal 46, 106, 124, 141, 163, 219, 225, 256, 272, 295, 296, 315, 358
Chesapeake & Ohio Canal Mus. 170
Chesapeake Bay Bridge 281
Chesapeake Bay Model 220
Chesapeake Beach 237
Chesapeake Biological Laboratory 316
Chesapeake College 365
Chesapeake Junction 306
Chesapeake Ranch Club 64
Chester Mill 77
Chester River 104
Chestertown Tea Party Festival 88
Chesterwood 40
Chestnut Grove 3
Chestnut Woods 3
Chew's 364
Chicken raising 356

Chilberry Hall 1
Childs, George W. 89
Chillum Castle Manor 89
Chimney Rock 72
Chincoteague Bay 14
Choptank Bridge 115, 164
Choptank Island 332
Choptico Indians 78
Christ Church 79
Christ Episcopal Church 66, 94, 200
Christ Protestant Episcopal Church 271
Christian Church Cemetery 184
Church Hill 128
Church of the Brethren 237, 340
Church of the Presidents 241
Church World Service of the Nat'l Council of the Chruch of Christ 237
Churchill, Winston (Sir) 143, 332, 341
City Hall 23
Civic Center 23
Civil War 266, 322, 342 351, 358
Civilian Conservation Corps 349
Claggett Diocesan Center 60
Claggett family 91, 259
Claggett, Thomas (Bishop or Rev.) 16, 103, 324, 333, 341
Claiborne, William 91, 153, 195
Clara Barton House 158
Clark, John 92
Clark's Switch 330
Clarysville Inn 93
Clay, Henry 135
Clemson family 205
Clemsonville 205
Cleveland, President 114, 241
Clifton 13
Clifton Park 19
Clifton Textile Mills 163
Clopper, Francis 94
Clopper's Mill 94
Cloverland Dairy Farm 340
Coach House Inn 61
Coaches Island 269
Coast Survey 322
Cockburn, George (Sir or Adm.) 155, 174
Cockey, John 94
Cockey's Tavern 351

Coke, BIshop   1
Cokesbury College   1
Colbourn Creek   217
Cole family   94
College Park   198, 276, 340
College Park Airport   95
Columbia   182, 242
Columbia Pike   96
Commercial Fisheries Biologi-
    cal Lab.   249
Communications Satellite Corp.
    92
Concord Point   174
"Coney"   208
Confed. Soldiers' Home   260
Confluence & Oakland RR   147
Congoleum plant   70, 75, 135
Conneway Hill   15
Conococheague Creek   57, 359
Conowingo Dam   17, 218, 243,
    324
Conrad's Ferry   356
Constellation   18
Convention Center   23
Cook, Ebenezer C.   97
Cookerly's Tavern   235
Coole Springs of St. Marie's
    81
Corbett, Isaac   98
Corner family   95
Corrigan, Douglas   221
Cosca Regional Park   94
Courthouse Point   245, 248
Coventry Episcopal Church   284
Cowenton   354
Cowper, William   247
Cox, Samuel   43
Cox's Point   16
Coxtown   210
Coxville   169
Cozy Restaurant   332
Crab Houses   269
Crabtown   102
Cracklintown   203
Cramer, George   346
Crampton   318
Crampton Gap   152
Crampton, Thomas   100
Creager, John   287
Cresap, Colonel   235
Cresap, Daniel   101, 110, 283
Cresap, Joseph   101
Cresap, Michael   247
Cresap,(Col.) Thos.   106, 246, 247
Creswell's Ferry   270
Crimea   19
Crisfield High School   313
Crisfield Historical Mus.   102

Crisfield, John Woodward   101
Crisfield Seafood Lab.   102
Crocheron, Nathan   102
Crochet's Ferry   58
Crone, Margaret   222
Cross Keys   30
Cross Roads Church   151
Crouse Mill   263
Crouse, Nancy   222
Crow Rock Falls   177
Crown Cork & Seal   148
Crownsville Sta. Hospital   104
Crystal Beach Manor Hs.   104
Cumberland Bone Cave   98
Cumberland Narrows   210
Cumberland Valley RR   124
Cunningham Falls State Pk.   72
Cunningham's Cross Roads   74
Curtis Creek Mining, Furnace &
    Mfrg. Co.   157
Custom House   24
Cylburn Park   19

Dahlgren, M.V.   318, 367
Dames Quarter   112
Damned Quarter   112
Dancer's Image   230
Daniels Company   109
Dans Mountain   358
Dans Mountain Wildlife Mgmt.
    110
Darne, William   111
Daughters of Charity   130
Davis' Warehouse   2
Dawson family   112
Dawson, Frederick   131
Dawson Manor   130
Dawson, William   130
Deal Island Wildlife Mgmt.
    Area   113
Dean, Aquila   17
Decatur, Stephen   45, 50
Declaration of the Ass'n of
    Freemen   314
Defoe, Daniel   51
Deep Creek Lake   153, 214
Deep Landing   162
Deer Creek   97
Deer Creek Friends' Meeting
    House   110
Deer Park Hotel   114
De Kalb's Pottery   175
Delaware Bay   83
Delmarva Fox Squirrel   344
Delmarva Peninsula   121
Delmarva Power & Light Co.
    344
Denton's oyster pkg. plt.   58

Dept. of Game & Inland Fish 185
Detrick, Major Fred. L. 137
Devil's Backbone County Pk. 56
Devil's Island 112
Devon cattle 320
Dickerson 225
Dickey, W. J. 244
Dickeyville 30
Dickinson, Charles 165, 172
Dickinson family 165
Diffenbach, F. (Dr.) 216
Dielman's Inn 236
Diocesan School of the Episcopal Church 299
Dividing Creek 276
Dixon, Jeremiah 219
Doncaster 59
Dorchester Town 90
Dorsey family 14, 117
Dorseys 126
Doub, Mr. 117
Double Pipe Creek 263
Double Pipe Creek Village 115
Doubleday publishers 313
Doubs 70
Doughoregan estate 182
Douglas, Charles R. 177
Douglass, Frederick 337, 364
Dowden's Ordinary 92
Dower House 294
Downey Branch 75
Down's Cross Roads 150
Downs, William 150
Drayton 319
Dred Scott decision 2
Druid Hill Park 19, 228
Drum Point Pond 118
Du Val family 159
Dubois, Father John 230
Duke of Marlborough 211
Dulaney, Patrick 142
Dundalk 254
Dundalk Marine Terminal 119
Dunkard 314
Dunker Church 311
Du Pont estate 132

Eagle Rock 15
Earhart, Amelia 221
Earl of Dorset 117
Early, Jubal 142, 356
Eastern Neck Island 195
Eastalco Aluminum Plant 60
Eastern Shore Early Amer. Mus. 182
Eastern Shore RR 102

Eastern Shore State Hosp. 66
Eastern Shore Stainless Steel 119
East Nottingham 63
Eckhart Mines 123
Eden, Governor 8
Eden, Sir Robert 203
Edentown 115
Edgewood Arsenal 42, 172
Edison, Thomas 231
Eight Mile House 93
Einstein, Albert 241
Elder, William 230
Eldersburg 261
Electric crossing bell 332
Elizabethtown 167
Elizabeth Hager's Town 167
Elkins 160
Elk Ridge 51
Elkridge Landing 125
Elk River 83, 99
Ellengowan 330
Ellicott, John, Jos., Andrew 127
Ellicott Mills 127
Elvaton 355
Ely, Thomas 109
Emerald Hill Estate 351
Emerson, Isaac 58
Emmanuel Church 87
Emmanuel Episc. Church 106
Emmit, Samuel, Wm. 129
Emmitsburg 334
Emmitsburg Junction 293
Emory Grove 160
Energy Research & Development Agency 109
England, John 278
Enoch Pratt Free Lib. 24
Episcopal as name for C. of E. 87
Episcopal Church 362
Equitable Trust Bank 252
Ernest A. Vaughan Wildlife Management Area 157
Essex 100
Eutaw Place 31
Evart 131
Evergreen House 21
Everhart, Lawrence 222
Evitts Creek Village 131
Ewell 313
"Experiment" 302
Exxon 244

Fairchild Aircraft 168
Fairfax stone 273
Fair Hill 247

Fairmount   179
Fairview   53, 132
Fairview Mill   133
Fairview Mountain   93
Falling Branch   135
Farmer, Joseph   278
Farmwalt family   338
Faul, M.E.   228
Fawn Grove   123
Federal Bldg. Complex   323
Federal Hill   31
Federalist Party   134
Fell's Point   19, 31
Fenwick Isl. Lighthouse   134
Ferry Point   209
Ferry, The   124
Fiery family   133
Fifteen Mile Creek   208
Fink, Adam   135
Finley, Samuel   352
Fire Museum of MD   212
Firestone, Harvey   231
Fishing Bay   129, 266
Fishing Creek   86, 180, 205, 228
Fitzgerald, F. Scott   292
Fitzhugh, Col.   89
Flag House and Mus.   28
Fleecy Dale   251
Fleming Park   40
Flint, Mr.   135
Flintstone   347
Flintstone Hotel   135
Floyd, Anne Olivia   294
Foard's blacksmith shop   204
Foote, Rear Adm. Andrew Hull   137
Ford, Henry   231
Forest Grove   150
Forest Inn   136
Forestry Management Section of University of MD   264
Forktown   148
Forks, The   340
Fort Cumberland   54, 105
Fort Cumberland trail   106
Fort Detrick   144
Fort Frederick   283
Fort Frederick State Park   46
Fort Hill   283
Fort Hill Mountain   112
Fort Howard Veterans' Hosp.   139
Fort Lincoln cemetery   50
Fort McHenry   18, 19, 24, 136
Fort (George) Meade   10, 244
Fort Pendleton   160

Fort Pleasant   105
Fort Severn   7
Foster's Mills   252
Fountain, Marcy   56
Fountain Rock   299
Four Corners   321
Fowble, Frederick   141
Fox Catchers' Hunt Cup Meet   132
Fox Gap   52, 318
Fox, George   122
Fry   17
Francis Scott Key Bridge   136
Franklin Academy   284
Franklin, Henry D.   330
Franklinville   330
Frederick County   318
Frederick Co. C. College   144
Frederick Co. Hist. Soc.   144
Free State   vii
Freedom of Conscience Monument   300
Freeland, John   146
French & Indian War   106, 137
Frenchtown   3
Friend, John   147
Friendship   146, 317
Friendship Airport   37
Friendship House or Hall   121
Friends' Meeting House   64
Fritchie, Barbara   72, 142, 143
Frizzell, Nimrod   147
Frost Mansion   147
Frost, Meshach   147
Frost Town   147
Frostburg   261
Frostburg State College   55
Fulton, Charles C.   149
Fundenberg, Daniel   205
Funk, Henry   149

Gaither, Elisha R.   340
Gale, Dr.   151
Gale, George   354
Gale, Richard   151
Galloway, John   151
Galloways   151
Gamber, William Snyder   151
Gambrill State Park   72
Gambrill, Dr. Steven   151
Ganey's Wharf   115
Garrett, John   308
Garrett, John W.   114
Garrett, Robert W.   152, 153
Garrett, Thomas   60
Garrett Community Coll.   214

Garrett Co. Fair Grounds 214
Garrett Co. Hist. Mus.   242
Garrett Co. Hist. Soc. 182
Garrettson, Freeborn   3, 302
Gardenhour, Jacob   43
Garland Dinner Theater   96
Garrison's Landing   49
Gary, James S.   109
Gateway to the West   234
Gath 152, 154, 203
Gathland State Park   100, 318
Geddes   87
Geddes-Piper House   88
General Electric   96
George's Creek Coal Co.   209
George's Creek Valley   110,
  350
George's Creek Village   155
George's Run   41
Georgetown 146, 346
Georgetown Cross Roads   150
Georgetown University   236
Germans 312
Germantown 257
Giddings, Elizabeth   346
Gilbert, Benjamin F.   327
Gilbert Memorial Park   327
Gilmor, Robert   159
Gilpin, Samuel   40
Gilpin's Church Tower   40
Gilpin's Rocks, Falls   40
Ginseng 304
Ginseng Run, Hill   304
Glade Valley Farms   230
Glenn Martin Aircraft Co.   221
Glenn Martin Plant   131
Glendale 159
Glenelg Country School   159
Glenellen Academy   185
Glenn, Judge Elias   157
Glenn, John   159
Glens   73
Glenville 159
Gnegy family   160
Goddard, Dr. Robert   160
Goldsboro House   165
Goode, John   79
Gorman, Senator   160
Gormania 160
Gorsuch, Edward   161
Gorsuch, Stephen   161
Goshen Mills   203
Goucher College   336
Goucher Hall   1
Gough, Harry Dorsey   258
Govans   32
Governor's Cup   100

Governor Emerson C. Harring-
  ton Bridge   90
Governor Henry W. Nice Memo-
  rial Bridge   273
Governor Run   64
Grace Church   312, 329
Graham, Curtin   161
Grand Nat'l Point to Point
  Horse Race   62
Grant, President   241
Gravelly 256
Great Falls   272
Great Meadows, PA   55
Great Valley   349
Greater Baltimore Industrial
  Park   94
Greater Washington Glass Show
  94
Green Hill Church   354
Green marble quarry   67
Green Ridge   286
Green Ridge State Forest   334
Green Spring   47, 165
Greenbelt Park   164
Greenberry, Nicholas   164
Greenbriar 318
Greenbriar Village   164
Greenbriar Swamp   60
Greenhead 146
Greenmount Cemetery   20, 141
Greensboro 115
Greenspring Valley   82
Greenspring Valley Hunt & Golf
  Club   154
Gretna Green   126, 265
Grey's Hill   162
Grimes, John   180
Grove, Robert Moses (Hefty)
  209
Guilford   32
Gunpowder Cemetery   178
Gunpowder River   346
Gunpowder State Park   82, 166
Gurley Town   146
Gwynns Falls   224
Gwynns Falls Park   19

Hager, Capt. Jonathan   167
Hager's Fancy   167
Hagerstown Almanac   168
Haines, J. B. & Co.   165
Halfway House   325, 360
Hall, Nicholas   235
Hallowing Point   255
Halls Cross Roads   1
Halltown 218
Hamburg 149

Hamilton 32
Hammerman Area 82, 166
Hampden 32
Hampstead 216
Hampton mansion 336
Hancock vii
Hancock, Joseph 170
Handy, Isaac 303
Handy, Major Levin 303
Hanging Rock 93
Hanover Pike 360
Hanoversville 170
Hanson, John 250
Hanson Junior High Sch. 250
Happy Harbor 146
Harbaugh brothers 297
Harbaugh Valley 297
Habor Place 24
Harbor Queen 6
Hard Crab Derby 102
Hard Scrabble 350
Harding, President 283
Harford Community Coll. 42
Harford County Executive 191
Harford County Hist. Soc. 41
Harford County Park 123
Harford, Henry viii, 171
Harford Town 61
Harley's Postoffice 61
Harmony 165
Harned, Joseph E. 241
Harney, General 172
Harney 225
Harper's Ferry 218, 352
Harper's Ferry Rd. 110
Harrison, Frederick 11
Harrison, President (Wm.Henry)
    173, 241
Harrison, Thomas 173
Harry Lundeberg School for Sea-
    men 261
Hart 184
Hart. Joseph 173
Harwood's Choice 360
Havre de Grace 324
Hawkins Point 136
Hayes, Rutherford B. 222
Hay's House 42
Haystack Mountain 55
Head of Chester 224
Head of Elk 126
Head of Severn 224
Hebb, Dr. 175
Henryton State Hospital 176
Hensel, William 111
Henson, Josiah 212
Henson, Matthew 233

Herman, Augustine 52
Herold, David 93
Herring Bay 132
Herring Run Park 19
Herrington Manor Area 325
Herrington Manor State Park
    214
Herringtown 238
Hickman Town 177
"High Balling" 114
High Rock 177, 318
Highland gathering 132
Highlandtown 33
Highland View Academy 228
Highlands 56, 321
Higman's Mill 224
Hills of Linganore 207
Hillsboro, Lord 178
Hilton estate 73
Hilton Inn 9
His Lordship's Kindness (Man-
    sion) 294
Hoffman, William 178
Hog Creek 235
Hog Rock 72
Hole-in-the-Wall 169
Holland Island 103
Hollingsworth 125
Hollingsworth Tavern 126
Holy Trinity Protestant Epis-
    copal Church 124
Homeland 33
Homewood 21
Honga 180
Hood College 144
Hood, James 180
Hoop Pole Mountain 230
Hooper, Henry 180
Hoopersville 180
Hooversville 190
Horse Range Farm 220
Horsehead Tavern 181
Horsey, John C. 217
Houghton, Arthur A. 365
Howard County Fair Grds. 350
Howard County Hist. Soc. 129
Howard House 128
Howad Hunt Club 159
Howard, John Eager 139, 181,
    217
Howard R. Duckett Dam 255
Howe, General 126
Hoye, Charles E. 182
Hoyes 305
Hoyes Crest 15
H. U. D. 157, 298, 306, 333
Hugg-Thomas W'life Refuge 326

Hughes Creek   66
Hughes, Edward   109
Hughes Methodist Church   353
Hughesville   80
Hungerford, Charles   291
Hungerford's Tavern   291
Hunt Club   272
Hunting Creek   107, 183, 206
Huntington City   53
Hurlock   117
Hurlock, John M.   183
Hurricane Agnes   109
Hussey, Obed   340
Hutton   101
Hutton family   184
Hutton Switch   184
Hyatt, Christopher, Jesse, Seth
    184
Hyattsville   276, 341
Hydrographic Office   323
Hyer, Tom   321

Idlewild Mills   185
Ijams Mills   185
Ijams, Plummer   185
Immanuel Lutheran Church   216
Independence   51
Indian George   154
Indian Queen   49
Indian Head   232
Indian Head Junction   186
Indian Springs   366
Inner Harbor   33
Inverness   40
Ireland   17
Irving College   216
Israel Creek   77

Jackson, Andrew   165, 172
Jacksonville   260
Jacques, Lancelot   165
Jamestown   99, 248
Jarrett, Luther   188
Jefferson Island   269
Jefferson, Thomas   245, 276
Jericho covered bridge   189
Jerusalem   149, 231
Jessups   190
Jessup's Cut   190
Job, Andrew   51
Job Corps   362
John Brown's Farm   110
John Brown's Raiders   13
Johns Hopkins Hosp.   24
Johns Hopkins University   24
John's Point   360
Johnson, Joe   285

Johnson, Roger   341
Johnson, Thomas   71, 142, 165
Johnson's Cross Roads   285
Jones Falls   82, 198
Jones, John Paul   7
Jones, Tom   182
Jonestown   17
Jousting   217, 271, 333
Julia A. Purnell Mus.   314
Jump family   191

Kaiser Aluminum   169
Kansas   133
Keedy, John & Samuel   192
Keller, Geo. W.   181
Kelly Springfield Tire Co.
    107
Kelso Gap   15
Kenilworth Aquatic Gardens   5
Kennedy, President   261
Kennedy Farm   110
Kennedy Highway Bridge   174
Kennedys   332
Kent County Hist. Soc.   88
Kent Island   87
Kent Fort Manor   195
Kent Narrows   195
Key family   196
Key, Francis Scott   9, 69,
    142, 196, 204
Key, John Ross   58
Keyser's Ridge   99
Keysville   58
Kilgore Rocks   135
Kilpatrick's Cavalry   313
King, Abraham   196
King and Queen Seat   291
King William's School   6
King's Corner   215
King's England, The   v
King's Gift   118
Kingston Hall   196
Kingston Landing   359
Kingsville Inn   197
Kirby's Wharf   359
Kitty Knight House   155
Knapps Narrows   332
Knowles Station   193
Koontz   222
Koppers Company   157
Krauss, Leonard   173
Kreight family   133
Krise family   293
Kruschev   332

Labadie Tract   73
Labadists   73

Ladew, Harvey   198
Ladies' Seminary   136
Lafayette (General)   42, 45,
   98, 126, 135, 184, 197,
   259, 286
Lafayette's Army   110
Lafayette's troops   17
Lake family   199
Lake Ford   100
Lake Linganore   207
Lamb's Knoll   318
Lanham family   199
Lanier, Sidney   266
Lansdowne   37, 130
Lansdowne Christ'n Church   200
Lapidum   270, 324
Latrobe, Benjamin H. II   331
Laurel factory   201
Laurel Race Track, Raceway   201
Lavender Hill   252
Layhill   239
Layton family   203
Le   Compte   Wildlife   Refuge
   344
Leakin, J. W.   19
Leakin Park   19
Lee, David   190
Lee, Robert E.   137
Lehigh   340
Leighton, Benjamin F.   362
Leiter family   203
L'Enfant, Pierre Charles   89
Leonardtown   300
Levitt   103
Levitt & Sons   42
Lewis Shore Road   246
Lexington Market   24
Lexington Park   302
Liberty Reservoir   37, 242
Licking Creek   257
Licksville   70
"Limbo"   180
Limekiln   70
Lincoln   267
Lincoln, President   143, 196,
   310, 312
Lindbergh   221
Linthicum, Abner   207
Liquified Natural Gas Terminal
   99
Little Bennett Creek   207
Little Choptank   208
Little Crossings   71, 162
Little Deal   113
Little Heiskell   168
Little Italy   33
Llangollen   50

Lloyd, Edward   9
Lloyd, John M.   93
Lloyd's Tavern   93
Lloyd family   364
Lloyd House   337
Lloyd St. Synagogue   22
Lloyds   364
Loblolly pine   308, 357
Loch Raven Reservoir   37,
   166, 274
Lock Pump House   86
Locust Point   33
Lonaconing   155
Long Marsh   186
Long Meadows   247
Loomtown   362
Lord   197
Lord Baltimore   65, 122, 151,
   300
Lord Baltimore Hotel   26
Lord Chesterfield   87
Lorna Doone   185
Lostland Run   273
Loudon Heights   12
Love Point   91
Lovely Lane Methodist Church
   22
Lovers' Leap   359
Lower Cross Roads   91
Lower Ferry   259
Loyola Retreat House   182
Loyola University   25
Loys   248
Lucifer matches   332
Ludlow's Ferry   273
Luke   350
Luke family   211
Luransville   101
Luther, Martin   212
Lutheran Church   216
Luthern Church tower   329
Lutheran Churchyard   313
Lutherville Fem. Seminary   212
Luthworth   230
Lynch Cove   40
Lyons Creek   10
Lyric Opera House   28
Lyttonsville   191

Mack trucks   168
Madison, President   57
Makemie, Francis   276, 284
Manokin Presbyterian Ch.   276
Manokin River   216, 276
Manor   232
Manor Chapel   298
Margarettsville   52

"Marietta"   159
Marlborough   341
Marlborough Academy   211
Marquis of Lansdowne   200
Marriott, General Wm.   217
Marshall   310
Marshall family   217
Marshall Hall   263
Marshall Plantation   217
Marshyhope Creek   58, 185
Marston   304
Martin, Glenn   286
Martin-Marietta Co.   221
Martin Mountain   286
Martinak, George   218
Mary Garrett Children's Hosp.
   229
Marydel   90
Maryland Airport   268
MD Agricultural College   95
Maryland Assembly
MD Capital Yacht Club   180
Maryland Charter   349
Maryland Day   301
MD Dept. of Motor Vehicles
   157
MD Dept of Nat. Resources   220
MD Game & Inland Fish Comm.
   286
Maryland Historical Soc.   28,
   219, 221
MD Historical Trust   303
MD House of Correction   190
Maryland Inn   8
Maryland Institute   25, 215
Maryland Institute for Men
   55
Maryland Midland RR   196, 346
Maryland Mining Co.   104
Maryland Nat'l Bank Bldg.   25
MD Nat'l Capital Park & Plan-
   ning Commission   227
Maryland Oyster Festival   204
Maryland & Pennsylvania RR
   136, 291, 310, 321
Maryland Regiment   138
Maryland State Fair   333
Maryland State House   233
Maryland State Police   260
Maryland Science Center   28
MD State Reformatory for Women
   190
MD State Teachers' Coll.   53
Maryland T.B. Hospital   297
Maryland Yacht Club   133
Mason, Charles   219

Mason & Dixon   176
Mason-Dixon Line   vii, 218
Mason-Dixon Markets   93
Mattapany Estate   255
Maugan, Jonathan & Abraham 220
Maxwell, Elizabeth   51
May, Major Wm.   305
Mayo, Isaac, U.S.N.   220
McCall Printing Co.   159
McCarty family   241
McClellan saddle   287
McCormick & Co,   253
McCormick, Cyrus B.   340
McCormick Spice Co.   25
McCoy's Ferry   165
McCulloch, Mrs. John S.   158
McCullough, Samuel   214
McCullough's Path   15, 321
McDonough, Maurice James   267
McGrath   200
McHenry, Dr. James   214
McKinstrey, Samuel   215
McNally, Brother Dan   110
McShane, William   118
Meade, General   263, 267, 329
Mechanicsville   1, 151, 247,
   332
Medford, Henry   123
Medford's Wharf   90
Medical Hall   91
Mee, Arthur   v
Meeting House   127
Meeting-House Landing   265
Memorial Stadium   25
Mencken, Mrs. H. L.   351
Mencken House   21
Meredith House   66
Meredith's Crossings   176
Merritt Point   40
Merryman family   176
Methodist Church   228
Methodist Church camp meeting
   ground   348
Methodist Episcopal campground
   160
Methodist Episcopal Church
   351
Methodist settlement   302
Meyerhoff (Jos.) Sumphony Hall
   28
Middleton Episcopal Ch.   212
Middletown   222
Middletown Valley   189
Midland   110 155
Midway   237
Milburn Landing   265

Milford Mill Industrial Pk. 260
Miller, Mr.   224
Miller, George   224
Miller House   167
Milton Hall or Academy   319
Milton Inn   319
Mink Hollow Pumping Sta.   255
Mitchell, Dr. I.Abraham   126
Mitchell's Cross Roads   353
Mitchell's Store   353
Mockley Point   263
Model RR Club   124
Modular Housing Corp   277
Monitor   71
Monocacy   101, 225
Monocacy cemetery   40
Monocacy Trail   206, 225, 237
Monocacyville   172
Monroe, President   261
Montgomery County   337
Montgomery Co. Hist. Soc. 292
Montgomery Courthouse   291
Montgomery, General Richard 226
Montpelier Mansion   201
Montrose   361
Montrose School   361
Monument Knob   349
Moravian Town   161
Morgan State College   338
Morgan State University   25
Morgantown Generating Sta. 273
Morris, Geoge & Wm.   185
Morris, John G.   212
Morris Mechanic Theater   28
Morris, Robert   169, 250
Morse, Samuel   285
Moscow   154, 155
Mother Seton House   21
Mount Airy   252
Mount Airy Tunnel   229
Mount Ararat Farms   270
Mount Calvert   16, 81
Mount Clare Mansion   21
Mount Gilboa Church   245
Mount Gilead Church   360
Mount Harmon   120
Mount Ida   129
Mount Lubentia   201
Mount Misery   309
Mount Pleasant   147
Mt. Olivet Cemetery   142
Mt. Olivet Cemetery, Baltimore 304

Mount Royal Station   26
Mount St. Mary's College   130
Mount Savage Iron Co.   231
Mount Vernon   33
Mount Washington   33
Mount Zion   191
Mountain Inn   133
Mountain View Cemetery   310
Movie "Showboat"   104
Mudd, Dr. Samuel   40
Muddy Creek   100
Muddy Creek Falls   325
Mulberry Grove   250
Mullikin   225
Mullins, Andrew, House   350
Murray's Mill   206
Muskrat trapping   117
"My Lady's Manor"   311
My Lady's Manor Racecourse 225
"My Lady Sewell's Manor" House 307
Myerstown   222
Myrtle   157

Nail factory   339
Naill, David W.   243
Nanticoke Indians   343
Napoleon   361
Narrows   107
Nassawango Creek   234
National   68, 155, 222
National Agricultural Center 276
National Agricultural Lib. 44
National Aquarium in Baltimore   28
National Bird Banding Office 256
National Bureau of Standards 150
National Capital   358
National Capital Parks and Planning Comm.   350
Nat'l Capital Trolley Mus. 202, 239
National Cemetery   310
Nat'l Colonial Farm   2, 60
National Freeway   107
Nat'l Geographic Soc.   150
Nat'l Indoor Tennis Championship   304
Nat'l Institute of Health   46
Nat'l Oyster Shucking Contest 204
National Park   163, 311

National Park Service   250
National Pike   55
National Plastics Co.   244
National Register of Historic
    Places   109, 209, 267, 268,
    278, 308
Nat'l Wildlife Refuge   313
Native Dancer   297
Natural History Landmark   100
Nature Conservancy   12,   38,
    100
Naval Academy   6
Naval Academy Dairy Farm   151
Naval Air Test Center   302
Naval Communications Sta.   82
Naval Hospital   46
Naval Ordnance Lab.   178
Naval   Photographic   Interpre-
    tation Center   323
Naval reservation   267
Navy Aerodynamics Lab.   67
Navy Applied Math Lab.   67
Navy Ship Research & Develop-
    ment Center   67
Navy's transmitter facil.   164
Neck Meeting House   115
Nemacolin   154
Nemacolin's Path   55
Nemesis   235
New Ark, The   235
New Bremen   251
New Freedom   189
New Leeds   203
New Lisbon   207
New Tavern   173
New Town   87, 189, 265
New Yarmouth   120
Newmarket   219
Newmarket Academy, The   121
Newport   308
Newton's or Newtown Trap   189
Newtown   236
Newtown Neck Manor House   236
Nike Missile Site   176
Nine Bridges   56
Norris, Edward   237
North Branch   160
North Point   254
North Potomac   272
North Star   337
Northeast   270
Northeast Creek   40
Northern   Central   RR   146,
    345, 354
Northwest Branch Regional Park
    202
Northwest Fork Bridge   134

N.W. Fork of the Nanticoke   134
Northwood   34
Nottingham Lots   351
Noxema   48

Oak Grove   212
Oakhill Cem., Georgetown   335
Ocean City   363
Ocean Downs Raceway   244
Ocean Steam Co.   243
Octagon House   111
O'Donald, Mr.   146
Oella   350
Ogle, Samuel   42
Old Anglers' Club   104
Old Baltimore   1
Old Bohemia Church   347
Old Bohemia Hist. Soc.   347
Old Durham Church   187
Old Dutch Church   187
Old Fields   274
Old Frenchtown   146
Old Germantown   156
Old Line State, The   vii
Old Otterbein U. M. Church   22
Old St. Paul's Cemetery   250
Old Stone Church   203
Old Town   17, 34, 160
Old Trinity Church   90
Old Trinity Graveyard   196
Oldfield Point   246
Oldfields School   158
Oldtown   334
Olmstead, Frederick Law   322
Olney theater, inn   247
O'Neill, John   174
Orchard Park   40
Ordinary Point   195
O'Toole, Richard J.   332
Otterdale Mill   263
Overlea   252
Owings Mills   295
Owings, Samuel   248
Oxford   36
Oxford cemetery   250
Oxon Hill   323
Oxon Hill Children's Farm   250
Oxon Hill Manor   250

Paca Family   1
Paca, William   9, 365
Paca's Island   364
Paine, Thomas   193
Painter's Mill Music Fair   248
Palmer, Edward   153
Palmer, Gerald C.   251
Palmer's Island   153

Pancoast, Caleb   207
Parke family   252
Parson family   253
"Parson of the Islands"   113, 253
Partridge Hill   126
"Partridge Trap"   336
Patapsco   360
Patapsco Female Seminary   128
Patapsco State Park   254, 326, 362
Patapsco Village   254
Patriarch of Maryland, The   92
Patterson, Betsy   320, 361
Patterson, George   320
Patterson Park   20
Patterson, William   361
Patuxent Naval Air Test Center   76, 205
Patuxent River   118, 240
Patuxent State Park   10
Peabody Institute   25
Peale, Charles Wilson   88
Peale Museum   28
Peary   233
Peerless Rockville Historic Pres. Ltd.   292
Peggy Stewart   6
Pekin   228
Peninsula Methodist Conference   52
Penmar   177
Penn, Wm.   122, 352
Penn Central RR   324
Pennington's Point   146
Pennsylvania Electric Co.   113
Pennsylvania RR   259
Pennsylvania Station   26
Pennsylvania Steel Co.   118
Perdue   303
Peregrine's Mount   16
Perkins Hospital   190
Perry, Capt. Richard   258
Perryman family   258
Perrymansville   258
Persimmon Point   57
Peter Pan Restaurant   342
Petersville   222
Phillips family   245
Phoenix   148
Pier 6 Concert Pavilion   29
Pierceland   190
Pig Town   115
Pike, Zebulon   260
Pike's Peak   260
Pimlico   34
Pine Knob   318

Piney Point Lighthouse   261
Pipe Creek Mill   263
Pipe Creek Quaker Meeting Hs.   339
Pipe Creek Settlement   339
Piscataway Indians   76
Piscataway Park   263
Pitts, William   263
Pittsburg Plate Glass   107
Plank Road, The   338
Pleasure Island   173
Plyer's Mill Road   353
Plyer, George   353
Pocomoke State Forest   265
Poe, Edgar Allen   20
Poe House   21
"Point, The"   319
Point Look-In   266
Point No Point   266
Point of Rocks   70
Police Academy   220
Polo Club   272
Pomfret Siding   267
Pompey Smash   343
Poole, John   268
Poplar Fields   129
Poplar Hill Mansion   303
Poplar Island   269
Poplin's or Popley's Island   269
Port Covington   34
Port Deposit   146, 218
Port Tobacco   200
Porter, Doctor G. E.   209
Post Pavilion   96
Postal Museum   351
Potomac   262, 356
Potomac Edison Power Co.   358
Potomac Edison Pow'r Plt.   115
Potomac Heights   186
Potomac Hollow   38
Potomac marble   117
Potomac River   347
Potomac River Bridge   80, 200, 227
Potomac River Festival   59
Potomac River Museum   95
Potomac (Yacht)   66
Potter family   358
Potter's Landing   358
Powhattan   361
Preakness   221
Presbyterian Church   111, 216
Presbyterian Church in America   352
Presidents' Tree   327
Preston   274

Preston Lumber Co.   101
Prettyboy Reservoir   37, 178
Price, Mordecai   274
Prince Frederick   255
Prince George's Co. Lib.   184
Principio Creek, Village   278
Proudfoot's   241
Public Landing   315
Punch Hall
Purse State Park   233

Quakerism   111
Quakers   274
Queen Anne   91, 170
Queen Charlotte   81
Queen City   107
Queen City Station, hotel   107
Queen Henrietta Maria   vii
Queponco   235
Quirauk Mountain   318

Ramsey House   143
Randall, Thomas & Christopher
   283
Raskob family   262
Raven, Abraham   208
Raven Rock   318
Rawlings, Col. Moses   283
Rays   283
Reaper   339
Reckord, Henry   283
Redemptionist Fathers   185
Reister family   284
Reister, John   284
Reister, Philip   284
Remington Arms Co.   286
Reno, General   141
Reno Monument Road   52
Repudiation Day   142
Resurrection Scholasticate 89
Retreat House   216
Revolution   266
Revolution, guns for the   190
Revolutionary War   125
R.F.D. Service   351
Rhodes Point   313
Rhodes, Richard E.   286
Richards Oak   287
Richards, Richard   169
Richards, Capt. Richard   216
Richardson, Col. Wm.   156
Ridgely family   170
Ridgeville   229, 252, 287
Rigbie, Col. James   45
Rinehart, William   215
Ringgold, Major Samuel   287
Rising Sun   173

Ritchie, Governor   139
River Brethren or Brethren in
   Christ Church   287
River Bridges   176
Riverdale Presbyt'n Ch.   288
Riversdale Mansion   287
Riverside Park   101, 106
Robert E. Lee Park   199
Robert Island   200
Robert Morris Inn   250
Rochambeau   126, 259
Rochambeau's troops   17
Rock Creek   203
Rock Run Mill   290
Rockhold or Rockhole Creek   112
Rockland Farm   290
Rocks State Park   113
Rocky Gap State Park   131
Rocky Gorge Reservoir   118
Rocky Point   16
Rod & Reel Club & Marina   86
Roddy   248
Rodgers Bros.   293
Rodgers Forge Elem. Sch.   293
Roe, James   293
Roe's Crossroads   293
Roesville   293
Rogers, James Harrison   184
Rogers, John   259
Rogers Tavern   259
Rogers, Will   107
Rogues Point   313
Rohr, David, Frederick   293
Roland Park   34
Roosevelt, Pres.   221, 269
Roosevelt, Theodore   135
Rose Hill Manor   142
Rose, Joe   294
Rosebud Perfume Co.   362
Rosecroft Raceway   250
Rosewood State Hosp.   248
Rosewood Training School   295
Ross Borough Inn   95
Roth Rock   15
Rouse Co.   96
Royal Oak   295
Rumsey, Benjamin   191
Rumsey, James   347
Rumsey Mansion   191
Rumsey's steamboat   12, 71
Rush, Benjamin   352
Rush, Richard   57, 296
Russian Embassy   262

Sadler family   322
Safeway   199
St. Andrew's Episc. Ch.   276

St. Anne's Episcopal Ch. 8
St. Augustine Episc. Ch. 297
St. Barnabas 124
St. Barnabas Church 203
St. Bartholomew's Ch. 354
St. Clement Island 95
St. Dominic's Graveyard 182
St. Francis Xavier 155
St. Francis Xavier Cath. Ch. 347
St. George's Church 343
St. Helena Island 309
St. Ignatius Catholic Church 78, 299
St. Ignatius Church at Chapel Point 295
St. James Church 57, 225
St. James School 299
St. James's Church 336
St. John's College 6
St. John's Graveyard 113
St. Joseph Institute 130
St. Joseph's Church 2, 98
St. Leonards Creek 300
St. Luke's Episcopal Ch. 91
St. Mark's Episcopal Ch. 259
St. Mark's Reformed 312
St. Mary Anne's Episcopal Ch. 238
St. Mary's Lutheran 312
St. Mary's Catholic Cem. 40
St. Mary's City 298, 299
St. Mary's Church 38, 312
St. Mary's College 185
St. Mary's County Hist. Soc. 204
St. Mary's Square 302
St. Mary, Star of the Sea 180
St. Matthews Episc. Church 306
St. Michaels 19, 295
St. Michael's Church 147
St. Michael's Point 266
St. Michael's Prot. Episcopal Church 302
St. Michael's River 223
St. Paul's Cemetery 20
St. Paul's Church 16, 336
St. Pauls Episcopal Ch. 289
St. Paul's P. E. Church 22
St. Paul's School 58
St. Peter's Church 40
St. Thomas Church 248
St. Thomas Episcopal Ch. 103
St. Thomas Episcopalian Ch. 154
St. Thomas's Church 170
Sandy Hill 321

Sandy Hook 219
Sandy Hook Bridge 189
Sandy Point State Park 85
Sandy Spring 353
Sappington 151
Sassafras River 99
Sater's Church 58
Savage, John 306
Savage River STate Forest 46, 235
Scholl, Jacob 92
School for the Deaf 142
Scott, General Winfield 359
Scott's Old Field 41
Seabrook 199
Seagram 285
Second Army 139
Secretary Creek 307
Selbysport 147
Semmes, Raphael 233
Seneca 296
Seneca Point 80
"Seneca Red" 308
Seneca School House Mus. 308
Sequoia 90
Seton Hill 34
Seton, Mother Elizabeth 130, 230
Seventh Day Adventists 327
Sewell, Henry 307
Seymour, Gov. John 203
Shad Landing State Pk. 265
Shangri La 66
Sharpe, Gov. Horatio 310, 311, 354
Sharpsburg, Battle of viii
Sharpsburg Landing 315
Shaw, Maj. Andrew Bruce 38, 228
Shaw, William 154
Shawnee Old Town 246
Shelby, Capt. Evan 307
Shenandoah Trail 163
Sheppard, Moses 189
"Sheppard's Old Fields" 203
Sheppard-Pratt Hospital 189
Shepperd 232
Shepherdstown 12
Sherman Fairchild Technology Center 156
Shorewood Estate 150
Shot Tower 25
"Show Boat" 135
Shrewsbury Church 193
Sideling Hill 286
Sideling Hill Creek 261
Sideling Hill W. M. A. 312

Simmons, Isaac   146
Sinepuxent Bay   243
Singer, Anna Brugh   167
Skipton   246
Slabtown   206
Slaughter Creek   329
Smallwood, General   313
Smallwood, Brigadier Wm.   276
Smith, Christopher   313
Smith, Denis A.   298
Smith Island   102
Smith, Dr. James   260
Smith, John   101, 349
Smith, Capt. John   16, 180,
    271, 313
Smith, Leonard   59
Smith, Samuel G.   314
Smith, "Stuffle"   313
Smith, William   87
Smithfield   222
Smithson   235
Smithson, Rev. R.   235
Smithsonian Inst.   126, 269
Snouffer, George   266
Snow Hill   274
Snowden family   201
Snowden, Richard   201
Snowdens   227
Snyder's Landing   315
Social Security Complex   361
Soc. for the Pres. of MD An-
    tiquities 170, 259, 364
Soc. for the Restoration of
    Port Tobacco   272
Solomon, Capt.   316
Solomons   64, 255
Somers Cove   101
Somerset Co. Court Hs.   116
Somerset Co. Hist. Soc.   276
Somerset, Mary   317
Somervell's Island   316
Sotterly Mansion   179
Sotweed   97
Soucksville   337
South Delta   67
South Mountain Inn   318
South River Club   319
Southside (boat)   249
Spa Creek   123
Spaniard Neck   319
Sparks family   319
Sparrow, Thomas   319
Sparrows Point   254
Sparrows Pt. Steel Mills   18
Spencer Island   200
Spencer, William   319
Spesutie Church   258

Spitz, Armand N.   127
Spurriers Inn   349
Spring Gardens   169
Spring Grove Hosp. Center   325
Spring Grove State Hosp.   73
Spring Hill   89
Spring Mills   320
Springfield State Hosp.   320
Stansbury's Mill   123
Stanton's Mill   162
State Wildlife M'gment Area
    186
Steam Engine Machine Wks.   168
Stearn's Tavern   74
Steel Pone Creek   321
Steppingstone Museum   215
Sterner's Tavern   71
Steuben Glass   365
Steuart Petroleum Co.   261
Stevens Landing   264
Stevensville   57
Steward, Stephen   352
Stewarttown   191
Steyer, John   321
Stockton, Richard   352
Stone Chapel   304
Stone Chapel Meth. Church   154
Stonewall Jackson   143
Stony Creek   247
Stoneywood Nature Center   291
Stottlemyer, James   231
Strawbridge, Robert   304
Street family   321
Strong, Gordon   322
Stuart, General   314
Stuart, JEB   180
Sue Creek   16
Sugar Loaf Mountain   225
Suit, Samuel Tyler   323
Suitland   228
Sullivan, Yankee   321
Sulphur Springs   236
Summer Hill   287
"Summer White House"   261
Sumner, Maj. Gen. Edwin V.   140
Sunshine   101
Surratt Tavern   94
Surrattsville   93
Surratt, Mary   93
Susquehanna   259
Susquehanna & Tidewater Canal
    175
Susquehanna Lower Ferry   174
Susquehanna Power & Paper Co.
    110
Swallow Falls State Pk.   231,
    324, 366

"Swans Mill" 325
Swartz, Mano 13
Sykes, James 325

Talbot Co. Hist. Soc. & Mus.
  122
Talbot, George 16
Talbot, Grace 327
Talbot Resolves 122
Talbot Town 121
Taney family 328
Taney, FredK. & Raphael 328
Taney, Roger (Brooke) 2, 278,
  328
Tangier Island, VA 102
Tasker, Benjamin 42
Tawneytown 328
Tayler, Thomas 329
Taylor, Gen. Zachary 330
Teackle, Littleton Dennis 276
Teackle Mansion 276
Tecumseh Statue 7
Temple family 330
Terra Rubra 196
Thayersville 113
Third Haven 336
Third Haven Meeting Hs. 122
Thistle 185
Thomas. Gov. Francis 259
Thomas. John B. 340
Thomas Johnson Bridge 256
Thomas. Joshua 113, 253
Thomas, Philip 331
Thomas Viaduct 126, 285
Thompson, Prof. Herbert 185
Thompson, Richard & fam. 269
Thompson, Willards 357
Thrasher, J. R. 222
Thrasher Museum 222
Thurmont 220
Thurmont Vista 72
Tiber Creek 127
Tidewater Inn 122
Tilghman, Col. Frisby 333
Tilghman, Matthew 92, 332
Tilghman Packing Co. 38
Tilghman Seafood Packing Co.
  14
Tilghman, Tench 20, 250, 289
Timonium Racetrack 333
Tobacco Stick 215
Todd 139
Todd, Thomas 254
Tolchester 132
Tolchester Beach Improvement
  Co. 334
Toll House 202

Tom Thumb 128
Tome Institute 270
Tome School 16-17
Tomlinson family 71, 208
Tomlinson, Joseph 284
Tomlinsons 162
Toms Creek Presbyterian Ch.
  334
Tonoloway Creek 140
Tonoloway Station, Ridge 361
Town Creek 247
Town Hill 247, 286
Town Hill Mountain 47
Town Ridge 312
"Town that fooled the British"
  302
Townsend, George A. 152, 154,
  234, 276, 285, 314
Townsend House 73
Townsend Memorial Arch 100
Towsom 18
Towson, Ezekiel 335
Towson family 335
Towson, Genl. Nathan 335
Towson State University 336
Towsontown 335
Tracey's Station 157
Transtown 246
Trap, The 189
Trappe 4
Trappe Landing 336
Trappist Monastery 336
Treaty Oak 91
Tred Avon Ferry 249
Tred Avon Yacht Club 249
Tridelphia Reservoir 255
Trinity Church 52, 300, 341
Truman, President 269
Truman, Vice-President 221
Trummelstown 266
Trump, Van 337
Tubman, Harriet 60
Tuckahoe Bridge 178
Tuckahoe Creek 337
Tuckahoe State Park 337
Tuckahoe weed 337
Tucker House 77
Tudor Hall 140, 204
Turkey Point 16
Turkey Point Light 125, 338
Turn in the Road 353
Turner, Albert 235
Turner's Gap 318
Tuscarora 70
Tydings Park 175
Tylerton 313

Tyson family   189
Tyson, General   158
Tyson, Isaac   315

ULM   248
Uncle Tom's Cabin   212
Unicorn Woollen Mills   339
Union Corner   61
Union County   340
Union Hospital   93
Union Hosp. of Cecil Co.   132
Union Mfg. Co.   244
Union Meeting House   351
Union Mills   263
Union Mining Co.   231
Union Schoolhouse   199
Union Square   35
United Nuclear   262
University of Baltimore 26
University of MD   73, 95,
   276, 287, 304. 364, 365
University of MD, Eastern
   Shore   277
University of MD Hospital   26
Upper Ferry   270, 290
Upper Marlboro   276
Upperco   13
Upperco family   341
Utica Mills covered bridge 342
U.S. Agent of Vaccination   260
U.S. Army Corps of Engineers
   220
U.S. Army Ordnance Mus.   1
U.S. Army Radio Receiving Sta.
   200
U.S. Arsenal   260
U.S. Bureau of the Census   323
U.S. Coastguard Res.   266
U.S. Dept. of Health, Educ. &
   Welfare   292
U.S. Fidelity and Guaranty
   Trust Co. Bldg.   25
U.S. Frig. Constellation   29
U.S. Naval Installation   299
U.S. Naval Ordnance Sta.   186
U.S. Naval Research Lab.   86
U.S. Naval Test Pilot School
   255
U.S. Navy   298
U.S. Navy's Explosive Disposal
   School   322
U.S. Public Health Serv.   258
U.S. Veterans' Hosp.   258
U.S. Weather Bureau   323
Utie, Capt. Nathaniel   320
Utie's Hope   320

Vagabond Players   129
Valley Store Museum   167
Van Horn, Congressman   180
Vanderbilt family   297
Vaughan, Christopher   169
Vaughan, Samuel   129
Veirs family   344
Veterans' Administration 344
Victor Cullen School   297
Vienna   117
Vinnacokasimmon   343

W.P.A.   205
Wagner family   123
Waldorf   80
Walker, George   346
Walker's Switch   345
Walnut Grange   201
Walter Reed Army Hosp.   136
Walters Art Gallery   29
Walters Station   345
Waltersville   48, 161
War Memorial   22
War of 1812   viii, 125, 335,
   352
Warehouse Landing   265
Warfield, Chas. Alex.   159
Warfield, Wallis   158
Warner, Brainard H.   193
Warrior Mountain   286
Warrior Mtn. W.M.A.   347
Warriors' Path   135, 347
Warwick Creek   307
Washington basketball team 201
Washington Bible College   200
Washington Biologists' Field
   Club   264
Washington College   87
Washington County   318
Washington County Hist. Soc.
   167
Washington County Lib.   167
Washington, D.C.   ix
Washington, General   252
Washington, George   48, 80,
   87, 106, 126, 162, 173,
   187, 197, 203, 217, 226,
   227, 235, 247, 263, 272,
   277. 289, 310, 328, 347,
   349, 350, 358
Washington Hall   270
Washington Hotel   277
Washington Junction   267
Washington, Martha   259
Washington Monument   22, 53,
   318

Washington Co. Mus. of Fine Arts 167
Washington Suburban Sanitary Commission 118
Washington's troops 364
Waters Store 149
Watersedge Beach 40
Watkins Regional Park 201
Watson's Island 153
Watts Creek 218
WAVE Recruit Training Command 17
Waverly 35
Waverly Novels 153
Wax Museum 9
Weaver Stone Co. 62
Webster Field 299
Weems, Mason Locke 47
Weise, John 360
Weller, Jos. & John 332
W. Nottingham Academy 352
West River Landing 151
West River Sailing Club 151
Western Branch 81
Western Publishers 66
Western Maryland Coll. 351
Western Maryland RR 30, 70, 107, 196, 207, 257, 295, 339, 358, 361
Western Maryland RR Hist. Soc. Mus. 339
Western Maryland Station 168
Western Maryland trains 170
Westinghouse Corp. 325
Westminster 177, 252
Westminster Churchyard 20
Westvaco Corp. 211
Wever, Caspar 352
Weverton 12, 318
Weverton quartzite 353
Whaley, Capt. Peter 353
Whaleyville 353
Wheaton (Capt.) 353
Wheaton Regional Park 353
Whitaker, George P. 278
Whitaker's Mill 51
White, (Father) Andrew 78, 236, 271, 298
Whitegrounds 175
White Haven 90
White Marlin Capital of the World 243
White Marsh Park 54
White Plains Park 355
White Rocks 254
Whitehaven 341
Whiteley family 354

Whitemarsh Cemetery 250
Whitemarsh Church 169
White's Ford 356
Whittier 72, 143
Wickes, Lambert 120
Wicomico & Pocomoke RR 263
Wild World 225
Wildlife Review 256
Wiley Mfrg. Co. 270
Willard, Daniel 357
Wiley Mill 263
Will 359
William Preston Lane, Jr. Memorial Bridge 85
Williams, Otto Holland 358
Williamsburg 291
Willis, John A. 358
Wills Mountain 210, 286
Wilson, John 203
Winans family 19
Winchester 350
Winchester Pub. Shooting Center 159
Winchester, Wm. 169, 350
Windsor Hills 35
Wingate, Urim G. 360
Winter 166
Winter's Run 14
Wisp Ski Area 214
Wolf, Jacob D. 360
Wolf Rock 72
Wolfe, George "Hooper" 358
Wolfs Mill 263
Wood Island 200
Wood, Joseph 362
Wood Land 289
Woodberry 35
Wooden, Benjamin 360
Woodlawn Cemetery Co. 361
Woodlawn Hotel 292
Woodlandtown 100
Woodmont Gun Club 361
Woods Town 362
Woodsberry 362
Woodsborough 362
Woodstock College 161, 362
Woodward, Wm. 42
World Trade Center 18, 26
World Weather Center 67
Wright Bros. 95
Wright, Orville 221
Wright's Chance 77
Wye Church 365
Wye East River 59, 364
Wye Institute 365
Wye Island 364
Wye Mills 363

Wye Narrows   364
Wye Neck   364
Wye Oak   363
Wye Oak State Park   363
Wye Plantation   364
Wyman Park   20

Yoder's Locker Plant   162
York   313

York Road   196
Yough Glades   241
Youghiogheny River   113, 325

Zihlman, Fred N.   367
Zittles   367
Zollinger, Servilla   297
Zollingers Town   297
"Zubrun"   215

SUPPLEMENTARY INDEX

Allen's Fresh   368
Allen's Mill   368
B & O RR   368, 370
Baltimore (Southern Hotel)
   368
Baltimore Harbor Tunnel   368
Baltimore Beltway   369
Barnes, General James   371
Barton   371
Big Run State Park   371
Bushwood   368
Bushwood Wharf   368
CSX   368, 372
C & O Canal   370
Camp Upton   303
Chesapeake Appreciation Days
   370
Curtis Bay   368
Edmonston   369
Ellicott's Mills   368
Fort McHenry Tunnel   369
Francis   Scott   Key   Bridge
   369
Friends' School   371
High Rock   371
Jarboesville   205
Kensington   369
Locust Point   368
Lynn, Capt. David   208
Ma & Pa RR   369
MD & PA RR   369
Menhaden   309
Middleham   Episcopal   Church
   212

Morman Temple   369
Muirkirk   369
Myers, Peter E.   371
Myersville   371
New Germany   371
Pemberton Hall   303
Phila. Wilmington and Balto. RR
   246
Pleasantville   370
Port Covington   372
Port Wicomico   368
Potobac   271
Relay   368
Sandy Hook   370
Sandy Mount   370
Sandy Point State Park   370
Sandy Spring   370
Savage (surveyor)   371
Savage Mountain   371
Savage River Reservoir   371
Savage River Sta. Forest   371
Shriver, Andrew & David   371
Smithsonian Building   308
Society of Friends   371
Stuart. JEB   371
Swamp, The   309
Union Mills   371
Western Maryland RR   372
Wheeling   368
Wm. Preston Lane Memorial Bridge
   370
Wiley (Company)   369
Zekiah Swamp   368